A Concise History of Columbus, Ohio and Franklin County

Chester C. Winter

Copyright © 2009 by Chester C. Winter.

Library of Congress Control Number: 2008903094
ISBN: Hardcover 978-1-4363-3381-8
Softcover 978-1-4363-3380-1

1. Columbus, Ohio
2. Franklin County, Ohio
3. History-Columbus, Ohio
4. History-Franklin County, Ohio
5. History-Ohio

Registered with the Library of Congress, 2008
Winter, Chester C., 1922—

Includes pictures, figures, tables, references and index
Pbk: acid-free paper

All rights reserved. No part of this book may be reproduced or transmitted in any form or by any means, electronic or mechanical, including photocopying, recording, or by any information storage and retrieval system, without permission in writing from the copyright owner.

This book was printed in the United States of America.

To order additional copies of this book, contact:
Xlibris Corporation
1-888-795-4274
www.Xlibris.com
Orders@Xlibris.com
48719

Dedication

This book is dedicated to all those that came before us and made a positive contribution to Columbus and Franklin County. They merit our deepest gratitude.

Chester C. Winter

Acknowledgements

The author is profoundly grateful to his wife, Mary, who edited this book and helped in many ways the process of publishing. Most of the illustrations came from the archives of Columbus Metropolitan Library with the expert assistance of Andrew Miller. Photos pertaining to The Ohio State University and its members were made possible by the help of Michelle Drobik. Jennifer Wilkinson arranged for the photos from the Columbus Museum of Art. Many books and pictures of Columbus by other authors were reviewed with gratitude to their sources and are listed in the references. A myriad of relatives and friends provided help in the use of the computer in writing and in the preparation of tables, figures and illustrations. This book was not produced alone.

Contents

Chapter 1   Pre-Columbus—Ohio Territory before Statehood 1

  The Relationship of Columbus to Virginia
  Northwest Territory—The Congressional Ordinances of 1785 and 1787

Chapter 2   Settlement of Franklinton—1797—Forerunner of Columbus 5

  Early Growth of Franklinton
  Women in Early Ohio
  Franklinton during the War of 1812
  Early Churches in Franklin County

Chapter 3   First Capitals of Ohio and Early Columbus 13

  First Capitals of Ohio
  Selection of Columbus as Final Capital—1812
  Early Development of Columbus
  Penal Institutions
  City Government
  Early Roads and Bridges
  Early Road Connections to and from Columbus

Chapter 4   Formation of Franklin County and Townships 26

Chapter 5   State and Federal Governments 31

  State Houses in Columbus
  The Ohio Judiciary
  Ohio's First Members of Congress
  First Franklin County Members of Ohio Legislature
  Ohio's First Governor

Chapter 6   Columbus in the Mid-Nineteenth Century 37

Witchcraft Madness
Franklin County's Early Newspapers
Early Taverns and Coffee Houses in Columbus
Notable Visitors to Early Columbus
Columbus Feeder Canal
Columbus in the 1830's
Columbus City Markets
Columbus Hotels
Early Political Campaigns
Early Theatrical Presentations in Columbus
City, County and State Fairs
The First Museum
Gas Lights in Columbus
Banks
Fires in Columbus
Waterways, Dams and Reservoirs
Floods in Columbus
Railroads and Depots in Columbus
Columbus from 1840 to the Civil War (1861)

Chapter 7   German Immigration to Columbus 59

German Village
Lazarus Stores
Schoedinger

Chapter 8   Benevolent Institutions in Columbus/Franklin County 68

The Columbus Poor House
Home for the Aged
Mental Institutions in Columbus
Idiot Asylum
State School for the Deaf
State School for the Blind
Franklin County Children's Home
St. Vincent Orphanage
Care for Disturbed Children
  Salesian Boys and Girls Club of Columbus
  Buckeye Ranch
  United Methodist Children's Home

Chapter 9   Early Churches, Seminaries and Cemeteries 74

    Early Churches in Columbus
    Lutheran Seminary
    Pontifical College Josephinum
    Cemeteries in Columbus

Chapter 10 Columbus during the Civil War 77

Chapter 11 Post-Civil War Columbus 82

    Immigrant Villages
    African-Americans in Columbus
    Entertainment in Columbus
    Sells Brothers Circus
    The Hartman Era
    Electric Plant
    Early Refrigeration
    Water and Waste Management
    The First Telephones in Columbus

Chapter 12 Progressive Era (1880-1915) 100

    Economic, Political and Social Changes in Columbus
    YMCA
    YWCA
    NAACP and Urban League

Chapter 13 World War I, Roaring Twenties, Great Depression and
             World War II 103

    World War I
    Roaring Twenties
    The Great Depression
    World War II Changes

Chapter 14 Medical Education and Treatment in Columbus 106

    The Ohio State University College of Medicine
    The Ohio State University College of Dentistry
    The Ohio State University College of Nursing

Columbus Hospitals
　　　　The Ohio State University Hospitals
　　　　　　Rhodes Hall
　　　　　　OSU Hospital East
　　　　　　The Tuberculosis Hospital
　　　　　　The Psychiatric Institute and Harding Hospital
　　　　Nationwide Children's Hospital
　　　　Riverside Methodist Hospital (originally Protestant and White Cross)
　　　　American Kidney Stone Management (AKSM)
　　　　Grant Hospital
　　　　Mount Carmel Hospitals and College of Nursing
　　　　St. Ann's Hospital
　　　　Doctor's Hospitals
　　　　Select Specialty Hospital
　　　　Mercy Hospital
　　Early Epidemics

Chapter 15 Education in Columbus 119

　　Esther Institute
　　Public Schools
　　Columbus School for Girls
　　Columbus Academy
　　University School
　　Wellington School
　　Sectarian Schools
　　Montessori Schools
　　Charter and "On-line" Schools in Columbus
　　Early College
　　Metro High School

Chapter 16 Colleges and Universities in Franklin County 127

　　The Ohio State University
　　Other Colleges and Universities in Franklin County
　　　　Capital University
　　　　Columbus College of Art & Design
　　　　DeVry University
　　　　Columbus State Community College
　　　　Franklin University
　　　　Ivy Tech Community College
　　　　Ohio Dominican University

OSU, Mt. Carmel and Capital Schools of Nursing
Otterbein University

Chapter 17 Libraries and Newspapers in Franklin County............................ 142

    Columbus Metropolitan Library
    State Library of Ohio
    Ohioana Library
    Palatines To America National Library
    Online Computer Library Center (OCLC)
    Chemical Abstracts Service
    Current Central Ohio Newspapers and Magazines
        The Columbus Dispatch
        The Columbus Call and Post
        Weekly Newspapers and Magazines

Chapter 18 Historical and Genealogy Societies... 146

    Columbus Historical Society
    Franklin County Genealogical & Historical Society
    Ohio Historical Society
    Columbus Jewish Historical Society
    Palatines To America

Chapter 19 Cultural Activities... 148

    Columbus Association for the Performing Arts (CAPA)
    Center of Science and Industry (COSI)
    Columbus Museum of Art
    Columbus Metropolitan Club
    League of Women Voters
    Junior League of Columbus
    Kelton House
    Snowden-Gray House
    An example of luxurious homes built in the Olde Town East district.
    Columbus Landmarks Foundation
    The Jefferson Center for Learning and the Arts
    The Columbus Club

Chapter 20 Notable Persons in Columbus 155

    Early Notable Architects in Columbus

Notable Persons in Arts and Science in Columbus
Notable Clergymen in Columbus
Notable Political Figures in Columbus
Notable Business Persons in Columbus

Chapter 21 Current Large Columbus Companies... 189

Abercrombie & Fitch
American Telephone and Telegraphy Company (AT & T)
American Electric Power (AEP)
Anderson Concrete
Advanced Drainage Systems (ADS)
Big Bear Supermarket (now defunct)
Big Lots
George Byers Automotive Company
Cardinal Health
Columbia Gas
Columbus Dispatch Publishing Company
Columbus Life Insurance Company
Columbus Steel Castings
Commercial Vehicle Group
CompuServe (AOL)
Continental Realty
Core Molding Technologies
The Crane Group
Delphi Automotive Systems
Diamond Innovations
Dominion Homes
Donatos Pizza
Don Casto Organization
DSW Shoes
Germain Motor Company
Glimcher Realty Trust
Grange Mutual Insurance
Hexion Specialty Chemicals
Highlights for Children
Huntington Bank
J.P. Morgan-Chase (formerly Bank One)
Lancaster Colony Corporation
Limited Brands

Liebert Corporation
Lucent Technologies (formerly Western Electric, now part of Alcatel)
M/I Homes
Midland Life Insurance Company
Motorists Mutual Insurance Group
National City Corp. (its branch in Columbus was formerly BancOhio)
Nationwide Insurance Company
NetJets
Outsourcing Solutions
Pinnacle Data Systems
Pizzuti Companies
Plaskolite
Real Living
R.G. Barry
Ricart Automotive Group
Ross Laboratories
Roxane Laboratories
Ruscilli Construction Company
Safelite Group (Belron U.S.)
Schottenstein Stores
R.W. Setterlin Building Company
State Auto Insurance
Sterling Commerce
W.W. Williams Company
TS Tech North America
Wendy's
Westinghouse Electric
White Castle
Worthington Industries

Chapter 22   Columbus Chamber of Commerce, Visitor's Bureau,
             Convention Centers and Arenas 216

Chapter 23   Columbus Tall Buildings 219

  Wyandotte Building
  Atlas Building
  LeVeque Tower
  Buckeye Building
  Continental Center

    8 East Broad Street
    16 East Broad Street
    One Nationwide Plaza
    Three Nationwide Plaza
    Fifth-Third Center
    Franklin County Municipal Courthouse
    Capitol Square Office Building
    Rhodes State Office Tower
    Vern Riffe State Office Tower
    Huntington Center
    Borden Building
    Midland Building
    The Columbus, a Renaissance Hotel
    Motorists Mutual Building
    One Columbus Center
    William Green Building
    Key Bank
    Former Union Store

Chapter 24 Columbus City Halls 230

Chapter 25 Entertainment in Columbus 232

    Columbus Theaters and Arenas
    Columbus Symphony
    Opera Columbus (formerly Columbus Opera)
    BalletMet
    The King Arts Complex and the Pythian Theater
    The Lincoln Theater
    Franklin Park Conservatory
    Vaud-Villities
    Columbus Zoo and Aquarium
    Television in Columbus

Chapter 26 Commercial and Professional Sports and Recreation 240

    The Columbus Clippers Baseball Team
    Blue Jackets Hockey Team
    Columbus Crew Soccer Team
    Columbus Destroyers Arena Football Team

Columbus Sports Figures
Metropolitan Parks and Recreation
Fort Rapids Indoor Waterpark

Chapter 27 Notable Restaurants in Columbus 248

Maramor
Marzetti's
Presutti's
Jai Lai
Current Notable Restaurants Originating or Headquartered in Columbus
    Bob Evans Restaurants
    Clarmont
    Handke's Cuisine
    Damon's International
    Max & Erma's
    Cameron Mitchell Restaurants
    Refectory
    Bravo and Brio (Bravo! Development Inc.)
    Lindey's
    Rigsby's Kitchen

Chapter 28 Philanthropic Organizations 254

Salvation Army
Volunteers of America
Goodwill Columbus
The Columbus Foundation
Heinzerling Foundation
United Way
Charity Newsies
LifeCare Alliance

Chapter 29 Urban Renewal by Columbus 259

Urban Renewal
City Center Shopping Mall
Columbus Metropolitan Housing Authority
Columbus Area Commissions

Chapter 30 Cities and Villages in Franklin County 266

   Suburban Cities

      Bexley   *New Albany*

Bexley

Dublin

Gahanna

Grandview Heights/Marble Cliff

Grove City

Groveport

Hilliard

*Powell

New Albany

Pickerington

Reynoldsburg

Upper Arlington

Westerville

Whitehall

Worthington

   Incorporated Villages in Franklin County

      Amlin
      Brice
      Canal Winchester
      Harrisburg
      Lockbourne
      Minerva Park
      Obetz
      Riverlea
      Urbancrest
      Valleyview

   Unincorporated Communities in Columbus and Franklin County

      Clintonville-Beechwold
      (German Village presented elsewhere)
      Huber Ridge
      Lake Darby
      Lincoln Village
      Linworth
      New Rome
      San Margherita
      Victorian Village

Chapter 31 Demographics of Columbus and Franklin County 302

Map 1 Columbus is centrally located as the capital of the state of Ohio (outlined) which is in the northeast quadrant of the United States

Illustrations

Map 1	Columbus, Ohio in relation to United States	xvii
Map 2	Ohio land districts before statehood	3
Fig. 1	Bas relief of Lucas Sullivant	5
Fig. 2	David Deardurff house	6
Fig. 3	David Beers house	7
Fig. 4	Oberdier house	8
Fig. 5	Location of Columbus in Refugee Tract	14
Fig. 6	Lyne Starling	15
Fig. 7	John Kerr	15
Fig. 8	First state penitentiary	19
Fig. 9	Third state penitentiary	21
Fig. 10	Eighteen counties when state created in 1803	26
Fig. 11	Final Ohio counties and years they were organized	27
Table 1	Reorganization of Franklin County Townships	28
Fig. 12	Second Franklin Court House	29
Fig. 13	Franklin County Judiciary buildings	29
Fig. 14	Third Franklin County Jail	30
Fig. 15	Current Franklin County Townships	30
Fig. 16	First state buildings	32
Fig. 17	Current State Capitol	33
Fig. 18	The Judiciary Center	34
Fig. 19	Thomas Worthington	35
Fig. 20	Second City Market	44
Fig. 21	The Broadway and James Theaters	47
Fig. 22	The Keith Theater	47
Fig. 23	The Ohio State Fair-1890	48
Fig. 24	Columbus floods-1898 and 1913	53
Fig. 25	First Columbus railroad station-1851	54
Fig. 26	Second Columbus railroad station-1897	55
Fig. 27	Current railroads in Franklin County	56
Fig. 28	William Shephard	58
Fig. 29	Born brewery	61
Fig. 30	Simon, Fred and Ralph Lazarus	65

Fig. 31	Camp Chase	78
Fig. 32	Lincoln's cortege in Columbus-1865	80
Fig. 33	Lighted arches, downtown-1880s	81
Fig. 34	Renovated former 1880s postoffice into law office	81
Fig. 35	Heavy industrial pollution, in Columbus-1880s	83
Fig. 36	Columbus Buggy Company-1900	85
Fig. 37	Franklin County trolley and interurban lines-1955	86
Fig. 38	Villages of Italian, Milo-Grogan and Weiland Park	88
Fig. 39	Olentangy Amusement Park	92
Fig. 40	Samuel Hartman	94
Fig. 41	Hartman Hotel-1908	95
Fig. 42	Park, Seneca and Southern Hotels and Atlas Bldg	96
Fig. 43	Chittenden Hotel and Theater	97
Fig. 44	Deshler Hotel	97
Fig. 45	Second Neil House Hotel	97
Fig. 46	Third and last Neil House Hotel	97
Fig. 47	View of downtown Columbus-1907	101
Fig. 48	St. Francis Teaching Hospital-1851-1955	107
Fig. 49	OSU Medical Center today	108
Fig. 50	First Central High School-1862	120
Fig. 51	Second Central High School-1924	121
Fig. 52	First North High School-1892	121
Fig. 53	University Hall, OSU-1873	127
Fig. 54	OSU President Karen Holbrook-2002-2007	130
Fig. 55	OSU President E. Gordon Gee-2007-	130
Fig. 56	Ohio Stadium in detail	131
Fig. 57	Air-view of current Ohio Stadium	132
Fig. 58	Coach "Woody" Hayes	133
Fig. 59	Coach Jim Tressel	135
Fig. 60	Heisman Trophy winner Archie Griffin	135
Fig. 61	Heisman Trophy winner Eddie George	136
Fig. 62	Coach Fred Taylor	136
Fig. 63	Coach Thad Matta	137
Fig. 64	Basketball star Jerry Lucas	137
Fig. 65	Basketball star John Havlicek	138
Fig. 66	Myers home-1896	152
Fig. 67	Charles Lindenberg home	156
Fig. 68	George Bellows, Jr.	156
Fig. 69	George Bellows painting	156
Fig. 70	Emerson Burkhart	157
Fig. 71	Portrait by Emerson Burkhart	157
Fig. 72	Eric Gnezda	159

Fig. 73	Bob Marvin	161
Fig. 74	Elijah Pierce	161
Fig. 75	Painting by Elijah Pierce	161
Fig. 76	Aminah Robinson	162
Fig. 77	A work by Aminah Robinson	162
Fig. 78	Alice Schille	163
Fig. 79	Painting by Alice Schille	163
Fig. 80	Drawing by James Thurber	164
Fig. 81	James Thurber	164
Fig. 82	Washington Gladden	166
Fig. 83	James Rhodes	170
Fig. 84	David Deshler	173
Fig. 85	John Green Deshler	173
Fig. 86	Alfred Kelley	178
Fig. 87	William Neil	181
Fig. 88	Hannah Neil	181
Fig. 89	Eddie Rickenbacker	182
Fig. 90	Dave Thomas	185
Fig. 91	Buildings around Capitol Square	220
Fig. 92	Aerial view of downtown Columbus today	221
Fig. 93	Wyandotte building	222
Fig. 94	Statue of Christopher Columbus	230
Fig. 95	"Old" City Hall-1872-1921	230
Fig. 96	Palace Theater	233
Fig. 97	Ohio Theater	233
Fig. 98	Martin Luther King Arts Complex	235
Fig. 99	Franklin Park Conservatory	237
Fig. 100	Nationwide Arena	241
Fig. 101	Jack Nicklaus	242
Fig. 102	Metropolitan Parks and Trails	245
Fig. 103	Public & Private Golf Courses in County	247
Fig. 104	Columbus Athletic Club	247
Fig. 105	Cameron Mitchell	251
Fig. 106	City Center Mall	261
Fig. 107	Columbus Neighborhood Commission Areas	265
Fig. 108	Franklin Counties Cities	266
Fig. 109	Capital University in 1850	267
Fig. 110	James Kilbourne, founder of Worthington	286
Fig. 111	Communities in Franklin County	296
Fig. 112	Travel distances between Columbus & Ohio towns	305
Fig. 113	Statistical comparison, Columbus & Indianapolis	306
Table 2	Cost of living and of homes in Franklin County	307

Table 3	Populations of Columbus and Franklin County	308
Table 4	Populations of Counties in Columbus Metro Area	309
Table 5	Columbus Mayors	310
Fig. 114	Mayor M. E. Sensenbrennor	310
Fig. 115	Mayor Michael Coleman	310
Table 6	Rankings of Franklin County Banks	311
Table 7	Forbes Magazine's Ranking of Technology Centers	311
Table 8	Commercial Real Estate Developers in Central Ohio	312
Table 9	Central Ohio General Contractors	312
Table 10	Largest Employers in Central Ohio	313

References 315

Preface

This book is about a young city and its surroundings carved out of a wilderness two hundred years ago. It is about a state capital that continuously has grown and is now the largest city in Ohio. It is about buildings in and around capitol square. Many of the tall buildings produce a recognizable skyline, especially when colorfully illuminated at night. It is about businesses that were created, some prospering, others fading away. Some have a fascinating history to relate. But, the book is also about people who lived in Columbus and Franklin County and whose contributions often made their names and the city of Columbus indelibly written in the annals of history. Their talents were in a wide variety of fields. Some became national figures. A few earned international recognition, but most lived in an unassuming and dignified fashion, a characteristic of Mid-Western inhabitants.

Chapter 1

Pre-Columbus—Ohio Territory before Statehood

The Relationship of Columbus to Virginia

The history of Columbus is a continuum of the discovery of North America by Europeans and the predominance of British embedment in the eastern seaboard colonies of the United States. The Jamestown Virginia Colony was the first permanent settlement in the United States in 1607. The Virginians, once firmly established, began to search westward for more fertile land and better opportunities for obtaining wealth. The Virginia Colony, like those in Massachusetts, Connecticut and New York, claimed that their western boundary extended to the Pacific Ocean. They did not know what lay beyond the mountain chain that became known as the Appalachians. Early, the high mountainous ridges served as a barrier to exploration and migration.

The Ohio Territory was claimed by three European countries in it early history. It was included with the claim of the New World for Spain by Christopher Columbus in 1492. Of the contents of this land, he had no realization. Thus, the first possessor of the city, county and state for over one hundred and sixty years was Hispanic. But, this changed hands when the land along the Ohio and Mississippi Rivers was explored by the French in the 1600's. They claimed ownership of the Ohio Territory for ninety years under the name of New France with its capital in Quebec. The French were expelled by the British after the French and Indian War (1756-1763). Virginia, on behalf of the British Empire, then asserted her claim to trans-Appalachian territory with an ill-defined western boundary. In 1763, both England and authorities of the Colonies declared that the trans-Appalachian territory belonged to the native American Indians (the original and now fourth owners). Westward moving settlers believed otherwise and proceeded to infiltrate the Ohio Territory to make claims of ownership for themselves.

Northwest Territory—The Congressional Ordinances of 1785 and 1787

The Continental Congress, a loose confederation of the thirteen colonies during the Revolutionary War period, recognized the potential value of land between the Ohio and Mississippi Rivers largely based on the explorations of Christopher Gist and George Washington in the 1750's. Since 1763, when the French were forced out of North America, both the British and the Colonial governments affirmed Indian ownership of land west of the Alleghany Mountains. The Colonies, having defeated England, and now exclusively in charge, recognized the inevitable and signaled a change in their official policy concerning the Indian-occupied territory. Congress passed two ordinances that proclaimed ownership of the Northwest Territory and a desire to stimulate land sales (and revenue) and settlement of this area. The Ordinance of 1785 stipulated how the land beyond the Ohio River was to be surveyed; thus, the Seven Ranges of future Southeast Ohio were laid out and divided into townships. The center for this activity was at Fort Steuben located between Pittsburgh and Wheeling on the western bank of the Ohio River. There, soldiers were stationed to protect the surveyors, remove unlawful settlers (squatters on government property), and to open the first land-sales office in the territory. The Northwest Ordinance of 1787 gave substance to how the Northwest Territory was to be organized, governed and have land set aside for schools and religious purposes. It was to be free of slavery. In order for the United States to become a reality after the Revolutionary War (1776-1783), the colonies had to relinquish their western land claims. Only Virginia and Connecticut were allowed to keep portions of their western territorial claims. A Connecticut group had purchased the Western Reserve (1786) bordering on Lake Erie and centered in Cleveland. Virginia was allowed to form a "Military District" extending northward from the Ohio River in order to give war veterans payment in the form of land grants. A few veterans claimed their land and settled on and developed their parcels, but most of the recipients sold their land warrants to eastern speculators. The Virginia Military District (1784) was a large fertile territory between the Scioto and Little Miami Rivers, extending northward from the Ohio River to the origin of the two boundary rivers (near present day Kenton, Ohio). The tract had to be surveyed so that the land could be purchased in an orderly and legal fashion from the owners.

The surveyors of the Congressional land tracts used the New England Township as a model for parceling the acreage. Each township contained thirty-six sections; each section was one square mile, or six hundred and forty acres. Initially, the allowable purchases of land could be for no less than six hundred and forty acres at two dollars per acre. Few settlers could afford to buy, let alone develop, that large and expensive portion of land. Therefore, development of the Northwest Territory did not start in earnest until Congress, in 1804, reduced the minimal

Map 2 Ohio Land Districts before Statehood
—from *Ohio Lands*, State of Ohio

An examination of Map 2 reveals that Franklin County and Columbus were developed on land in four districts: Virginia Military, U.S. Military, Refugee Tract and Congressional Lands. When land was acquired and laid out to be Columbus in 1812, the future new capital of Ohio was entirely in the western end of the Refugee Tract.

acreage that could be purchased to one hundred and sixty acres at one dollar and twenty-five cents per acre. Finally, a settler who squatted on a few acres and developed the land over a five year period by clearing the trees and building a cabin could file a claim and own the land free. The Indians were always a menace, and surviving that threat plus wild animals, disease and harsh weather, allowed only the hardiest to stay alive. Needless to say, the first settlers were courageous and hardy. After all, many were survivors of Indian warfare in Kentucky and raids into the Ohio Territory. Fifteen additional land offices were opened throughout the state beginning with Cincinnati, Marietta and Chillicothe. One of the first federal land agents was Thomas Worthington, who lived in Chillicothe, and dealt primarily with the Virginia District land grant.

Chapter 2

Settlement of Franklinton—1797
—Forerunner of Columbus

Fig. 1 Bas relief of Lucas Sullivant on his tombstone. Founder of Columbus.

Lucas Sullivant was a Virginian, of Irish descent, who had moved to Kentucky with his parents. There he explored the wilderness, became quite knowledgeable about frontier existence and Indian fighting. He was described by his son as muscular, well proportioned, of erect posture and a very active nature. He had a firm and decisive manner, was courteous and forceful in obtaining his objectives, and exerted great influence in his community. He became a surveyor for the Virginia Military District and plotted land west of the Scioto River in the locale of its fork with the Whetstone River (now called the Olentangy River). He accepted payment for his work in the form of 6,000 acres of land centering at the junction of the Whetstone and Scioto Rivers. (The name Scioto is of Indian origin, believed to mean *many hairs*. The Indians saw a lot of hair on the water's surface after the deer came to drink during molting season.) Sullivant formed a village on the west side of the rivers and named it Franklinton (1797) after one of the founding fathers of our republic, Benjamin Franklin. Its township was also named Franklin and extended south to the Franklin County line. The land had been occupied by

Mingo, Shawnee and Wyandotte Indians who established villages in the area and raised corn in the fertile ground. They were also hunters and traders. Much later the Amish would foresee a rich future in farming around nearby Plain City. One of the first streets in the new village was named Gift Street. The lots on this street were free to anyone willing to occupy and develop the property. Only the Deardurff and Oberdier homes on this street remain today. For transportation purposes, the river junction seemed a highly favorable site for a town. But, from health aspects and annual flooding, the swampy, mosquito infested "flats" turned out to be a disaster. In fact, in the first year of its existence, the town was washed away by the flood of 1798. The village was rebuilt, but many moved to higher ground "hilltop" to the west. Nevertheless, Franklinton was the forerunner of Columbus (1812), to be located on the east side of the Scioto River just below its confluence with the Olentangy River.

Lucas Sullivant married Sarah Starling, daughter of Colonel William Starling in Kentucky before migrating to Ohio. Starling gave Lucas financial security and influence in their Kentucky settlement. Sarah was nineteen and sixteen years younger than her husband. She arrived in future Franklinton with hope and fortitude that was soon tested by hardships and endangerment from hostile Indians. Two of Sarah's lifelong servants, Arthur and Humphrey, were her former Kentucky slaves. She bore Lucas three sons. Her sister and her husband, Lucy and James McDowell, and her brother, Lyne Starling, joined them in Franklinton. Lyne Starling was six and one-half feet tall, had red hair and an aristocratic demeanor. Upon arrival in Franklinton, his brother-in-law placed him in the county clerk's office. In partnership with Sullivant, he became a wealthy merchant, trader and land owner. Lucas Sullivant died in 1823. His bust is preserved on his gravestone in Green Lawn Cemetery.

Fig. 2 David Deardurff House-1807.
—from Columbus Metro Library

The early Deardurff house (1798) was constructed with twelve inch wide walnut logs making it durable for living as well as for protection. Abraham Deardurff, his wife and their five children farmed and traded with the Indians. In 1815, he started east carrying a large sum of money. He was never seen again in Franklinton; he was found stabbed to death near the Virginia border. His son, David Deardurff, was a good carpenter and built his home of similar material in 1807. Early in its existence, it served as a postoffice.

Adam Hosec was the first postmaster in Franklinton, obtaining a federal contract in 1805. The first mail service was to Chillicothe, performed by a teenager, Andrew McElvain. It took three days for a round trip to Chillicothe with an overnight stay halfway. The small mail pouch was held high while wading or swimming through streams. High water could delay delivery for up to two weeks. Mail to the eastern states took several weeks; the irregular schedule was dependent upon the weather and other circumstances. Prepayment of postage was not required until 1816. Then, rates became established depending upon weight and distance. A single sheet carried under forty miles cost eight cents. The maximum rate was twenty-five cents for over five hundred miles. While James Kilbourn was Congressman, he secured the first post office in Columbus in 1813 with Matthew Matthews appointed postmaster.

Fig. 3 David Beers cabin constructed in 1804 still stands near Norwich Avenue and High Street.
—from Columbus Metro Library

Remnants have been found where Columbus was destined to be located: ruins of Robert Ballentine's saw mill (1800), ruins of Robert White's distillery (1800) and John Bricknell's cabin. The latter had been a captive of Indians for a lengthy period. David Beers' cabin (1804) built near Glen Echo Ravine, a short distance north, is preserved today near Norwich Avenue and High Street. The Oberdier House was a substantial two-story brick house built in 1808 on northwest corner of West Broad and Gift Streets in Franklinton and is the oldest brick house remaining in downtown Columbus. Today, it is occupied by the Franklin County Genealogical and Historical Society. General Harrison visited there among other residences during the War of 1812, and sometimes it is called the Harrison

House. It was never Harrison's headquarters, which is believed to have been a few blocks to the west.

Fig. 4 The Oberdier or Harrison House still stands at the northwest corner of Gift and Broad Streets.
—from Columbus Metro Library

Early Growth of Franklinton

Due to floods and disease, Franklinton's growth was stagnant for several decades. The village's population reached 1,510 in 1840, and in 1850 it was only 1,827. When able, the inhabitants moved to the hilltop immediately west of the town. There, they were free from flooding and less susceptible to other swamp related conditions. Franklinton was inhabited initially by farmers and laborers. Most worked on Sullivant's farm and in nearby stone quarries.

A large cave-like outcropping of limestone near present day Marble Cliff produced a strong stench when first encountered. The odor was found to arise from hundreds of rattlesnakes that had molted their skins and were producing eggs for their young. This hazard was overcome later by stationing hogs at the entrance of the caves. Swine thrived on eating the snakes.

The sub-soil limestone in the Scioto River Valley came from the sediment produced during the Devonian period, over three hundred and fifty million years ago, when the area was covered by a lake, and accounts for the productive quarries and highly fertile top-soil in the region. In 1998, Franklin County ranked fifth statewide in the production of limestone, sand and gravel. These products have been used principally for road building and commercial construction. Sand and natural gas in Central Ohio led directly to its glass industry. In contrast, the sub-soil of the Olentangy River Valley consists mostly of shale, making its soil more acid and less fertile. The principal water source for Columbus was originally from the Scioto River watershed, and the first waterworks was located at the junction of the Scioto and Olentangy Rivers in 1871. As the demand for water grew with the increase in population, the Griggs Dam (1905) and the O'Shaughnessy Dam (1925) were constructed on the Scioto River to form huge reservoirs. Smaller dams were built on the Big Walnut and Darby Creeks. Finally, in 1954, Hoover Lake behind a new dam on the Big Walnut Creek made it the chief source of water for Franklin County. It is anticipated that several more dams and reservoirs in Delaware County, and well-fields in Pickaway County, will be needed to supply water to the rapidly rising population of Columbus and Franklin County.

Fish were plentiful in the rivers, and large numbers were harvested by using net seines or a brush drag. Animals were plentiful also, and hunters killed them for food, for sport and to protect their crops. Grand hunts by large numbers of citizens were organized, a custom continued for over a century, and the number of game dwindled. Deer would come to the rivers at night, and hunters would approach in canoes with bright lights that seemed to blind and paralyze the animals so that they were easy to shoot. Today, deer are protected by law and have become problems by eating shrubs, flowers, crops and causing auto accidents. Riflemen have been hired to cull the herds legally. Squirrels became such a nuisance that a squirrel hunt in 1822 reduced the critters by twenty thousand in the burgeoning town (Franklinton was not declared a city by the state legislature until 1834).

The few Indians in the region brought fruit, vegetables, deerskins and fur to trade with the settlers for whiskey, trinkets and odds and ends. Whiskey was produced by many of the settlers and served as the chief item in bartering. Rarely were wines, French brandy and Jamaica spirits imported. Many settlers viewed whiskey as safer to drink than water and it often was used as medicine for various ailments and fevers whose causes were unknown. The opinions of church congregations and their pastors were divided in its use. Cash was scarce and used to buy such necessities as salt and luxuries like tea, sugar and light weight items from the east. The scarcity and value of money were illustrated by the reward of one cent offered for delivery of a run-away slave. Trade would not advance until there were better roads and improved means of transportation.

Later, the raising, curing and shipping of broom corn occupied some of the residents. A race track was built at the south edge of the town. Mr. Sullivant's large mill later became known as the Ohio Manufacturing Company employing half-a-dozen men. A small cemetery on the north edge of Franklinton, beside the Scioto River, was the final resting place for the first pioneers. It remains today. Later, the remains of Lucas Sullivant and his wife, Lyne Starling, and General Foos and his wife were reburied further south in Green Lawn Cemetery. Sullivant's large land-holdings were left to his three sons, William, Michael and Joseph. William's share included a ridge on the Hilltop that became known as Sullivant's Hill. William Starling Sullivant's large cabin on Broad Street, a mile west of the Scioto River, commemorated by a historic marker, became the modern site of the Graham Ford auto agency. William Sullivant's interest in botany made him an expert in the plants of Central Ohio. His published work was illustrated by his second wife, Eliza, who was an accomplished artist. She died in 1850 at the age of thirty-four. Her portrait etched in stone marks her grave site in Green Lawn Cemetery.

In 1807, a small log jail surrounded by thirteen whipping posts and a larger log courthouse were erected in Franklinton. Lucas Sullivant was the contractor. Within a few years the log structures were replaced with brick buildings. The first official in the infant town was a marshal. Later, law officers wore pewter badges on civilian clothes. Navy blue uniforms were not worn until 1868.

The first Academy opened in Franklinton had a curriculum that included English Grammar, Geography, Bookkeeping, "Measuration," Geometry, Trigonometry, Surveying, Navigation, Algebra and Astronomy. Only students whose parents paid the school teacher attended.

Women in Early Ohio

Life for women on the frontier in early Ohio was challenging, dangerous and often life-shortening. Most came along with their husbands, family or male friends. It may have been without choice, and travel was often by foot and complicated by pregnancy. Sentimental objects such as family heirlooms, china, furniture and things other than necessities were left behind. Their first shelters were primitive, and the climate was often harsh. Insects, wild animals and savage natives were a constant menace. They faced illness of themselves and their family with little medical aid. Moreover, they were often the chief care-giver to the ill and disabled. In addition to bearing and raising children, they helped with farm chores, tended gardens, made clothing, prepared food, churned butter and made soap and candles. Their life was often lonely, and depression was common. Because of financial necessity, infirmary of spouse or widowhood, they often performed traditional male duties. Life expectancy was short. To reach the age of forty was nearly a miracle. When employed as school teachers, they were expected to remain unmarried. If carrying out a man's job, they were paid less. In many locales they had few freedoms such as educational opportunities, the right to vote, serve on juries or in public office and do certain types of work. They were frequently offered menial jobs. They were the necessary but unsung heroes in the development of Ohio. As noted in the front of this book, it is dedicated to those who made a positive contribution to Columbus and Franklin County. Women are at the top of the list.

Franklinton during the War of 1812

The War of 1812 commenced on June 18, four years before Columbus became the state capital. On that date, 1,200 acres of town lots in Columbus were first made available for purchase. The U.S. senators voted nineteen to thirteen to declare war, but Ohio's senators, including Thomas Worthington, were against it. Worthington thought the nation was too ill-prepared for such military action. Once the country entered the conflict, Worthington gave it his full support. The local settlers were more enthusiastic, hoping the war would in some way end the danger of Indian raids. The British were still encouraging the Native Americans to reclaim the Ohio land, alarming the settlers to a considerable degree. Despite the defeat of Tecumseh's Confederation of Indians at Tippecanoe in Indiana in 1811, the residents of Franklinton were in somewhat of a panic, and a stockade and defensive ditch were placed around the courthouse, and supplies were stockpiled. Governor Meigs ordered three regiments of soldiers to be raised in Dayton, Urbana and Franklinton. Regimental Generals were Duncan McArthur, James Findlay and Lewis Cass, each serving under General William Hull. Forts were built every twenty miles between Urbana and Maumee. Dense forest and the Great Black Swamp caused great hardship, and it took a long time for the men to reach Fort Detroit, their destination. Franklinton served as a headquarters for the "Northwest Army." Troops came and went creating considerable commotion. Commissary officers collected food and forage for the men and their horses. Local products were sold to the army at inflated prices making some merchants prosperous for a short period. The Worthington Manufacturing Company headed by James Kilbourne was an example. The company made uniforms and saddles and other items required by the military. General William Harrison visited Franklinton many times during the war. He met with Ohio Indian chiefs in Sullivant's backyard. One of the most influential Wyandot Indian chiefs, Tarhe, "The Crane," swore allegiance to the American cause. Most of the Indians sided with Great Britain. No Indian or British raids occurred in Franklinton during the war. Some British prisoners were taken to a makeshift prison on a sandbar in the Scioto River south of Columbus. No vestige of the prison remains. Hull surrendered to the British at Detroit on August 8, and the American troops returned in disgrace. The British commander allowed the Indians to massacre the American prisoners and wounded. Lucas Sullivant placed scouts in Logan County to warn of any approaching hostilities. General William Henry Harrison replaced Hull, but the American forces under General Winchester and Colonel Lewis suffered another defeat before Harrison took command on the battlefield and successfully captured Detroit. Much of the American success can be attributed to Commodore Oliver Perry whose fleet defeated the British on Lake Erie and ferried militia to the Detroit area. A huge Victory and International Peace Monument stands on South Bass Island commemorating his triumph. Tecumseh was killed in Canada in the Battle of the Thames River in 1813, and the war in Ohio ended.

Early Churches in Franklin County

The majority of early settlers were Scotch-Irish and Protestant. The first church in Franklinton was Presbyterian (1806). It was a log cabin on River Road, and The Reverend James Hoge was its pastor for fifty-one years. The "Old First" church moved to several locations in Columbus before settling in its present location at 1101 Bryden Road. In the early history of the church, the membership reached six hundred. Today, there are about two dozen members. The second church in Franklinton was Methodist (1814). It was used also as a school. In Columbus, the Trinity Episcopal Church first met in Lincoln Goodale's home/store in 1817. The church was built near East Broad Street and Pearl Alley in 1833 at a cost of ten thousand dollars. During the Civil War, female church members made uniforms for the Union soldiers. The German Lutheran Reform Church was established in 1821, and the first Baptist Church was started in 1825. St. Remigius was the earliest Catholic Church in Columbus in 1833 (its name changed to Holy Cross in 1848). St. Patrick's Catholic Church had its origin in 1852. The first Jewish temple, B'nai Israel, with a reform congregation, was dedicated at Main and Third Streets in 1870. Before that, their synagogues were in rented quarters. Joseph Goodman was the first salaried rabbi (1853). The low salaries of clergymen made holding other occupations mandatory.

The Wesley Chapel was organized as a Methodist Society and constructed on High Street near Gay Street on land donated by William Neil in 1846. Characteristic of that denomination, the interior was stark, without trappings or adornments, and pastors changed every two or three years. At first the sexes sat in divided sections. Later they were permitted to sit in the same pew. Rules relaxed further, and a choir and organ were allowed. One new clergyman was surprised by the attendance of Governors Salmon Chase and William Dennison who greeted him on the platform in honor of his father, Governor Allen Trimble, whom they had known. The Chapel burned in 1883 and was rebuilt elsewhere.

Chapter 3

First Capitals of Ohio and Early Columbus

First Capitals of Ohio

The first capital of the new state of Ohio (1803) was Chillicothe in Ross County. The Democratic-Republicans or anti-federalists (the "Chillicothe junta") were able to wrest the location away from Cincinnati, which was Federalist dominated, the most populous city and capital of the Northwest Territory (1787-1803). Chillicothe remained the capital until 1810. The stone county courthouse was used by the House of Representative and a newly erected brick annex was utilized for the Senate. For political considerations, the seat of government was moved to Zanesville for two years (1810-1812). Zanesville, in anticipation of the move, had constructed a brick edifice expressly for a state house. Then, the capital returned to Chillicothe for four more years (1812-1816). When it became apparent that the population growth of Cleveland and other Lake Erie towns would counterbalance the growth along the Ohio River, a more central location within the state was sought for the capital. In 1810, the state legislature appointed five commissioners to examine sites within forty miles of the center of the state and to select the most suitable place for a permanent seat of the state government. The most serious contenders for the capital were Franklinton, Worthington, Sells' property, Lancaster, Newark, Delaware and Circleville. The commissioners chose a site owned by John and Peter Sells, four and one-half miles west of Worthington (present day Dublin). The state legislature was open to any other offer of land and money for the capital. Worthington made a strong offer of $25,334, subscribed by 135 individuals. Four owners of Wolf Ridge, a forested piece of land on the east bank of the Scioto River and in the western portion of the Refugee Tract prevailed in their bid, and their location was selected (see area in map of Franklin County on p 14). They had secured several thousand acres from the original owners, John Halstead, Martha Walker, Benjamin Thompson, Seth Harding and James Price. The property was called Refugee Tract because it had been made available to Canadians who suffered property loss due to their allegiance to the cause of American independence. None of the original land grantees had set foot in the Ohio Territory. The four entrepreneurs offered twenty acres of land to

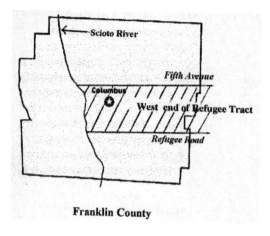

Fig. 5 Location of Columbus

the state for its permanent capital and were willing to spend up to $50,000 to erect state buildings. They agreed also to lay out a town upon the acreage. Ten acres were to be used for placement of state buildings and the remaining ten acres to be utilized for a penitentiary. This obviously indicated the importance and priority of law enforcement and punishment. No other town or group of people could match this offer. The state also made January 1815 the completion date for the penitentiary and December 1817 the date the state buildings must be finished. Any overrun of the $50,000 cost of buildings was to be the responsibility of the state. An agreement between the four proprietors and the legislature included supervision of the lots around the statehouse plot and of the platting of the new town of Columbus by a director appointed by the state legislature. The new seat of state government was guaranteed by law to remain in Columbus until 1840, suggesting the site would be permanent, but with a limitation release date. The owners of Wolf Ridge speculated that they would redeem their money and make a profit from sales of 1,200 acres turned into lots around the new capitol building. Since Columbus was guaranteed to be the capital for at least twenty-four years, this seemed a reasonable risk of their venture capital.

Between 1837 and 1846, considerable discussion was held among legislators about moving the state capital to a more central location. Newark, Delaware and Mount Vernon were mentioned. Columbus businessmen were alarmed, but nothing came of the notion after the legislature resolved the issue by a vote of seventeen to sixteen to keep Columbus as the permanent capital.

Selection of Columbus as Final Capital—1812

Similar to Washington D.C., Columbus was created specifically to be a capital city. It was carved out of the wilderness in 1812 in a state established only nine years earlier on the frontier. There was neither such precedence in any state nor one since.

Columbus was founded in the western portion of the Refugee Tract. This federal tract of land in the Ohio Territory was established by Congress from which to give land grants to residents of Canada and Nova Scotia, who in support of the American Revolution had been forced to flee from their homes. This large rectangular piece of land measured forty by four and one-half miles whose western boundary of its width was the Scioto River, and its eastern edge was the Muskingum River at Zanesville. The northern border of its length was the present Fifth Avenue and the southern boundary was the present Refugee Road, each in Columbus. The extreme western portion of this tract was in Franklin County (organized in 1803 by the legislature which extended from Pickaway County on its southern boundary to Lake Erie as its northern edge). The Franklin County dimensions lasted five years (1803-1808), after which Delaware County was formed to make up a new northern boundary of Franklin County. Early settlers in the area were William and John White, George Turner, William Hamilton, James Johnston, David Nelson, Colonel Edward Livingston, John Hunter, William Shaw, John Starr, Nathaniel Hamlin and John McGown. They farmed the land before Columbus was laid out. Their names suggested all were of British heritage.

General Joseph Foos, an officer in the War of 1812, a Franklinton judge and tavern owner, named the new capital Columbus after the discoverer of the "new world." The town's one square mile tract was bounded by North Public Lane (present day Nationwide Boulevard) on the north, South Public Lane (now Livingston Avenue) on the south, east Public Lane (today Parsons Avenue) on the east and the Scioto River on the west. The land was relatively flat and swampy with many springs and small ravines that cut through to the river. One intermittent stream, south of the capitol grounds was called Hayden's Creek. There were ponds that needed draining and filled with gravel. Trees were plentiful and would need to be cleared to make room for state buildings, churches, stores, taverns and homes. It was higher ground than Franklinton and was the chief reason that the new site was selected over its nearest contender. Another advantage was that the land was undeveloped, and a new city could be platted. Finally, Lucus Sullivant and nearby Franklinton had powerful influence with the legislature.

Early Development of Columbus

Fig. 6 Lyne Starling
—Columbus Metro Library

In 1812, the new state of Ohio accepted fifty thousand dollars worth of state buildings on twenty acres from Lyne Starling (Franklin County), James Johnston (Washington County), Alexander McLaughlin (Muskingum County) and John Kerr (Ross County) for their right to subdivide their public land in Columbus and to sell lots. The town was platted by Joel Wright and Joseph Vance.

Fig. 7 John Kerr
—Columbus Metro Library

Unfortunately, in 1879, the original plat map that had been in storage in the court house vault was destroyed by fire. A few of the first lots were given away. Soon the price of the one and two acre lots ranged from $200 to $1,000. Advertisements by the real estate speculators suggested that the lots were composed of fertile land, were located on a river that was easily navigable, and were connected to Lake Erie via a road (actually an Indian trail). The price was set with one-fifth down payment and the remainder to be paid in four equal installments with eight percent interest due with each annual payment. The first purchasers of lots were: Jacob Hare, Peter Putnam, George McCormick, George Harvey, John Shields, Michael and Alexander Patton, William Altman, John Collett, William McElvain, Daniel Kooser, Christian Heyl, Benjamin and George Pike, William Long, Townsend Nichols and Dr. John Edmiston. Soon there were many foreclosures. The depressed economy in 1820 brought the selling price for the less desirable lots to seven dollars. One foreclosed buyer contested the legal action. Lyne Starling, the seller and defendant, hired Henry Clay to represent him. Clay, a Kentuckian, practiced in U.S. court cases in Columbus. But, when he became U.S. Secretary of State in 1825, he separated himself from the case. The court decided in Starling's favor.

Newcomers located chiefly on High, Front, Broad, Town, State and Rich Streets. Front Street was visualized as the principal location for residences. The Worthington Manufacturing Company with Joel Buttles as manager erected a small brick building on High Street across from the state house for the sale of dry goods, hardware and groceries. McLene & Green opened a general store in a small log cabin on the south side of East Rich Street.

In the earliest days of Columbus, many legislators stayed in private homes. John Collett established a two-story brick tavern in 1813 on the west side of South High Street near the corner of State Street (Lion and Eagle). Volney Payne was its first manager until Collett took over from 1814 to 1816 when he sold the tavern to Robert Russell. The tavern's name was changed to the Globe in 1818. Russell finally closed his tavern in 1847. Other early tavern owners were Daniel Kooser, McCollum (Black Bear) and the Day brothers. The last tavern gained the nickname of War Office due to frequent brawls. The Columbus Inn, a "respectable tavern," was opened at the southeast corner of South High and Town Streets. Isaiah Voris started the White Horse Tavern. In 1816, James Gardiner began the Ohio Tavern on Friend Street (future Main Street). The many inns were necessary to provide lodging for the many newcomers and legislators in the new state capital.

Christian Heyl made the three-day journey from Lancaster to Columbus in 1813 with two heavily loaded wagons pulled by two five-horse teams. He built an oven in one of the three stalls of his small log cabin at the southeast corner of Rich and

High Streets and started the first bakery in Columbus. Firewood conveniently came from his lot. Two years later, he built the Franklin House nearby and managed the tavern for twenty-eight years. Gradually, Columbus acquired many of its first industries and businesses from Franklinton.

Of the original four proprietors responsible for the creation of Columbus, John Kerr died first, in 1823. He had been a councilman, the second mayor of the city (1818-1819), associate judge of the Court of Common Pleas and president of the Franklin Bank. He left a large family and estate. Alexander McLaughlin lost his fortune in 1820; at one time he was considered the wealthiest man in the state. Before he died in 1832, he supported himself by teaching in a country school. James Johnston also lost his fortune in 1820 and moved to Pittsburgh, Pennsylvania where he died in 1842. Lyne Starling was the most successful, living as a bachelor until his death in 1848, age sixty-five. He toured Europe in 1818. He donated $35,000 for the creation of Starling Medical College in 1842, the forerunner of The Ohio State University College of Medicine. Since the new village of Columbus was on the east bank of the Scioto River, directly across from Franklinton, a ferry service was used until a toll-bridge could be constructed to join the two villages (present Broad Street Bridge). A wooden bridge was built by Lucas Sullivant under charter from the state legislature. Sullivant collected the tolls. There was no toll for using the bridge if one could prove that it was used to attend church. Due to rot and damage, the bridge had to be rebuilt in ten years. Construction of streets on Indian trails and the necessary state buildings began. The tree stumps left after tree removal presented obstacles to horses and wagons. In 1815, two hundred dollars was raised by subscription for removing these obstructions on High Street. Other chief hazards to travel were the deep and treacherous ruts produced by wagons during rainy periods. High Street, parallel to the river, was made the main north/south thoroughfare. It had been part of an old Indian trail extending from the Ohio River to Lake Erie. Broad Street became the primary east/west artery. The first state house was constructed at the northeast corner of High and State Streets. Later, it would be reconstructed a few yards north and east of this corner. Springs were found a few hundred yards north of the center of town producing a stream. Following improvements, a street was placed there named Spring Street. Other early streets (e.g., Water Street and Center Alley) underwent name change later to current usage. High Street was one hundred feet wide, Broad Street was one hundred and twenty feet wide and the other streets were eighty-two feet in width. Growth was slow in the new capital until roads were improved. Transportation in Central Ohio was curtailed due to use of irregular Indian trails and the weather. Needless to say, it was an ordeal to travel to Columbus at this time. The village of Worthington, organized in 1803, was twelve miles to the north, and Granville was thirty miles northeast in Licking County. Zanesville was the largest settlement forty-three miles to the east, and Chillicothe was thirty-five miles directly south of Columbus. Dayton, fifty miles west was the largest community in that direction. The nearest post office was in Chillicothe. Weekly mail was brought to Joel Buttle's store for distribution. Matthew Matthew was postmaster for two years to be followed by Buttles who served for fifteen years. The first mayor of Columbus was Jarvis Pike, age twenty-two (1816-1817). He was designated by Governor Thomas Worthington to remove tree trunks from the capital's streets. When remuneration was not forthcoming, Pike sued the state for his compensation. In addition to the mayor, the other first governing officials were a recorder, treasurer, surveyor, marshal, clerk of the market, an appraiser and a lister. Nine councilmen were elected from which the mayor was selected. When Columbus became a city in 1834, it was divided into four wards, each with three councilmen. In 1852, the number of councilmen for each ward was reduced to two.

The first meal-making device was a block mill made by burning a large hole in a log. The corn was pounded into meal and sifted through a deer skin that was punctured with several holes. The first sawmill for the new capital was erected by Richard Courtney and John Shields in 1813 on the west side of the Scioto River south of Franklinton, and the first flour mill followed in 1816 nearby. Corn was the first crop planted. Soon, water-powered mills for sawing lumber and grinding corn and a distillery were improvised. The first water mill was erected by Robert Balentine. The first whiskey distillery was built by Benjamin White, who incidentally was the first sheriff of Franklin County. Hoster's brewery and a tannery were started at this time. Later John Blenkner, another German brewmaster, opened his beer making company. The breweries were located adjacent to the Scioto River, southwest of the public square. This area, when further developed, would be called the Brewery District. Salt was obtained from a spring several miles distant. Its value was such that cash was often required for purchase. The manufacture of cotton yarn by use of horse-power started in Columbus in 1821. A woolen mill was commenced in 1822.

In its first years, Columbus had no sewage system or street cleaning service. Some animals were kept on the citizens' premises. Waste material from homes was dumped on the edge of lots or buried or directed to the Scioto River. When the canal came to Columbus, an aqueduct was constructed over the canal to carry sewage to the Scioto River. Horses deposited their excrements on the streets. These biological hazards produced an odor offensive to all. Soon persons were appointed to keep the streets free of sewage and manure, and ordinances were passed regarding where animals would be allowed. Until the 1970's, Columbus had the nickname of "cow town." The first substantial brick sewer was constructed in 1848 and lasted for one hundred years. Today, Columbus and the county have several water treatment plants and solid waste disposal facilities.

Columbus was incorporated as a Borough in 1816 with a census of just over seven hundred. When the county courthouse site was moved across the river to the Borough of Columbus in 1824, the old courthouse in Franklinton was converted into a school. Three judges presided over the new County Common Pleas Court. The first physician to settle in the capital was Dr. John Edmiston, followed by Drs. Parsons, Ball and Goodale. The first homes and businesses were located on High or Broad Street. In 1814, the first marriage took place in Columbus. It was performed for Jane Armstrong and George B. Harvey. The first public market opened on South High Street in 1814. The hitching posts outside the market were often crowded. Included were Indians with horses, well-laden with furs and maple sugar for trade. A second larger market was built on State Street in 1817. The proprietor lived above it. Soon the living quarters were turned into an amusement and gaming business. A new market was placed on the same site but without a second floor in 1829. The first school was a small structure on Public Square and opened in 1814; students were taught for a fee. The earliest teachers were: Uriah Case, John Peoples, Mr. Whitehill and W.T. Martin. Several lawyers located in the new village in 1815 (David Smith, Orris Parish, David Scott and Gustavus Swan). Most of the new homes were close to the south and east sides of the new state house.

The mercantile trade in the new village included such items as dry goods, notions, glassware, tinware, saws, munitions, shoes, boots, shawls, saddles, books, Bibles, pocketbooks, umbrellas, groceries, spices, medicines, tobacco and whiskey. The latter was used frequently for bartering since currency was scarce. The clothing of the first citizens of the frontier town was usually homespun. Some wore outer garments made of deerskin.

Penal Institutions

Fig. 8 The first state penitentiary.
—from Columbus Metro Library

Following English and Colonial custom, whipping and fining were the punishments for crime. This was changed to imprisonment in early Ohio statehood. The first state penitentiary was located on a ten acre lot on Scioto Street (now 2nd Street) at Mound Street, near where the Cultural Arts Center now stands. It was constructed in 1813-1815 as one of the first state buildings, indicative of the pressure to incarcerate evildoers before attending to political matters. It was a three-story brick building with a basement that contained a kitchen, an eating room for prisoners and a cellar for storing perishables. The bricks were made from clay, found in abundance in the nearby Indian mound (Mound Street) that also contained bones, utensils and trinkets. The keeper or warden resided on the first floor. There were thirteen cells on the second and third floors. A one hundred feet square yard was enclosed by a high stone fence. This prison was replaced in 1818 with a brick structure several times larger. It included blacksmith, cooper, and other workshops. Other occupations by the prisoners were shoe making and tailoring. Gradually weaving, cigar making, broom construction, stove manufacturing, furniture making, and the building of wagons were introduced as well as work on public buildings and roads. The new establishment had a kitchen and eating facilities on the first floor and over fifty unheated cells and a hospital section on the second floor. Five solitary cells were below ground, accessed only by a trap door. The entire prison was enclosed by high double stone walls. The original prison was renovated into quarters for the keeper. Every year, escapes occurred. In 1822, the inmate population included one hundred and three white men, one white woman and nine African-Americans.

In the first decades of Columbus, citizens were called for watchman duty much like being called for jury duty. The watchmen were responsible for lighting street lamps and arresting drunk or suspicious persons found loitering after ten p.m. Suspicious persons were described as vagrants, idlers, disorderly or lewd individuals. They were turned over to the town marshal. Punishment varied, but one historian relates that for extreme punishment, men, women and children were whipped until their backs resembled raw beef. Then, they were tied face down on the cold ground while shovels of hot ashes and coals of fire were sprinkled on the bleeding flesh. Other forms of punishment included dunking, hanging by the wrists and handcuffing inside sweat boxes. Some inmates died from this punishment. Surprisingly, pardons were common. Later, the practice of religious faiths was encouraged, and a chapel and chaplains were made available.

The third penitentiary, similar to the previous one, was constructed on the northwest side of Columbus on West Spring Street in 1834 at a cost of $93,300. An annex and other buildings were added over the next hundred years. Its first occupants were one hundred and eighty-nine prisoners transferred from the old prison. The former prison was converted into a state armory and finally razed in 1855. The new penal institution, the state's largest, had twenty-four feet high walls and could hold seven hundred prisoners. Prisoners labored in silence during daylight hours and were locked in solitary confinement at night. Gradually, cells for women were added, and federal prisoners were kept by contract. Upon admittance, new inmates were searched, stripped and deloused. Instead of fingerprinting, they underwent

Fig. 9 The third state penitentiary was opened on West Spring Street in 1834 and used until 1979.
—from Columbus Metro Library

Bertillon measurements that included many of the skull. Warden Elijah G. Coffin (1886-1900) introduced military-style regulations, so that prisoners marched to meals and to their cells at night. They were served meals in shifts. They were forced to keep their cells neat. Cholera swept through the prison in 1849-1850, causing forty-three deaths. Two doctors in attendance died also. More humane treatment of prisoners gradually occurred so that by 1900 the penitentiary was considered to be a model prison. Well-connected inmates on "Bankers' Row" were given large, airy cells and special privileges. The "new punishment" consisted of a hard box to sleep on and bread and water for food. The electric chair replaced the gallows for executions in 1897. One prisoner, a 250-pound woman, brought her baby to the execution chamber. The first execution took place in 1844; the use of an electric chair ceased in 1963, after three hundred and fifteen prisoners had been executed by this method. Since then, lethal injection has been used. By 1910, indoor recreation rooms had been installed, a feature of more humane treatment during the progressive era. Women were transferred to a new women's reformatory in Marysville in 1913. The largest fire, thought to be started by inmates, occurred in 1930 killing three hundred and twenty-three inmates. Amazingly, damage amounted to only $11,000. Riots accompanied by fires, the taking of hostages and deaths of inmates and guards punctuated the history of the old penitentiary. Famous prisoners included William Porter (a.k.a. "O.Henry"—authored *Gift of the Magi,* while jailed three years for embezzlement), George "Bugs" Moran, a Chicago mobster, and Confederate General John Morgan, charged with stealing horses. The latter and thirteen of his raiders escaped by digging into a ventilation tunnel and then through an inner wall and finally climbing over the outer wall by means of a hook and blanket rope during a rainy and dark night. Morgan and an accomplice took a train to Cincinnati and then a skiff across the Ohio River to freedom. The Morgan cell block remained a feature in tours for visitors for many decades. The electric chair was also a popular tourist item. "Going up to Columbus" often meant serving hard time in the state penitentiary. The badly deteriorated penitentiary was ordered closed in 1979 by order of federal Judge Robert Duncan. The prisoners were transferred finally in 1984, primarily to the Mansfield state prison and some to the Southern Ohio Correctional Facility at Lucasville. The Northeast Ohio Correctional Center, opened in Youngstown in 1997 and owned and operated privately, is a medium-security prison for the state. Today, a parking garage, serving the Nationwide Arena, occupies the old penitentiary site.

In Columbus, the first law enforcement officer was the Village Marshal, who also acted in charge of night watchmen. In 1834, the position became less political by becoming an elective office. After 1850, city and county jails were separate. An ordinance in 1868 provided for twenty-five policemen in navy-blue uniforms. By 1900, civil service exams eliminated some of the influence of politics in appointing policemen. The Old Town Street police station was severely damaged by the 1913 flood. In 1930, a new Central Police Station was built at Gay Street and Marconi Boulevard and rebuilt in 1991. It now opens at the southeast corner of Long Street and Marconi Boulevard.

City Government

In the beginning, the state legislature stipulated the governance of Columbus. A mayor and a few minor officials were elected. In 1834, the mayor and a sizeable city council were elected from wards or divisions of the city. The number of councilmen grew to twenty-two. In 1914, a new city charter reduced the council to seven, and they were to be elected citywide. Other elected officials are Auditor, City Attorney, Clerk of Court and Municipal Court Judges. The mayor and council then appointed the necessary officials to manage the city. The mayor's cabinet came to include Departments of Technology, Finance, Public Service and Public Utilities. In turn, the department heads appointed the Directors of Parks and Recreation, Commerce, Health and Civil Service. Today, the term for the mayor and councilpersons has been increased to four years.

For a century, Columbus and Franklin County operated under a Justice of the Peace system. In 1916, the state's General Assembly created the Columbus Municipal Court. Further changes in state law gave the court countywide jurisdiction in 1955, and a change in name to Franklin County Municipal Court in 1968. The fourteen Municipal Court Judges and six Magistrates in the General Division of the court have county wide jurisdiction over all cases up to $10,000 in fines; criminal, traffic, jury and non-jury trials; and hearings involving misdemeanor cases. In 1992, an Environment Division was established to enforce building, housing, health and safety codes or resolve disputes involving environmental issues. This Division has one judge. The Clerk of Court performs financial and management duties for both Divisions. Administrative offices oversee juries, case assignments, probation services, court reporters, security, bailiffs, language interpretation, vehicle immobilization and volunteers. In 1979, the court's facilities were transferred from City Hall to the Franklin County Municipal Court building at 375 South High Street. Two dozen courtrooms are provided for court functions.

The clerk's office is composed of seven divisions that occupy four floors. A new county courthouse is in the planning stage.

Early Roads and Bridges

Lucas Sullivant built the Broad Street toll bridge over the Scioto River in 1816. It was inherited by his son, Joseph, who in turn rebuilt it in 1826. When the National Road came to Columbus in the mid-1830's, private citizens raised $8,000 dollars and the County paid $2,000 dollars to buy the bridge franchise from Sullivant. The national government then built a new bridge that was free for all to use. It had two tracks for wagons and a walkway on each side. Toll bridges were built over Alum and Big Walnut Creeks. They were unprofitable and were abandoned when they became unsafe. In 1923, a new and straighter road was constructed of crushed rock from Columbus to Worthington (present High Street). Also, in that year, the Franklin County seat was moved from Franklinton to Columbus. In 1823, the official name of the Whetstone River was changed to the Olentangy River as part of a movement to recognize Indian heritage.

Some of the early street names in Columbus underwent change with time. North Street became Naghten and much later Nationwide Boulevard. South Street is now Livingston Avenue. East Public Lane changed to Parsons Avenue. Friend Street became Main Street. Other city center street names such as Rich, Town, State, Gay, Spring, Mound and Long have survived. Some alleys were named for trees: Hickory, Elm, Maple and Cherry. All of our presidents' names have been used for streets in Columbus except Buchanan, Bush and Polk. Both the first and last names of Alexander Hamilton have been utilized. Jack Nicklaus's name is attached to the I-270 outerbelt. Interestingly, a Dr. Young purchased the Indian mound (later Mound Street) and built a house atop the forty foot mound. Several families lived there before it was flattened to build a road and to facilitate traffic. Clay removed from the mound was used to make bricks.

Early Road Connections to and from Columbus

In 1826, the state legislature passed a road bill that allowed a company of men to form a joint stock company for the purpose of building a toll-road, the *Columbus and Sandusky Turnpike*. It was to be constructed of stone, gravel, wood and other suitable materials. The bill said nothing about the native clay mud it produced which the public soon experienced. The eighteen-foot wide road stretched one hundred and six miles, passing through Worthington, Delaware, Marion, and Bucyrus, and took eight years to construct (1828-1836). James Kilbourne was in charge of surveying, and Orange Johnson was a commissioner and principal agent in charge of construction. Congress donated thirty-one thousand and eight hundred dollars and forty acres to the state to be used in the project. It cost $74,376, raised by private subscription. The state appointed an inspector who pronounced the road satisfactory. The users of the turnpike complained loudly about the impassable conditions after rains and tore down the toll gates as often as they were re-erected. This caused the legislative act to be repealed (1845), and the state then proceeded to build its own highway of real gravel on the bed of the old road-free for use by the public. The turnpike proprietors sued the state for damages, but the bill for reimbursement was lost in the legislative chambers. Other toll-turnpikes that lasted for short periods of time were *The Columbus and Worthington Plank Road, The Columbus and Portsmouth Turnpike, The Columbus and Harrisburg Turnpike, The Columbus and Johnstown Turnpike, The Columbus and Sunbury Turnpike, The Columbus and Granville Turnpike,* and *The Columbus and Groveport Turnpike.* Short turnpikes were built as connecters between the larger roads. The collected tolls barely paid the stockholders for their efforts; none of whom made any great profit. Most turnpikes were money losers. The longer roads were operated by each county through which they passed, having their own shareholders. Obviously, the building of private roads was highly speculative, and, eventually, the road building costs had to be shared by the taxpayers.

Road building was expensive, and states could little afford such projects. Therefore, the earliest efforts were carried out by private consortiums, and tolls were exacted for their use. It was recognized by the more astute national leaders that a good crushed rock road was needed to connect the east to the old Northwest Territory. An expenditure bill to construct such a national highway was signed by Thomas Jefferson in 1806. The first ten miles out of Cumberland, Maryland was not completed until 1811. The second stretch reached Wheeling, Virginia in 1817. Construction restarted in 1825, and, by 1833, the road entered Columbus, Ohio. Again its progress was stalled. It entered Columbus on Friend Street (later renamed Main Street) and veered sharply north to Broad Street in Bexley before continuing west, passing the Capitol and crossing over the Broad Street/Scioto River bridge. Later, the road upon entering Columbus, continued on Main Street until it reached South High Street before turning north to Broad Street. These routes were fought for by businessmen. Repairs on this interstate road were financed partially by charging tolls every ten miles. Initially, a rider and horse cost three cents; persons in a stage were charged four cents and coaches eighteen cents. The charge for cattle was higher than for sheep and hogs. Tollgate keepers were appointed by the governor and received their salary from gate receipts. By 1842, the road was macadamized, and coaches sped along at six miles per hour. Accidents and overturns occurred. Coaches and their floors would become mud caked, windows would break and curtains became torn and dirty. Some coaches leaked badly. A long blast of a horn announced the arrival of mail. As more settlers arrived, the roads and modes of transportation were improved. The National Road was also called U.S. 40, and, eventually, during the Eisenhower administration would become superseded by interstate highway I-70 that went on to Indianapolis and St. Louis before proceeding through Kansas City and ending abruptly in Utah. The National Road has been maintained in an improved condition as a scenic route and for servicing small towns. It is still Main Street in Columbus. Workers on the road were mainly Irish immigrants and a few were from Germany. Enough workers stayed in Columbus to swell its population significantly.

Chapter 4

Formation of Franklin County and Townships

When Ohio statehood was born in 1803, seventeen counties were recognized. Nine counties had existed in the Northwest Territory prior to statehood. The nine counties and their principal towns were: Washington (Marietta)-1788, Hamilton (Cincinnati)-1790, Jefferson (Steubenville)-1797, Adams (West Union)-1797, Ross (Chillicothe)-1798, Clermont (Batavia)-1800, Trumbull (Warren)-1800, Fairfield (Lancaster)-1800 and Belmont (St. Clairsville)-1801.

Fig. 10 The seventeen Ohio Counties when state entered Union in 1803.

After Franklin County was split off from Ross County in 1803, four townships were carved within the new county in the same year with Franklinton serving as county seat. Franklin Township occupied the southwest quadrant, Darby Township was in the northwest portion, Harrison Township in the southeastern part of the county, and Liberty Township was in the northeast quadrant. Each township had at least one Justice of the Peace. Lucas Sullivant acted as the first county clerk. The southern county boundary was shortened when Pickaway County was placed between Ross and Franklin counties in 1810. Likewise, Delaware County was created in 1808 to form the new northern border, thus removing Lake Erie as Franklin County's first northern limitation. Today, the northern boundary of Franklin County is found at Lazelle and County Line Roads. The southern delineation is Hiner and London-Lancaster Roads. Tippett, Dixon and Taylor

Roads are on the eastern edge and Big Darby Creek flows along most of the western border.

Fig. 11 The final Ohio counties and the years they were organized.

The formation of new townships began early, and their future names and principal towns are listed (Table 1, page 28). The land east of the Scioto River that was in the Congressional District and occupied the southeast corner of Franklin County, became Hamilton (Lockbourne) and Madison (Groveport) Townships.

The United States Military District occupying the northeast corner of the county included Plain (New Albany), Jefferson (Gahanna), Mifflin, Blendon (Westerville), Sharon (Worthington) and Clinton (Clintonville) Townships. The Refugee Tract starting at the Scioto River and extending directly east became Montgomery and Truro (Reynoldsburg) Townships. Later, Montgomery Township became Columbus and part of Franklin Township.

In the Virginia Military District, situated west of the Scioto River, Jackson Township (Grove City) and Pleasant Township (Georgesville and Harrisburg) were split off of the south end of Franklin Township in 1815. Norwich (Hilliard) and Prairie (Alton and Galloway) were separated from the west side of Franklin Township. Washington Township, the northernmost portion of Franklinton in the old Virginia Military District, became the site of Dublin. Upper Arlington and a portion of Worthington were located in Perry Township, split off of northeastern Franklin Township. Brown Township in the Virginia Military District was the last township to be formed in Franklin County in 1830 (along Darby Creek).

Table 1. Franklin County Townships
(* original townships; • current townships)

Name	Date of Origin	Location	Principal Town
*Franklin•	1803	Southwest	Franklinton
Pleasant•	1807—from Franklin	Southwest	Georgesville
Norwich•	1813—from Franklin	Northwest	Hilliard
Jackson•	1815—from Franklin	Southwest	Grove City
Prairie•	1819—from Franklin	Westcentral	Alton/Galloway
Brown•	1830—from Franklin	Westcentral	None
*Darby	1803	Northwest	Dublin
Washington•	1809—from Darby Franklin and Liberty	Northwest	Dublin
*Harrison	1803	Southeast	Groveport
Hamilton•	1807—from Harrison	Southeast	Lockbourne and Liberty
Madison•	1809—from Hamilton	Southeast	Groveport
*Liberty	1803	Northeast	Worthington
Plain•	1810—from Liberty	Northeast	New Albany
Sharon•	1806—from Liberty	Northcentral	Worthington
Montgomery•	1807—from Liberty	Central	Columbus
Truro•	1810—from Liberty	Eastcentral	Reynoldsburg
Mifflin•	1811—from Liberty	Eastcentral	Airport
Clinton•	1811—from Liberty	Northcentral	Clintonville
Blendon•	1815—from Liberty	Northeast	Westerville
Jefferson•	1816—from Liberty/Plain	Eastcentral	Gahanna
Perry•	1820—fromLiberty/Washington	Northcentral	Upper Arlington & Worthington

Due to subdivisions, the names of Darby, Harrison and Liberty disappeared. Of the original township names, only Franklin was retained.

The Franklin Township courts were moved from Franklinton to Columbus in 1824 and were located in the U.S. Court House until 1840. A federal Court House had been erected in 1820. Part of the building funds was provided by citizens' donations. The building was torn down in 1850 when the U.S. District Court was moved to Cincinnati. Most townships had their own post office, churches, schools, small stores and mills. Revolutionary War veterans were given warrants for land in the Military and Refugee portions while Congress sold lots from its Congressional Tract to obtain revenue.

Fig. 12 The second Franklin County Courthouse (1887-1974)
—Columbus Metro Library

The first Franklin County Courthouse was built in 1824. In 1879, fire destroyed the building and many of its records. Plans had already been underway to build a new courthouse and it was completed in 1887. It would last nearly a century before it was razed to make way for a new Courthouse.

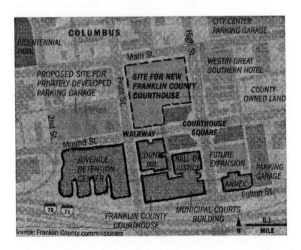

Fig. 13 This map shows the location of the Franklin County judiciary buildings in 2007. The site for the new Franklin County Courthouse is shown just northwest of Courthouse Square. All buildings will be connected by underground tunnels. Green space will be an important part of the complex.

Fig. 14 This is the third Franklin County Jail, opened at 36 East Fulton Street in 1889. It replaced the second county jail constructed in 1865. This jail was closed and razed in 1971.

—from Columbus Metro Library

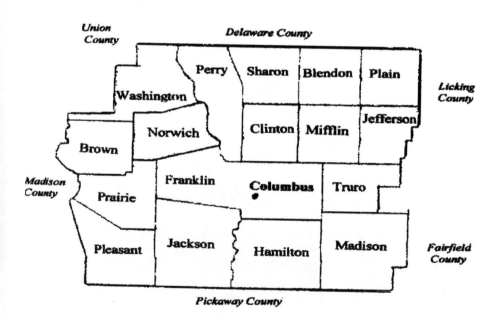

Fig. 15 Current Townships in Franklin County.

Chapter 5

State and Federal Governments

State Houses in Columbus

In 1816, all state offices were removed from Chillicothe to Columbus, and the first legislative session opened in December in the newly constructed State House. It was located on the southwest corner of State House square, facing High Street to the west and State Street to the south. Its base measured seventy-five by fifty feet. The foundation consisted of locally quarried limestone. Upon this rested brick and wood work. The bricks were made near the site from clay dug from a large adjacent Indian mound (from which Mound Street received its name). The two lofty stories had a central square roof upon which rested a balcony with railed walkways and a bell and clock tower. From the balcony, spectators could view the city and the Scioto River. Rising above the tower was a steeple, ending one hundred and nine feet from the ground. The main floor contained the House of Representatives, two committee rooms and a gallery. The Senate chamber and two committee rooms occupied the second floor. The interior had solid oak trimmings, and oiled and waxed walnut floors. Large wooden columns were painted in imitation of clouded marble. Large stone slabs with patriotic inscriptions were placed over doors.

The State Office Building was directly north and adjacent to the State House. It was a plain two-story brick structure with a stone base one hundred and fifty feet long and twenty-five feet wide. The Governor, Secretary, Auditor, Treasurer, Quarter Master and Adjutant General had offices in the building which were shared by other officials and a library. It, too, ended existence in 1857 when it was razed to make room for a new State House. A third building in line and north of the office building was the United States Court House. It conformed in size and composition with the first two buildings in the state house square. It contained two jury rooms, a court room and offices for the Clerk and Marshal. It was built in 1820 and torn down in 1855 when the Federal Court House was moved to Cincinnati. County offices were to be found in a long one-story brick building behind the Court House.

Fig. 16 First State Buildings
—from Columbus Metro Library

In this scene of the first state buildings, the observer is looking east and the buggy is traveling north on High Street. The west entrance of the first State House (on the right) faces South High Street with its south side (not seen) toward State Street. The middle building is the state office building. The third building on the left is the United States Courthouse.

Jervis Pike had been instructed by Governor Worthington to remove trees from the state house square between 1815 and 1816. When Pike was not paid, he had the Governor arrested and conducted before Squire King, and the matter was settled without trial. This episode has been a matter of jest since. The remainder of the state house grounds was farmed for four years and enclosed with a rough rail fence. The fence was replaced by a neat and substantial fence of cedar posts and white painted rails. Several elm trees were planted in a decorative pattern. In 1839, still another fence of ungainly rough boards, twelve feet high was erected to serve as a semi-prison since prisoners worked on the new buildings. The old white fence was purchased by several citizens and appeared around their lots.

The state used thirty-five thousand dollars of the fifty thousand dollars given by the proprietors for the construction of the state buildings. Part of the labor was furnished by local prisoners. The legislature ordered a return of $15,000 to the four proprietors with a note of thanks. The State House, built of brick, lasted until 1837 when deterioration and fire required its removal. Masses of documents and minutes were lost, but all of the clerk's papers were saved.

The second State House was controversial from the beginning. Plans for its construction commenced in 1839 when $200,000 was allotted by the legislature.

In fits of stops and starts, it was completed eighteen years later after spending an overrun to $2.2 million. Henry Walter designed it in the Greek Revival style. Local limestone and brick were used by penitentiary inmate laborers. Its magnificence was celebrated by refreshments and a gala night long dance to the accompaniment of two bands. Salmon P. Chase was the first governor to meet in the new state house in 1857. President-elect Abraham Lincoln visited the capital city in 1861 on his way to Washington. He was entertained and spoke in the new capitol building.

In the 1990's, a several million dollar renovation of the State Capitol took place. Now, gleaming marble and fancy oak and gold leaf adorn its interior. Ohioans can view its charm with pride.

Fig. 17 Current State Capitol, built in 1857 and renovated in the 1990's.
—from Columbus Metro *Library*

The Ohio Judiciary

Through most of its history the Ohio Supreme conducted its business in shared quarters. Beginning with statehood in 1803, the three justices, appointed by the legislature, traveled on horseback to each county across the state to hear cases. Once a year the full court met in the State House. After 1851, all cases were heard in the State House. In 1901, the court moved to the Judiciary Annex (now the Senate Office Building) and shared space with the Attorney General's office. The Annex was built next to the statehouse. In 1974, the court moved to the new Rhodes State Office Tower on East Broad Street. These quarters proved to be insufficient.

The final move of the judiciary was to the State Departments Building at 65 South Front Street. It was renovated in 2004 and became the sixteen-story Ohio

Judiciary Center. The original Front Street state office building was designed by Harry Blake of Cincinnati and finished in 1932 at a cost $5 million. In that year, a natural gas explosion damaged and killed eleven workers. Repairs cost $750,000. Initial tenants included the Industrial Commission, the State Library and the Departments of Agriculture, Public Works, Industrial Relations and Taxation.

The ground floor lobby of the Judiciary Center is decorated with mosaic ceilings, designed light fixtures, and bronze plaques of Indian Chiefs Tecumseh, Pontiac, Little Turtle and Logan. For reasons unknown, Blue Jacket is left out. Immediately south of the lobby is the Visitor Education Center. The Grand Concourse on the first floor leads into the centrally placed Supreme Court Room. Bold and muted murals, appointed with walnut and marble, depict Ohio history in Renaissance, Rococo and Art Deco styles. Paintings and friezes illustrate a panorama of early Ohio events and its people. Significant developments in Ohio law are also carved into the court's bench. Seats can accommodate visitors and hundreds of school children who are brought on tours to see the court in action and to marvel the artwork. There are two hearing rooms on the first floor and a law library and reading room on the eleventh floor. The remainder of the building contains a Court of Claims, the Ohio Judiciary Conference, Ohio Criminal Sentencing Commission, the Board of Commissioners on Grievances and Discipline, the Client's Security Fund and many offices for those involved in judiciary tasks.

Fig. 18 The Judiciary Center
(LeVeque Tower in background)

Today, all seven Supreme Court judges including the chief justice are elected by the citizens of the state in a non-partisan ballot and serve a six-year term. The court hears cases appealed from the twelve district courts, the Tax Board and the Public Utilities Commission. It also hears cases involving interpretation of the Ohio Constitution and death penalty appeals and is the last resort for sundry legal disputes.

Columbus has courts that handle Common Pleas, Probate, Domestic Relations, Juveniles, Claims, and Municipal/County cases. Some of the cities in the county have a Mayor's Court that settles minor disputes and violations of city codes and infractions related to use of automobiles.

The first judges in Columbus were: Wyllis Silliman-Common Pleas, 1803; John Dill, David Jamison and Joseph Foos-Associate Judges, 1803. Other first appointments were William Rankin-Probate, 1851; Prosecuting Attorney-Reuben Bonam, 1805; Lucas Sullivant-Clerk of Court, 1803; Joseph Dixon-Coroner, 1805; Commissioners—John Blair, Benjamin Sells and Arthur O'Harra, 1804; Surveyor-Joseph Vance-1803; Recorder-Lucas Sullivant, 1804; Treasurer-Jacob Grubb-1803; County Collector-Benjamin White, 1803; and Assessor-James Kilbourne, 1825.

Ohio's First Members of Congress

According to the federal constitution, an Ohio representative to Congress was to be chosen for every 30,000 citizens. Ohio was eligible to elect only one representative in 1803. Jeremiah Morrow of Warren County was chosen; he received only two votes in Franklin County. The first Representative to Congress from Franklin County was James Kilbourne of Worthington in 1812. He served two terms. The first U.S. senators were Thomas Worthington and John Smith, both chosen by the legislature.

Fig. 19 Thomas Worthington
"Father of Ohio Statehood"
—Columbus Metro Library

First Franklin County Members of Ohio Legislature

The first representative to the state legislature from Franklin County as a sole district was John Blair in 1808. Likewise, the first Franklin County person elected to the Ohio Senate was Joseph Foos in 1810. He served five additional terms although not consecutively (1812-1828).

Ohio's First Governor

Edward Tiffin, from Chillicothe, and brother-in-law of Thomas Worthington, was elected to be the first governor of Ohio (two terms, 1803-1807). He was an admirer of Thomas Jefferson.

During this early era in Ohio, two future presidents of the nation were born in the state: Ulysses Grant in Point Pleasant (1822) and Rutherford Hayes in Delaware (1822).

Chapter 6

Columbus in the Mid-Nineteenth Century

Witchcraft Madness

In 1810, an historic event took place fifteen miles north of Franklinton near the banks of the Scioto River. A peaceful, harmless, elderly Wyandot Indian Chief, Leatherlips, lived in the vicinity. He was accused of participating in witchcraft by the Shawnees and was sentenced to death by the Prophet (brother of Tecumseh, living in Indiana). The witchcraft charge was concocted because Leatherlips refused to join Tecumseh's confederation to oppose the settlers. A party of executioners arrived and pronounced sentence on the old man. Thereupon, Leatherlips ate a full meal, washed and adorned himself in his best finery and was made to kneel next to a freshly prepared grave. He shook hands with the spectators, sang a death prayer and was then beaten over the head until lifeless. Drops of sweat that appeared on his brow were pointed out by the Indians as proof of his guilt. He was immediately buried in his regalia. A number of settlers were present but unable to intervene. Today, a monument at the site commemorates the event.

Franklin County's Early Newspapers

Editing a newspaper was precarious in early Ohio. Supplies were difficult to obtain. Local news was often stale by the time a weekly paper went to press. Much of the news was gossip and unreliable. News dispatches from the east coast were usually two or three weeks late, and foreign items were delayed one to three months in reaching Columbus. Reporters and editors moved away, and replacements were uncertain. Owners and editors changed frequently among dozens of papers. Subscriptions for newspapers were nominal, but cash was not readily available, and bartering was the most frequent form of payment. Although a day of the week was set for printing, this was not dependable, due to illness, weather, other priorities and inconvenience. When the legislature was in session, the issuance of the newspaper was more certain. Special events like fires, elections, war events, murders and unexpected calamities were treated by issuing "extras." These were often in the form of a hand bill and free to subscribers. Irregularity and inaccuracy was the rule in publishing the news. Printing was done with hand presses until steam power was introduced in the mid 1830's. The introduction of telegraphy produced a big change in journalism including an added expense. The papers became bi-and tri-weeklies and finally dailies became standard in the 1840's. The introduction of railroads and better highways increased the transmission speed of news. The new state constitution of 1851 introduced the office of State Printer and it was filled usually by a Columbus newspaper publisher. When political emotions were heated, especially during war time, mobs would vent their dislike of a newspaper or its editor by use of arson, vandalism or physical harm. Occasionally, a publisher was beaten, killed or fled from the city.

The first Franklin County newspaper originated in Worthington in 1811. It was called the *Western Intelligencer,* and its publisher was James Kilbourne, the principal founder of Worthington in 1803. Kilbourne had purchased a printing press in 1809 but it remained idle for two years. His printing operation was moved to Columbus in 1814, and its proprietorship passed to P.H. Olmstead, Joel Buttles and Ezra Griswold, Jr. They continued the editorial policy of supporting the federal government and changed the name to *Western Intelligencer and Columbus Gazette.* The newspaper eventually became *The Ohio State Journal* (1839) after merging with the *Western Stateman,* the *Columbus Sentinel,* the *Ohio State Bulletin* and the *Ohio Political Register and Western Calendar.* The change in editors and owners was frequent. In 1812, James B. Gardiner commenced publication of the *Freemen's Chronicle.* Gardiner is considered the first newspaper publisher in Columbus. He pledged to support religion, liberty, law and the rights of individuals. Its advertisements included those of businessmen R.W. McCoy, Henry Brown, Starling & Delashmut, L. Goodale and Samuel Barr. Other advertisers were Archibald, saddler; Richard Courtney, tailor; Samuel Culbertson, hatter; George Skidmore, blacksmith; Matthew Bailey, shoemaker, Samuel King, tanner; David F. Heaton, tailor; Orris Parish, lawyer and John Ball, physician. Military men advertising in the paper included Brigadier General Joseph Foos, Colonel Edward Livingston, Brigadier Inspector Gustavus Swan, First Lieutenants Jacob Reab and John McElvain, and a Third Lieutenant looking for deserters. A third paper, the *Ohio Monitor,* existed twenty years, from 1816 to 1836. It supported the Democratic Party. One paper had the interesting name of *Ohio Register and Anti-Masonic Review.* Most of the smaller papers were merged or sold to the larger newspapers. A Baptist weekly called *The Cross and Journal* existed from 1838 to 1849. Other short-lived papers were started for the sole purpose of supporting presidential candidates and ceased after the elections. During the presidential campaigns of William Henry Harrison in 1840 and 1844, the *Tornado,* the *Ohio Tribune* and the *Whig Battering Ram* were examples of newspapers that ceased publication after the elections. Some opposed the Know-

Nothing Party (*Continental*) and others were for abolition of slavery (*Columbian*) or for temperance (*The Alliance*). Still others were printed in German; the best known was the *West Bote*. In the 1940's, Columbus could claim that half of its population was of German ethnicity. There were many other newspapers that had short runs. Some were published weekly, bi-weekly or monthly by fraternal, educational, industrial, medical and legal organizations.

Early Taverns and Coffee Houses in Columbus

State gambling prohibitions did not deter the presence of pool tables and roulette wheels in the capital city. In addition to many taverns, several coffee houses (Eagle, Globe and Swan) were frequented chiefly by politicians and lawyers where they commented on the weather and exchanged local and national gossip. Wine and mint juleps were also served. Women and blacks were noticeably absent except as waiters. One popular black waiter was captured by his former owner and taken back to Kentucky. Patrons of the Eagle bought his freedom, allowing his return to Columbus. Drunkenness was common and often tolerated despite local laws against lewd and disorderly behavior which the seldom seen marshal failed to enforce, especially after ten p.m. The Eagle coffee house also had bathing facilities. Water was pumped from a well using power provided by a captive bear on a treadmill.

Notable Visitors to Early Columbus

President James Monroe visited Columbus in 1817 as part of a national tour. He was the first president to travel across the Appalachian Mountains. He was escorted by local cavalry and a reception was held in the State House. Speeches and dinners punctuated the exciting occasion. It was noted that the president wore plain clothes and was sunburned from travel by horseback. He was quoted as observing that Columbus was an "infant" city.

New York Governor DeWitt Clinton visited Columbus in 1825. He had been invited to attend the opening ceremonies for the Ohio-Erie Canal at Licking Summit near Newark.

Another famous visitor, Charles Dickens, came to Columbus during his tour of the new country in 1842. He described the beautiful country as richly cultivated with abundant harvest. He described Columbus as "clean and pretty" but found the inns to be dull and quiet. He also frowned on the "temperance hotels."

In 1833, Edwin Stanton, soon to become a distinguished Ohioan, spent most of one year working in a Columbus bookstore. During his time in Columbus, he met his future wife and decided to become a lawyer. After a successful legal career elsewhere, he served as Attorney General under President James Buchanan and as Secretary of War under President Lincoln during the Civil War. He was appointed to the U.S. Supreme Court by President Grant but died before serving. A statue of Stanton is on the statehouse grounds, one of a cluster of "Ohio's Jewels."

President-elect Abraham Lincoln visited Columbus in February 1861, enroute to be sworn into office in Washington, D.C. A brass band and military escort met his train and conducted him to the state house as people waved and cheered. He addressed the assembled legislators and then the populace from the steps of the capitol. He then greeted citizens in the rotunda. After dining at the governor's house, he received local and state politicians in an after dinner reception. Finally, he returned to the state house where he again exchanged small talk with the electorate. He also received news that the Electoral College had selected him officially to be president. The following morning, on his forty-ninth birthday, he was escorted to the Union Station, where an awaiting train took him to Pittsburgh via Steubenville. Four years later, his funeral train brought him back to Columbus where he lay in the rotunda for viewing by thousands before the train took him on to Springfield, Illinois for burial.

Other notable visitors were General and Mrs. John Fremont, ex-President Millard Fillmore, ex-Senator John Bell, the Prince of Wales, Horace Greeley, Ralph Waldo Emerson, General G.T. Beauregard, Martin Van Buren, Vice-President Richard M. Johnson, Daniel Webster, General Winfield Scott, Senator Charles Sumner and Edward Everett.

Columbus Feeder Canal

Stimulated by the success of the Erie Canal in New York, Ohio decided to connect Lake Erie to the Ohio River. Plans called for two canals. The eastern canal ran from Cleveland to Portsmouth, passing through Akron, Massillon, Dover, Coshocton, Newark, Lockbourne, Circleville, Chillicothe and Waverly. The western canal began at Toledo and proceeded southward to Cincinnati through Defiance, Piqua, Dayton and Hamilton. All of these towns benefited businesswise. Columbus lacked a canal at first because the upper Scioto River area lacked sufficient water to supply a canal. Two years after the Ohio-Erie Canal with a large reservoir at Buckeye Lake was completed, plans were carried out to connect with Columbus. In April 1827, ground was broken for digging a ten-mile feeder canal to connect Columbus with the Ohio-Erie Canal at Lockbourne. A ceremony was held that included local and state dignitaries, a military unit, ceremonial first spade-digging, speeches and refreshments. The connecter canal was finished in four years. Prisoners from the state penitentiary did part of the work for which many were granted pardons. Local farmers and Irish and German immigrants made up most of the work crews. Immigrant workers were paid thirty cents a day plus room and board and a ration of whiskey. The most difficult work was making a canal dam on the Scioto River, the Columbus locks, the four-mile locks and the locks at Lockbourne. New York Governor DeWitt Clinton of Erie Canal fame, visited Columbus in 1825 after attending a ceremony in Newark that signaled the start of building the Ohio-Erie canal. Another ceremony accompanied by a gun salute and speeches took place when the first canal boat arrived in Columbus in September 1831. Lady and gentleman passengers and a band cruised in the first boat back to Chillicothe at a comfortable speed of four miles an hour. The locks slowed travel time considerably. A person could travel faster, but less comfortably for a short distance, by horseback or buggy. The boats were between sixty and eighty feet in length, and twelve feet wide. There were three types; freight only, passenger only, or a combination of the two. They had a draft of two feet and could transport a cargo up to sixty tons. The canal bed was sixty feet wide with a channel thirty to forty feet wide. Periodic locks to raise or lower the boats were only fifteen feet wide and were constructed of wood and stone. A tow-path along one side of the canal was used by horses or mules and driver to pull the boats. Animals had to be changed every twelve to fifteen miles. Droughts, floods, ice, storms, tornadoes and wall or lock breakdowns hampered the voyages. The passenger boats had a parlor, sitting room and outside deck where passengers could socialize and eat food prepared in the kitchen. The main business office and warehouse for the Columbus Feeder Canal was adjacent to the Broad Street Bridge over the Scioto River. All passengers embarked and disembarked there. In the winter season, ice-skating and races took place in the vicinity. Warm weather allowed a band to play for dancing in the warehouse. Business was brisk until the railroads came in the 1840's. State bonds were sold to finance the canals, although they were managed privately. In the end, no profit was made by the collective canal system which ended in the 1860's. Some of the channels were dynamited during the great flood of 1913 to impede the flow of water into southern Ohio. Fragments of the locks and canals still exist, and some are maintained for tourist and historical interest. Canal boat rides are available.

Columbus in the 1830's

The population of Columbus expanded slowly to 2,435 by 1830. Its growth doubled in the next four years, and Columbus became incorporated as a city in 1834. The city now had over five thousand citizens including ten attorneys, eleven physicians, one dentist, eight clergymen, thirty-six merchants and nine taverns/hotels. Twenty-three of the merchants dealt in dry goods and groceries, three were druggists, two were booksellers, two had tin and hardware stores, three were wholesale grocers, and one each dealt in shoes, hosiery, jewelry, liquor and an auction house. Some of the stores sold leather items, hats and combs. Others were employed as blacksmiths, livery stable and animal caretakers, surveyors, politicians, teachers and road builders or toll collectors. Small manufacturing plants were making their appearances. Many worked at more than one job. Often, wives and children partook in family enterprises. The primary reason for the city's growth was the tremendous importance of the National Road (Route 40) and the feeder canal coming to Columbus which made it easier for people, animals and commerce to enter and leave the capital.

In 1843, a distillery was converted into a starch factory (C. Colgate & Co.) that eventually employed fifty men and consumed over two hundred bushels of corn per day. A fire destroyed the factory in 1852, and it was rebuilt. It represented one of the first large businesses in Columbus. In 1832, the Columbus Insurance Company was incorporated; it failed in 1851. The Clinton Bank of Columbus was chartered in 1833. Other banks followed. The leaders in the community were on boards of directors of the banks. The Clinton bank dropped the name Columbus in 1854 when the bank became privately owned. A theater made its appearance in 1835 and lasted six years.

As an example of medical care in this period, there were about eight botanical practitioners who used herbs to cure ailments. Some of the medications were administered with the use of steam. 1833 was the year of the cholera epidemic. About two hundred residents died. Many citizens fled to the countryside. No epidemic since has caused more deaths. Epidemics of smallpox, cholera, measles, other childhood diseases and dysentery occurred sporadically and often. Pollution was suspected and ordinances were passed to clean property and provide better methods of waste disposal. Unknown at the time, water supply was the chief culprit and usually was badly contaminated. Most of Columbus sewage was dumped into the Scioto River.

Life expectancy in the early 1800's was twenty-five years shorter than today. The birthrate was high as was infant and youngster mortality. Childbirth was often fatal for the mother. Cancer was not recognized as such but probably was as frequent as today. Medications were virtually poisonous to the sick. They often contained toxic heavy metals such as mercury, bismuth and antimony. The use of herbal medication was common. Vaccination for the prevention of smallpox had been introduced for fifty years but was not often practiced and in some areas outlawed. Quackery in the practice of medicine was commonplace. Doctors and hospitals were essentially unregulated. Hospitals were not safe havens, and admission to a hospital was looked upon as a sentence of death. Injuries contributed heavily to disability and demise. Epidemics of fever and unknown entities often kept a high proportion of the populace disabled with a high death rate. Another century would pass before medical science would advance remarkably due to better anesthesia, asepsis, antibiotics, miracle drugs, organ transplantation, endoscopic and robotic surgical advances and body imaging.

The economy in the early years of Columbus was often depressed. Recessions and panics were frequent and often nationwide. Local banks and even some businesses issued monetary notes that often became worthless. Cash was scarce, and bartering was common. During hard times, many became unemployed and lost their businesses or homes when unable to pay taxes. Sheriffs were kept busy auctioning off property of people unable to pay taxes or mortgages. Land speculators could accumulate large amounts of real estate in this fashion. Many unemployed moved westward to seek their fortune. Newcomers filled their places, and the number of inhabitants grew steadily. The populous was decidedly in flux. The successful and/or the wealthy were the most immobile segment of the citizenry.

In the 1830's, real estate sold briskly, and Columbus participated in the national land speculation craze.

Several men decided that silk manufacturing would be profitable. They set out a large field of mulberry trees in Franklin County, introduced "silk worms" and built a large factory. This experiment was abandoned as unprofitable, as was a sugar beet project in the county.

The legislature passed an act in 1838 that provided for erecting a new State House. The corner stone was laid the following year. Convict labor was used. Due to a scandal, the act to build a new State House was repealed in 1840 after expending $41,585.

There can be no doubt that the entrance of the Ohio-Erie canal and the National Road into Columbus in the 1830's contributed mightily to the economy and brought Columbus and Central Ohio out of the long recession that followed the War of 1812. Farm produce and commercial products that had been bottled up for lack of transport now flowed east, south and north. New businesses included a barber, the selling of musical instruments, carriages, glasses, millinery, drugs, watch and clock making, jewelry, china and glassware, candies, and the production of a business directory. The rampart speculation in buying land warrants, the sale of lottery tickets from eastern states and the issuance of notes by many banks came to an abrupt halt when another panic and recession occurred in 1840.

Columbus City Markets

In the first years of the new capital, farmers and Indians brought their produce to sell from their wagons in a haphazard fashion on South High Street. Mounting congestion caused the city fathers to try a different arrangement. The first "city market" was opened in 1830 on the southwest corner of State and Front Streets on land purchased by the city.

Fig. 20 Second City Market
—from Columbus Metro Library

Several decades later, a new market (above) at Town and Fourth Streets was a long two-story building with six brick pillars on each side. A wide isle in the center allowed customers to buy from farmer's stalls on each side. Over three hundred farmers sold fresh vegetables, meat and fish during the summer season with stalls overflowing up and down the street from either end of the market building. The farmers' wives used this opportunity to buy goods at the local shops. Due to lack of currency, bartering was a popular mode of commerce. The second floor was used for city offices and a council chamber. A small jail was located adjacent to the market.

A new North Market (third), located on Vine Street, just off North High Street in the Short North, replaced the second City Market in the 1960s when the Mohawk urban renewal project dictated removal of the former venerable market building. The old market site is now occupied by the bus depot.

Columbus Hotels

Numerous hostelries had been part of the central Columbus landscape from the beginning. Early inns were crude two-story brick or log structures covered with clapboards to protect them from the elements. Clients shared a large room as sleeping quarters with no privacy. Some shared the same sleeping pad. In 1835, Robert McCoy, owner of a dry goods store, tore down his tavern, and replaced it with a substantial three-story hotel, named the American House. Its amenities of good food, private rooms and banquet facilities far outdistanced the competition, and McCoy became rich. The hotel's location, on South High Street, across the street from the state capitol, was convenient to legislators. After forty years of business, the hotel gave way to more modern structures and became a store front with inexpensive rental rooms in the back. Even this arrangement played out in the 1920's, and the space was occupied by retail businesses. Eventually, the Riffe State Office Tower was erected on the former site of the American House.

In the Goodale Park area, Park hotel was built in the 1850's to accommodate the nearby train travelers and wealthy politicians. Two governors resided in the Park Hotel while they were in office: Governors Richard Bishop (1878-1880) and George Hoadley (1884-1886). The hotel had a name change to Northern Hotel and, after its decline, it was demolished to make room for freeway I-670 in 1957. The area had ceased to be a desirable place to live, and for a period of time it was known as "Flytown."

By 1840, the economy cooled, and land and building prices fell. The economy returned to normal in 1846, and a new economic expansion lasted for seven years. The population increased, and small towns sprang up in Ohio. Farming continued to be the most popular occupation, aided by improved transportation of products to market by better roads, the canals and railroads. From 1840 to 1849, a paper mill was opened but failed to survive. A fire was partly responsible for its demise. Fires were a scourge due to the many wooden buildings and inability of firemen to do little more than watch.

Early Political Campaigns

During the national election periods, torch-light parades were held with slogans, floats, hoopla, flag waving, singing, inflammatory speeches and considerable imbibing of spirits. The most notable early campaign was for General William Henry Harrison in 1836, and, again in 1840, when he was the successful Whig candidate for president. Harrison had a long career as an administrator in the

Northwest Territory, as Governor of the Indiana Territory, and as a successful Indian fighter during the War of 1812. He was Ohio's favorite son, living his twilight years in North Bend, Ohio. The Whigs, under the leadership of Henry Clay, had replaced the old Federalist Party which had rarely been successful on the frontier. This was natural, since the Whigs attracted bankers, businessmen, large land owners, farmers, the socially conservative and some disgruntled Democrats. They favored a strong central government, a National Bank based on tight currency supported by gold and silver currency, a high tariff to enhance eastern manufacturers, and federal support for roads, bridges, canals and lighthouses.

Most of the new settlers favored the Democratic Republicans who were followers of Thomas Jefferson and Andrew Jackson and organized the modern Democratic Party in 1832 under Jackson. The Democrats stood for states' rights, a low tariff, a decentralized banking system with an abundance of paper money; they opposed monopolies, "easterners" and privileges for the wealthy. Their supporters were chiefly common men comprised of laborers, farmers, immigrants and religious fundamentalists. On the opposite side of the political spectrum, Third Parties such as the Liberty Party (1839) and the Free-Soil Party (1848) attracted some voters and their birth forecast the coming Civil War but did not alter the outcome of national elections. The most prominent candidate emerging from the Free-Soil Party was Salmon Chase, future governor of Ohio, U.S. Senator, cabinet secretary and Chief Justice of the federal Supreme Court. It would be several decades before Columbus again would spawn a national political leader.

Early Theatrical Presentations in Columbus

Traveling troupes of actors appeared in Columbus as early as 1827. Musicians played during intermissions. A requirement for a city license to stage a play and religious criticism chilled these early theatrical efforts.

The fifteen hundred seat Columbus Playhouse, on the west side of North High Street between Broad and Gay Streets, opened in 1835. Admission was one dollar for one of two tiers of box seats, fifty cents for seats in the "pit," and twenty-five cents for "colored" persons. It was frequented by the legislators and more affluent citizens. The elite had private boxes with cushioned seats and backs. They also had the privilege of using a private salon that made available food and drinks during intermissions. Traveling theatrical groups, minstrels, lectures and recitals provided the entertainment. Wintertime was the best season for the theater. It closed in 1841 and was remodeled into a city hall. Later one half of the building was removed, and the remainder became private dwellings.

The Comstock Opera House was opened on the west side of South High Street between Town and Rich Streets in 1864. Its four-story Italianate architectural style theater seated twelve hundred and was useful also for important public meetings. Isaac Eberly remodeled it in 1891. It was demolished by fire in the following year; fortunately there were no fatalities. This was the same year of the Chittenden Hotel fire which destroyed four city blocks, one of the worst fires to date. By 1910, there were six theaters: Great Southern, Hartman, Grand, Colonial (present Palace), High Street and Keith's. The Exhibit, at 155 North High Street was formerly a nickelodeon, a theater with an admission charge of a nickel. Keith's Theater at the northeast corner of Gay and Pearl Streets was the place for vaudeville

Fig. 21 The Broadway and James Theaters on the west side of North High Street.

Fig. 22 The Keith Theater at northeast cornerof Gay and Pearl Streets.

—from Columbus Metro Library

City, County and State Fairs

In 1845, the Columbus Agricultural Society was organized for the express purpose of holding an annual two-day fair to exhibit flowers, fruits and vegetables grown by its members. A lot was purchased as a site to plant gardens and to exhibit their harvest. Prizes were given by judges for the excellence of exhibited items. Each member of the society was required to pay dues of one dollar per year, but twenty dollars would secure a life membership. Soon, the initiation fee was increased to two dollars. The county contributed a small sum annually, and tickets to the fair were sold. Later, the county built an improved thoroughfare from the National Road (Main Street) to the fairgrounds. The Society also promoted improving the science and practice of horticulture. A cholera epidemic prevented the fair from being held in 1849 and 1850. As an outgrowth of this organization, a State Fair on its own grounds in Columbus was initiated. For a few years the State Fair was rotated around the state, meeting first in Cincinnati in 1850. It soon became a permanent fixture in Columbus and, by 1886, settled on its grounds at 17th Avenue and I-71. The old fairgrounds had been at Franklin Park, and, in 1895, a conservatory was erected on the site. The county organized the Franklin County Agricultural Society in 1851, and its fair settled in Hilliard.

Fig. 23 The Ohio State Fair in 1890 at its present location.
—from Columbus Metro Library

The First Museum

The first museum opened in Columbus in 1851 and consisted of six wax figures and a few paintings. It gradually gathered more paintings, wax figures, specimens of beasts, birds and other curiosities.

Gas Lights in Columbus

The Columbus Gas Light and Coke Company was incorporated under state law in 1846. Its prime purpose was to illuminate city streets and buildings. In 1850, the city gave the company the right to use streets and alleys for laying gas pipes. For this privilege, the city had to pay only two-thirds the price paid by private citizens for its gas.

Banks

Columbus, from its inception, has had hundreds of financial institutions. Most were short-lived or failed; they were high risk ventures. Not only banks, but business companies offered their own commercial notes, and their value fluctuated widely dependent upon local and the national economy. Recessions and financial panics occurred with some regularity-about every ten years. A customer could lose most of his savings. Some banks made their owners rich and locally famous. Examples are David Deshler, William Sullivant, William Neil, W.B. Hawkes, F.C. Sessions, J.A. Jeffrey, Ephraim Sells, C.D. Firestone, Orange Johnson, Joel Buttles and P. W. Huntington. These men were successful businessmen in Columbus. The founders of banks were not required to have appropriate experience or capital. Records were apt to be chaotic. Some of the original banks are still alive today, perhaps under a different name. P.W. Huntington and D.W. Deshler founded the P.W. Huntington and Company at the northwest corner of High and Broads Streets in 1866 on the site of the former Deshler Savings Bank. Following Deshler's death in 1869, the bank moved to the southwest corner of Broad and High Streets where it still exists today as Huntington National Bank. For decades, the banks were unregulated by state or federal governments. It took over one hundred years for this problem to be corrected properly. Today, deposits in banks, savings and loan institutions and some commercial companies are guaranteed up to certain amounts by federal law, a practice unknown in the 1800's. This has led to customer confidence and stability in financial circles. Several states had their own bank, and Ohio established its state bank in 1845. In 1852, the Columbus office of the state bank began the replacement of torn, mutilated or unfit bank notes. Forgery was not uncommon and much easier to accomplish than today.

(See the index for current banks and their histories.)

Fires in Columbus

The early buildings in Columbus were constructed chiefly of wood. It was only a matter of time before they became engulfed in fire and burned to the ground. At first, the local citizenry fought the fires by hand with pails of water. Soon volunteer bucket brigades were organized into companies. The fire units were competitive and social and often involved in brawls. Volunteers were exempt from jury duty. In 1822, a cluster of eight buildings was destroyed by fire. This so frightened the City Council, that it reorganized fire companies and built more fire stations. Pumping equipment evolved from hand power to steam engine pumpers. By the mid-1850's the fire companies became professionalized with uniformed firemen and fire wagons. Large cisterns of water were located at strategic street intersections. Despite these measures, the Brotherlin and Halm Chair and Cabinet Company burned to the ground in 1856, as did the Columbus Tub and Pail firm in 1858. The first major conflagration occurred on presidential election night in 1860 when the Neil House Hotel burned to the ground. Other memorable early fires were: the courthouse in 1879, the 14th Regiment Armory in 1888, the Opera House and the Chittenden Hotel in 1892. Fires in 1879 were considered to be started by arsonists although none were apprehended despite the offering of rewards to informants. Fires in that year, in addition to the courthouse, included Monypeny's warehouse, several stables, barns and outbuildings. Damage was heavy and fire fighting ineffective but without loss of life. The militia was called out and streets were patrolled for a few nights. Orders were given to shoot arsonists on sight. None were spotted. In the last decades of the nineteenth century, Columbus had about fifty fire signal boxes and key holders located strategically throughout the city. The alarm was set off by unlocking the box and pulling the hook down slowly. The Central Engine House receiving the signal from the numbered box would sound an alarm repeatedly with a special cadence and number of gong strikes to arouse volunteer fire fighters to go to the proper location. Ultimately, many fire stations were built, fulltime firemen were salaried, and modern equipment was introduced and administrated by the Columbus Division of Fire. Today, a Fire Museum and Educational Center is located in the renovated Fire Station No. 1 at 260 North Fourth Street. Fortunately, major downtown fires have not spread widely to other buildings and have had little loss of life. That is until 1930, when prisoners set a fire in the state penitentiary that caused three hundred and twenty-two trapped inmates to perish. In 1936, five firefighters lost their lives when the Oddfellows Hall was destroyed by fire. This is the largest number of firefighters killed by fire in Columbus to date.

Waterways, Dams and Reservoirs

With an average annual rainfall of thirty-eight inches in Central Ohio, Franklin County seems insulated from a lack of water supply. A severe, prolonged drought could test this premise. Future plans call for adding reservoirs in Delaware and Pickaway Counties to accommodate the rapid population growth in Franklin County.

Franklin County has four major rivers or creeks coursing north to south. The Scioto and Olentangy Rivers flow through the center of the county; Big Walnut Creek is in the east side; and Big Darby Creek passes through the west side. There are many smaller streams and ravines. All water flows south from headwaters in counties north of Franklin County. The Olentangy River merges with the Scioto River near the center of the county, while Big Walnut Creek enters the Scioto below the Franklin County line. Big Darby Creeks joins the Scioto at Circleville in Pickaway County. None of these rivers was consistently navigable for trading purposes. Some of the earliest settlers brought their possessions and purchases up the Scioto River to Franklinton, largely because the roads were so bad. A few attempts were made to send barges of produce to New Orleans via the waterway.

However, the Scioto River didn't have enough water year around to be included in the Ohio-Erie Canal route in the mid-1800's. Columbus had to settle for a feeder canal connected to the Ohio-Erie Canal. The first effort to provide a water supply to local citizens was the digging of a well at the junction of the Scioto and Olentangy Rivers in 1871.

The Scioto River is the largest river in Franklin County and the longest in Ohio. It measures 231 miles and drains a 6,510 square mile area. Its name is of native Indian origin meaning "hair river"; the Indians noted molting deer hair on its surface. For comparison, the Great Miami River, measuring 171 miles, is the second longest river in Ohio. The fifth longest river, which has a larger watershed of 8,038 square miles, is the Muskingum River. As expected, the Muskingum has a greater propensity for flood damage. The Scioto River begins in Auglaize County to the north, and passes through Hardin, Marion and Delaware Counties before entering Franklin County near Dublin. For purposes of serving as a major water supply for Columbus and some of its suburbs and for flood control, two major dams and some smaller dams were constructed on the Scioto. The first reservoir was formed above Griggs Dam erected in 1905 on the western edge of Upper Arlington. The artificial lake also provided opportunities for motor boats, sailing, water skiing and fishing, and today is the home for Leatherlips Yacht Club. The Griggs reservoir held five-billion gallons of water. By 1908 an enormous filtering and water-softening works was completed. It included six lime saturators, two mixing or softening tanks, six settling basins, ten mechanical filters and two clear-water reservoirs. In 1925, the larger O'Shaughnessy reservoir was formed above a dam of the same name at Glick Road. It lies entirely in Delaware County. A five megawatt, two-turbine generator hydroelectric plant was built at this dam site in 1987 to furnish electricity for Columbus municipal buildings and street lights. Eventually, the Columbus Electricity Division formed a joint venture with American Electric Power and now sells its electricity to that company.

After the Scioto River enters Franklin County near Dublin, and passes southward through downtown Columbus (more precisely Franklinton), it leaves the county between Grove City and U.S. 23. It enters the Ohio River at Portsmouth after passing through Circleville, Chillicothe and Waverly. The Scioto has risen above flood stage many times producing considerable damage. The worst floods in the history of Columbus occurred in 1898 and 1913. Since then, the dams and a floodwall protect the city.

Of the other three large streams coursing through Franklin County, the Olentangy River is longest (88 miles long), Big Darby Creek is the most scenic (79 miles long) and the Big Walnut Creek is 74 miles in length. Hoover reservoir was formed from Big Walnut Creek above the Hoover dam, built in 1954, and extends northward into Delaware County. It is the major water supply for the Columbus and Franklin County and provides recreational opportunities. The smaller Alum Creek is also dammed with a smaller reservoir above Lewis Center Road in Delaware County. Big Walnut is joined by Alum, Rocky Fork and Blacklick Creeks at Groveport before leaving the county to immediately enter the Scioto River in Pickaway County. Little Walnut Creek enters the southeast quadrant of Franklin County from Fairfield County, passes through Canal Winchester and Groveport before entering Pickaway County. Westerville obtains some of its water from its own small reservoir near Ohio Route 3 and the Lakes Country Club.

The Olentangy River arises from the north in Morrow County and passes through Crawford, Marion and Delaware Counties before entering Franklin County. The Olentangy River has a dam and reservoir in Delaware County for flood control and passes through Worthington and The Ohio State University before joining the Scioto River in downtown Columbus. It is scenic as it passes through Worthington and Riverlea. The river is popular with canoeists and is lined with pathways.

Floods in Columbus

The low land along the west side of the Scioto River was always subject to frequent flooding. This doomed Franklinton from becoming the state capital or even developing along with its higher neighbors. Franklinton was only a year old when its first encounter with high water occurred in 1798. The devastation prompted Lucas Sullivant, the settlement's founder, to move to the hilltop further west. People and small businesses continued to reestablish themselves in the "bottoms" attracted by cheap property prices. As time went on, limitations on development, and the high cost of flood insurance, restricted growth in the area. The flood waters of March 1913 wiped out property for miles along the river; it reached twenty-five feet in depth. Besides staggering property loss, over ninety people lost their lives. The disaster prompted civic and state leaders to take stern measures in controlling the rivers in the state by building dams and reservoirs. Still, another flood in 1939 took a heavy toll. The federal Army Corps of Engineers, finally, began construction of the 7.2 mile Franklinton floodwall in 1993. The north end of the wall begins at I-670, crosses U.S. 315 and continues to Frank Road, its southern terminus. It was completed finally in 2004 after sporadic federal funding, at a cost of $134 million. The Veteran's Memorial Hall and Center of

Science and Industry are now protected from menacing waters. Nevertheless, in 2006, a four-inch rain resulted in flooding in Franklinton because of failure of a water pump that was needed when the flood gates are closed. Meanwhile, Franklinton has been bedeviled by the infiltration of drug abusers, petty criminals and low property values. It remains to be seen whether the historic village can recover some of its value.

Fig. 24 Downtown Columbus in floods of 1898 (left) and 1913 (right) before the flood wall was built.
—from Columbus Metro Library

Railroads and Depots in Columbus

The introduction of rail transportation literally changed the economy and the face of towns and cities. Now, perishable products could be transported great distances. The speed of trains far surpassed that of horse drawn wagons and canal boats. The canal system disappeared almost as quickly as it was completed in Ohio. Highway transit would also benefit from the competition of trains. The railroad empires were principally paid for privately, while road, bridges and tunnels were heavily endowed by the government from tax revenue. The building of rail lines produced an immense need for laborers, and the great influx of immigrants fitted nicely with this need. Most of the railroads took advantage of the Irish immigration, and soon an Irish enclave grew around Union station. North Public Lane was the center of "Little Ireland" and was dubbed "Irish Broadway." Later, the lane was renamed Naghten Street and still later Nationwide Boulevard. Likewise, the rail center attracted small hotels to the northern edge of Columbus away from earlier desirable locales south of Capitol Square. When the automobile era arrived, the small hotels withered, giving way to motels, and the Irish ghetto dissipated, blending into the populace.

Fig. 25 The first railroad station in Columbus opened in 1851 and is shown here.
—from Columbus Metro Library

The first railroad entering Columbus was the Columbus and Xenia line, constructed in 1848-1849. At Xenia, the line connected with the Little Miami Railroad going to Cincinnati. The first passenger train was placed in operation in 1850. While the railway station was owned by the company, the depot grounds were shared by other rail lines. The first Union Station, built in 1851, was a long barn at Naghten and High Streets with two cupolas on its roof (site now occupied by the Hyatt Regency Hotel). Later a turntable for locomotives and repair shops were added. The grand opening of the Cincinnati, Columbus and Cleveland line occurred in 1851. Grand celebrations were held at Columbus and Cleveland when a train with 425 passengers including the governor made the trip in nine hours with a stop in Shelby for dinner. On the return trip, the engine ran into a cow. A train to Zanesville was started in 1852, and the Columbus, Piqua and Indiana railroad was opened in 1853. Access to Pittsburgh was made possible by connection with a rail line from Columbus to Wheeling. The building of the Hocking Valley Railroad made possible the moving of coal, iron and timber to Columbus, which guaranteed the introduction of iron foundries and the manufacturing of such items as vaults and buggies. Wealthy men like Alfred Kelley and William Neil were early financial supporters of Columbus railroads and gave great impetus to their development. Kelley was President of the Columbus-Xenia line with an annual salary of five hundred dollars. He was able to attract out-of-state funds by selling bonds in New York City. The attraction to ill-affording investors also was a source of depressions and panics when rail companies failed as they were wont to do. Even famous financiers such as Jay Cooke lost their fortunes when their railroad investments folded. Since the railroads were the biggest industry in the country, a strike could be a serious matter for the nation as well as for the workers. During a formidable depression beginning in 1873, the railroad workers went on strike nationwide and by 1877 it spread to Columbus. Emotions among workers and management became red-hot. Railroad equipment was damaged, and people were injured and a few killed. For the first time, the nation was so paralyzed that President Rutherford Hayes called on the army to run the railroads and end the strike.

The second Union Station, more pleasing to the eye, was constructed in 1875, and serviced five railroads meeting at the Columbus hub. Forty-two daily trains were spread over eight tracks. Passenger traffic was heavy. During the first years, when the locomotives were fueled by coal, the stations, passengers and railroad cars were dirty and unpleasant. The trains frequently brought street traffic to a halt. Citizens loudly complained. Overhead structures were built to obviate the congestion problem. A third Union Station, more elaborate in design, was built and opened in 1897. The architect was Daniel Burnham who had helped design the Columbian Exposition in Chicago in 1893. It was designed in the colorful Beaux Arts style, and it contained rest rooms, a smoking room, a restaurant, and baggage rooms. Subways were used as concourses to guide passengers to their trains. A second important station was built on West Broad Street reducing congestion in the main station.

Fig. 26 The second and last Union Railroad Station was completed in 1897 and razed in the 1980's.
Only the central arch was saved and placed in the Arena District.
—from Columbus Metro Library

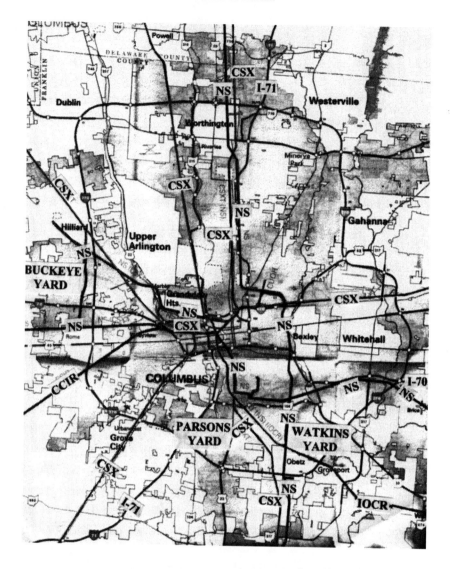

—adapted from State of Ohio map

Fig. 27 Map of Franklin County showing current railroads and railroad yards in relation to interstate highways I-70, I-71 and I-270.

In recent years, three railroad companies, Norfolk Southern, CSX and Conrail share all rail lines traversing Franklin County. Conrail does not own rail lines but leases their use from CSX and NS. There are three marshaling yards: Buckeye (NS) near Hilliard, Parsons (CSX) south of Columbus and Watkins (NS) near Obetz. A fourth yard is in Pickaway County near the southeast boundary of Franklin County.

The second centrally located, major railroad station was constructed at 379 West Broad Street in Franklinton in 1896. The well known local architects, Joseph Yost and Frank Packard, designed an eye-catching station for the Toledo & Central Ohio Railroad. The structure had a pagoda-like tower, Italian marble floors and fireplaces, and a skylight. It was abandoned in 1929 when the railroad was sold. The Volunteers of America bought the structure in 1930 and used it for a thrift store. Eventually, the boarded-up building was purchased by the city's Capitol South Community Urban Redevelopment Corporation in 2003, who visualized its restoration into an office complex with a small attractive park.

The Union Station was remodeled extensively in 1928-9. Mail transportation was now an important business for the railroads. More freight was hauled, and refrigerated cars were added to transport fresh fruits and vegetables. Coal fired steam engines were replaced eventually by diesel fueled motors. Today, the Union Station and passenger trains are long gone in Columbus superseded by automobiles, buses, trucks and airplanes. A remnant of the ornate Union Station entry edifice may be found situated in Arch Park in the Arena district, a reminder of yesteryears. The razed station was replaced by a convention center and the Hyatt Regency Hotel. Long freight trains, primarily Norfolk/Southern and CSX lines, carrying coal through the outskirts of Columbus from southern Ohio to Lake Erie plants are witnessed many times today. Most trains pass over roads in elevated fashion. After World War II, Central Ohio persons desiring express rail travel to Chicago or New York, drove to Fostoria to catch these trains. Passenger trains are infrequent in the Middle West today.

During the first half of the twentieth century, Columbus had an important railroad freight car manufacturing company. The Ralston Steel Car Company occupied about forty acres between the eastside rail lines and present day Bexley. The company built low cost housing around the plant for its workers who were mostly Eastern Europe immigrants and African-Americans. The compact area was essentially a "company town." Neighborhood stores provided a source of purchase by credit. The company ceased to exist after World War II.

Columbus played a major role in the labor movement since both the American Federation of Labor in 1886 and the United Mine Workers in 1890 were founded in the city. The headquarters of the UMW was in Columbus at High and Chestnut Streets until 1895.

Columbus from 1840 to the Civil War (1861)

Expenditures for a new State House was approved in 1838, but it was not finished until 1857, nineteen years later. During the interim, the old State House was consumed by fire in 1852. A large mass of documents, journals, and other records were lost in the conflagration. A new county Court House was finished in 1840 at a cost of $44,000.

On July 4, 1842, a balloon ascended from the State House for over a mile in altitude. It landed in Newark. These balloon ascents were used to celebrate the 4th July intermittently for several years. The person in the balloon was called an "aeronaut." One ascent was made with the pilot on horseback. One aeronaut dangled twenty feet below the balloon carrying an American flag. The propellant was hot gas.

Fig. 28

In 1852, William Shephard, M.D. (Fig. 28) established the Water Cure and Medical Infirmary, also known as "Shephard's Sanitarium," for the treatment of "invalid females." This medical facility flourished for several years. Shephard was raised on a farm in New York and attended Canandaigue Academy. He studied medicine in Rochester and received his doctor's diploma from the Eclectic Medical College of Cincinnati in 1852. The sanitarium was reputed to be the largest and most thoroughly equipped institution of its kind in the Midwest and received hundreds of patients. He served in the Ohio General Assembly but was an unsuccessful candidate for Congress. He was a trustee of the Children's Home for four years. He had interests in the Alum Creek Ice Company, flour mills, a grocery store and real estate. Among his charities, he provided Gahanna with a public library and reading room.

Chapter 7

German Immigration to Columbus

Germans immigrated to the United States and Ohio in increasing numbers in the nineteenth century. Constant military action in Europe, accompanied by economic hardship, religious persecution and the scarcity of land available to each succeeding generation motivated young Germans to come to America. Revolutions, as in 1830 and 1848, brought some upper-middle class and well educated immigrants, although most were of the working class. The promise of rich land and the opportunity to attain wealth and freedom from government oppression outweighed any frontier hardships reported by earlier immigrants. Each failed revolution in Germany produced a fresh wave of immigrants. In 1812, the first documented German to arrive in Franklinton was Christian Heyl, a baker, at Rich and High Streets. His success provided him with means to build and manage a hotel for twenty-eight years on the site of his bakery. Ultimately, it was called the Swan Tavern. His son, Lewis Heyl, established Esther Institute in 1852, a private academy for girls. In 1814, Gottlieb Lichtenegger and Conrad Heyl, who were carpenters, arrived in time to work on the construction of the original state house. Subsequent Germans arrived slowly but increased in numbers steadily. By 1830 a sizeable number of Germans settled as an enclave on the south side of the capital city. Germans knew it as *Die Alte Sud Ende* or The Old South End. When the population of Columbus reached 18,000 in 1850, German-Americans owned one-third of all Columbus property. They had come up the Scioto River from the south and over Zane's Trace from the east. Most German immigrants settled in Pennsylvania for a few years or for a generation or more before moving on to Ohio or other points westward. The National Road (U.S. route 40) reached Columbus from the east in 1833 enhancing travel. A branch of the Ohio-Erie canal came at about the same time, followed by the railroads in the 1850's. All forms of transportation construction attracted German laborers, some of whom settled in Columbus. A sizeable number came to farm, and many were middle-class craftsmen and tradesmen. They were responsible for making brooms, tools, many bakeries and brick factories. A few had artistic skills. The Columbus Watch Company was a sizeable operation. Schmidt's Sausage Plant and later Schmidt's restaurants are examples of original German businesses which are alive and well today. The Great Southern Hotel was started by a group of German businessmen in 1896 to help develop the southern part of downtown.

In the late 1840's, some Columbus Germans rushed to California to seek their fortune in gold. Others went to Nebraska where they settled in New Columbus. The last part of the town's name survives today.

Generally, German immigrants had a reputation for working hard, loving music, drinking beer, and enjoying life especially on festive occasions. Most came from the Rhenish Palatinate and the states of Baden and Wurttemberg via the Rhine River and through the English Channel seaports. They brought with them many old-world customs and religious faiths. They built Catholic (St. Mary's, 1871), Lutheran (Trinity, 1848) and Methodist ("Old First"-Livingston, 1843) churches in South Columbus. Early church services were conducted in German. Likewise, the German language was used in some Columbus schools (German Central, Lewis Heyl's Seminary School for Girls) and colleges (Capital University and the Theological Seminary for German Lutherans). *Der Westbote* (1843-1918), outstanding among many newspapers printed in German, kept the community updated on local and old world events. The original German homes gave way to small brick two-story structures, adorned with carved limestone steps and lintels. The small yards were graced with flower boxes, and, in the backyards, vegetables and grapes were grown. Wrought iron fences were placed for beauty not for isolation. The homes reflected unpretentious, orderly and frugal citizens. Shops and beer parlors were intermingled with the homes. Breweries (City, Capital City, Wagner, Blenkner, Hoster, Born, Schlegel and Schlee) sprang up in South Columbus immediately west and adjacent to German Village allowing easy access for workers and owners. Child labor from German Village was common. This area became known as the Brewery District. Most breweries had a stable of horses and wagons for delivery of beer to saloons and restaurants. Later, the horse-drawn wagons were supplanted by fleets of motorized trucks. A railroad line brought transportation facilities directly to the breweries. Later, refrigeration cars were introduced. During the era of the canals, the breweries found their location favorable for use of this mode of transportation.

On festive occasions and in advertisements, August Wagner often dressed in the costume of King Gambrinus, the "patron saint" of beer. A statue of King Gambrinus was displayed in front of the Wagner brewery, where Gambrinus and Augustiner beers, Robin Hood Ale and Mark V light beer were made. (After the brewery closed in 1974, having been bought out by a Pittsburgh competitor, the statue remained on its pedestal on the site for a lengthy period. Today, the statue has been moved to South Front Street in front of Brewers Yard Park). Skilled brew masters were imported from Germany. Some of the breweries became quite large,

Fig. 29 Columbus had several large breweries from 1850 until prohibition in 1920. Shown above is the Born Brewery.
—from Columbus Metro Library

employing hundreds of German immigrants. Due to an excess of breweries some merged. The original breweries are long gone, victims of prohibition in 1919 and the Great Depression ten years later. Only the large national breweries survived prohibition and re-commenced beer making after the repeal of the Volstead Act in 1933. Local breweries that sprang up after 1933 were the Washington, Franklin, August Wagner and the Ohio Brewing companies. Only Wagner had survived during prohibition by turning to the production of soft drinks. German owners of breweries were often prominent citizens and involved in other pursuits. Nicholas Schlee was vice-president of the Central Bank and owner of the Lyceum Theater. Conrad Born, Sr. was a butcher and realtor. Conrad Christian Born was a director of the Columbus Malleable Iron Company. Conrad Edward Born was president of the Century Discount Company. Louis Hoster was a city councilman and opened the first woolen mill on West Mound Street. Louis Philip Hoster was president of the Columbus Structural Steel Company. Carl L. Hoster owned the Chittenden Hotel. Carl J. Hoster was a director of the Hayden Clinton National Bank and the Columbus Driving Park Association. His father, George J. Hoster was married to Mary Sheldon, an aunt of President George H. Bush. Charles L. Resch held several important positions in the Capital City Brewing Company and opened a restaurant and tavern. He was Sheriff of Franklin County from 1913 to 1917. Columbus now has one of twelve Anheuser-Busch Breweries (since 1968), that produces nine million barrels of beer annually. Smaller hometown breweries currently are Barley's, Gordon Biersch, Elevator and Columbus.

The German immigrants were often pacifists, understandably so, because of their forced participation in European wars. They did not relish fighting in wars but as loyal Americans did not avoid enlistment. An exception was the Mexican War when one of four companies volunteering from Columbus was composed entirely of German-Americans. The Know-Nothing political party in the 1850's, with an anti-immigrant and anti-Catholic agenda, produced resentment in the German community. This came to a show down in 1855 when the Germans were marching as a quasi-military unit in the Fourth of July parade. Jeering and rock throwing from spectators precipitated gunfire, and one onlooker was killed. Several Germans were arrested but, subsequently, released without being charged. Such hostility soon subsided when cooler heads prevailed.

Again in the Civil War, Germans, especially those in Turner gymnastic clubs, volunteered for military service. They fought as units under German commanders. German-Americans were persecuted again during World War I when Germany was on "the other side." There was a diminution of teaching the German language in public institutions, German language books were burned, and the use of German in street names and publications was changed to English names (e.g., Germania Street became Stewart Avenue). Ohio passed a law in 1917 that discriminated against Germans. It was spearheaded by then governor, James M. Cox, a vitriolic anti-German. The Ohio Supreme Court found the law to be unconstitutional. Over time, the German language has not been retained by the younger generations of ethnic Germans. Membership clubs open only to German-Americans for socializing, eating, singing, and dancing were to be found in South Columbus. The most prestigious German club in Columbus, founded in 1848, the Maennerchor ("men's chorus"), sent its singing group on tours to Europe and to national contests. The winner was often given a large, ornate, silver drinking cup. The Maennerchor Club, opened in 1921, still exists today, known for its German cuisine and dancing, although no longer exclusive. Its membership has dropped from 3,000 to 700 today. After a three-year experiment of relaxation of its dress code and opening its membership to the public, it returned to private membership in 2007. Its singing groups are still energetically active. German ladies had their own singing group (Damenchor) and an independent society called the Columbus Liederkranz. The Germania Society, formed in 1866, also provided social and gymnastic pleasures (*Turn Verein* or "Turner Clubs"). Other groups that provided social gatherings as well as a chance to practice their skills were orchestras, opera, bands, literary, garden, crafts, drama and quasi-military units. Occasionally, special musical festivals were held to celebrate special events (*saengerfests*).

Jews were in the minority among those with religious beliefs and made up between one and two percent of the German immigrants to Columbus. As life in Germany became more strife-ridden and restrictive, Jews with enough savings were encouraged by the Jewish publication, *Allegemaine Zeitung des*

Judentums, and by returned immigrants and relatives to find a new home and opportunity in America. At first, the majority came from southwestern and southern Germany. The first two Jewish immigrant families settling in Columbus were the Gundersheimers and Nusbaums. Lacking financial means, the earliest German Jewish immigrants in Columbus were street peddlers. Gradually, many were employed in or owned their own department stores. Some became tailors, grocers, jewelers or held clerical positions. Beginning in 1880, Jewish immigration ranks swelled noticeably from Eastern Europe and Russia. Some store signs began to be printed in German and Yiddish. Flytown, "a tough, colorful, immigrant neighborhood", near the short north factories and railroads, was populated by laborers, mostly Italian, but supported by a few Jewish store owners. Gradually, the Jewish newcomers congregated in the Near East of downtown. While the educational and occupational background of Jews was diverse, they contributed significantly to the arts, education, skilled crafts and religious aspects of the Columbus culture. Most of the latter were of the reform branch of their religious faith, but synagogues were established also to accommodate followers of the orthodox and conservative beliefs. Assimilation was slow and most married within their faith. Some families followed old world tradition of arranging marriage by parents or matchmakers. The more affluent Jews gradually settled further east in Columbus, notably in Bexley. This community became known for its high standard of living and its education system. Both men and women had their social organizations (Young Men's Hebrew Association, Young Ladies Hebrew Association, B'nai B'rith and Free and Accepted Mason). They also had singing, sewing, coffee, drama, literary and philanthropic groups. The most enduring and largest of these organizations has been B'nai B'rith.

German Village

German Village is a restored community in the short south end of Columbus where Germans were the earliest, predominant ethnic group. The renovation of its homes and shops took place in the 1960's. This privately funded venture, largely due to the energetic leadership of Frank Fetch, attracted national attention, and is registered nationally as an historic site. Its boundaries are: Livingston Avenue on the north; Grant, Jaeger and Lathrop Streets to the east; Nursery Lane on the south; and, High Street/Pearl Street to the west. Old world charm can be seen in its restaurants, bookstores, shops, brick homes and furnishings and bricks streets; it is a popular tourist destination. The *Book Loft* is a prime example of a uniquely arranged business and successful attraction. The thirty-two room bookstore was opened in 1977 on South Third Street, stretching to City Park Avenue. Formerly, its name was the *Village Owl,* fronting on City Park Avenue in 1974.

Young professionals enjoy living in the renovated historical village that has been rescued from neglect and migration of its residents to the suburbs. The German Village Society conducts an annual Haus and Garten Tour. A senior center and the Golden Hobby Shop reside today in the former Third Street School. Today, German is the predominant ethnic ancestry in Columbus as elsewhere in parts of Ohio. Columbus is known for this ethnicity, although outranked in percentage by Cincinnati, St. Louis and Milwaukee. Easily visible to the careful observer, vestiges of our German forbearers grace our Ohio state capital city today. A notable example is the library/headquarters of a national German genealogy organization, *Palatines to America* on Weber Road.

Schiller Park and Beck Park were created in German Village for entertainment that included playgrounds, courts for tennis, basketball and baseball, picnics, fishing, boating, plays by the Actors' Theatre Company and band concerts. Schiller Park, named for the famous German poet, originated as City Park in 1867 after several citizens bought twenty-three acres of Stewart's Grove for that purpose. Due to anti-German sentiment during World War I, the name was changed to Washington Park in 1918. In 1930, after emotions had cooled, the park's name reverted to Schiller.

A German-American who became mayor of Columbus for six terms (1891-1894 and again in 1912-1919), George Karb, was thoroughly liked. His popularity arose partly from his friendly greeting of people on the street. He habitually addressed men, "Good morning, Colonel." He was a stately figure in his long black coat, wing collar and pince-nez glasses. He had a strong voice and was a favorite speaker for all occasions. In addition to being a successful politician, he was a pharmacist, oil-company executive, banker, city councilman and sheriff. He easily survived the anti-German hysteria during World War I and, in fact, was instrumental in cooling emotions.

Lazarus Stores

Among the German immigrants to Columbus in the mid-1800s was Simon Lazarus, who arrived in Columbus from Germany in 1848. He peddled clothes and odds and ends from a street cart. In 1851, he opened a one-room clothing store at the southwest corner of Town and South High Streets. He also served as the first rabbi of Temple Israel having been trained as such in his native land. Following the Civil War, Simon intuitively recognized the veterans' need for civilian clothes and increased his wealth by meeting this need. To facilitate service, industrious proprietors slept in the back of their stores. Nothing was allowed to stand between them and a trade. Simon instituted home delivery by wagon. Fred Sr. and Ralph joined their father's business, and the name of the store changed to S. Lazarus & Sons. Upon Simon's death in 1877, the store's name changed to

Fig. 30 Simon Lazarus and sons, Fred and Ralph Lazarus.
—from Columbus Metro Library

F. and R. Lazarus. In 1909, the store was relocated across the street to its permanent location as a six-story department enterprise with a clock tower that could be seen from some distance. It now had a children's section, an escalator, chirping canaries, a soda fountain and separate entrances for gentlemen with a private elevator. The store became a Columbus landmark, reaching one million dollars in sales by 1912. Its popularity was enhanced by a sales policy of allowing full return of merchandise without questioning. They acquired the motto "square-dealing clothiers." A steam engine allowed the announcements of weather predictions twice daily by means of a coded series of horn blasts. In 1928, the company bought Shillito's department store in Cincinnati. In 1929, Lazarus affiliated with Filene's of Boston and Abraham & Strauss of Brooklyn to form the holding company, Federated Department Stores. Bloomingdale of New York joined the federation in 1930. Each member of the conglomerate functioned independently. They became the first national chain to establish a credit union. Fred Lazarus was the chief proponent of lengthening the holiday shopping season by convincing President Franklin Roosevelt in 1941 to move Thanksgiving Day back to the fourth Thursday in November. In 1946, a housewares and appliance store was added on the former site of the Columbus Auditorium. In the following year, the first of several parking garages was added. Since then, a number of enlargements and face-liftings have occurred. Progress brought a bookstore, a circulating library, cooking lessons, charm classes for teenage girls, reading for children, entertainment for all, and twelve restaurants in the central store. Christmas decorations, Santa and a Talking Tree attracted families from great distances. The first satellite store opened in Westland Mall in 1962. Northland, Eastland and Kingsdale Mall stores followed in 1964, 1966 and 1971, respectively. In 1986, the headquarters of Lazarus and Shillito-Rikes was moved to Cincinnati. This meant a loss of nine hundred jobs in Columbus. In 1988, an attempted hostile takeover by Canadian Campeau forced the loss of more jobs. By now, the corporation had opened additional stores in other cities in Ohio, Indiana and Kentucky. The City Center Mall opened adjacent to Lazarus in 1989 with a covered over-the-street walkway, bringing a significant rise in sales. In 1995, Federated merged with Rich's and Goldsmith's, and the headquarters moved to Atlanta. Federated's latest acquisition was May Company in 2006. In 1997, a Lazarus store opened in the Mall at Tuttle Crossing, and a portion of the downtown store made room for the Ohio Protection Agency. Two more satellite stores opened in the malls at Polaris Fashion Place and Easton Town Center in 2001. Macy's was added to the Lazarus store name in 2003, and, in 2005, the Lazarus name was dropped altogether. The competition from peripheral malls, mega-stores such as Wal-Mart and population shift to the suburbs had taken its toll. The downtown store closed in 2004 by gifting a large portion of the building to the city and selling its parking lots and garage for $5.7 million. The city has renovated the store building into a science and art center sponsored by Ohio State University and Battelle Institute, and it continues to house the Environmental Agency. The Lazarus family provided additional executive talent through the years; namely Robert Sr., Charles and Robert Jr. Charles Lazarus, the last family member to head the Lazarus stores died in May 2007. He became Chairman Emeritus in 1981, and had received many honors and honorary degrees as well as serving on many boards of corporation and philanthropic organizations. Many members of the Lazarus family had been generous in gifting philanthropies, civic ventures and the Community Chest in Columbus. Most citizens regret the gradual demise of a legendary department store.

Schoedinger

F. Oscar Schoedinger was a prominent early German immigrant and businessman. He had expertise in carpentry and opened the F.O. Schoedinger Company that specialized in roofing and sheet metal products.

Another Schoedinger, Philip, immigrated to this country in 1829, and as a craftsman, opened a casket making company in 1855. In 1865, he and a partner established the Schoedinger & Brown Mortuary on South High Street. A new location, the former home of renown Columbus physician, Dr. Starling Loving, became the Schoedinger Chapel at 229 East State Street. It was the first chapel opened expressly for the purpose of conducting funeral services and one of the earliest in America of such magnitude. It is also the oldest continuously owned family business in Columbus. Today, the belltower at this location stands as a city landmark. Schoedinger was one of the first funeral companies to offer an air-conditioned building and the first to offer guaranteed advance funeral arrangements. Six generations have remained active in managing eleven funeral chapels and crematories and Kingwood Memorial Park (since 1986) on U.S. Route 23 in southern Delaware County. A recent addition to the cemetery has been named Whispering Waters Cremation Garden.

Chapter 8

Benevolent Institutions in Columbus/Franklin County

The Columbus Poor House

It was an English custom to place paupers and debtors in prison, where they would be cared for in a stark manner by the state. England decided to empty their prisons of some of these indigents in the 1700's by allowing them to immigrate to America and Australia. This was how much of Georgia was populated initially. Ohio followed the Anglican method of dealing with the destitute by passing a legislative act in 1831 that allowed counties to establish Poor Houses at their discretion. Some called the houses infirmaries, others called them homes for sick paupers. In 1833, Columbus opened a Poor House on farmland one mile north of the town near where the Scioto and Olentangy joined. A Board of Directors, appointed by County Commissioners, hired a superintendent and physician for the care of the indigent. The superintendent lived on the grounds and had free access to farm products raised by the paupers as part of his pay. He furnished his own farming equipment. The turnover of superintendents was frequent. In 1840, the Poor House was moved into Columbus, and administration of the Poor House, now called an Infirmary, was relegated to just a physician. A keeper was hired also. In the late 1840's, a City Hospital was erected on the Infirmary grounds. Plans were made to move the Infirmary to larger acreage two miles east of downtown Columbus. In 1856, the Infirmary expenses were $9,800, with an average occupancy of sixty-eight inmates. One hundred and sixty people were admitted, and one hundred and forty were discharged, and twenty-six died in that year. The old infirmary was razed in 1968.

Home for the Aged

A Columbus Home for the Aged was constructed in 1888 using money raised at a charity ball. Mrs. William Monypeny was the principal catalyst for the benevolence. At first, only widows were admitted; later, men were allowed to live in the home, regardless of background. After the home was abandoned, the 300 Spruce Street building was renovated and occupied by Moody-Nolan Ltd, an architectural/engineering/design firm, in the 1980's.

Mental Institutions in Columbus

Mental illness was ignored during the first decade of Ohio's existence. This changed in 1815 when the state legislature passed a law that said "harmless lunatics" should be committed to county poorhouses, and the "dangerously insane" should be placed in local jails. Many of the individuals so afflicted remained at home under the vigilance of their families. Between 1835 and 1837, a group of local physicians, clergymen and civic leaders led by Dr. William Awl agitated for the state to build a home for the insane. This was constructed with prison labor in 1839 on a thirty acre site off the north side of East Broad Street, one-half mile east of the capitol building. With the addition of three more wings, 450 inmates were housed. Dorothea Dix, a foremost worker in the field of mental health, pronounced the Columbus facility one of the best in the nation. According to the styles of the era, patients were uniformed and fed like prison inmates. A large amusement hall allowed theatrical performances to be created by the patients for entertainment and therapy. On November 17, 1868, one of the worst fires in Columbus completely demolished this institution. Miraculously, only six perished. It was replaced by the Central Ohio Insane Asylum in 1877 on the Hilltop, west of the city. The old site was developed into an attractive park-like residential complex. Gradual deterioration of the huge west side institution, known as the Columbus Psychiatric Hospital, caused it to be demolished in 1996; it was replaced by buildings for the Ohio Department of Transportation. Three cemeteries were left on the grounds. All tombstones are of identical shape and size with name, date of birth and death. Those that are unnamed have the word "Specimens" inscribed on the stones. The county spends over $900 million per annum on its entire budget. Today, the county remains responsible for the care of the mentally retarded, the mentally disabled and those physically disabled. Children and family services, including legal expenses, account for most of the budget. Well over one-third of revenue (42%) comes from taxes (79% property and 21% sales).

Idiot Asylum

The state legislature created an asylum for the feeble-minded in 1838. Some of the patients were subsidized by their parents, others by the taxpayers.

State School for the Deaf

In 1832, the state began renting houses in various locations for dwelling places for the deaf (and dumb). The dwellings were centralized in 1834 by erecting a three-story main structure plus a barn and outbuildings at 450 East Town Street. A new emphasis was placed on education for the deaf and dumb. The residents were taught work skills and sign language was used. A gymnasium and power plant were added. In 1866-1868, a new building for the school was constructed that had been designed by George W. Bellows, Sr., father of the renown artist, George Jr. A hospital was added in 1906. After 1929, the school was moved to rented property on North High Street, and the previous building was used for commercial offices. The students were taught non-industrial occupations including cooking, housekeeping, sewing and book binding. One student, William Cauley, became a well-known frontier scout in the Rocky Mountains region. In 1953, a new school for the blind was built on the spacious grounds of a former golf course facing Morse Road where it remains today. Vocational classes expanded into auto body repair, auto maintenance, business office education, printing, masonry, graphics arts and commercial baking. Special support services included speech therapy, auditory training and occupational therapy. The original school on East Town Street burned down, and in 1981 that space was turned into a park with a topiary garden arranged into a representation of Georges Seurat's *A Sunday on the Island of La Grande Jatte*. Today, forty-five professional staff members educate an average of one hundred and forty-five students who range in age from three to twenty-two years. Computer, media, art and behavior management have been added to the curriculum. During after school hours, students may participate in intramural sports, clubs, cheerleading and other recreational activities. A full range of health care is provided by physicians and registered nurses in a sixteen-bed health facility.

State School for the Blind

Ohio was the first state in the nation to open a school for the blind in 1839 on East Main Street with its entrance facing Parsons Avenue. Students were taught many disciplines including playing musical instruments and piano tuning. Dr. Asa Lord introduced a system for grading students and teachers, using minimal standards. Some graduates became well known musicians. A second school, enlarged to accommodate more students as the result of the Civil War, was constructed in 1874 in the ornate style of the era with several steeples and clock tower. The third school was opened on North High Street in 1953. Its spacious grounds were shared with a school for deaf on a former golf course. The old school on Main Street became the headquarters of the state Highway Patrol. When they left, the building was renovated and used by the state Department of Health, its current occupant. It was damaged by fire in 2001.

Franklin County Children's Home

A home for orphaned or neglected children in Franklin County was opened on Johnstown Pike near Woodland Avenue in 1880. It included several multi-storied structures and spacious grounds. It closed and was superseded by Franklin County Village in 1951. The building was razed in 1955.

St. Vincent Orphanage

The St. Vincent de Paul Orphan Asylum was opened in 1875 at 1490 East Main Street. It was enlarged in 1894. It was converted into a Catholic children's service center upon closure of the orphanage in 1973. The nuns remained in the buildings until 1994.

Care for Disturbed Children

Salesian Boys and Girls Club of Columbus

The Salesians of St. John Bosco, a Catholic religious order, started the Salesian Boys Club for poor and/or troubled boys in 1970. A five-story red brick building at the corner of State and Sixth Streets, built in 1925 for the Knights of Columbus, was donated for use by the club. The non-sectarian club is open to youths of either sex between six and eighteen years of age. Entrance and departure is voluntary. The philosophy of the caretakers emphasizes education, positive values, caring and compassion. Young people are accepted as unique individuals living in an adult world of real fears and pressures. The intentions are to be fair, thoughtful and respectful of young people's values. Demands are to be reasonable and just. Compliance is not achieved by force but by firm, friendly persuasion. It is believed that even the most troubled youth can be touched by kindness. The young people are challenged to live genuine and good Christian lives. In addition to a paid professional staff, some are Salesian Brothers including the Director, but many are volunteers. Outside schools are used but the club provides, in addition to free food and shelter, a gym, swimming pool and two computer labs. A board of trustees of community leaders governs the club. The club's name became Salesian Inner City Boys Club in 1974 and, finally, Salesian Boys and Girls Club of Columbus in 1993.

Buckeye Ranch

Buckeye Boys Ranch was a charitable, non-profit, mental health facility founded by a group of women in 1961. Their mission was to care for emotionally, socially and behaviorally disturbed boys, ages 10 to 18. A residential house was erected for this purpose on 150 acres of land purchased at 5665 Hoover Road near Grove City. The name of the private organization was changed to Buckeye Ranch in 1994 to reflect the addition of girls. Dr. Les Bostic served as executive director for many years. Funds are provided by individuals, corporations, foundations and fund-raising events. For two decades, the service board sponsored the Buckeye Tennis Classic, attracting some of the great players. Currently, Hoops for Healing Team is a support group spearheaded by Coach Thad Matta of The Ohio State University basketball team. The Buckeye Ranch Film Festival is another fund-raising event. The Ranch has an on-site school system with a principal and fifteen teachers; eleven with bachelor degrees and five with master degrees or beyond. The student/teacher ratio is six/one. Classroom studies are enhanced by an athletic center, an outdoor swimming pool, athletic fields, an equestrian program and a creative arts center. The school is closely affiliated with and supported by teachers from the Southwestern School District of Franklin County. Ninety students are enrolled of which fifty-one percent are African-American, forty-five percent are Caucasian and the rest of mixed race. Twenty-five percent of the students are disabled. The expenditure per student averages $16,385 per year compared with a state average of $9,050. Seventy percent of the money goes for instruction, compared with fifty-six percent statewide. Comprehensive health care is provided in addition to any necessary psychological and psychiatric therapies. The Ranch has a working agreement with Ohio State University Hospitals to admit youths exhibiting acute psychiatric disorders to its medical facility, a specialized unit for children. It has a similar arrangement with Children's Hospital pertaining to physical illnesses. Hearing impairment is evaluated and treated. Spiritual guidance is ecumenically available. A foster-care service is a valuable asset.

United Methodist Children's Home

The United Methodist Children's Home was started as a faith-based orphanage in 1911. Its forty-two acre campus is located in the middle of Worthington. Today, troubled youth of both sexes between six and eighteen are received for care, nurture, treatment, education and skill building to overcome years of abuse and neglect. Hope, positive goals and important family values are instilled in the context of unconditional love. Between fifty and sixty students spend from three to six years in dormitories on the residential-like campus at 1033 North High Street. The staff, besides traditional teachers, includes social workers, nurses, art therapists and psychologists. Seventy percent of the staff has bachelor's degrees. Every student is reviewed twice a month to allow the staff to share information and develop programming for the child. The Worthington School System provides classroom instruction on the UMCH site. Some students attend school off-campus. The Home has received accreditation from the national Council of Services for Families, indicative of quality care and service. UMCH believes it benefits its students by being located in the midst of a close community culture. It has hosted "neighbor night," and offers campus tours and lunches. The Worthington Administrative Center also has a satellite facility in Reynoldsburg for its Treatment Foster Care and Adoption Program.

Chapter 9

Early Churches, Seminaries and Cemeteries

Early Churches in Columbus

Protestantism was the dominant religion in the new state capital. The first church in Columbus, in 1814, was Methodist. The small wooden building was converted into a school when a new brick church was constructed in 1825. Afro-Americans separated from the white congregation in 1823 and built a brick structure on Long Street in 1840. German Methodists met separately in 1844. Several branches of the Methodists split-off in early years. The Presbyterians first met in Franklinton under the leadership of Lucas Sullivant in 1806. They moved to Columbus in 1816 and built their first church at Spring and Third Streets. They, too, had several spin-offs into separate congregations. The Episcopal Church was organized in 1817 by Bishop Philander Chase. The Universalist Society of Columbus was formed in 1837 and acquired an abandoned German church in 1845. The first Baptist Church in Columbus started in 1825. They occupied their first building in 1830. Other protestant churches were German Lutheran (1821), German Reform (1846), Trinity German Evangelical Lutheran (1848-rebuilt in 1856 and is oldest Protestant church still in use today), German Evangelical Protestant (1842), Welch Methodist (1848) and German Evangelical (1858). The first Roman Catholic Church, St. Remigius (later called Holy Cross), was organized in 1833. Columbus became the second Ohio Catholic Diocese in 1868 under Bishop Sylvester Rosecrans. Catholics came with the first wave of Irish and German laborers. They built the German St. Mary's Catholic Church in German Village in the 1840's and the Irish St. Patrick's Catholic Church at Grant and Naghton Streets in 1855. German Jews organized their first congregation in 1852. While conducting their services in Hebrew, their records were in German. They were not numerous enough to have a Temple (B'nai Israel-reformed) until 1870. Greeks arrived late, and they were given a charter by the state for an Orthodox Church in 1910. Today, their Annunciation Cathedral is located at 555 North High Street. Several African-American churches, mostly Methodist and Baptist came into existence in the 1840s.

The Methodist Wesley Chapel was an historic structure built in 1846 on a lot donated by William Neil. It was a two-story, Federalist style, brick building erected on North High Street just north of Gay Street. In 1857, its members numbered one hundred and fifty. It was a participant in the "underground railroad" and served as a meeting place for various groups.

Lutheran Seminary

The Theological Department of Capital University was started in 1830, in Canton, Ohio, as a German Theological Seminary of the Lutheran Church. It moved to South Columbus in 1832 where it was housed in log cabins. The seminary's first president and founder was Rev. William Schmidt. He performed his work without formal salary. The first seminary buildings were erected in 1833 on the south side of Columbus. Capital University received its charter in 1850. After the Civil War, Capital University moved into a building near Goodale Park on land gifted by Dr. Lincoln Goodale. In 1876, the University moved again to rural east Columbus (Bexley), where it would permanently reside.

Pontifical College Josephinum

The Pontifical College Josephinum was established by Father Joseph Jessing in Columbus in 1898. Jessing was a Prussian war veteran who entered the priesthood in 1870 after immigrating to the United States in 1867. His first assignment was to Sacred Heart Church in Pomeroy, Ohio. In Pomeroy, he established an orphanage for boys called Saint Joseph Orphanage funded by a German newspaper which he wrote and published. The orphanage was relocated to downtown Columbus to be closer to rail transportation. Due to the demand for priests, Jessing started classes in 1888 leading to ordination to priesthood (high school, two years of college and four years of theology). In 1892, Pope Leo XIII granted direction of the seminary to be from the Vatican, the first pontifical seminary outside of Italy and independent of local Diocese control. The seminary is incorporated under the laws of Ohio and received its most recent approval from the Vatican in 1996. The early education of priests was aimed to service German immigrants but, after World War I, shifted to preparing priests for dioceses that lacked seminaries. The high school was closed in 1967. In 1931, the seminary moved to a one hundred-acre location north of Worthington and thirteen miles from downtown Columbus. A landmark Gothic-style edifice was erected among surrounding buildings. From the hundreds of students, many from abroad, over fifteen hundred priests have been educated at the Josephinum. The college also provides continuing education classes for lay persons, teachers, deacons, liturgical musicians, directors of religious education and priests. The college is fully accredited by commissions of higher education.

Cemeteries in Columbus

The North Graveyard, organized after a gift of land from John Kerr in 1821, was the city's first public burial ground. It occupied one and one-quarter acres off North High Street. It was for Caucasians only. Before that a small cemetery existed in Franklinton. The Columbus burial ground was enlarged in 1830 and again in 1845. In that year, all lots were sold. The East Graveyard was opened on Livingston Avenue, one and one-half miles east of the State House, in 1839. The Catholic Burying Ground in northeast Columbus became available in 1846. Interments were prohibited in the latter after 1856 on the basis that it contaminated the water supply. Green Lawn Cemetery was situated in Franklin Township, one and one-half miles west of the State House. Opening in 1849, it grew to eighty-four acres, the largest to date in Columbus. Lucas Sullivant was one of the trustees. It is the only one of the first four cemeteries still in active use. Eighty-five percent of stockholders voted to deny African-American burials in Green Lawn in 1856. This does not pertain today. Union cemetery was opened a few miles north of downtown Columbus in 1806. It was between the Olentangy River Road and the river. In 1946, a new addition was added on the other side of the River Road. Many notable citizens of Columbus are buried in this cemetery. The largest Catholic cemetery is St. Joseph Cemetery in southern Franklin County near Lockbourne on State Route 23. It was established in 1912. An older, smaller Catholic burial ground is Mt. Calvary Cemetery that opened in 1865 near Mound Street in Franklinton. An increasing number of Franklin County Catholics are buried in Resurrection Catholic Cemetery in southern Delaware County on State Route 23. It is only a few decades old. The first Jewish Cemetery was East Grave Yard (1852) at Meadow Lane and Livingston Avenue, one-half mile east of downtown Columbus. There are twelve other cemeteries for those of the Jewish faith. The largest non-denominational cemeteries in Columbus have sections set aside for Hebrew burials.

Chapter 10

Columbus during the Civil War

When the American Civil War commenced in 1861, Columbus had a population just over 18,000. Abraham Lincoln had been in office only a few weeks. He was not the candidate of choice in Columbus, rather Stephen Douglas, the Democratic contestant, won the majority of votes. William Dennison, a Republican, won the governorship. Lincoln called for volunteers, and Ohio responded with 30,000; 17,000 over their quota. Their arrival in Columbus caused great commotion. Provisional camps were set in most cities and larger towns. Government buildings and private homes were used for the first arrivals. The state arsenal was nearly empty holding only a few worn harnesses, out-of-date muskets and some rusting artillery pieces. The first hastily built camp in Columbus was in Goodale Park and called Camp Jackson (after President Andrew Jackson). Shortly thereafter the camp was moved five miles west and renamed Camp Chase after Senator and former Governor Salmon Chase. The southeast corner of the one hundred and sixty acre camp was the juncture of present Hague and Sullivant Avenues. The main entrance was off Broad Street. The volunteers swamped the capital city, and there was an extreme shortage of housing, clothing, food, water, sewer facilities, equipment and clerical help. When the first western battles took place, Confederate prisoners began to flow into Camp Chase. At first the captured officers, upon promise not to escape, were allowed to roam freely and attended the theaters, legislative sessions and visit private homes. Some even had slaves as valets. Later the officers were removed to Johnson Island Prison off the shore of Lake Erie near Sandusky. The barracks constructed for the prisoners were primitive, the food very ordinary and the guards ill-trained. Later Union parolees became guards. Sanitation was lacking, and epidemics, especially smallpox, plagued the camp with a high death rate. Curious civilians could pay a fee to visit the camp. Relatives were permitted to send gift packages. These relaxed conditions soon changed when word arrived of ill-treatment of Union prisoners in southern camps. The camp not only had 26,000 troops at its zenith but became the largest northern prison. Today, the Confederate cemetery with 2,260 headstones is the only remnant of the camp. A commemorative ceremony is held annually on Confederate Memorial Day.

Fig. 31 Camp Chase, the largest northern prison camp during the Civil War. The only vestige of the camp today is a Confederate Cemetery.
—from Columbus Metro Library

In honor of Ohio's Civil War heroes, a cluster of six statues were erected on the statehouse grounds. Those chosen were: Salmon Chase, James Garfield, Ulysses Grant, Phillip Sheridan, William Sherman and Edwin Stanton. Statues of Rutherford Hayes and William McKinley were added later.

In 1863, The United States Barracks, or Columbus Barracks as it was more commonly referred to, was built on the near east side of the capitol on land purchased from William Neil. It was the forerunner of Fort Hayes (named after former Governor and later President Rutherford Hayes in 1922). Its huge acreage extended from its Cleveland Avenue entrance on its west side to Hamilton Road on the east and from its southern boundary of Fifth Avenue to an artillery range on the northern side, occupied by Port Columbus Airport today. The land was purchased from the heirs of Robert and William Neil. It was used initially during the Civil War as an induction center, arsenal and armory. Through the years, the base enveloped large recreational facilities, a commissary/post exchange/lounge, mess hall, drill hall/recreational center, hospital, YMCA, a parade ground/park with band stand, houses for officers, barracks for enlistees and an admission and administration center. It was the size and encompassment of a sizeable village. It reached its zenith during World War I, when it contained stables for officers' mounts. It still persists as an employment center and for non-military tasks. Columbus has placed an alternative high school on the premises that emphasizes the fine arts. The ancient shot tower now houses a high school art museum, one of the few in the nation. Unfortunately, some of the remaining buildings are crumbling and have been vandalized and used as a refuge by the homeless.

Tod Barracks was another Civil War facility located at Swan and High Streets immediately north of the union railroad station. Its large enclosure held a parade ground, six lodging houses, a guardhouse, a dining hall, a kitchen and officers quarters. Built in 1863 and named after Governor David Tod, it served as a recruiting center, a receiving place for the sick, wounded soldiers and a jail.

Several small temporary camps made their appearance in Columbus to handle the excess recruits: Camp Lorenzo Thomas (where Olentangy Village is now); Camp Lew Wallace (immediately north of Camp Thomas); and Camp Tod (three miles west of downtown). African-Americans were camped near Delaware, Ohio. In 1864, the national draft selected men from the Columbus area.

In April 1861, Senator Stephen Douglas, enroute from Washington D.C. to Illinois, made two speeches in Columbus in support of the war. He died a few weeks later of typhoid fever. The Lincoln administration, in adhering to the "spoils system," rewarded several local men with political plums. John Grenier, editor of the *Gazette,* was appointed receiver of Public Monies for the New Mexico Territory. William Dean Howells, editor of the *Ohio State Journal,* was made Consul to Venice, Italy. Richard P. Baber, a Republican Party politician, secured a paymaster's job with the army. Noah Swayne was made a Justice of the Supreme Court. Surprisingly, it was business as usual in many areas of the community. In the elections of 1862, the Democrats came out on top in Columbus and Ohio, as a reflection of the unpopularity of the war. Several of the most vociferous opponents were imprisoned and banished from Ohio. The political atmosphere reversed in the elections of 1864, and Lincoln and his party were sustained.

The most famous state penitentiary prisoner during the war was Confederate General John Morgan who was captured near Cadiz, Ohio after a raid with several hundred men that terrorized citizens in southern Ohio. He was charged with being a horse thief rather than being treated as a prisoner of war. Morgan escaped from the Ohio penitentiary after being held a few weeks, and returned to military duty in Tennessee. His escape was enhanced by stealing clothes from the Lazarus store and receiving $1,000 in bills from his sister who hid them in a Bible mailed to him.

The Ohio volunteer units fought principally in the western theater under General William Tecumseh Sherman who grew up in nearby Lancaster. After news of intense fighting in Tennessee reached Columbus, a businessman gathered medical supplies and rushed with them to the war front. Three governors served Ohio during the war. William Dennison was replaced by David Tod in 1862. Tod, a Democrat, was the candidate of the Union Party, a combination of Republicans and Democrats who supported the war. Democrat John Brough became the second Union Party governor in 1864. He died in office in 1865. Democrats and others who opposed the war became known as "copperheads," named after the poisonous snakes that inhabited the state. Their leader was Clement Vallandigham, congressman from Dayton. He was arrested on charges of sedition and banished to the Confederacy. Escaping into Canada, he ran unsuccessfully for Governor of Ohio in the 1863 election from Windsor, Canada. He made President Lincoln very uncomfortable during that election, and Lincoln failed to carry Columbus in his victory over General George McClellan. Among other opponents of the war was newspaper publisher Samuel Medary. His paper, *The Crisis,* was vehement in its anti-war editorials. Union soldiers raided the newspaper office and closed it down. Other civilian citizens formed a number of societies to aid the war effort. Conversely, merchants able to produce materials needed by the army achieved huge profits. Foreign immigration into Ohio slowed to a trickle during the war. Following Lincoln's assassination in 1865, his funeral train came to Columbus, and the coffin was carried in a procession to the State House where it was placed in the rotunda for a few hours for public viewing. It was estimated that 50,000 people, walking four abreast, viewed the president. The shock and mourning over the president's death was intense in Columbus.

Fig. 32 Artist's portrayal of Lincoln's cortege following his assassination in 1865. Note new State House to left. The unfinished new City Hall is in the rear.

—from Columbus Metro Library

The chief newspaper in Columbus during the 1860's was the *Ohio State Journal,* supporter of the Republican Party and the Union during the war. The *Columbus*

Gazette also was loyal to the northern cause, but the *Ohio Statesman* was in favor of the Democratic Party and neutral toward the war. The German language paper, the *Westbote*, a supporter of the Democratic Party, was in favor of gradual emancipation of slaves and opposed abolitionist agitators.

Industry turned to producing war materiel and supplies for soldiers. Some businessmen became wealthy. The building of fine homes continued in spite of a shortage of building supplies and workers. The Neil House, the largest downtown hotel, was rebuilt in 1862. An opera house and schools were constructed as if the war was not a hindrance.

Lyceum lectures by visiting speakers were discontinued as were Maennerchor concerts. Although operas in the new Opera House and theatrical productions continued, home-town talent was resorted to for producing "benefits" for the Soldiers' Aid Society. The State Fair continued each year.

In 1863, laborers received $1.50 a day; carpenters, $1.75, stonemasons, $2.00; and bricklayers, $2.50. Vegetables and fruit were plentiful, and even fresh oysters arrived from the Chesapeake region. A few people vacationed in Europe. In contrast, relief organizations were busy, and a large number of women volunteered their services. Considerable aid was provided families whose men were in the military service.

Fig. 33 Lighted arches were placed over North High Street in the 1880's, extending from the center of Columbus into the Short North area.

Fig. 34 The former Post Office (1887) was renovated in the 1980's, and is now the Bricker & Eckler law office.

—from Columbus Metro Library

Chapter 11

Post-Civil War Columbus

Columbus in 1870 had a population over 31,000 citizens and was becoming more industrialized. Improved roads, the state canal and the railroads opened avenues for trade with the east and south and promoted immigration. The Ohio State University was founded in 1873. It was made possible by a congressional act giving public land to each state according to its number of congressmen. In return, the university had to emphasize the teaching of subjects in agriculture and mechanics (engineering). A survey of the city revealed over thirty churches, over one hundred saloons, nearly fifty physicians, fifty-five attorneys, seven book stores, seven tanneries, thirteen drug stores, and over one hundred and twenty grocery stores. Provisions were made to care for the infirm, poor, deaf, blind and mentally deficient. Sewers were built, and streetcars were introduced. Lagging behind was the medical service and purity of water supply. Typhoid fever, cholera and infectious diseases took terrible tolls. By 1897, Columbus had its first skyscraper, the Wyandotte Building, on West Broad Street one block from High Street. Reform was slowly taking place in politics and social issues. Technology added the telephone to telegraphy. Lighted arches were placed over High Street, and amusement parks thrived. Sports were gaining momentum. Columbus was humming.

The Ohio Centennial (Northwest Territory) was a large exposition held from September 4 to October 19, 1888. Although the state was only eighty-five years old, the exhibition was designed to proudly demonstrate the material and educational progress and growth of Ohio. On over one hundred acres, two miles northeast of the city, the exposition grounds held a beautiful park, lakes, drives, walks, a speed and exhibition track and pleasure attractions. The Central Building and its annexes contained many exhibits of fine arts, music, floral displays, manufactured products and any ware a merchant might wish to show. The Power Hall held demonstrations of heavy machinery and boilers. A General Headquarters and Executives Building was used for conducting business, meetings and conventions. Thirty-six smaller buildings provided stalls, pens and cages for farm animals and birds, and a speed ring for races and demonstrations. Thousands gathered to participate in or view the exhibits.

It was no coincidence that the Grand Army of the Republic held its 22nd annual encampment for a week in Columbus beginning on September 10, 1888. The GAR was a veterans group to aid soldiers and lobby in their behalf. A quarter of a million veterans showed up for the week-long celebration. Reduced railroad fares, no increase in hotel rates or food services, and all the hospitality Columbus could muster made the reunion a glorious affair. Activities centered at Franklin Park, the old fairgrounds, one mile east of the Capitol. Camp sites were named for states with numbered "streets" and tents. Straw for bedding, firewood and water were provided free. The Capitol, opera houses and school buildings were at their disposal. A program of events and entertainment was published daily. Police protection, electric lights and means to remove waste was also complimentary. Women Relief Corps were located in apartments and churches. The citizens of Columbus donated one hundred thousand dollars to defray expenses. The grand parade took place on September 11. A highlight of the week was a speech by Army General William Tecumseh Sherman which included the famous phrase, "Boys, War is Hell!" The city decided to glamorize the occasion by placing wooden arches over downtown High Street, spaced every half-block and illuminated with gas lights. After the veterans left, the city decided to keep the arches for safety at night. When electricity became available, the arches were replaced by steel and electrically lighted. Columbus was known worldwide as the "Arch City." Finally, in 1914, the arches were removed, and street lights were installed. What goes around, comes around, and in 2004, new arches were restored on High Street in the Short North area with mixed citizen response.

Fig. 35 After the Civil War, industries sprang up along the Scioto River creating much smoke and heavy pollution of the river. This picture shows the Main Street (closest) and Broad Street Bridges and the Ohio Penitentiary on West Spring Street in the upper left.

—from Columbus Metro Library

After the Civil War, Columbus developed a thriving vehicle trade. In fact, by the turn of the century, Columbus became known as the "Buggy Capital of the World." The major entrepreneurs in this enterprise were George M. Peters, and the Benns brothers, William and John. Having experience in buggy repair, painting and shoeing horses, the three formed a carriage manufacturing company at Town and Third Streets called the Peters, Benns & Company in 1865. They believed that success lay in the use of an assembly-line system of labor and the use of steam power. Despite the low production costs allowing low sale prices, the business floundered. The partners differed over the production philosophy. Peters was joined by his brother, Oscar, and Clinton D. Firestone in forming a new company in 1871 named the Iron Buggy Company. The new company manufactured buggies and dash boards utilizing the "duplicate plan." They sold the company in 1875 and formed two new companies called the Columbus Buggy Company and the Peters Dash Company located at the northeast corner of Wall and Locust Streets. Sales increased annually, allowing expansion to several buildings along the P.C. & St. L. rail lines. By 1892, their annual sales were two million dollars, and they employed twelve hundred men who made one hundred vehicles and fifteen hundred carriage dashes per day. In the early 1900s, the company occupied the entire quarter of a block at the southwest corner of High and Naghten Streets (now Nationwide Center). Before the end of this vehicular era, Columbus would have twenty-two buggy manufacturing companies. Peters and Firestone were among the socially elite in the city. A devastating fire and an economic depression in the 1890s took its toll of the Peters and Firestone companies. Oscar Peters committed suicide. The company reorganized, and, in 1903, the Columbus Buggy Company began to manufacture an electric vehicle called the Columbus Electric. It looked similar to the horse-drawn buggy with a convertible fabric top. It functioned quietly, had a maximum speed of twenty miles per hour and limited operating time. The chief disadvantage was the time expended to recharge the batteries and their short life. This limitation would hamper the use of electric vehicles for a century. In 1907, they produced a gasoline engine car called the Firestone-Columbus. Competition from the Ford Model-T and the flood of 1913 caused the company to fold in that year. Allen automobiles were manufactured in Columbus from 1919 to 1923 when the company went out of business. Columbus was not destined to be an automotive manufacturing center like Detroit and Cleveland. The city was too far away from the steel industry.

As the transportation hub of Columbus enlarged with the advent of a canal, improved roads and the railroads, so did the hostelry business grow. At the corner of High and Naghten Streets (today Nationwide Boulevard), near the Union Station, the six-story Davidson Hotel was built in 1878 to provide lodging for the affluent railroad and carriage travelers. It ceased to exist in 1916 due to the decline in rail passengers. The Norwich Hotel had a similar existence. Only, the empty Seneca Hotel on East Broad Street remains as a condemned landmark but with the possibility of being renovated into condominiums. The Seneca was named after a prominent business man, who had been the center of the Irish community that made up to twenty-five percent of Columbus in the last half of the nineteenth century.

Fig. 36 The Columbus Buggy Company plant was the largest in America (1900). This site is now occupied by Nationwide Insurance buildings.
—from Columbus Metro Library

Columbus had trolley lines, first horse drawn in 1863 and later powered by electricity (1891). The cars not only were numbered but were painted in various colors to identify their routes. In 1806, a newly promoted motorman, President Richard Nixon's father, Frank, had his feet frostbitten riding in the raw winter weather. He led a worker's effort to get the open motorman's vestibule enclosed and heated like the interior of the trolleys. Strong company opposition forced Nixon to leave for California. Unrest continued into 1910, when the streetcar workers struck, and the resultant violence forced the governor to call on the National Guard for protection. The workers' cause was lost.

The early streetcar companies had individual routes with single destinations. Consolidation occurred, and by 1903 the Columbus Railway & Light Company was the sole operator. Its name changed to Columbus Railway, Power & Light Company in 1914. In 1937, the company's new name was Columbus & Southern Ohio Electric. Streetcars were gradually replaced by electric trolley buses with overhead wire-lines during the period 1933-1948 allowing boarding at the curb. At this time, the company's electric and transportation operations were separated and the Columbus Transit Company was formed. The electric buses were exchanged for gas engine powered buses in 1965. In 1973, our present COTA (Central Ohio

Transit Authority) became the sole provider of public transportation supported by local taxes. Today, the system has 234 buses that make 4,214 stops on 53 routes. There are 380 shelters and 24 Park & Ride locations. Forty nine thousand rides were made weekly, 4,000 by disabled. In 2006, Mayor Michael Coleman of Columbus, proposed a return of trolleys to downtown Columbus streets, connecting the Short North to the Brewery District with the Arena District in its midst. The projected cost has held it up. For years a rapid transit, light rail system has been suggested for Ohio, and again the cost has not found favor with the public. Several interurban stations in downtown Columbus served as hubs for connections to all Central Ohio towns (Worthington-Delaware-Marion; Westerville; Gahanna; Newark; Zanesville; Canal Winchester; Grove City; London; Springville; Groveport; Lancaster and Circleville).

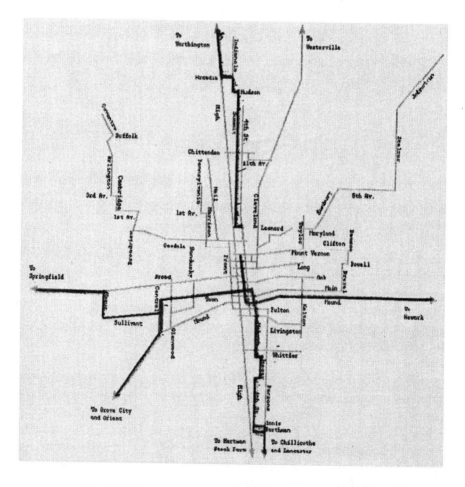

Fig. 37 Trolley and interurban (heavy) lines—circa 1955.
—from http://hometown. aol. com

Immigrant Villages

Italian Village, although predominately settled by Italian families, was a melting pot of Irish, German, Greek, other southeast Europeans immigrants and African-Americans. A short distance northeast of downtown Columbus, it has ill-defined boundaries. It spreads out a mile in each direction from its center at the intersection of Fourth Street and First Avenue. The southern boundary is I-670 and the northern limit is Fifth Avenue. High Street bounds it on the west and Conrail tracks on the east. The immigrants were drawn to Columbus, primarily after the Civil War, to work on the railroads, in the quarries, in Italian restaurants, on construction projects, landscaping and in manufacturing companies. Their common denominator was their poverty. They put their roots down near their places of employment: Jeffrey Manufacturing, Clark Grave Vault and Auto Equipment Company, Timken Roller Bearing plant, Berry Bolt Works, John Amicon Produce Company, Smith Brothers Hardware, several bakeries and other smaller businesses. WPA work helped them survive the Great Depression in the 1930's. Number Four Fire Station was a source of food, clothing and toys during hard times. Few owned cars, and the streetcars were their main mode of transportation. The focal point for the Italians was their place of worship, weddings and general fellowship, St. John the Baptist Italian Catholic Church. It was founded in 1898 on the corner of Hamlet and Lincoln Streets by Reverand Alexander Cestelli, a professor at the Pontifical College of Josephinum. Services were conducted in the Italian language, and music and pre-mass musical processions were provided by an Italian band and choir. Unusual, there was no Italian school. Rather, the students attended nearby Sacred Heart School, or one of several public high schools. An annual Italian Festival, founded by Father Casto Marrapese in 1980 as a fund raiser for a cultural center on the church grounds, also bonded those of Italian heritage. The church still gives classes for those wishing to learn the Italian language. The fact that a neighborhood Village is named Italian is a testament to the determination of that ethnic group, more than most immigrants, to maintain their traditional heritage and beliefs. Other groups of Italians settled in Milo-Grogan (between railroad tracks on west, north and east and I-670 on the south; it is transected by Cleveland Avenue), "fly town," (west of Goodale Park), the "hilltop," (western Franklinton), Grandview Heights, Marble Cliff and San Margherita. The first three settlements were within walking distance of each other as well as to the North Market, Ft. Hayes and Union Station. The main lines of the railroads cut through the area.

A second generation Italian, Gene D'Angelo, played in the Italian Band, attended Ohio State University, was a long time general manager of WBNS television station, a strong supporter of the arts and a civil leader in Columbus. His daughter,

Beverly D'Angelo, became a singer and actress in motion pictures. The southeast quadrant is now being developed into apartments, condominiums and shops called Jeffrey Place.

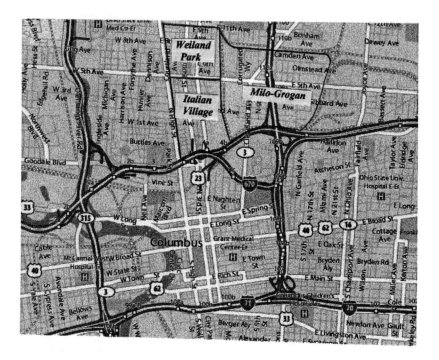

Fig. 38 The neighborhoods of Weiland Park, Milo-Grogan and Italian Village.

Flytown was a twenty-five square block area west of Neil Avenue and extending south of Goodale Street to railroad tracks, industrial plants and the state penitentiary. Olentangy River formed its western limits. It was a port of entry for immigrants of seventeen nationalities who were aided by relatives and other immigrants who preceded them. Numerous shops, saloons and rental rooms were to be found on West Goodale Street. Nearby industry and the railroads were sources of employment. St. Francis of Assisi Church on Buttles Avenue served the community, especially Italians. In 1898, the First Neighborhood Guild was the first settlement house sponsor in Columbus. Henry Godman, owner of a large shoe company gave $10,000 to build the settlement house. Today, the Godman Guild is still active in charitable efforts.

At the turn of the twentieth century, it was recognized world-wide that respiratory illnesses such as tuberculosis flourished in environments that allowed close contact between individuals and poor sanitation. In response, sanitariums sprang up in outdoor, sunny, clear-air, high altitude sites in the Alps and Colorado. It was a popular notion that the human body, placed under such advantageous conditions could develop a resistance to certain diseases and cause them to be arrested. In 1907, a group of nurses in the Instructional District Nursing Association of Columbus, in keeping with this belief, established an outdoor, summer camp of tents to provide fresh air for underprivileged infants and toddlers living in the crowded tenement houses and poor neighborhoods. The babies were given proper food, hygiene, medical care and relief from the summer heat. The first baby camp was adjacent to St. Anthony's Hospital. The second year's camp was next to the Godman Guild Settlement House in Flytown. Next, it was moved near Mercy Hospital on South High Street in 1909. Thereafter, the location was on Sullivant Avenue between Townsend Avenue and Helen Street. In 1911, the tents were replaced by wooden shelters. City water, ice, and phone service were provided gratis by Columbus and altruistic companies. As many as sixty infants were given these privileges at any one time. The camps were funded by donations from individuals, corporations, the three major local newspapers and fund-raising events. The camps ceased operations after 1938, when tuberculosis began responding to quarantine and medicinal treatment.

Flytown was polluted from nearby plants and gradually deteriorated with the constant change in its populus. The Columbus Redevelopment Authority declared Flytown blighted in the 1950s, and the area was gradually cleared of homes and businesses. The Goodale Expressway demolished the southern portion of the area. Thurber Towers, Westminster Terrace, a shopping area and a few apartments sprang up off the southwest corner of Neil and Buttles Avenues, attracting a new group of people and are active today. The Presbyterian Retirement Services, the Galbreath Company and national insurance companies have infused the renamed Thurber Village with financial support.

African-Americans in Columbus

African-Americans came slowly into the new capital in the first half of the nineteenth century. They lived near their employment along Peter's Run which is occupied now by the I-70/I-71 freeway, running east and west, parallel to Livingston Avenue, and separating German Village on the south from downtown Columbus on the north. Land was cheap and undesirable due to the malodorous tanning business operated by the Peters. Sewage in the Run was an additional unpleasantness. As downtown business pushed south, the African-Americans moved to the short east, centering on Mt. Vernon Avenue and East Long Street where they continue to be concentrated today. They had their own churches and schools before desegregation, which has taken over one hundred years to accomplish.

Milo-Grogan, Linden South and Weiland Park are other depressed areas that have a high percentage of black occupancy. The city has an active program of demolishing or repairing vacant homes. Defunct businesses are likewise targets of this program. As an example, former Columbus Coated Fabrics, about thirty buildings at East Fifth and Grant Avenues in Weiland Park, underwent demolishment in 2007 to make way for over five hundred condominiums and apartments. State grants were made available for this project (Clean Ohio Fund). Ohio State University undertook the building of a $10 million laboratory day-care center in Weiland Park at the southeast corner of Summit Street and Seventh Avenue in 2007. It is located next to the new Weiland Park Elementary School at 211 East Seventh Avenue. The center accommodates eighty-eight children including twenty pre-schoolers and ten infants and toddlers. All will come from low-income families. The center will offer family counseling, wellness services, a classroom for OSU students and researchers, and an art studio with a kiln. Overhead observation areas with headphones and two-way windows will facilitate teaching. Over half of the cost is being provided privately from fund-raising and corporate donations. The Schoenbaum family, owners of the Shoney Restaurant chain, gave $2.5 million. One million dollars each was given by JPMorgan Chase and Proctor & Gamble. Lowe's provided a rooftop deck. Columbus invested $300,000 to redesign the adjoining Weiland Park and elementary school.

African-American Albert L. Brooks opened a mortuary in his home at 295 North 21st Street in 1923. Although it changed locations several times, it remained in the family for several generations. The Brooks-Owens Funeral Home on East Main Street represents eighty-four years of service by a black owned business in Columbus.

After World War II, federal funds and tax abatements helped the development of small businesses and public housing. A Playhouse and venue for speakers and other performances was opened at the Martin Luther King Jr. Center, helping to draw the community together, socially and culturally. President Jimmy Carter came to Columbus and pronounced the public housing community efforts a model for the nation. Unfortunately, poor construction and maintenance caused the high-rise dwelling to be abandoned. Today, African-Americans make up fifteen percent of the population of Columbus, and one of their own is Mayor Michael Coleman, serving his third term, and frequently mentioned as a candidate for governor.

Entertainment in Columbus

Sells Brothers Circus

Beginning in the 1830's, small animal acts, some with male acrobats, were brought to Columbus from the east. The larger groups had a parade with at least one elephant and a band. The average ticket for admission cost twenty-five cents and half-price for children under twelve.

Ephraim, William, Lewis and Peter Sells opened a circus in Columbus in 1871. Prior to that, they had engaged in auctions and a small traveling side show. They mortgaged their property in order to buy equipment, animals and the services of "Cannonball George Richards," whose specialty was to be shot from a cannon at each appearance. A parade of horse-drawn animal cages opening the show was not popular, so they substituted elephants at the head of the procession. By 1881, their eight elephant act was the main attraction. The popularity of their show reached its zenith in 1890. They found it necessary to use a train to move the second largest circus around the country. Their headquarters, where they wintered, was called Sellsville located just south of the present day Ohio State University. Misfortune struck the circus while touring Australia when their animal menagerie was decimated by disease. After the four brothers died, the family heirs sold the show in 1905 to J.A. Bailey of later fame as the Ringling Brothers, Barnum and Bailey Circus. The advent of the modern circus was their legacy.

Peter Sells built a mansion near Goodale Park in 1895 that was designed by Frank Packard, famed Columbus architect. The outside appearance is quite distinct; it looks like a circus big top. Some of the interior walls were adorned with circus posters. Rumors circulated that animals were kept in the basement, and that a carousel was placed on the third floor. Local historians now consider both notions to be myths. Following the death of Sells' widow, the house had many owners that included The Fraternal Order of Police, United Commercial Travelers and the House of Hope for Alcoholics. The most recent owner renovated the 7,400-square-foot "Circus House," and its market price in 2007 was $1.4 million.

The industrial revolution and the proliferation of inventions after the Civil War provided more leisure time and money to spend. It was not unusual for people to become occupied in their spare time with sports and amusement activities. Circuses, vaudeville acts and amusement parks became the vogue. Trolleys and the automobile allowed easy transportation of large numbers to these events. Four major amusement parks were opened on the north side of Columbus. They were: Olentangy Amusement Park, the Indianola Amusement Park, the Minerva

Amusement Park and much later, Wyandot Lake. The first three are long gone and Wyandot is now merged with the Columbus Zoo.

Fig. 39 The Casino and Theater, Olentangy Amusement Park.
—Columbus Metro Library

A premier Columbus destination was the Olentangy Amusement Park which opened in 1893 and functioned until 1937. The Park was located off North High Street, half-way between downtown and Worthington. Hundreds were attracted to its rides, boating, games, pony track, train ride, picnicking, dancing and food. Some of the more popular rides were a figure-8 roller coaster, two ferris-wheels, a merry-go-round, a loop-the-loop, a circle-swing and a shoot-the-chutes. A theater which seated over 2,200 hosted vaudeville, plays and musicals. The park was only open during the summer months. The buildings were highly decorative. The amusement center was owned initially by Robert Turner who sold it to the Columbus Streetcar Company in 1896 who, in turn, used it to enhance its trolley business. Two streetcar tracks coursed through the entrance arcade. In 1899, the park came under the ownership of the Dussenbury brothers who, in turn, sold the venture to Lester L. LeVeque in 1938. In 1947, he converted all except the swimming pool into an apartment complex known as Olentangy Village. The High Street front contained several shops.

At one time, for a short period, there was a Cyclorama of the Battle of Gettysburg exhibited at the corner of Sixth and Long Streets.

By 1900, Columbus had three major parks for leisure strolls, picnics, bird-watching, observation of flora and trees, and in some locations, boating and refreshment stands. The oldest was Goodale Park on the near north side. City Park was one mile to the south, and Franklin Park was two miles east of the Capitol.

A baseball field, also known as Recreation Park was located two miles south of the Capitol. All could be reached by trolley cars.

Dancing thrived in private clubs and public halls such as Valleydale and nearby Buckeye Lake. Both attracted nationally famous dance bands.

Horse racing has been carried out at the Driving Park (short distance east of downtown), Beulah Park in Grove City and Scioto Downs, south of Columbus on U.S. Route 23. The last two tracks were allowed to have pari-mutual wagering. National Trails is a drag-racing track twenty-five miles east of the city on U.S. 40. Barney Oldfield thrilled onlookers in his customized racing auto at the Columbus Driving park in the early 1900's. He claimed he could beat any airplane. Even Jesse Owens, the star sprinter in the 1936 Olympics, raced against horses at the Driving Park.

Beginning in the 1840s, people became interested in riding in hydrogen filled balloons. Richard Clayton provided the rides and demonstrations in Columbus. After World War I, thousands attended air shows that included dirigibles. Charles Lindbergh teamed with Henry Ford to fly mail and passengers in Ford tri-motor planes. Their Transcontinental Air Transport Company opened for business in 1929 with a celebrity flight out of Port Columbus. Soon, it merged with Trans World Airline with an important stop in Columbus. Port Columbus grew continuously and has expanded with new and longer runways, new flight towers and more concourses and gates. It always has been located east of Columbus, between Stelzer Road and the I-270 outerbelt, and is the eastern terminus of I-670, a freeway to downtown Columbus.

Before the advent of motion pictures, entertainment was provided by vaudeville and stage shows, fairs and demonstrations by magicians. One of the most notable performers of magic was Howard Thurston. He was born in Columbus in 1869. His father was a carriage maker who also made mallets for tenderizing meat. Young Thurston peddled the mallets and newspapers on the street and was a hotel bellhop. Due to his adult height of five and one-half feet and slight build, he considered being a jockey. Briefly, he thought also of being a minister. Instead, as a teenager, he ran away from home and joined a circus. He developed a side show using card tricks. As he toured the world and expanded his repertoire, he developed the reputation of a talented magician. His shows became lavish with pretty ladies, humor and stage illusions. He made a Whippet automobile filled with beautiful women disappear and floated an assistant above the stage who disappeared over the footlights. At the height of his career, a ten-box car show with two separate tours was required to entertain his amazed, overflowing audiences. He wrote an autobiography, *My Life of Magic,* which sold well. Competition from

Hollywood-made movies, the Great Depression and naïve investments reduced his fortune. He died in Miami, Florida in 1936 of a massive stroke.

Competition for the entertainment trade was located principally in downtown Columbus For example, the Bott Brothers at 141 North High Street installed a billiard parlor, bowling alley, a buffet and sold bar supplies. Their emporium featured the finest glass and woodware available. The business lost popularity and closed in 1923. Two years later, the Clock Restaurant opened on the premises.

The Hartman Era

Fig. 40

Dr. Samuel Brubaker Hartman (Fig. 40) was one of the most infamous citizens of Columbus during a period from 1890 to 1917, the year he died. He was born in 1830 on a farm in Lancaster County, Pennsylvania. In 1847, he graduated from Farmer's College in Cincinnati, the equivalent of high school. He served a medical apprenticeship under Dr. Shackelford in Medway, Ohio near Dayton, earning his way by selling German Bibles. He completed further medical studies in Cleveland and New York. He commenced the practice of medicine and the manufacture of medical devices in Lancaster, Pennsylvania. In 1882, he moved his practice to Columbus. In 1890, he gave up his career as a physician to produce and distribute a patent medicine labeled Pe-Ru-Na., claiming to have received the formula from an Indian Chief during a dream. This enterprise began in Dayton but was moved to Columbus where he built a large plant to manufacture the "medicine." He advertised the mixture as a cure for "catarrh" which he said afflicted the sinuses, throat, respiratory tract, digestive tract, kidneys and other internal organs. He gave lectures on his theory of what caused diseases and why his elixir could cure all disorders. Produced at a cost of fifteen cents a bottle, it sold for one dollar. The business was doing poorly until Frederick Schumaker, a sales expert, married Hartman's daughter. Schumaker became vice-president and director of advertising for his father-in-law's business. A million dollar advertising campaign for Peruna (name change) resulted in a highly successful business empire. Hartman's thirty-five hundred acre farm south of Columbus included a dairy, vineyards, cattle, poultry, grain, houses for his workers, the owner's mansion ($100,000), a power plant and an interurban line to Columbus complete with trolley cars and repair shops. Veterinary students from Ohio State University practiced judging livestock on his farm which was a national showplace. In Columbus, he built the six-story Hartman Sanitarium and hotel in 1908, originally intended for his patients. The hotel stood at the northwest corner of Fourth and East Main Street. The top floor contained an ornate dining room and an adjacent ballroom and lounge. It also included living quarters for the Hartman family, and they preferred it over his farm mansion. A ten-story Hartman office building with a connected theater was built on East State Street and was the venue for major concerts, theatrical productions and movies. There, the world premiere of Eugene O'Neill's *A Moon for the Misbegotten* was held. This building complex was demolished in 1971 to be replaced by offices at Capitol Square. The Hartman Hotel has been preserved. It eventually came to be used as a warehouse, government offices, a branch of Huntington Bank and was renovated into business offices in 1999-2000. The ceiling was damaged by a fire in 2000. Today, the farm no longer is productive and contains a sand and gravel quarry and some buildings that include an abandoned school house and former quarters for training state patrolmen. After the death of Hartman in 1917, the Federal Drug Administration belatedly confirmed the ingredients of Puruna to be twenty-eight percent grain alcohol, burnt sugar for color and fruit for flavor. It was particularly popular in "dry" or "temperance" states. Prior to this, in 1905, *Collier's Weekly* attempted an exposé of the "miracle cure." His exploitation of gullible patients is an example of the ability of medical quacks to influence minds by persuasive lectures, testimonials, advertisements and the pleasurable effects of alcohol, much to the embarrassment of Columbus. During Hartman's final years, he gave generously to Columbus organizations, especially those involving the arts. The Columbus Museum of Art was a prime benefactor. After Hartman's death, the business closed, and his farm and holdings were administered by a trust.

Fig. 41 The Hartman Hotel, built in 1908 at the northwest corner of Fourth and East Main Streets, still stands, having been renovated into an office building.
—Columbus Metro Library

Fig. 42 The Park Hotel (name changed later to Northern) is shown in upper left. The Seneca Hotel is shown in upper right. The Southern Hotel is seen in the lower left. The Atlas building is in the lower right. It was first known as the Columbus Savings and Trust Building. The last three buildings remain standing. The Southern Hotel and Theater and the Atlas building are in full use today. The Seneca Hotel building has been condemned and is vacant (there is a plan to restore and use the building).

—from Columbus Metro Library

Henry Chittenden, a successful Columbus man, built a fashionable hotel at the northwest corner of West Spring and High Streets. The cost was $300,000, a considerable amount of money at that time. The complex included an attached Henrietta Theater. It was next door to the Park Theater, creating a theater-dining-hotel district. While William McKinley was governor, he made the hotel his home. By 1893, a new Chittenden Hall of six stories was under construction immediately west of the original hotel and containing the Henrietta Theater. A fire, from an electrical cause, broke out and within twenty-four hours the entire Chittenden complex was in ruins. Undaunted, Chittenden rebuilt, and, in 1895, opened an eight-story, three hundred room new hotel with a theater. Today, the hotel is gone, replaced by the thirty-three story William Green Office Building.

Fig. 43 Chittenden Hotel and Theater-1893   Fig. 44 Deshler Hotel-1915

Fig. 45 The second Neil House Hotel was constructed on South High Street opposite the State Capitol in 1862 after the first Neil House was consumed by fire on election night 1860.

Fig. 46 The third and last Neil House was built in 1925 and closed and razed in 1980. It was replaced by the Huntington Center.

—from Columbus Metro Library

Electric Plant

Columbus began illuminating its central streets with candles in 1840. Gas street lights were introduced in 1844. In 1896, the Columbus City Council agreed to issue bonds up to $300,000 for an experimental municipal light power plant to service street lights and city owned buildings. Its headquarters was with the city water works. The superintendent was paid $120 per month, and all others were employed for $100 per month. The plant closed in 1900 after spending $68,000 for what it considered an uneconomical venture. Nevertheless, in a change of mind, the city built a new power plant that opened in 1905 with its Division of Electricity building at the corner of Gay and North High Streets. In 1987, the city built a more efficient and modern five megawatt hydroelectric plant at the Scioto River's O'Shaughnessey dam on Glick Road. Over 10,000 gallons of river water fuel its twin turbines that generate electricity. Today, it services the municipal government needs plus about 14,000 other customers. Recently, the divisions of electricity and water were combined. The Division of Power and Water is located at 3500 Indianola Avenue and has current annual revenues of forty million dollars and one hundred and forty employees. For years, revenues from sales of electric power paid for all expenses. Even today, the street lights of Columbus are provided free to its citizens. In recent years, the taxpayer's aid is needed for some of the expenses to operate the Division of Electricity. It cooperates with its competitor, American Electric Power, and utilizes their lines for transmission and distribution.

Early Refrigeration

The Crystal Ice Manufacturing Company was a large and successful business in the 1890's. Water was obtained from artesian wells, boiled into steam which passed through pipes submerged in cold water. In the next step, steam was converted back into water causing lime, magnesium, sulphur, iron and other minerals to be removed. After filtering the reclaimed water through charcoal and sponges, over one hundred and twenty tons of water per day were frozen in zinc cans by placing the cans in salt water vats that had small pipes carrying ammonia and anti-hydrate gas to absorb heat and reduce the temperature to ten degrees below zero. The ice blocks were then loosened with warm water sprinklers, removed and stored. Also, this made possible the storage of enormous amounts of food until modern refrigeration appeared in 1910. Before that, some homes had zinc lined passage ways to receive eighteen inch ice cubes into their kitchens. A cheaper, less sophisticated and less sanitary way to refrigerate, was to cut large blocks of ice from lakes and rivers and store the ice in sawdust. The ice would then be delivered to home ice boxes through the use of ice wagons.

Water and Waste Management

Sewage and the means of disposal of it was a major drawback in living in early Columbus. It wasn't until after the Civil War that the city came to serious grips with the problem. In the 1870's, an effective system of sewer pipes was built to carry household and business waste into the Scioto River. This coincided with the installation of lavoratories, faucets, toilets and bathtubs in homes. A major supplier of fixtures for these indoor conveniences at this time was the Columbus Brass Company on North Sixth Street, one of the largest producers of such parts in the Midwest. The company survived a devastating fire in 1893, and their products are still in use today.

Today, Columbus and its suburbs have three modern and reliable water treatment plants: Dublin Road near downtown, Hap Creamean in the far north and Parson in the far south; and two solid waste disposal facilities (Southerly Wastewater Treatment Plant and the Jackson Pike Wastewater Treatment Plant). They service one million people through the use of 6,159 miles of sanitary, storm and combined sewers.

The First Telephones in Columbus

Francis Sessions and George Twiss opened the Columbus Telephone Exchange in 1879, the first in the capital city. It was located in the Sessions Building at the southwest corner of Long and High Streets. Sessions and Twiss became aware of the invention of the telephone through a demonstration of the new invention by Alexander Graham Bell at the Philadelphia Centennial Exposition in 1876. The use of the telephone was made possible by the prior introduction of the use of electricity. Charles Williams introduced the first telephone company in Boston in 1877. Sessions and Twiss made their own demonstration in Columbus in the same year and started their company two years later. At first, male operators were used; they could listen in on the conversations. The conversation was activated by speaking and listening through a protuding aperature in a box. Western Union became owner of this first telephone exchange in Columbus in 1879, and they later sold it to the Midland Telephone Company who in turn sold the business to Central Union Telephone Company. Operating a telephone exchange turned out to be more suitable for women. During this time period, women were employed in a few livelihoods such as the garment industry, cleansing establishments and teaching, otherwise they were expected to be stay at home wives, housekeepers and raise children.

Chapter 12

Progressive Era (1880-1915)

Economic, Political and Social Changes in Columbus

From the beginning of statehood, Columbus lagged behind in improving economic, political and social conditions for the laboring class, women and minorities. After the Civil War, agitation gradually increased to bring these issues to the forefront. The labor problems were abetted by the formation of the American Federation of Labor in 1886 and the United Mine Workers in 1890, both originating in Columbus. Strikes occurred sporadically with loss of life and property. While management and anti-union believers usually came out on top in public opinion, some improvement could be seen in safety, health, working hours, wages, minority hiring and child labor. Women were not allowed to vote, perform certain occupations, or receive wages equal to men. On the other hand, they were expected to be meek, sweet, gentle, happy, sober, virtuous, punctual, frugal, morally uplifting and, if married, a helpmate. Women organized into clubs, marches and political parties to promote women's suffrage, improvement in their working conditions and opportunities. They were often joined in their efforts by the advocates of prohibition. Notable women in Columbus in these attempts were Clara Reynolds, Lucille Curtis, Alice Johnston, Harriet Bradbury, Mary Senter and Nannie Goode. These women were usually well educated, married to successful, affluent and supportive husbands and highly motivated. Only a very few females attended college, wrote magazine articles or published books. Their success finally came in the form of two national amendments to the constitution. The Volstead Act (Prohibition) and the Women's Suffrage Act were both enacted in 1920. Before this, in 1917, Columbus had granted municipal suffrage to women. Washington Gladden, a Congregational minister in Columbus, was the leading male in this political sphere. He marched with the strikers, spoke at rallies and in the pulpit regarding social problems and served on the city council. The Initiative, Recall, Referendum, secret ballot and public ownership of utilities were other progressive reforms that were on the political horizon to be adopted. A few women were beginning to wear the new Gibson Girl style of shorter skirts, had loose girdle-less waist lines and bobbed their hair.

Fig. 47 The viewer is facing southwest, looking at the buildings extending from the corner of High (1) and Broad (8) Streets.

1. is South High Street and the unseen State Capitol would be to the left.
2. is the second Neil Hotel.
3. is the twelve-story Harrison Building.
4. is the Huntington Bank.
5. is the nine-story Wheeler Building (1895-1975).
6. is the eleven-story Wyandotte Building (1897-).
7. is a bank preceding the Deshler Hotel.
8. is West Broad Street.

Of these 1907 buildings, only the Huntington and Wyandotte exist today.

YMCA

The YMCA (Young Men's Christian Association) started in England in 1844. It was introduced to Columbus by Henry Carrington, an attorney and son-in-law of Lucas Sullivant. Its mission was to provide physical training, educational classes and encourage moral uplifting. Lodging, food and programs were healthful, safe and inexpensive. A five-story building was built on Capitol Square. In 1924, a new building (largest YMCA structure in the world) was relocated to its present site at Front and Spring Streets. It happened to be the site of the boyhood home of General Irvin McDowell of Civil War fame. In the 1980's, the "Y" underwent a sixty million dollar renovation. Both Franklin University and Capital University Law School received their start there. Over the years, it has served millions of youths. Its physical facilities are open to older adults. In 1998, the Y spread to the suburbs. Grove City, Gahanna and Hilliard have satellite facilities, soon to be joined by a site in southern Delaware County. The Ohio State University Medical Center furnishes rehabilitate services to the four suburban facilities. The Y took in $33 million in 2005 from corporate and private donors, individuals, fees and a small amount from the government and foundations. Its expenditures were $32 million.

YWCA

The Columbus YWCA (Young Women's Christian Association) was established in 1886. It is located in a large building at 65 South Front Street. During its existence, it has supported, housed, fed, nurtured and mentored thousands of women. Among its most prominent services is the help provided to women in times of crisis such as rape and domestic violence. It furnishes shelter for families, provides child care, promotes youth development and fitness and works to eliminate racism. The "Y" provides a safe place to empower and build strong leaders, and a place for advocates for civil and women's rights. The organization has the basic belief that all people have value, and, therefore, wish to give full access and opportunity for the potential to contribute to the best of personal ability. The Columbus chapter receives financial support from United Way, the Community Shelter Board, the City of Columbus and the Franklin County Board of Commissioners.

NAACP and Urban League

To meet the social and economic needs of a rapidly growing African-American population in Columbus, several groups were formed. The NAACP (National Association for the Advancement of Colored People), founded in 1909, used confrontation in its efforts. The Urban League was less abrasive. Nimrod Allen, an African-American clergyman, educated at Wilberforce College and Yale Divinity School, came to Columbus in 1915, to head a branch of the YMCA. Six years later, he was appointed to head up the Urban League, an organization of whites and blacks, formed to expedite job training and placement, improve education and housing and improve race relations. He directed these activities with some success for thirty-three years. These groups are funded by corporations, individual gifts and philanthropic organizations.

Chapter 13

World War I, Roaring Twenties, Great Depression and World War II

World War I

The United States aided the Allies from the war's beginning in 1914 into 1917. When German submarines continued to sink our ships, the U.S. declared war and participated in the last eighteen months of the conflict. For nine months the U.S. drafted and trained soldiers before sending them to Europe. As factories converted to producing war materiel, shortages of food, clothing, fuel and durable goods occurred. Victory gardens were started to overcome food shortages. Columbus participated in all domestic emergency programs to help the armed services. Women were occupation replacements for men who had gone into the service. Others joined the Red Cross or one of the volunteer services, and a few entered the military. Columbus-born Elsie Janis, a Broadway singing and dancing star, was the first woman entertainer permitted by the government to perform on the war front. The government built the Defense Construction Supply Depot on the East side of Columbus between Whitehall and the major rail lines. It continues today as a major defense installation.

In typical war hysteria, the German ethnic group underwent severe harassment. German street and business names were dropped or converted to English. The use of the German language in church services and school classes was banned. German books were burned. Some Germans, personally or in business, were shunned. The state legislature, urged by Governor James Cox, passed a law discriminating against German Americans. Fortunately, the state Supreme court declared it unconstitutional. In an unusual divergence of public opinion, Eddie Rickenbacker, a German American from Columbus, was proclaimed a war hero after shooting down twenty-six German planes.

Roaring Twenties

After World War I there was prosperity accompanied by excessive speculation in the stock market, a relaxing of conservative morals, increased crime, ignoring of prohibition, the introduction of jazz and further liberation in women's attire. The "flapper" was seen in a few quarters as a young, thin, woman attired in a short skirt, rolled down stockings, bobbed hair and dancing the Charleston, a popular jerky dance step. Columbus was somewhat aloof to this trend and slow to change. The mood was seen as an Eastern Establishment culture. Offsetting the shift in morality was a resurgence of fundamentalism in religion; that is, a literal interpretation of the Bible. Ohio was in the middle of the "Bible Belt." The purchase of automobiles tripled during the 1920's. There was also a marked increase in the purchase of consumer goods, contributing to lower savings and adding to personal debt. Labor devices became more abundant. Mass production of newspapers, magazines and advertising and increased attendance to motion pictures contributed to shaping public opinions. Columbus was a recipient of the migration of southern African-Americans and Appalachians who came expecting to improve their lot in life.

The Great Depression

During the Roaring Twenties, the economy other than agriculture roared upward. Many people who had never entered the stock market before decided to give it a try. Often they borrowed money or mortgaged their property to make investments or gamble by buying stocks. Clients were allowed to buy equity "on the margin" that required as little as twenty-five percent cash. When the crash came in 1929, those owing mortgage payments or had invested heavily in now worthless stocks, were unable to meet their obligations. This was compounded by loss of jobs. Companies and banks failed. Unemployment rose to thirty percent. The government under President Franklin Roosevelt tried to relieve the situation by instituting welfare-like programs. One such plan, the WPA (Works Plan Administration), made jobs available to Columbus laborers who in turn built much needed public buildings. Two such projects were the new Federal District Courthouse and Post Office, constructed in 1937. The judiciary structure, now called the (Judge) Joseph Kinneary Courthouse, is still in use. The new post office was built on Twin Rivers Drive at the fork of the Scioto and Olentangy Rivers.

World War II Changes

World War II (1941-1945) brought big and swift changes to Columbus. It became a recruiting center, and industries changed overnight from producing consumer goods to wartime needs. Victory gardens, war bonds and transportation alterations attracted strong public support. Ft. Hayes was activated and Ohio State University had an active Reserve Officers Training Corps program. After the war, returning students received federal aid (GI Bill). Again, anti-German sentiment affected a large ethnic segment of the residents but not as severely as in previous conflicts. Port Columbus Airport became a center of air force activity with the opening of the Curtiss-Wright aircraft plant on its south side in 1941. Eventually, the name would change to North American and still again to Rockwell-North American Company, as a builder of Navy training planes. It eventually closed in the 1980's. Space in the huge plant was given to Lustron Corporation for its post-war production of prefabricated, porcelain-clad steel houses, patterned after uses in constructing White Castle hamburger buildings and Standard Oil stations. They were assembled with plumbing and electrical systems ready for outside connections. Federal financial support was supplied by the Reconstruction Finance Corporation. Lustron closed in 1950. Its demise was quickened by the decision of many cities not to permit acceptance of such structures in their communities for esthetic reasons.

Chapter 14

Medical Education and Treatment in Columbus

The first female physician in Columbus was Mahala Pike Senter who was trained in Vermont and moved to Columbus with her husband in the 1840's. She was not allowed to practice medicine due to local prejudice and her strong liberal expressions. She did act as a midwife on occasions.

During the 1830's, Dr. Hiram Todd, the first dentist in Columbus, spent his first few years as an itinerate practitioner in the surrounding countryside. He used a number of simple instruments to pull teeth or fill cavities. He used whiskey for anesthesia. Before he died in 1884, chloroform, nitrous oxide ("laughing gas") and ether became available for his use. His son, William, followed in his footsteps. The Ohio State College of Dentistry also began as an offshoot of Dr. John Bain's Dentistry College in Bainbridge, Ohio, in 1892. It became part of the Starling Ohio Medical College in 1907 and co-existed with the new Ohio State College of Medicine in 1914.

The Ohio State University College of Medicine

The Ohio State University College of Medicine traces its origin to 1834, when it began as the Department of Medicine in Willoughby University of Lake Erie, in Chagrin Falls, in northeast Ohio. The name Willoughby was chosen because a few faculty members had trained in Dr. Westel Willoughby's medical school in Newport, New York. Although Willoughby would never set foot in Ohio, he did offer guidance and sent books (they are now held in OSU's Medical Heritage Center). The new school soon found itself in strong competition with Western Reserve's medical school, some twenty miles away. Seeking a change in venue, the Willoughby school petitioned the state legislature to change its charter to enable it to move to Columbus. The transfer took place in 1847, and the new medical school was renamed after its chief benefactor, Lyne Starling, who donated $35,000. The initial faculty contributed $13,000, and an additional $7,000 came from the public. The first classes were conducted in small remodeled houses and

Wesley Chapel near Gay and High Streets. Total tuition plus room and board for one year amounted to about one hundred dollars.

A teaching hospital was built in 1851 to provide patients for student instruction in the new medical school. It was an ornate, Gothic-style, five-story brick and stone building featuring several towers. It was located at the northwest corner of Sixth and State Streets. The Columbus Police Department donated $1,400 for installation of an elevator. William S. Sullivant and Dr. L. Goodale were among its trustees. In 1865, the Sisters of the Poor of St. Francis took over management of the hospital, and its name became St. Francis Hospital, the first hospital in the United States constructed specifically for teaching medical students.

Fig. 48 St. Francis (teaching) Hospital (1851-1955).
—from Columbus Library

In 1876, a faculty split caused one group to form the Ohio Medical College who concentrated their teaching in the Protestant Hospital on Park Street near Goodale Park. In 1907, the two medical colleges reunited to become the Starling and Ohio Medical College. They utilized both the Protestant (later called White Cross Methodist) and St. Francis Hospitals. In 1914, the college merged yet again with Ohio State University to become its Medical College, with teaching concentrated in St. Francis Hospital and a decade later in the newly constructed Starling-Loving (University) Hospital at 310 West Tenth Avenue on the OSU campus. St. Francis was razed in 1955 and supplanted by a new structure named Grant Hospital. Meanwhile, the OSU Starling-Loving Hospital was superseded in 1951 by a new and enlarged University Hospital, a few steps away, on the OSU campus. The principal University Hospital was named Rhodes Hall after the Ohio Governor who was very beneficial in obtaining state funds for the new university hospital. The old Starling-Loving Hospital remains in use for offices and laboratories.

The OSU Medical Complex has expanded greatly with the addition of over twenty buildings, and has become nationally recognized as a foremost teaching, research and patient care center. Its pediatric teaching is carried out in Nationwide Children's Hospital on a separate campus. Today, the Health Center includes Colleges of Public Health, Dentistry, Nursing, Pharmacy, Optometry, Allied

Medicine and Veterinary Medicine. Skilled cardiovascular treatment including heart and lung transplantation is provided in the Richard M. Ross Heart Institute. The James Cancer Center is one of the top twenty cancer treatment centers in the nation. The Neuroscience Institute is renown for its management of neurologic and neurosurgical needs. Thirteen of the College of Medicine departments were in the top ranks among Medical Schools in the latest *U.S. News and World Report* listings.

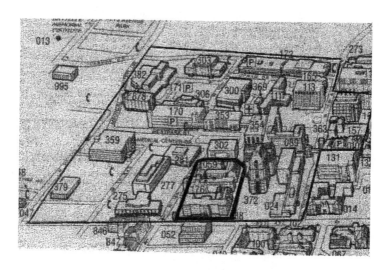

Fig. 49 The OSU Medical Complex today.
The small outline of buildings in lower center is the original medical center from the 1920's (Hamilton-176 and Starling-Loving-059 Halls).
Some of the numbered buildings are: Rhodes Hall-354; James Cancer Hospital-372; Clinic Building-300; Ross Heart Research Institute-113; Doan Hall-089; Starling/Loving Hall-176; Davis Research Center-382; and Dental College-024.

The largest college on the OSU campus, with twenty-one buildings, highest number of faculty and most sizeable budget, is the College of Medicine. Many of its faculty, departments and hospitals rank with the best in the country. One hundred and forty-five faculty from the one hundred and eighty-two central Ohio physicians have made the list of "Best Doctors in Central Ohio." In 2005, University Hospital was selected along with 176 others from 6,000 hospitals nationwide as one of "America's Best Hospitals," and thirteen specialty departments were rated among the best in the nation. In 2007, the medical school completed the largest one-year and five-year increase in ranking as well as total research funding. In patient care, the University Health System Consortium ranked the OSU health care system among the top five in the country. Four notable Deans, during the past fifty years, have had a tremendous impact upon the advancement of the quality of the faculty and students and the expansion of the physical facilities. They are: Charles Doan, Richard Meiling, Manuel Tzagournis and Frederick Sanfilippo, all M.D. s. Much of the current success may be attributed to the former Senior Vice-President and Executive Dean and CEO of the medical center, Dr. Fred Sanfilippo. He presided over the College of Medicine and Public Health, University Hospital, OSU Physicians and the OSU Health System, the James Cancer Hospital, the Richard M. Ross Heart Institute, the Davis Institute, the Richard J. Solove Research Institute, University Hospital East, OSU Harding Hopspital, and a network of community care sites. The free-standing cancer hospital has been designated as one of three-dozen Comprehensive Cancer Centers in the nation by the National Institute of Health. It is currently undergoing expansion. Dr. Arthur James was the principal force in developing the James Cancer Hospital, opened in 1985. He received all of his education in St. Clairsville, Ohio and The Ohio State University, complemented by an internship at Duke University Medical Center and a cancer fellowship at Memorial Hospital in New York City. He was instrumental in getting the state legislature and Governor James Rhodes to provide the funds to build the comprehensive cancer hospital that bears his name. Richard J. Solove, a graduate of the OSU College of Pharmacy and successful real estate developer, donated over $20 million to establish the Solove Cancer Research Institute, opened in 1990, and a Chair in Surgical Oncology. The Heart Institute was named for the Ross family, founders of Ross Laboratories now owned by Abbott Laboratories. The Ross family, some of whom graduated from OSU, gave generously to the medical center.

In an effort to enroll candidates from racial, ethnic or low-income minorities, the College of Medicine holds an M.D. Day Camp for three weeks each summer. The camp is open to twenty-four high-school sophomores, juniors and seniors interested in a health-science career. Applicants must have at least a 3.0 grade-point average and a math and science average of 3.3 or higher.

Little known or remembered today, The Ohio State University's first on-campus medical school was opened in 1914 as a homeopathic institution. It enrolled as many as thirty-nine students and enlarged to eighty-seven beds. It was located in a refurbished dormitory house on Neil Avenue just south of Hamilton Hall. It was supported by money from Cleveland sources and Charles Kettering of Dayton. A four-story brick building was constructed for its use in 1916. Attached to it was the Payne School of Nursing and a dietetic service. It closed in 1922 when OSU decided it couldn't support two medical schools. They reluctantly relinquished Kettering's substantial financial support. The homeopathic hospital building was incorporated into a larger Starling-Loving hospital building in 1925 (still in use).

Among the distinguished professors in the history of the medical college, two warrant special attention-Dr. Charles Doan and Dr. Robert Zollinger.

Dr. Charles Doan graduated from Hiram College in 1918. His M.D. degree was obtained at Johns Hopkins University in 1923. From 1925 to 1930, he was a research scientist at the Rockefeller Institute where he worked with Florence Sabin on blood cells and the lymphatic system. In 1930, he was appointed Professor and Chairman of the Department of Medicine in the Ohio State University College of Medicine. He continued his research with Professor Bruce Wiseman on blood dyscrasias, the role of the spleen and leukemia. In 1944, he assumed the deanship of the medical college. In 1952, he also occupied the chairmanship of the hematology division in the department of medicine. In 1960, the American Medical Association bestowed upon him one of its highest honors, the Distinguished Service Award.

Dr. Robert Zollinger, Sr. was born in 1903 on a farm near Millersport, Ohio. He rode his pony to a one-room schoolhouse near his farm. He used the same transportation to attend high school in Millersport where in addition to excelling in academics, he played basketball. He used his pony in a business he formed, delivering milk and vegetables to neighbors. He wanted to attend West Point Military Academy, but instead he attended The Ohio State University and its Medical College and became a physician. He interned at Harvard's Peter Bent Brigham Hospital in Boston. He received his surgery residency under Dr. Elliott C. Cutler at Western Reserve University Hospital in Cleveland. He followed Cutler back to Boston where his chief became the Moseley Professor of Surgery at Harvard. Together, they published an *Atlas of Surgical Operations* that went through seven editions. He was an Assistant Professor of Surgery at Harvard when World War II broke out. He joined the Harvard Surgical Unit in 1941 where he rose to the rank of Colonel and command of the 5th General Hospital, fighting in Normandy, France and Germany. He earned the Legion of Merit and three battle stars. After the war, he returned to Harvard, but within a year he was appointed Professor and Chairman of the Surgery Department at Ohio State University. He held this position for thirty years before retiring as an Emeritus Professor. In 1955, his research with Edwin Ellison led to the discovery of the Zollinger-Ellison Syndrome, a relationship between pancreatic tumors and peptic ulcer disease. He became president of many surgical societies and received honorary degrees and/or fellowships from several American universities and from universities abroad. His fame led him to be in demand for lectures around the world. In 1977, he was recognized as the Outstanding Doctor of Medical Science in the United States. He turned down the presidency of his alma mater. He taught medical students and trained surgeons. He was especially stern with surgical residents. He had a passion for photography and was a stickler for producing the finest visual aids for lectures. He published over 340 articles and was the Editor-in-Chief of the *American Journal of Surgery* from 1958 to 1986. His outside interests were growing roses and gourds. He was president of the American Rose Society as well as one of its judges. He died of pancreatic cancer in 1992. He requested that his tombstone should include the words, "teacher, surgeon, soldier and farmer." His son, Robert M. Zollinger, Jr., M.D., became a prominent surgeon and medical educator in Cleveland.

The Ohio State University College of Dentistry

The Ohio State University College of Dentistry began as an offshoot of Dr. John Bain's Dentistry College in Bainbridge, Ohio in 1892. In that year, it became a department of the "Ohio Medical College" in Columbus, starting with ten dental students. Two women entered the dental school in 1900, and, at the end of its first decade of existence, 354 dental students had graduated. During this period, Dr. Gillette Hayden matriculated and later founded the specialty of periodontology. Another distinguished dentistry graduate of OMC was Dr. Frank Casto who gained the additional degrees of M.D. and G.Ph. He became Dean of the Western Reserve School of Dentistry and President of the American Dental Association. OMC merged with its rival, Starling Ohio Medical College in 1907. In 1914, The Ohio State University acquired the two medical schools in Columbus and formed its own Colleges of Medicine and Dentistry. In 1925, the Dental college was moved from off campus to Hamilton Hall in the OSU Medical Center, and it became more physically allied with the OSU College of Medicine. In 1950, a new Dentistry building (Postle Hall) was completed on the medical campus. The College of Dentistry installed a Division of Oral Surgery in the new University Hospital. Currently, the Dentistry College has eight core subjects taught during a four year period leading to a doctor of Dental Surgery degree: Endodontics, Oral Biology, Oral and Maxillofacial Surgery, Orthodontics, Pediatric Dentistry, Periodontology, Primary Care and Restorative and Prosthetic Dentistry. Currently, there are one hundred and four students per class, about one-half the enrollment by the 1980s. Faculty and students participate in dental research. Students are offered the opportunity of entering a seven-year clinic-research track leading to D.D.S. and Ph.D. degrees. National health agencies have given $5.6 million to dental research. More than $2 million from private foundations supports the Ohio Project which is a major outreach effort to provide dental care to underserved populations. The Division of Dental Hygiene offers a baccalaureate degree, the only dental hygiene school in Ohio to do so.

The Ohio State University College of Nursing

Befitting the size and scope of OSU, the College of Nursing, founded in 1914, offers comprehensive and high quality nursing education, including emphasis on leadership, research, training midwives, nurse practitioners, nurse-specialists, nurse-administrators and community, business, state and national policy advisors. It is one of six colleges in the medical complex. Classroom courses are enhanced by state-of-the-art audio-visual, computer technology and broad clinical opportunities in the OSU hospitals and libraries. In addition to the basic RN-BSN degree, MS and PhD degrees are offered. Courses in continuing education are available to graduates.

Columbus Hospitals

The Ohio State University Hospitals

The Ohio State University Hospital is really a complex of many hospitals. The main hospital was built in 1951 and has since been named *Rhodes Hall*. It is joined with *Doan Hall*, containing staff and research offices. The Ohio State Hospitals complex is ranked among the top hospitals nationwide. One hundred and forty-five of its staff have been rated among the "Best Doctors in Central Ohio". The complex includes a radio-imaging unit, a heart institute, a neurology/neurosurgical institute and a physical medicine/rehabilitation/ musculoskeletal institute, an emergency unit, a helicopter ambulance service and an outpatient clinic.

An important ancillary hospital in the OSU Health complex is *Ohio State University Hospital East*. It started under different names. It was first known as St. Anthony's Hospital, opened in 1891, on the corner of Hawthorne Street and Taylor Avenue, on the near east side of Columbus. It was briefly aligned with St. Francis Hospital before the latter was razed in 1955. It underwent ownership and name change to Park Hospital when rebuilt in 1955. In 1999, it became Ohio State University Hospital East. It is a full service hospital with an emergency room and outpatient facilities, but it is known best for its excellent orthopedic service.

*The Ohio Tuberculosis Hospital (*later named *Means Hall)* was built on the OSU Medical Campus in 1951, but independently state owned, emphasizing the seriousness of tuberculosis at the time. It was used also for teaching nurses and medical students. Its mission ceased after a decade, when tuberculosis was no longer prevalent. The hospital was turned over to the university to be used for various departments of the hospital complex. It still stands but is scheduled to be razed and replaced by a new cancer hospital tower.

Also, in 1951, the *Columbus Psychiatric Institute and Hospital (Upham Hall)* was erected along side the Tuberculosis Hospital on the OSU Medical Campus. In addition to acute psychiatric patient care, it was made available for training nurses and doctors. It was razed in the 1990s and replaced by a neuropsychiatric institute. For a short time, an annex for mental patients was located in Worthington, well known previously as *Harding Hospital*. In 2004, the Worthington facility was closed, and its activities were transferred to OSU's neuropsychiatric institute which in turn was renamed Harding Hospital.

Nationwide Children's Hospital

Columbus Children's Hospital was founded as a charitable institution by a group of women in 1892. A mansion at the corner of Miller and Fair Avenues near Franklin Park was converted into the first Children's Hospital in 1894. The Pleasure Guild and Twigs were formed to raise financial support. New hospital buildings were constructed at its present location on Livingston Avenue in 1924. Since then, the hospital has grown into one of the nation's ten largest children's hospitals and pediatric research centers. Although a private facility, it is closely affiliated with the OSU College of Medicine and serves as its pediatric department. Its campus is off East Livingston Avenue and takes up several city blocks. The bed capacity is 323. Over fifteen thousand surgeries are performed annually. The research budget is over $31 million. Of the over 4,800 employees, over 800 are medical staff. Hundreds of volunteers help the staff, and many organizations raise funds to support the hospital. In 2006, one of its largest contribution was a $50 million naming gift from Nationwide Insurance Company and the hospital now bears that name. In 2007, *U.S. News & World Report* ranked Nationwide Children's Hospital twelfth among the top pediatric hospitals in the nation.

Riverside Methodist Hospital (originally Protestant and White Cross)

The Protestant Hospital was opened in 1892 at Dennison and Third Avenues. It was operated by a group of local Protestant churches. It was relocated in 1898 to nearby Park Avenue, adjacent to Ohio Medical University, facing Goodale Park to the west. The hospital's dormitory and training center for nurses was nearby at 98 Buttles Avenue. The facilities were acquired by the Methodist Episcopal Church in 1922 and renamed White Cross Methodist Hospital. The hospital was closed in 1961 and demolished in 1970. It was replaced by Riverside Methodist Hospital at West North Broadway Street and Olentangy River Road in 1961. At that time, its School of Nursing became affiliated with Ohio Northern University. RMH has achieved a reputation as one of the best hospitals in Ohio, with continual expansion. It has the largest number of beds, sees the largest number of emergencies and does the most surgical procedures of any single hospital in Columbus. It ranks fifth in the United States in number of patient admissions per year. It is especially known for its McConnell Heart Care Center and is among the one hundred top hospitals in the U.S. in cancer care. The hospital is also among the top ranked in neurological and orthopedic specialties. The only electric lithotripter in central Ohio (AKSM), a privately owned and operated facility for the management of kidney stones, is located on the Riverside campus. The RMH staff is highly rated in the administration of medical care. In 1995, Riverside merged with Grant Hospital. Soon thereafter, Doctor's Hospital joined them in a health care complex called Ohio Health.

American Kidney Stone Management (AKSM)

The American Kidney Stone Management is a physician owned company that offers electric shock-wave lithotripsy treatment for the dissolution of kidney stones. It also utilizes the shock-wave method to treat heel-pain syndrome and various musculo-skeletal problems. It was started in Columbus 1984 by Dr. Henry A. Wise, who from its beginning has been the CEO and chairman of the board of this state-of-the art therapy. There are over eight hundred urologists in fifteen eastern states that share ownership and administer treatment by over thirty lithotripters. Special training is required to enable the physician to become skilled in administering treatment. The German invented lithotripter costs several million dollars. Some of the lithotripter machines are placed in mobile vehicles, making it possible for several hospitals to share their use. The Columbus lithotripter is housed on the campus of Riverside Hospital, but independently owned. The company also offers laser and other treatments for the management of prostate disorders.

Grant Hospital

Grant Hospital was opened at 125 South Grant Avenue in 1900 and owned by Dr. James F. Baldwin. Baldwin was a renowned surgeon, specializing in thyroid operations. He was highly organized as demonstrated by the system he developed for transporting patients to and from the local railroad depot. The hospital was rebuilt in 1961 near the site of the former St. Francis Hospital with a nursing school and office buildings. It has undergone several expansions. The last improvement occurred in 2006, when the sixteen-story Baldwin Tower office building was replaced by a $60 million, four-story annex containing sixteen operating rooms, support services and a new main entrance to the hospital. The hospital and its staff are among the nation's top rankings especially in orthopedics, cardiovascular diseases, breast cancer and ear, nose and throat diseases. It has a level I Trauma Center. Like University Hospital, Grant has a helicopter ambulance service and helicopter port. The hospital is part of the Ohio Health family that includes Riverside and Doctor's hospitals.

Mount Carmel Hospitals and College of Nursing

Mount Carmel Hospital West (at first named Hawkes Hospital after founder W. B. Hawkes, M.D.) opened on West State Street in 1886. It was administrated by the Sisters of the Holy Cross. A Nursing School was started in 1903 and continues to offer excellent classroom education and clinical opportunities in the three Mt. Carmel Hospitals. In 1990, the nursing school became the Mt. Carmel College of Nursing and in addition to the basic RN certification offered the degrees of MS and BSN. Six hundred and eight-four students are enrolled currently. The medical complex remains today as Mount Carmel West Medical Center with multiple new buildings and a staff of two thousand that serve a large patient population. It is the largest employer in Franklinton. Its sister hospital, Mount Carmel East, opened on East Broad Street in 1972 due to strong regional patient demand. It has been expanded several times. Both hospitals have physician office and rehabilitation facilities on the premises. In 2007, the New Albany Surgical Hospital, specializing in orthopedic and neurological procedures, merged with the Mount Carmel Health System that included, Mount Carmel East and West and St. Ann's Hospitals.

St. Ann's Hospital

St. Ann's Hospital was first opened in 1908 by the Sisters of St. Francis as the St. Ann's Infant Asylum to protect and care for orphaned infants and unwed mothers. It became St. Ann's Hospital for Women in 1920 and began providing maternity care. In 1950, the hospital was remodeled, expanded its maternity services and added gynecological care. A Department of Medicine and General Surgery was opened in 1951. The first male patient was admitted in 1972. St. Ann's Hospital relocated from downtown Columbus to Westerville in 1984 and joined the Mount Carmel Health System in 1995. Four years later, the hospital name was changed to Mount Carmel St. Ann's. In 2000, a cancer center was dedicated. A new Emergency Department was initiated in 2002. Finally, in 2003, St. Ann's opened a Women's Pavilion for comprehensive care.

Doctor's Hospitals

Doctor's Hospital (since 1938) and its satellite, Doctor's West (since 1962) are the only Osteopathic care centers in Columbus. They are affiliated with and share staff and the teaching medical students with the Osteopathic Medical School of Ohio University in Athens, Ohio (since 1976). They have expanded a number of times in size and services provided. They are now merged with Riverside and Grant Hospitals.

Select Specialty Hospital

This hospital had been a collection of units within five Columbus hospitals. When the renovation of Doctor's Hospital North on Dennison Avenue was completed in 2006 it became Select Specialty Hospital, one of the largest providers of long-term, acute hospital services in the country. The concept is relatively new and spreading across the nation. The hospital focuses on longer than usual specialized acute care for the medically complex, catastrophically injured or critically ill patients. The patients have access to a wide range of primary and support services, including critical care nursing, aggressive therapies, intensive respiratory care, laboratory and radiology services, bariatric rooms, negative pressure rooms, bedside dialysis and telemetry monitoring of all patients. All staff will be ACLS certified and approximately eighty percent of the nursing staff will consist of R.N.s. Sixty large private rooms opened in mid-2006, and another ninety-two beds became available in 2007. Twenty beds are in a high observation unit. The large rooms allow families to become an integral part of rehabilitation and recovery. The four core programs are: pulmonary/vent, medically complex, neuro/post-trauma and wound care.

Mercy Hospital

Mercy Hospital opened in 1907 on South High Street. The original structure was replaced by new buildings in 1970. Its name was changed to Community Hospital in 1991 under the ownership of a group of physicians. After years of financial burdens, its general services were reduced to emergencies only in 2001.

Other small hospitals existed briefly as private concerns. McKinley Hospital on East Town Street, started as Lawrence Hospital. It occupied the remodeled Charles H. Lindenberg mansion in 1900. The name change took place in 1921. Dr. John Alcorn opened an Eye, Ear, Nose and Throat Hospital on East Town Street in 1907. It closed in 1942. The St. Clair Hospital on St. Clair Avenue opened in 1910. Its proximity to the major rail lines and yards caused it to be the major medical care-server of their employees. It became a hotel-nursing home of that name in 1947. It began being used for senior citizen housing in 1976. Lincoln Memorial Hospital was built in 1958 and closed in 1971. It was started by a group of surgeons as a "for-profit" hospital. It soon became "non-profit" in order to receive insurance reimbursement. It could never attain Medicare accreditation. Some speciality groups have formed small outpatient facilities with overnight stays.

The Physicians Free Clinic, an affiliate organization of the Columbus Medical Association, has provided free outpatient medical care to indigent patients in

Franklin County since 1993. More than 30,000 uninsured people have been treated during its existence. Physicians volunteer their services without pay.

Penitentiary patients are attended in their infirmaries by subsidized staff and hospitalized primarily in the University medical facilities.

Early Epidemics

Lucas Sullivant, the most prominent early pioneer in Columbus, died of fever in 1823; he was fifty-eight. Other prominent citizens dying in that year were Judge John McDowell, Judge John Kerr and Barzillai Wright, keeper of the penitentiary. Cholera swept through the community periodically causing many deaths. The cholera epidemic of 1833 wiped out one-third of the population of Franklinton. The disease was believed to have originated in Asia, and the victims, through vomiting and diarrhea, went into a toxic state of circulatory shock leading to a quick demise. Travelers brought the disease to Columbus. The city in its panic, and not knowing the cause, resorted to cleaning up stagnant ponds and removing collections of trash and garbage and dead animals. Smudge pots were used to fight the unknown assailant thinking it might be airborne. People who were able fled to the rural areas. It was entirely unknown that the toxic cholera bacteria was ingested from the water supply and spread through human waste. More than one hundred citizens died including eleven state penitentiary inmates. The next epidemic of cholera was in the years 1849-1850. In this wave of the deadly disease, one hundred and sixty-two civilians died as well as one hundred and sixteen in the state prison. It would be several decades before the water supply would be made safe to drink, and a modern sewage system would be installed. Once the bacterial origin of the disease was identified and antibiotics became available (1940's), the scourge became a rarity in this country. A vaccine is available today to prevent only several strains of the disease, which is still endemic in parts of Asia, Africa and Central America.

Cholera had another interesting effect on Columbus. It caused a German immigrant and his family to settle in the city. Christian Jaeger was born in Germany in 1795. His father was a minister of the Reformed faith and died when Christian was four years old. The mother had enough accumulated money to see that her son received a good education. When he was sixteen, he was conscripted into the army to fight Napoleon who was on a rampage in Europe. After a two year stint in a military school, he rose to the rank of captain. Marriage resulted in a family of seven children. Due to political and economic uncertainly, Jaeger took his family to America and headed west toward Missouri. When they reached Lockbourne by canal boat, news of a cholera epidemic in the Midwest reached them, and they decided to stop temporarily in Columbus. Since the canal feeder line was closed, the family walked the eight miles and transported their luggage by wagon to the city. They liked what they found in 1834 and purchased a sizeable farm on the south side of Columbus near the German enclave in the city. The family prospered and eventually all eleven children reached maturity. Jaeger lived long enough to be recognized as a prominent citizen and have a street on the east edge of Schiller Park in German Village named for him.

Chapter 15

Education in Columbus

Education was highly prioritized in the development of the Ohio Territory. It was mentioned in the Congressional Ordinances of 1785 and 1787 and in the Ohio Constitution of 1802. Lot No. 16 of every township and one thirty-sixth of Ohio's land area was to be set aside or money from the sale of the land was to be used for schools. In addition, three percent of proceeds from the sale of public land was earmarked to support education. Between 1812 and 1820, several small schools were started and supported by parental subscriptions. Blacks were permitted to participate but few could afford the tuition. Although girls were allowed to attend, several "female academies" were started. Instruction for girls often centered on embroidering samples, needlework on satin and painting in watercolors. Frequently, school teachers stayed in the homes of parents and rotated among the subscribers. This was considered as part of their pay.

The Ohio General Assembly passed a bill in 1821 authorizing school districts and proposed local property taxation for the building of school houses. It was not until 1838 that the legislature passed an effective act creating a common school system. Until then, schools were private. In the 1840's, German language and Catholic schools sprang up.

The first school in Columbus was a small log cabin on public square. It was used by subscribers for a few pupils taught by a hired teacher. It lasted only a short time. Other subscription schools sprang up periodically and served the community until free public schools were provided by several acts of the legislature between 1827 and 1838. The first funds were limited, and schools were open for only a quarter of the year. The schools were located in rented homes. The younger students were taught by females; the older ones by males. The first Board of Education in Columbus was convened in 1845. The first public school buildings (three brick structures with six rooms in each) were opened in 1847. Instruction was divided into four grades: Primary, Secondary, Grammar and High. A separate high school was erected in 1853. A private German speaking school had opened in 1852. In 1855, thirty teachers making an aggregate of $16,292 taught 1,575 pupils. Private schools always existed.

Esther Institute

Esther Institute was a private academy that opened in 1852 as the Columbus Female Seminary under the management of its founder, Mr. Louis Heyl, son of the first German immigrant to Columbus in 1812. He was quite active in civic affairs and, in particular, education. The institute was placed in a new building in 1853 near the northwest corner of Broad and Fourth Streets and renamed the Esther Institute. Within five years it had one hundred and fifty students enrolled. It was not a financial success and closed in 1862. During the Civil War the school building was rented by the state to serve as a military hospital serving as many as three hundred fifty patients, including female prisoner of war. After the war, it became the Irving House hotel. In 1891, it became a parish house for the Trinity Episcopal Church. It was razed in 1916 to be replaced by the Columbus Athletic Club.

Public Schools

Fig. 50 First Central High School-1862

The first Central High School (left) opened in 1862 during the Civil War. It was located at 303 East Broad Street. Its mission narrowed in 1911, when its name was changed to The High School of Commerce. When a new Central High School was opened on the west bank of the Scioto River in 1924, the original school was converted to offices and finally demolished in 1928.

The second Central High School (Fig. 51) was situated on eighteen acres in Franklinton (where COSI now resides) and became a source of local pride. With the advent of suburban high schools, the prestige of Central diminished and its neighborhood deteriorated. It was closed to students in 1982 and lay in decay for seventeen years. In 1999, it was restored and converted into a new home for the Center of Science and Industry (COSI). Fig. 50

Fig. 51 Second Central High School 1924-1982
—all schools from Columbus Metro Library

Fig. 52

North High School (Fig. 52) opened at Dennison Avenue and Fourth Street in 1892. It was changed to Everett Junior High School in 1924 when a new North High School was built on Arcadia Avenue. It, too, changed status in 1979 and became North Adult Education Center. Likewise, South High School built in 1900 on Deshler Avenue was converted into Barrett Junior High School when a new South High School was constructed on Ann Street in 1924. West High School was built on South Central Avenue in 1908. It became Starling Middle School in 1929 when a new West High School opened at 179 South Powell Street. East High School was built at 1390 Franklin Street (later Bryden Road) and became Franklin Junior High School in 1923 when the new East High School was constructed on East Broad Street, its present location.

Columbus claims to have had the first kindergarten in the nation. It was commenced by Louisa Frankenberg in 1836. It did not flourish, and she returned to Germany to continue training in the Froebel system. Froebel took a keen interest in the Columbus initiative, and Frankenberg returned to Columbus in 1858 and restarted her kindergarten. The school was taught in the German language. A counter claim for beginning the first kindergarten in this country has been made in Wisconsin (Margarethe Schurz, 1856, also a German immigrant).

Indianola Informal School (now K through eight) at 140 East Sixteenth Avenue believes it was the first Junior High School (grades seven through nine) in the nation (1908). Richmond, Indiana also has made that claim.

Some of the early school houses still stand in a state of abandonment. Others were torn down and replaced by businesses and roads. All public schools, by law, were supported by property taxes.

In 2006, Les Wexler, founder and CEO of Limited Brands, announced a matching gift of up to $2 million to launch a non-profit Foundation to support Columbus Public Schools. This is a common practice in Ohio. Twelve Educational Foundations are found in Franklin County School Districts; the most heavily endowed are in Bexley and Upper Arlington. The money has usually been used to support the arts and extra-curricular activities.

In 1979, Federal Judge Robert Duncan declared Columbus schools to be segregated and ordered the busing of students to different schools as a remedy. Thus, desegregation was achieved at a tremendous expense to the taxpayer. Yet, it was easier than forcing a racial mix in residential areas.

To meet the educational needs of approximately sixty thousand public school children in Columbus, eighteen high schools, eighty-seven elementary, twenty-six middle schools, and several alternative schools of various types are currently in existence. The public schools are arranged in six districts, all administered by an elected school board which hires a superintendent and other administrators. Sixty-two percent of the students are African-Americans, while thirty-one percent are white, not including four percent of Hispanic origin. In school year 2005, Ohio Achievement Tests revealed that Columbus students averaged in the fiftieth percentile, compared with a state average in the seventieth percentile. About seven thousand students are enrolled in over fifty public charter schools at a cost of $7,286 per student. This money comes out of the public school budget. The enrollment in charter schools has increased steadily each year since they commenced in 1999. Several thousand additional students are enrolled in sixty-three private schools of all grades, and their tuition is paid for by the parents unless they come from failing public schools. The latter students are subsidized by the public school systems, beginning in 2006. Currently, in cooperation with DeVry University and Ohio State University, the Columbus Public School System established *Advantage Academy* to offer a high school graduation certificate and a degree of Associate in Applied Science to those finishing the tenth grade. Tuition is paid by the public schools. This is an effort to offset dropouts.

Columbus School for Girls

Mary Bole Scott and Florence Kelley established the Columbus School for Girls in 1898 as a finishing and college preparatory school. Its first two graduates went to Wellesley College. The site on Parsons Avenue was moved to a mansion at East Broad Street and Columbia Avenue in Bexley in 1946 where it remains today. The school was desegregated in 1957. The curriculum has expanded greatly over the ensuing years as has the physical appearance. Six hundred and fifty girls are now enrolled annually. The school consists of three campuses of one hundred and eighty acres with several buildings, athletic field and woodlands. In addition to classrooms, the buildings include a comprehensive library, theater, gymnasium and swimming pool. The faculty of ninety-eight members and fifty other personnel including coaches, provides an outstanding, well-rounded educational opportunity. Many of the alumnae, of this well-endowed institution, have had illustrative careers.

Columbus Academy

Area businessmen founded the Columbus Academy in 1911 to provide a college preparatory school dedicated to high intellectual, social, moral, aesthetic and physical development standards. It soon enrolled boys to attend five through twelve grades at its location along Alum Creek. Its motto has always been "In Quest of the Best." Chronic flooding problems forced the school to move from its location on Nelson Road to Cherry Bottom Road in Gahanna, where its original four acre size grew to two hundred and thirty acres. Gradually, the school expanded to include kindergarten along with Forms 1-4. Five new buildings include an administration hall and a theater. Girls were admitted in 1991. Today, the school has an excellent faculty and over one thousand non-segregated students. It met its latest endowment drive for seventeen million dollars. Its graduates have been admitted to top universities and are to be found among the business, civic and social leaders in the community.

University School

The Ohio State University School was established as a laboratory (research and experimentation) school in 1930, as a component of the teacher education program in the College of Education. It was an outgrowth of John Dewey's "progressive education" philosophy for educating youth and developing leadership which was gaining wide acceptance at this time nationally. Progressive Education rejected authoritative teaching methods in favor of those infused with democratic principles and values. It was hoped that students would develop social sensitivity, cooperativeness, creativity, and skills in utilizing such attributes in a democratic fashion. The student-centered curriculum had been demonstrated favorably in a laboratory school founded for practice teaching at the University of Chicago. A new building, Ramseyer Hall, was erected in 1932 for the school that included all grades from kindergarten to the university level. Initially, there were four hundred and eleven students from mostly middle and upper income groups from all parts of Central Ohio. A few scholarships were available for deserving low income families to balance the student body socio-economically. The school was funded by tuition and state monies. Although the school was viewed by many academic educators as a great success and a positive credit to the University, it was closed in 1967 for administrative reasons, some financial, some philosophical and some political.

Wellington School

Wellington is a coeducational, independent day school for students pre-kindergarten through grade 12. More than six hundred students are taught by a faculty of sixty-two. Twenty-two percent are non-white. The large campus includes a library and play fields. The school was founded by Kenneth B. Ackerman in 1982 in North Columbus at 3650 Reed Road. The college preparatory curriculum includes arts education, foreign languages and technology studies. One hundred percent of high school graduates move on to four-year colleges. Co-curricular programs are offered from fencing to chess, from sports to Columbus Little Theater. Accelerated, Honors and Advanced Placement courses are part of a demanding curriculum. The school is highly rated, and its graduates are prized by college admissions officials.

Sectarian Schools

Over fifty elementary and high schools supported by various religious denominations are present throughout Franklin County. They constitute a significant proportion of the student population. All are privately funded by tuitions and religious organizations.

Montessori Schools

The Montessori method of educating K-12 students was initiated in Italy in 1907 by Dr. Maria Montessori. She believed that children teach themselves and designed "prepared environments" in which children freely choose from a number of developmentally appropriate activities. The students are grouped in mixed ages and abilities in three to six year spans. There is constant interaction, problem solving, child to child teaching and socializing. Students are challenged according to their ability and should never be bored. Middle and high school teachers are required to take training courses plus, ideally, graduate work in an academic area or areas. Under age six, there are one or two 3-hour, uninterrupted, work periods each day not broken up by required group lessons. Older children schedule meetings or study groups with the teacher when necessary. Groups form spontaneously or are arranged ahead. They almost never take precedence over self-selected work. Children are free to move around the room instead of staying at a desk. There is no limit to how long a child can work with a piece of material. At any one time in a day, all subjects—math, language, science, history, geography, art, music, etc., may be studied at all levels. There are four Montessori schools in Columbus, pre-K through eighth grade.

Charter and "On-line" Schools in Columbus

In 1997, the state legislature made provisions for Charter Schools as an alternative to educate disadvantaged youths outside the traditional public school system. Thus, unruly, substance-abused and potential drop-out students, K-12, would be allowed to attend Charter Schools. The schools are sponsored and administered privately but receive their budgets from public school districts and additional financial support from the state. In 2004-2005, $7,286 was provided per charter student in Columbus. Three percent of the subsidy went to the sponsor; the remainder was for management, faculty, other school expenses and legal costs. In 2007, the Columbus Public Schools opened its own charter school in one of its unused school buildings for the first time. The school will serve students who are failing or are too old for the grade they are in. The school will be allowed to try innovative measures and will be overviewed by a special board. The district will not lose state basic aid. In 2005, more than 6,300 students from Columbus were enrolled in thirty-nine such schools. Studies have shown that teachers in charter schools, are less educated, receive lower salaries (exempt from state minimum), fewer are certified and stay with the school a shorter time as compared with public school teachers. The efficacy of charter schools has yet to be determined. Furthermore, teacher qualifications and the financial accountability in charter schools are being challenged by the state teachers' union; the case is now before the Ohio Supreme Court. Columbus Public School administrators and many parents are aggravated by the loss of tax money that was originally earmarked for public schools. In 2007, newly elected Governor Strickland indicated a lack of enthusiasm for charter schools.

A similar situation exists in Columbus regarding Electronic Classroom of Tomorrow ventures, in which the students receive virtually all instruction from the computer on-line internet. Again, this type of charter school is state supported. It, too, has yet to be proven to be a reliable form of education.

Early College

Two colleges in Columbus have joined charter schools to institute programs designed to ease the transition from high school to college and reduce the intimidation factor. This is more helpful to students whose parents did not attend college and, therefore, are unable to guide the student from personal experience. Thus, doors are opened to students who otherwise might never have entered them. This concept is called "early college" and is found in over one hundred and thirty schools in the nation. Ohio Dominican University has formed the Charles School by an attachment with the Graham Charter School in Clintonville. The Columbus State Community College has a similar arrangement with the Africentric High School to form Columbus Africentric Early College. Students will receive a high school diploma and up to sixty-two college credits, which could result in an associate degree. The classes are demanding and students receive personal attention. They are required to serve several intensive community-service internships, develop ties to their area, and it is hoped they grow into socially responsible, well-rounded adults. The college credits are free, and the students could be half-way to a college degree and will have learned how to navigate the higher-education system.

Metro High School

In 2006, a unique new high school was forged between the sixteen Franklin County School Districts, Battelle Memorial Institute and The Ohio State University. It is named Metro High School and located on university property at the northwest corner of Kenny and Kinnear Roads. Emphasis is placed on subjects of science, technology, engineering and mathematics (STEM). Sports, music and drama are to be provided by the students' home high schools, allowing the primary educational focus to be unfettered. Its tuition-free student body of one hundred would be derived from throughout the county on a proportional basis and of mixed intellectual ability. This will create a distinct advantage for the financial disadvantaged. The laboratory-like atmosphere will be supported by $1.2 million donated by OSU for building leases and involvement of university faculty in teaching and testing new methods. Battelle will donate $500,000 for startup costs. This fits in nicely with Gordon Battelle's will which stipulates that a sizeable portion of his Institute's profit be designated for the betterment of Columbus. Some state funding will be involved. Private businesses will provide tutoring and mentoring. This unprecedented partnership is believed the first of its kind in the state. A few schools of similar focus are currently available in other states and more are envisioned.

This review of education in Columbus reveals a progressive attitude in opening new doors for affordable access to improving the academic achievements and character building in our youth.

Chapter 16

Colleges and Universities in Franklin County

The Ohio State University

In 1862, Congress passed the Morrill Act, which gave states the right to sell public land in acreage proportional to their number of representatives to Congress; the proceeds were to be used to establish a college for the purpose of teaching agriculture and mechanics. Both Ohio University and Miami University were by-passed in favor of creating a new "land grant" institution, an idea favored and vigorously supported by former U.S. President and Ohio Governor, Rutherford B. Hayes. Thus, the Ohio Agricultural and Mechanical College was born in 1873. It was placed on farmland four miles north of downtown Columbus. Immediately, the university trustees decided to broaden the educational focus to include in its curriculum ancient languages, chemistry, geology, mathematics, modern languages and physics. They also decided to have an armory. These changes were fortunate, since agricultural interests in the state were outright hostile to the new school of higher learning.

Fig. 53 The first University Hall (1873) was replaced by this exact replica in 1971.
—Columbus Metro Library

The college opened with one building called University Hall. The original building was replaced in 1971 with a new administration building, a replica and the same name of the former building. Over one hundred buildings now make up the physical structure of the main campus of the university. The highly touted Fisher College of Business combines a six-building mini-campus with a hotel and dining room.

For fifty years, OSU would be the only state school designated for doctoral and research functions while the other state colleges would not offer instruction beyond a master's degree level. The Law School was initiated in 1891, the Graduate School in 1912, the Colleges of Medicine and Dentistry in 1914, and the Colleges of Commerce and Journalism in 1916. Today, there are fifteen colleges on the campus plus the University Hospital Complex, the James Cancer Hospital, a National Cancer Institute Comprehensive Cancer Center, the Richard M. Ross Heart Hospital and radio and TV stations. In 1916, OSU was inducted into the sixty-member prestigious Association of American Universities, the only public university in Ohio to be so honored to date. By the advent of the Great Depression in 1930, the university's enrollment reached 15,000. State and federal funding helped the school to endure hard times, and the enrollment continued to climb. In addition, OSU began continual efforts to increase private funding. By 2007, *U.S. News & World Report* ranked OSU among the top sixty U.S. universities and the best public university in Ohio. In the rating of hundreds of U.S. graduate schools, OSU was given the following ratings: Department of Public Accounting 9th, Department of Political Science 13th (4th by The London School of Economics), College of Business 17th, College of Education 17th; College of Engineering 26th; College of Medicine 31st, College of Nursing 32nd and College of Law 31st. All of the preceding colleges were ranked at the top among Ohio schools. The publication, *Dance Teacher,* listed OSU's Department of Dance at its top rank. China's Shanghai Jiao Tong University placed OSU 66th in their 2006 Academic Ranking of World Universities. When ratings were confined to the United States, the University of Florida's Lombardi Performance Measurements placed OSU twenty-sixth among all universities and eleventh among public universities and at the top of public universities in Ohio. In terms of spending for research, the university, in 2004, moved up from fifteenth among all U.S. universities to twelfth ($609 million), and ninth among public institutions in 2005. In 2006, the university spent $652 million for research with rankings still to be disclosed. This surge was led by the College of Medicine. Medical services leaped from fortieth rank to twenty-fifth in 2005. The university faculty currently includes a Nobel Prize winning physicist, twenty members of the National Academy of Sciences or National Academy of Engineers and one hundred and twenty-seven elected to Fellowship in the American Association for the Advancement of Science, and three became members of the Institute of Medicine. In the last twenty-five years, thirty-two faculty members have been awarded Guggenheim Fellowships, more than from all public and private Ohio universities combined. Since 2000, thirty-nine faculty members have been named Fulbright Fellows, the highest of any university in Ohio.

The Mershon Center for International Security Studies was founded in 1952 through the bequest of seven million dollars from alumnus, Colonel Ralph D. Mershon. The center also includes the archives of astronaut and Senator John Glenn. The archives of Admiral Richard E. Byrd are housed in the university's Byrd Polar Research Center. The world's largest repository of original cartoons is in the Ohio State Cartoon Research Library. The William Oxley Thompson Memorial Library is the main OSU library and operates the eighteenth largest research library in North America with a collection of 5.8 million volumes. The library system has forty-seven branches and specialty collections on-campus and eight sites off-campus. The Hilandar Research Library houses the world's largest collection of medieval Slavic manuscripts on microfilm. Theatrical efforts are supported by the Lawrence Lee Theatre Research Library. The Comprehensive National Resource Center offers a multiple area studies within Slavic, Eastern Europe and East Asian programs.

The Wexner Center for the Arts, designed by Peter Eisenman and Richard Trott, opened in 1989. It was made possible by a gift of $25 million from alumnus, Leslie Wexner. It is a comprehensive visual and performing arts center which focuses on new commissions and artistic residencies. The centerpiece work is Picasso's *Nude on a Black Armchair*, donated by Wexner, who purchased it for forty-five million dollars.

In addition to the Chadwick Arboretum on campus, there is an arboretum and horticulture campus in Wooster, the Stone Laboratory on Gilbralter Island in Lake Erie that provides studies in aquatic biology and The Large Binocular Telescope in Arizona. The twenty-ton, twin-mirror, $120 million telescope on Mount Graham is the largest in the world and is shared with the University of Arizona, the Research Corporation and institutions in Italy and Germany.

The university's original mission to focus on agriculture as its most important area of study has long ago diminished, but research in that field continues as well as an active agricultural extension service to farmers. OSU has an excellent College of Veterinary Medicine and Hospital.

The university offers over one hundred and seventy undergraduate majors, two hundred graduate fields of study and more than ninety professional programs. The student body on the Columbus campus has numbered well over 50,000 for

Fig. 54

several years ranking it consistently either first or second to the University of Texas. Several more thousands of students are enrolled in five branch campuses at Delaware, Newark, Marion, Mansfield and Lima. Such large enrollments has resulted in one of the largest alumni associations in the country. In 2004, the university moved up to ninth among all public universities in expenditures for research ($553 million dollars awarded and $518 million spent). The university's endowment is over two billion dollars. President Karen Holbrook (2002-2007) (at left) retired in mid-2007. She was the first female president in the history of the university. Her successful five-year tenure included a general rise in academic ratings and overhauling general undergraduate and graduate education requirements. Her accomplishments included a crackdown on rowdy behavior at tailgating and after-game parties by enforcing open-container and underage drinking laws, getting the city to ban upholstered porch furniture in the university area (used to feed fires during rioting), and the building of a university-area police substation. Due to the high student enrollment, there is a potential powder keg for explosive emotions. They usually occur after football games with evening rioting fueled by alcohol. Police have their hands full. The other major period of rioting occurred during the Vietnam War. The National Guard was called out to control the rampaging students who closed down the university for a few days and shortened the academic term.

Other achievements during President Holbrook's tenure were an increase in faculty salaries, diversity and research, an extension of health and other benefits to same-sex domestic partners of faculty and staff members, the transfer of academic advisors to student athletes from the Athletic Department to the Office of Academic Affairs, and opening Metro High School (see page 126).

Fig. 55

On September 1, 2007, sixty-three year old E. Gordon Gee (left), president of OSU from 1990 to 1997, was reappointed as president of the university. Before being recruited in 2007 to return to OSU, he had served for ten years as president of Brown and Vanderbilt Universities. He was the enthusiastic choice of the board of trustees, alumni, the governor and the student body. During his earlier period as president, he restructured the curriculum and academic programs, expanded selective admissions of students, created Campus Partners to improve neighborhoods near the campus, planned the construction of the Max M. Fisher College of Business, the Schottenstein Center, renovation of the Ohio Stadium and student recreation center, and launched a successful $850 million fund-raising campaign. His new seven-year contract called for a $775,000 annual base salary plus a home, car, expense accounts and many other perks. An additional deferred salary of $225,000 annually will add to his compensation if he remains president for five years. He is expected to mount a one billion dollar fund-raising campaign. Whether he will restructure the athletic program, as he has at other universities where he served, remains a mystery. He definitely desires to increase the integration of athletes into student life and academics. He is renown for his energy and always wearing a bow-tie.

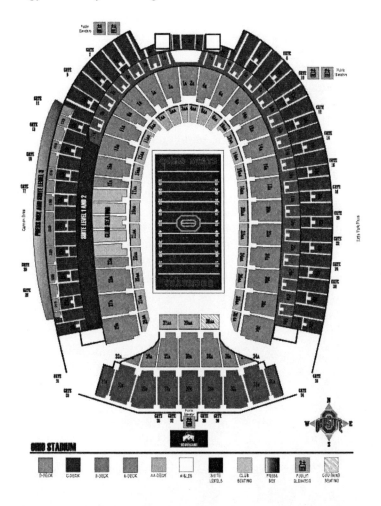

Fig. 56 An unique view of Ohio Stadium that has expanded from its original 66,000 seats when built in 1922 to over 106,000 today. The open end of the horseshoe shape has been filled in with seats. There are dormitory rooms beneath the stadium.

Tuition in 2006 was $8,666 for a full academic year. This is about a third of the average cost of tuition in a private school. A myriad of scholarships are available, especially for those in financial need. The university is in The *Princeton Review's* list of America's *150 Best Value Colleges*. In 2006, the freshman class of 6,122 contained the following percentage of high school graduates: forty-five percent from the top ten percent; seventy percent from the top twenty percent and ninety-five percent from the top thirty percent. Two hundred were high school valedictorians and two-thirds scored in the top fifteen percent of the pre-admission SAT test. During the past ten years, one-hundred National Merit Scholars were admitted. The percentage of students graduating in six years rose from 56% to 71%. The number of freshmen returning as sophomores increased from 86.5% to 91.5 percent.

Although the university has had many departments and world class professors, the athletic program, football in particular, has attracted the most publicity. The football stadium, known as "the horseshoe" because of its open-ended shape, was constructed in 1922. Its capacity was over 66,000. It was widely believed that the success of player Chic Harley led to building the stadium.

Harley grew up in Michigan but graduated from Columbus East High School in Columbus. Harley was only five feet and seven inches tall and one hundred and forty-five pounds in weight. But, he was tough and hard hitting. Due to his running and kicking abilities, his teams lost only one game during his high school career. He elected to play collegiate football under Coach John Wilce at The Ohio State University (1916-1919). Except for spending one year in the army during World War I, his skills and leadership led to his being selected for All-American honors for three years; his teams won two Big Ten championships.

Fig. 57 Current view of Ohio Stadium

In 2001, a massive reconstruction increased the stadium's capacity to over 106,000 (on left). It is always filled for football games that are televised, and fortunately so for the income, since the renovation resulted in a huge debt. The popularity of the "Buckeyes" was demonstrated by the attendance of 75,000 paying fans at the 2007 spring practice game. Due to the large university enrollment, Spring quarter graduation exercises are held in the stadium.

In 1998, a world class collegiate sports arena was opened on the OSU campus at the corner of Lane Avenue and Olentangy River Road. The $116 million multipurpose facility was privately and corporately funded. A large contribution from the Jerome Schottenstein family secured naming rights for the Value City Arena and the Jerome Schottenstein Center. Other substantial corporate sponsors were the Huntington Bank (for the luxurious second floor level *Huntington Club)*; the Kroger Company (*The Ohio State University Hall of Fame)*; and Nationwide Insurance Company (for extraordinary terrazzo floorscapes). The arena seats 19,500 for basketball, 17,500 for hockey and 21,000 for concerts. The arena has fifty-two luxury boxes. The designers were Moody/Nolan Ltd of Columbus. A record of 2.5 hours has been recorded as the time required for switching the playing floor from basketball to hockey. Special accommodations were built for basketball practice including two full courts, eight baskets for private workouts, a training and rehabilitation room, weight room, quality dressing rooms and laundry. A state-of-the-art accelerator and high tech treadmill is available for skaters.

The original campus was built on the Neil family farm, and today Neil Avenue transects the main campus. The expansive campus unfolds from North High Street on the east to Upper Arlington (North Star Avenue) on the west side. The Olentangy River divides the school's grounds. The northern boundary is delineated by Lane Avenue and Ackerman Road, while Eleventh and King Avenues and Kinnear Road form the southern limits.

Since football thoroughly dominates the athletic activities at the university, it seems fitting to mention its two most successful coaches and two outstanding players.

Woodrow *"Woody"* Hayes was born in Clifton, Ohio in 1913. He grew up in Newcomerstown, where his father was school superintendent. He is remembered by some of his classmates as showing a tendency toward being a bully. Perhaps this behavior was a foreshadowing of his coaching style to come. He played football in high school and at Denison University. His coaching career was confined to three colleges; Denison University, Miami University of

Fig. 58 —all images of OSU faculty and students by permission from OSU Archives.

Ohio and Ohio State University. During his career, his win-loss-tie record was 238-72-10, and 205-61-10 in the Big Ten Conference. His teams won four national championships plus the top title from the National Football Foundation in 1970. His record also included thirteen Big Ten titles, playing in eight Rose Bowl games, producing fifty-six All-American players, three Heisman Trophy winners, three Outland Trophy winners and two Lombardi Trophy winners. His most famous player was Archie Griffin, twice receiving the Heisman Trophy, given to best collegiate player of the year. Griffin was associate athletic director for many years. A number of Hayes's assistants became head coaches at large universities. The most prominent was Bo Schembechler at the University of Michigan, with whom he developed a classic rivalry. Hayes was noted for a fiery temper, throwing things, perfection in preparation, determination and inability to accept defeat. In efforts to instill perfection of play and accepting nothing less than winning every game, Hayes often verbally and physically abused his players. He accepted his coaching contracts on a one year basis; his salary was low. He scoffed at raises and always drove an out-of-date car or pickup. He left no action undone to get his players to graduate. On the other hand, he was a caring person whether it was for a player or stranger. He could be seen late at night in the hospital checking on the condition of his ill or injured players. He served as a Navy officer in World War II, and always expressed a love of history and the military. The university faculty had mixed feelings toward the coach. One year, they voted against his team going to the Rose Bowl. In the faculty lounge, one professor hurled insults at Woody and at football in general. Woody listened calmly and when he was done, Woody pointed his finger at the professor and said, "Okay, now you listen to me. What you say about me and about football may or may not be true. But I can tell you one thing that is very certainly true. I can do your job, but you can't do mine!" When a surgeon told Hayes he had inadvertently left a sponge in his abdomen during surgery, he smiled at the doctor and said, "Gee, that's funny. In twenty-eight years of coaching, I never made a mistake." He had many friends in high places including generals and presidents of the United States. Unfortunately, his temper led to an abrupt end to his coaching career. In a Bowl game being televised nationally, an opposing player intercepted a possible game-winning pass. Woody jumped out on the field and struck the player on the neck, causing no injury. The university had no recourse but to dismiss the coach. Later, Hayes was asked to give a commencement speech and receive an honorary degree from OSU. A campus street was named for him. Many of his players felt that next to their parents, he was the greatest person they knew. There is no question that he had a tremendous influence on his players, mostly positive. He died in 1987. Former President Richard Nixon, his personal friend, gave a eulogy at his funeral.

James Tressel (Fig. 59) was born in Mentor, Ohio in 1952. His father was a successful football coach at Baldwin-Wallace College in Berea, Ohio, where Tressel graduated in 1974 with honors. He played quarterback, winning all-conference honors as a senior. His first assistant coaching job was with Akron

Fig. 59

University (1975-1978), where he also received his master's degree. He spent the next two years as an assistant football coach at Miami University of Ohio. Following this, he was assistant coach at Syracuse University. In 1983, he joined Coach Earl Bruce as quarterback coach at The Ohio State University. In 1986, he was appointed head football coach at Youngstown State University where he remained until 2001, at which time he became head football coach at The Ohio State University. During his remarkable career of fifteen years at Youngstown, his teams won four national championships in Division 1-AA and qualified for the championship playoffs ten times. He was named Coach of the Year in one or more polls five times, and the Ohio Coach of the Year six times. He was very active in civic affairs at Youngstown, and the citizens returned their admiration for the coach in a myriad of ways. His career at OSU started with seven wins and five defeats, but the team beat Michigan and won the Outback Bowl. Then came the highlight of his career. In 2002, the team went undefeated (14-0) and beat Miami University of Florida in the Fiesta Bowl for the national championship. The team slipped to eleven and two in 2003 but won the Fiesta Bowl. In 2004, the team had an eight and four record and beat Oklahoma State in the season ending bowl game. In 2005, the team had a 13-1 record, losing only to Texas, the national champions. They won the Fiesta Bowl in 2006, beating Notre Dame. In 2006, the team was undefeated but lost the National Championship to the University of Florida in January 2007. During his first five years at OSU, the team had a nineteen game winning streak twice. He was selected as the Eddie Robinson National Coach of the Year in 2002, a repeat of the honor he received in 1994. His peers named him Ohio Football Coach of the year 2007. In his first twenty-one years as a head coach, his teams achieved an enviable record of 239-77-2. As in Youngstown, Tressel is heavily involved in Columbus civic affairs and is greatly admired by his many fans. His older brother, Dick, is his assistant at OSU.

Fig. 60

Archie Griffin (at left) was born in Columbus, Ohio, in 1954. He became a high school football star and played on the Ohio State University football team all four years of college. He was awarded the Heisman Trophy in 1974 and 1975, the only player to duplicate this feat. He was All-American in 1973, 1974 and 1975. He was the UPI College Player of the Year and Walter Camp Player of the Year in 1974. He was Big Ten Player of the Year in 1973 and 1974 and played in four Rose Bowl events. He is in four Halls of Fame: Collegiate, Rose Bowl, Ohio State Athletes and National High School. In 1975, he was the NCAA Top

Five Award Winner (includes excellence in athletics, academics and leadership). He played eight years for the Cincinnati Bengals in the National Football League. Upon retirement, he became Associate Director of Athletics at The Ohio State University. Presently he is the Director of the OSU Alumni Association. His college football coach, Woody Hayes, said of him, "He's a better young man than he is a football player, and he's the best football player I've ever seen."

Fig. 61 The 1995 Heisman trophy winner, OSU running back Eddie George.

Bill Willis was born in Columbus in 1921. He attended East High School in Columbus where he was an outstanding football player (Ohio Hall of Fame). His football talents as a two-way lineman at Ohio State University resulted in All-American and Collegiate Football Hall of Fame status. He became the first African-American to play professional football, preceding Jackie Robinson's entry into professional baseball by one year. From 1946-1953, he played for the Cleveland Browns coached by Paul Brown, again on both offensive and defensive lines. Quickness and solid tackling were his trademarks. He endured intense racial discrimination by hotels, restaurants and other commercial enterprises. He was a first-team All-league selection seven times and played in three NFL Pro Bowls. He was elected to the Professional Football of Fame. After football, he devoted his life to helping troubled young people. He joined the Ohio Youth Commission in 1964 and became its director in 1975, serving until 1982. He died in 2007, age 86. Ohio State University retired his football jersey number 99 in 2007 in recognition of his football ability and humanitarianism. That number and his name hang in the Ohio Stadium. OSU named its annual award for the team's top defensive player after Willis.

The OSU basketball program has also produced outstanding records. The 1959-1961 era saw achievement of the NCAA national championship in 1960 with no losses and a three year record of seventy-eight wins and six losses and two Big Ten championships. The "dream team" of 1960 had Fred Taylor (Fig. 62 at left) as coach and Jerry Lucas, John Havlicek, Larry Siegfried, Mel Newell, Joe Roberts and Bobby Knight as players. Elected to the Collegiate Basketball Hall of Fame were Lucas and

Havlicek as players, and Knight and Taylor as coaches. Lucas and Havlicek had exceptional careers in the professional ranks where they achieved membership in the Professional Basketball Hall of Fame.

Coach Thad Matta's teams of 2006 and 2007, likewise won two consecutive Big Ten championships, and the team was a finalist in the 2007 NCAA championship game.

Fig. 63 Coach Matta in a 2006 photo.

Jerry Lucas (at right), probably the greatest basketball player produced in Ohio, was born in Middletown in 1940. As a 230 pound, 6-foot-8 center, he led his Middletown High School team to seventy-six straight wins and two state championships. He recorded 2,466 points in high school and was coveted by over 150 colleges. He chose Ohio State University where he was coached by Hall of Famer, Fred Taylor, and teamed with another great, John Havlicek. His college career included a 78-6 record and three Big Ten championships. His team went to three straight NCAA finals and won the championship in 1960. He was three times All-American and College Player of the Year in 1961 and 1962. In 1960, he won an

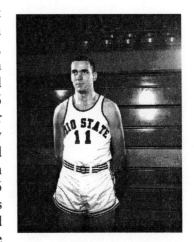

Fig. 64

Olympic team gold medal. His distinctive over-the-shoulder shooting style resulted in 1,990 college points and 1,411 rebounds. He acquired many individual game records. He was drafted by the Cincinnati Royals in 1962 and in 1964 became NBA Rookie of the Year with 17.7 points per game and a 52.7 shooting percentage. He subsequently played with San Francisco and New York teams, amassing 14,053 points, averaging 17 points per game and 12,942 rebounds. He led the New York Nicks to the NBA championship in 1973. He was an NBA All Star seven times (three on the first team). Lucas was the first basketball player to be elected to all four Halls of Fame (high school, college, Olympics and professional). He was elected to the Naismith Memorial Basketball Hall of Fame in 1980 and in 1996 was honored as one of the fifty greatest professional players. He was a gifted scholar with a photographic memory and gave lectures and wrote books on memory improvement.

Fig. 65

John Havlicek was born in Lansing, Ohio in 1940. He graduated from Bridgeport where he was an All-State basketball star in 1958. He attended Ohio State University from 1958 to 1962 and was team captain in 1962. In his prime, he was six feet, five inches tall and weighed one hundred and ninety-five pounds. The 1960 OSU team won the National Championship and they were runner-up in 1961. He was on the All-Big Ten Conference Team in 1961 and 1962. In the latter year he achieved All-American and All-Big Ten honors. He scored 1,223 career points in college. His entire professional career was with the Boston Celtics from 1962 through 1978. His team won four consecutive league championships aided by his excellence of play. His team won an additional four NBA championships. He was named the most valuable player in 1974, and he was named to eleven All-NBA first teams and second team seven times. He was also considered the best "sixth man" in NBA history. He set other records and received numerous honors. He was the first player to score one thousand points in sixteen consecutive seasons. He was described by his coach as "the guts of the team." Following his retirement in 1978, his number was immediately retired. He has been described as soft-spoken and modest. He formed a company to sell basketball paraphernalia and, of course, earned a sizeable pension.

Jack Nicklaus, illustrious golfer and OSU graduate is discussed in Chapter 26.

Other Colleges and Universities in Franklin County

Ohio Dominican University received its current name in 1968. Before that it was known as St. Mary's of the Springs College, organized by Dominican Sisters of the Roman Catholic Church in 1868 as an Academy for Women in Somerset, Ohio. After moving to the village of Shepard, on the eastern edge of Columbus, it became a college for women in 1911, the year Shepard was annexed to Columbus. After 1964, men were admitted. The school is known for its Conservatory of Music and preparation of teachers in its Department of Education. An athletic program was inaugurated in 2004, and football and other sports are played against other colleges. In 2007, the university entered into an agreement with the Graham charter school in Clintonville to form the Charles School. This arrangement was an attempt to smooth the transition to college, especially for those who might be intimidated by the idea of obtaining a higher degree of education. Up to sixty-two hours of college credit could be earned tuition free, and the student would be half-way toward a college degree. The requirement of internships and community involvement is intended to produce more socially and civic-minded, responsible adults.

Franklin University started in 1902 as a School of Commerce, sponsored by the YMCA. It was a two-year college specializing in business related subjects. Bachelor degrees started to be given at the end of four-year courses in 1921. The name, Franklin University, was adopted in 1933. The school separated from the YMCA in 1964, and moved to its permanent location on South Grant Street. Five downtown buildings and campuses in Dublin, Westerville and Worthington make up its physical facilities. Most of its ten thousand students have day-time jobs and attend classes at night. Over six hundred students are foreign citizens. Sixteen undergraduate majors are offered. An on-line program is provided especially for students in the armed services. Graduate programs can lead to MBA's and Masters of Science in Marketing, Communications and Computer Science. Three commencements are conducted annually. The University is accredited by North Central Association of Higher Learning.

Columbus State Community College is a large, two-year post-secondary school that was founded in 1963. The College grants Associate Certificates in technology, performing arts, writing and culinary, architectural, medical, nursing and law related subjects. Continuing education opportunities are free to senior citizens. An athletic program is offered with games against similar colleges. The campus on East Spring Street has over ten buildings that support nearly thirty thousand students that attend full or part time. Eight branches are located in central Ohio. Funding is obtained from tuitions and state subsidies. In 2007, the college formed an association with Africentric High School to provide high school students an opportunity for a smoother transition to college. Up to sixty-two college credits could be earned by attending the Columbus Africentric Early College without tuition. Special attention would be accorded by teachers selected to teach in the program. Thus, students are given the opportunity to attend college who might never have entertained such aspirations.

Columbus College of Art & Design was founded in 1879 as the Columbus Art School, as an adjunct to the Columbus Gallery of Fine Arts. It was viewed by many in its early years as a glorified finishing school for young ladies. It occupied a building at Long and North High Streets. In 1892, the school moved to the YMCA at 34 South Third Street, now site of the *Columbus Dispatch*. During the 1890's, Alice Schille was a student, teacher and became one of America's finest watercolorist. In 1914, the school relocated to a fine, old, three-story mansion at Washington Avenue and East Broad Street. The first building erected specifically for the school, Beaton Hall, opened at 44 North Ninth Street in 1930.

Its current name of CCAD was adopted in 1959. Ten years later the college was fully accredited and enabled to grant bachelor degrees in fine arts. Enrollment reached twelve hundred in 1978. A residence hall opened in 1985. A warehouse at Grant Avenue and Spring Street was renovated into classrooms and studios. Another large building, the Loann Crane Center for Design was completed in 2005. At the heart of the institution for forty-five years was Joseph V. Canzani. He retired in 1995 after teaching, and serving as the Dean and President. The college now has 2,600 students (1,300 full-time) on six campuses, providing instructions to children and adults of all ages. Students come from forty states and thirty countries. Their studies focused on the fine arts, advertising, computer animation, digital multimedia, fashion design, illustration and industrial design. The college is linked to Ohio Dominican University's educational programs. Over eighty full-time and one hundred and forty part-time teachers make up the faculty. In 1998, Dennison Griffith began his tenure as president of CCAD. He is a graduate of Ohio Wesleyan and The Ohio State Universities with bachelor and master degrees in fine arts. Past work experience includes being a painter, and working for the Ohio Foundation for the Arts and the Columbus Museum of Art. The annual budget is nearly twenty-five million dollars; eighty percent comes from tuition which is nearly $19,000 per student annually. Currently, the college is in a $12 million fund raising campaign with more than half subscribed. The main administration building is on North Ninth Street, but, a contract has been sealed to buy and renovate the Byers Automotive Dealership at 390 East Broad Street.

DeVry University can trace its roots to the establishment of the DeForest Training School in Chicago in 1931 by Dr. Herman DeVry. The mission was to prepare students for technical work in electronics, motion pictures, radio and later television. The name underwent two earlier changes: DeVry Technical Institute in 1953 and DeVry Institute of Technology in 1968. In 1957, the school granted associate degrees, and in 1968, bachelor degrees were added. DeVry was purchased by the Bell and Howell Education Group and expanded to eleven campuses in the United States and Canada. By 2003, B. A. degrees were offered in computer information systems, accounting, business administration and communications management. DeVry merged with the Keller Graduate School of Management in 1987. MBA degrees were added and, since 1998, have been offered via computer on-line. In 2002, the last name change to DeVry University received approval from The Higher Learning Commission of the North Central Association. Today, the University offers eighteen undergraduate and seven graduate degrees, and eleven certificates in technology and business. The University is unique in that it is publicly owned and trades its stock on the New York Stock Exchange. In 2003, DeVry acquired Ross University that is one of the largest medical and veterinary schools in the world. DeVry can now award M.D. and D.V.M. degrees at its Dominica Island campus in the Caribbean Sea. In 2007, DeVry added a branch of the Chamberlain College of Nursing based in St. Louis. Associate and bachelor degrees are offered. Selected students will be able to receive coursework on-line as well as clinical experience in their hometown. The college is the only for-profit nursing school in Columbus. It competes with schools of nursing at The Ohio State University, Mount Carmel Hospital, Columbus State Community College, Capital University and Otterbein College. The Columbus campus (since 1952) is located on Alum Creek Drive, where thirty-six hundred students are enrolled.

Capital University and Otterbein College are discussed elsewhere, under the cities of Bexley and Westerville respectively. *Ashland University* (2,500 students), *Central Michigan University* (150 students), *Mount Vernon Nazarene University* (750 students), *Kent State University* (170 students), *Tiffin University* (105 students) and *Park University* (230 students) have branch colleges in Columbus, leading to degrees in business or science. Nursing degrees can be obtained at The Ohio State University College of Nursing, Mount Carmel Hospital, Capital University, Otterbein College, Columbus State Community College and DeVry University. At one time both Riverside Methodist and Grant Hospitals trained and gave degrees to nurses. Neither hospital trains nurses today. *Ivy Tech Community College* on Central Avenue is a small business school for training technicians and assistants in libraries, schools, medical science settings and business offices.

Chapter 17

Libraries and Newspapers in Franklin County

Columbus Metropolitan Library

The Columbus Metropolitan Library has functioned for over one hundred and thirty years. Its mission is to promote reading and guide learning in the pursuit of information, knowledge and wisdom. This mission is accomplished through access to extensive databases, large collections of books and other media, reading clubs and language classes. The library has twenty branches as adjuncts to the main library on South Grant Street, plus a working agreement with Worthington's Northwest Library. The library collection contains over three million items on its shelves. It is one of the most used library systems in the country, and consistently ranks at the top of its class. Patrons borrow more than sixteen million items, make over eight million visits and ask over one million reference questions each year.

State Library of Ohio

Ohio has had a state library since 1817. In 1824, the only librarian was paid an annual salary of two hundred dollars, and three hundred and fifty dollars was appropriated for books. To develop lifelong learning among the citizens of the state and thereby strengthen the cultural and economic health of Ohio, the library has developed these priorities: to lead and partner in the development of library services throughout the state; to promote and enable resource sharing among libraries; and to provide access to information for Ohio's state government. A genealogy service has been included. Also, a Talking Book Program is equipped to play recorded books and magazines for the blind and physically handicapped. Workshops pertaining to the library's services are available to the public. The library recently moved from the Front Street State Building into spacious quarters in a renovated building on the grounds of the former Jeffrey Manufacturing Company at 274 East First Avenue.

Ohioana Library

The Ohioana Library Association is dedicated to collecting, preserving and promoting the works of Ohio's authors, artists and musicians. The library has a distinct array of books and materials based solely on their genesis in Ohio. The creative accomplishments of Ohioans are preserved in this library, which physically is a special section within the State Library at 274 East First Avenue in Columbus. The dissemination of information about the library's collection is made available to researchers, schools and the general public. Each year a reception is held at the library for Ohio authors whose works were published during the preceding year. At last count in 2006, the library held 45,000 books, 10,000 pieces of music and 20,000 biographic files, as well as a few special collections. Some of the better known Franklin County achievers of the Ohioana Awards were: James Thurber (x3), Arthur Schlesinger (x3) and Foster Dulles.

Palatines to America National Library

Palatine is an English word used as a general term for all German immigrants. The Palatines To America library contains thousands of books, magazines, maps, CDs and family records pertaining to German genealogy. The library strives to be a leader among family history societies in providing high quality and quantity research services. Although the library is private, non-member visitors may visit or use the facility by contributing a very modest fee. Since its inception on the Capital University campus in 1975, the library has grown rapidly. It has collected 120,000 American family names for reference. For the past decade, the library has been located at 611 Weber Road in Columbus.

Online Computer Library Center (OCLC)

OCLC Columbus-based, nonprofit, computer library center and research corporation was founded in 1967 in the main library of The Ohio State University. It is now located as an independent campus on the east edge of Dublin, on Frantz Road, off the northwest corner of the I-270-Outerbelt. Its original mission was to coordinate the library systems of Ohio's higher educational institutions in order to reduce costs. The first public library to use and help maintain the center was the Worthington Public Library. Its mission quickly expanded to worldwide collecting and disseminating of scientific, literary and educational knowledge and information. It contains over one billion bits of information shared by 57,000 libraries in 112 countries and territories around the globe. In addition to libraries, students, researchers and scholars share in the benefits. The company's database catalogue, *WorldCat*, is the foundation of its resources and reference sharing. Recipients, whether institutions or individuals, have access to biographies, abstracts, indexes or full text in print or electronic form. OCLC *FirstSearch* provides integrated access to over eighty databases and twenty-two hundred electronic journal titles. The company's interlibrary loan service has aided thousands in borrowing or lending. The division, *Preservation Resources,* gives high quality microfilming and digital services. The Library of Congress has been a recipient of this service. OCLC also publishes and updates the Dewey Decimal Classification, the most widely used classification of worldwide information. One thousand employees keep abreast of the latest advances in electronic processing in its endeavor. One of the founders and first President and CEO of OCLC was Fred Kilgour, recipient of the American Library Association's most prestigious honor, Honorary Life Member. In 2007, *Computerworld* named OCLC as one of the 100 Best Places to Work in technology.

Chemical Abstracts Service

This service began with its members housed in a single room in the Chemistry Department of The Ohio State University in 1907. The staff monitored, abstracted and indexed the world's chemistry-related literature. In the early 1960's, the service separated from the university and built its own large establishment on the northern edge of the university and now operates under the auspices of the American Chemical Society. Chemical Abstracts continued to grow and has become the world's largest such service. By year 2000, it had summarized 40,000 scientific journals and abstracted and indexed 725,000 articles. Its database included more than nineteen million abstracts of chemistry-related literature and patents, over twenty-seven million organic and inorganic substance records, and fifty-seven million DNA sequences. The sequence information comes from the GenBank of the National Institutes of Health. Chemical Abstracts has about 1,170 employees, many of whom are chemists. It represents a major scientific library source.

Current Central Ohio Newspapers and Magazines

The Columbus Dispatch

The only daily newspaper in Central Ohio is the *Columbus Dispatch*. The *Columbus Dispatch*, long politically conservative in its editorial policy, changed with the last publisher, Mr. John F. Wolfe II, in 1994. It is now more balanced politically and editorially often taking a reform and progressive posture. This stance is more fitting and acceptable to the political spectrum as the only daily newspaper in Columbus. (See Chapter 20, John Wolfe II and Ancestry).

The Columbus Call and Post

The *Columbus Call and Post* is a weekly newspaper and website produced by the Don King Productions, with sister *Call and Post* newspapers in Cleveland and Cincinnati. It is free and aimed at the African-American community. It has been in Columbus for many years and its business office is at 109 Hamilton Avenue.

Weekly Newspapers and Magazines

The Dispatch Printing Company (34 South Third Street) publishes a weekly paper, *This Week,* in twenty different suburbs. Its chief competitor is *Suburban News* published weekly for twenty-two suburbs. The latter is owned by CM Media Inc. (5257 Sinclair Road) which in addition publishes: *The Other Paper*, a weekly Columbus news and entertainment guide; *The Columbus Monthly*, a thirty-year old metropolitan news magazine; the *Official Columbus Visitors Guide* on behalf of the Columbus Chamber of Commerce; and *C.E.O.,* a monthly business magazine for central Ohio. *Senior Times* is published monthly.

Chapter 18

Historical and Genealogy Societies

Columbus Historical Society

The Columbus Historical Society was founded, belatedly, in 1990 to preserve Columbus's rich heritage and to educate residents and visitors through programs and publications. Community leaders and experts in various sectors participate in its endeavors. The Society is accumulating artifacts, collections and publications with the anticipation of having its own museum. The Society and its director are located at 51 Jefferson Avenue.

Franklin County Genealogical & Historical Society

The FCGHS Society collects and maintains research materials and sources primarily from Franklin County and some neighboring counties. A scant number of records pertain to the United States and a few foreign countries. The archives include some original records, obituaries, probated wills and an extensive index file of over 175,000 surnames. Many of these documents are available from computer on-line. The society's headquarters is in the Harrison or Jacob Oberdier House at 570 West Broad Street in Franklinton. The house is on the National Register of Historic Places; it is believed to have been built in 1807. It served as a frequent meeting place for General William Henry Harrison, commander of the Northwest Army in the War of 1812. Seventeen individuals owned the house at various times until it became the property of Columbus in 1973. Since 1985, the house has been leased to the FCGHS.

Ohio Historical Society

Ohio citizens gathered in 1822 and incorporated a society to remember and record Ohio's history. The group floundered and for a few years was primarily Cincinnati oriented. In 1885, Governor George Hoadly organized a new Ohio Archaeology and Historical Society that was private for three years. In 1912, it became funded by the state and met in the Ohio State Museum on the campus of

The Ohio State University. In 1970, it moved to its present location next to the state fair grounds near 17th Avenue and I-70. Byron Ireland designed the new Ohio Historical Center in the Brutalism style described as bold, imaginative, startling, utilizing form-textured concrete and having a plain massive appearance. The three story building shows each succeeding square floor to hang-out over its lower floor. The society's primary mission is to collect, organize, interpret and preserve Ohio's heritage in its museum and library. In addition to state funding, income is derived from private donations, grants, corporate gifts and a gift shop. The Ohio Village and Colonel Crawford Inn are close by and open on special occasions. The Society operates a statewide network of historic sites and museums.

Columbus Jewish Historical Society

The Columbus Jewish Historical Society was formed in 1981 by thirty members of the Columbus Jewish community. Its mission was to collect and preserve writings, photographs, oral histories and artifacts of local Jewish history and to use the material to present programs. Computer cross-filing is used to compile and check the accuracy of the collected items. Special attention has been given to local Jewish cemeteries. This effort has been expanded to include Southeastern Ohio and West Virginia. The society's archives is a valuable resource to researchers, historians and genealogists. The society's office is at 1175 College Avenue, Bexley.

Palatines To America

Palatines To America is a national genealogy organization devoted to the tracing of family roots of German ethnicity. The organization was founded in Columbus in 1975 where it continues to have its administrative center. The society's name is derived from the Palatinate (Pfalz) section of Germany from where most of the founders' ancestors immigrated, but the society pertains to all German immigrants regardless of country of origin. The society has promoted interest, research and study of the migration of German-speaking people to North America. In addition to the national group, there are eight state chapters, with over two thousand members. Regular state and national meetings are held for the presentation of education programs and the study of family ancestry. Its national headquarters and national library are located at 611 Weber Road in Columbus.

Chapter 19

Cultural Activities

After 1830, literary clubs, lyceums that sponsored lectures and historical and scientific societies made their appearance in Columbus. Some were for German or African American ethnicity. Some published pamphlets. Popular subjects for lectures were concerned with geography, religion, history, political issues and science. Membership in the clubs and societies was usually by election. Worthington resident, James Russell, constructed a large planetarium which he exhibited in the State House and in New York City. The Smithsonian Institute was petitioned to have him build one for them. The Mechanics Beneficial Society had a library, conducted debates, sponsored lectures in addition to giving medical aid to its members.

Columbus Association for the Performing Arts (CAPA)

CAPA was founded in 1969 to rescue and expedite the restoration of the Ohio Theater. Its success led to ownership and management of all of the other major downtown theaters: Ohio, Palace, Southern and the three theaters in the Riffe Tower. It coordinates and raises support for these performing artistic endeavors. It is funded from various endowments and corporate and individual gifts, but ninety percent of its income is derived from ticket sales and rentals. It operates with the smallest administrative staff of any comparable arts organization in North America. In its life span, CAPA has invested $34.8 million in capital improvements to the Ohio, Palace and Southern Theatres and has generated more than $121.8 million in operating revenue. CAPA repeated its success in theater rescue by saving and restoring the theater attached to the Southern (Westin) Hotel. The Ohio Theater at 55 East State Street serves as its headquarters and is now a Historic Landmark and the "Official Theatre for the State of Ohio." From 1998 to 2003, CAPA managed and programmed the Chicago Theater. Since 2001, it managed the Shubert Theater in New Haven, Connecticut. Its programs include jazz, world music, folk, country, classic music, comedy, dance, classic films, theater and family entertainment. It has produced the "Rhythm 'n' Zoo" concert series, and offerings in Cincinnati, Dayton and Toledo. Beginning in 1998, it launched the High 5 Tickets to the Arts for teen-aged students. Its diversity of world-class performance venues has enriched the Central Ohio community as well as benefiting the downtown economy. CAPA has received The Columbus Foundation Award as the City's outstanding philanthropic institution (1999), the Governor's Award for the Arts in Ohio (1995), the Greater Columbus Arts Council Award of Excellence (1994 and 1999), and the Columbus Landmarks Foundation's Organization of the Year Award in 2000.

Center of Science and Industry (COSI)

COSI, located in the renovated old Central High School on West Broad Street, is a cultural asset for Columbus. It was initiated in 1964 in the Veterans Memorial Hall which had been built in 1906 on East Broad Street. The Veterans Hall was used as a performing arts venue, later used to stage professional wrestling, and lastly as the home of the Franklin County Historical Society, and a Senior Citizens Recreational Center. COSI moved to its present location in 1999 to gain more room. Internationally renowned architect, Arata Isozaka, designed the new 320,000 square foot facility in the abandoned Central High School. Its first director was Sanford Hallock, who will be remembered not only as one of the founders, but for his enthusiasm and labor of love. Businessman Herschel Stephan, Historical Society Boardman Walter English and Preston Wolfe of the *Columbus Dispatch* were early boosters. COSI features interactive, discovery-based and themed exhibit areas, three theaters, an outdoor Big Science Park, the country's only high wire unicycle, a restaurant and a gift shop. Some exhibits combine science facts with learning through play. Favorite features are the Electrostatic Generator, Rat Basketball, the Foucault Pendulum, Total Knee Replacement Surgery, Dinosaur Dynasty, Coral Reef Adventure, the Battelle Planetarium, the Durell Street of Yesteryear and the Transparent Talking Woman. Over seventeen million visitors have passed through COSI. An extensive educational program includes in-depth field trips and outreach activities. Camp-In is an overnight experience for girls. Family Access memberships (five percent of memberships) are available to low income families for $20 per year. Other families pay $80 annually. COSI is supported by over 19,000 family members, donors, sponsors and large corporate partners. The staff is composed of 195 full-time team members, 183 part-time helpers and over 1,000 volunteers. The Columbus organization helped the start-up of Toledo's COSI which ran several years before closing in 2007.

Kathryn Sullivan, a recent CEO of COSI, was born in Patterson, New Jersey in 1951 but was reared in Woodland, California. In 1973, she received a B.S. degree with honors in Earth Sciences from the University of California, Santa Cruz. She received her doctorate in geology from Dalhousie University, Canada, in 1978. She spent one year, 1971-1972, as an exchange student at the University of Bergen, Norway. Her research included oceanographic expeditions and the study of faults off both shores of the United States. She joined NASA in 1978 and became an astronaut the following year. She participated in three shuttle missions, focusing on remote sensing projects; she performed a myriad of scientific experiments. She was the first woman to perform a space walk (1984). She was the payload commander for one of the first spacelabs. She logged over five hundred and thirty-two hours in space. In 1999, she became President and CEO of the Center of Science and Industry (COSI) in Columbus, Ohio, where she has exhibited a passion for teaching children and adults the importance of science, mathematics and technology. She stepped down from this position in 2005 but continues as a consultant. In 2006, Sullivan was appointed the first director of Ohio State University's new Battelle Center for Mathematics and Science Education Policy. The center is part of the John Glenn School of Public Affairs. It goal is to increase the number of students planning careers in science, technology, engineering, mathematics and medicine. She has received many honors, medals and commendations. They include membership in three halls of fame, three honorary degrees and presidential recognition under four different administrations.

David Chesebrough became the current President and CEO of COSI in 2006. He attained a bachelor's degree in physics and mathematics. He earned a master and a doctorate degree in science education. He held administrative positions at the Carnegie Museums in Pittsburgh and headed science museums in Buffalo and Binghamton, New York.

Columbus Museum of Art

The Columbus Museum of Art, located at 480 East Broad Street, was commenced in 1877. The collection contains mostly late nineteenth and early twentieth century American and Modern European art. It includes major works by Monet, Matisse, Picasso, Renoir, Hopper and O'Keeffe. Spectacular examples of impressionism, German Expressionism and Cubism are also part of the gallery acquisitions. The Museum is a repository for local artists such as Elijah Pierce, Aminah Robinson and George Bellows. The Museum has significant holdings in photography. Special exhibits and programs for children and adults are an integral part of its educational and cultural mission. The Museum enjoys excellent public and corporate support as illustrated by a $10 million gift from Robert and Peggy Walter in 2006.

Columbus Metropolitan Club

The Columbus Metropolitan Club was founded by a group of thirteen women in 1976 as a forum for neutral and unfiltered discussion of all aspects of local, state and national issues. It meets monthly, and membership is evenly divided among women and men of all social, racial, political, business, professional and religious persuasions. It addition to discussions of a wide variety of subjects by speakers and members, the club provides an excellent setting for "networking" for its members. Advertising, promotional and endorsement advocacy is prohibited. The club meets at the Athletic Club of Columbus at 136 East Broad Street, and the meetings are open to the public.

League of Women Voters

The League of Women Voters, founded in 1920, is a nonpartisan political organization that seeks to improve our democratic system of government through informed and active participation and impact public policies through citizen education and advocacy. There are Leagues in all fifty states, the District of Columbia, Puerto Rico, the Virgin Islands and Hong Kong. Hundreds of local and state Leagues nationwide include one in Columbus with headquarters at 17 South High Street. The League's mission is conducted through public meetings, newsletters and press releases. It does not support or oppose any candidate for public office. It recognizes that half of the voters are women and cherishes it success in obtaining women's right to vote through the Nineteenth Amendment to the United States Constitution (1920).

Junior League of Columbus

The Junior League of Columbus was founded by eleven women in 1923. Eight hundred and fifty members strong today, its mission has been to promote volunteerism; develop the potential of women of all races, religions and national origin; and improve communities through effective action and leadership of trained volunteers. Its purpose is exclusively educational and philanthropic. A substantial amount of money is raised annually and given to a myriad of worthy entities and projects. The League's headquarters is in the English House at 583 Franklin Avenue, close to the historic Kelton House which is owned and managed by the League. The League gives annual awards to Columbus women, outstanding for their accomplishments in community service.

Kelton House

The Kelton House, a Federal Revival mansion located at 586 East Town Street, contains a treasure of Victoriana. It was constructed in 1852 for Fernando Kelton, a dry goods and pharmaceutical wholesaler. In 1975, the home and gardens were acquired along with its antique furnishings from descendent Grace Kelton (1881-1975) by the Junior League of Columbus who maintains it as a museum, opens it to visitors and rents it to groups. Educational programs are available from volunteers. The house contains a gift shop. The Keltons had been active in civic affairs and patrons of the arts.

Snowden-Gray House

Philip Snowden, a successful dry goods merchant, had his home built in 1854. It is considered the finest example of Italianate architecture remaining in Columbus. In 1862, it was the residence of Governor David Tod. During the Civil War, Senator Andrew Johnson of Tennessee, who later became president, was a guest in the mansion. From 1865 to 1922, Columbus philanthropist, David Gray, lived in the home. After a fire in 1872, architect, George Bellows, Sr., supervised its rebuilding. The home was purchased by Kappa Kappa Gamma in 1951 for its national fraternal headquarters. It was registered as an historic place in 1980 as Heritage Museum at 530 East Town Street. Educational tours and an internship for college students are offered by the organization's foundation.

An example of luxurious homes built in the Olde Town East district.

Fig. 66 The Myers home was built on Bryden Road in 1896. The eighteen room ornate house was patterned after a castle in Germany. Frederick Myers immigrated to the U.S. at age thirteen and founded the United States Carriage Company that built horse-drawn carriages and hearses. They were made of the finest materials, satins and hand-carved ornaments.

—from Lea Ann Sterling's *Historic Homes of Olde Town, Columbus.*

Columbus Landmarks Foundation

A group of local residents interested in preserving Columbus's architectural heritage founded Columbus Landmarks in 1977. Its headquarters is at 61 Jefferson Avenue. The Foundation's mission is to educate the public, encourage responsible public and private sector enhancement of historic areas and structures, and to promote the highest standards in the design and construction of new buildings and spaces. The Foundation does not give grants but does make awards for outstanding achievement by an individual or groups. Some of the award recipients were designers of the Columbus Metropolitan Library Renovation, Greater Columbus Convention Center, Old Post Office Renovation, Central Ohio Fire Museum, St.

Mary's Church Restoration, Martin Luther King, Jr. Center for the Performing Arts and The Topiary Garden in Deaf School Park. Among their programs are walking tours to historic landmarks in Columbus. Membership includes over four hundred individuals and corporations dedicated to the mission of the foundation.

The Jefferson Center for Learning and the Arts

The Jefferson Center was created in 1975 as a non-profit entity to increase the number and quality of learning opportunities made available to the citizens of the Greater Columbus community by providing funds and facilities for the support of charitable, religious, educational and scientific organizations. Over one hundred and thirty people representing twenty-seven organizations perform their labor of love in the center. Some of the groups are: Columbus Metropolitan Area Church Council, Ohio Family Care Association, Columbus Council on World Affairs, Columbus Historical Society, Columbus Bach Ensemble, the Thurber Conference and Classrooms, Council for Ethics in Economics and The Academy for Leadership & Governance. The Academy has published several guidelines for civic leadership and is located at 65 Jefferson Avenue.

Jefferson Avenue is on the eastern edge of downtown Columbus, between Broad and Long Streets. The historic Jefferson Avenue was the site of the Ohio Lunatic Asylum in 1838. Over four hundred and fifty patients lived in the institution before it was destroyed by fire in 1868. The institution was then moved to West Broad Street in Franklinton. In the mid-1880's, Jefferson Avenue became a residential development called East Park Place. Broad avenues and a central park were notable features. Middle and upper class professional and business people lived in the area. Many of the homes were designed in the Italianate style with soaring ceilings, sweeping staircases and carriage houses in the rear for buggies and horses. The homes fell into disrepair until the avenue was placed on the National Register of Historic Places in 1983. Since then, eleven homes have been restored and occupied by various charitable and intellectual groups. The centerpiece is the home dedicated to the Vorys, one of the founding families. The Thurber House (77 Jefferson Avenue, where James Thurber lived as a youth) provides a position for a writer-in-residence, and conducts workshops for students. The board of trustees, consisting of leaders in business, religious and cultural domains of the community, has developed a master plan to detail future building, lighting and landscaping. New buildings and public art will grace the avenue. Each year six Jefferson Award grants are given to ordinary individuals in Franklin County who have made a difference in the community. Annual art and music festivals are also presented. Several art galleries are located in the homes. Neighbors are the Columbus Museum of Art, the Columbus College of Art and Design and the Columbus State Community College.

The Columbus Club

The Columbus Club, an exclusive male social group, was founded in 1887 and has met since then in the building at 181 East Broad Street. For twenty years, before the club house was purchased for $45,000, it was the residence of railroad contractor Benjamin E. Smith. It was considered one of the finest homes in Columbus, and two Ohio governors made it their residence. The exterior is constructed of bricks pressed in Philadelphia, which were individually wrapped in paper and shipped to Columbus. The club has been renovated several times in keeping with it use for social gatherings and fine dining. Adjacent property has been purchased for parking space. The club is private and limited to males who are recommended and voted into membership. Traditionally, all governors are honorary members. Women and non-members may be guests. On New Year's Day, the officers of the club receive members in a reception followed by a banquet in which females may be guests. Since its intent is purely social, politics are not favored as subjects for discussion. Famous people have been invited guests, but no news of their comments has ever been leaked to the press. The club's rules have undergone little change over one hundred and nineteen years.

Chapter 20

Notable Persons in Columbus

Early Notable Architects in Columbus

Frank Packard

At the end of the nineteenth century, Columbus became the home of one of America's foremost institutional architects. Frank L. Packard was born in Delaware, Ohio in 1866. As a youth, he worked as a chain carrier for the county surveyor and as an office boy for an architect. He attended The Ohio State University but graduated from the Massachusetts Institute of Technology in 1887. His career took off in 1892 when he began a partnership with Joseph Yost, already a prominent architect in Columbus. Yost left the partnership and moved to New York City in 1901. Packard designed over three thousand buildings and homes, some still standing today as historic landmarks. His schools include the Fair Avenue Public School, North High School, and at Ohio State University, Lord Hall, Hayes Hall and the Armory. Some of the other buildings he designed were: Congregational, Methodist, Presbyterian and Episcopal Churches, the Columbus Country Club, the Capitol Trust Building, the Chittenden, Seneca, and Virginia Hotels, the YMCA, the Columbus Savings & Trust Company, the Columbus Club, the Odd Fellows Temple and Elk's Club, several railroad and interurban stations, the Sells House, the Lindenberg House (used as the governor's residence, see below), the Huntington Building, the Chapel at Greenlawn Cemetery, Children's Hospital and the Franklin County Veteran's Memorial Hall (occupied by COSI for thirty years). The Veteran's building cost $250,000 to build and seated 5,000, one of the largest of its kind. Parkard died in 1923.

This Frank Packard house (Fig. 67) was built in the Georgian Revival Eclectic style at 1234 East Broad Street for Charles Lindenberg. The owner's fortune was made as a printer, manufacturer of fraternal societies' paraphernalia, and president of both the Columbus Brass and the Columbus Piano Companies. The State of

Ohio purchased the property in 1919 for $75,000 and had it remodeled for use as the governor's mansion. For thirty-six years it was occupied by ten governors. Its then languished as a book repository for the Columbus School System. After a short period as a restaurant, it became the property of the Columbus Foundation in 1988 and remains as its administrative office.

Fig. 67
—From Lea Ann Sterling's *Historic Homes in Olde Towne, Columbus.*

George Bellows, Sr.

Another architect of local renown was George Bellows, Sr. He was born on Long Island in 1829. His childhood was spent on the family farm with time for sailing and fishing. His architectural career began as a carpenter in Brooklyn. He progressed through the stages of design and building under R. A. Sheldon, and he moved to Columbus when the firm was commissioned to design and build the Starling Medical College and hospital in 1849. His work included high schools, commercial buildings, the county jail and homes. He may be remembered best for constructing the second Franklin County Courthouse at a cost of $460,000. The structure lasted until the 1970's. He was active in civic affairs and served as county commissioner for one term. His son, George Bellows, Jr., became an internationally known artist.

Notable Persons in Arts and Science from Columbus

George Bellows, Jr.

Fig. 68

George Bellows, Jr., was born in Columbus in 1882, son of an architect. He attended The Ohio State University for four years. There, he exhibited a talent for playing baseball. In 1903, he moved to New York City where he studied oil painting under Robert Henri. In 1906, he opened a

Fig. 69

studio and concentrated on painting realistic city street scenes, athletic events and unglamorous people, in what became known as the "Ashcan School." In 1908, one of his landscapes won the Hallgarten prize from the National Academy of Design. At age twenty-seven, he was the youngest artist elected to the National Academy. He married Emma Story in 1910 and began teaching at the New York Art Students League. During the next three years he was recognized with eighteen honors and awards from leading international art institutes. He was now considered a foremost artist of his generation. He began spending summers painting in the country sides of New England, Mexico and California. He was deeply moved by events in World War I. He illustrated several novels written by H.G. Wells. He developed strong humanitarian sentiments and contributed art work to the radical journal, *The Masses."* In 1919, he moved to the Chicago Art Institute. Late in life he experimented with lithographs. He died in 1925 in New York City, probably from neglected appendicitis. His best remembered paintings are *Stag at Sharkey's, Dempsey and Firpo, Blessed are the Peacemakers, The Pic-nic, The Cliff Dwellers, The Circus, Men of the Dock, The Crucifixion, Ringside Seats, River Front, Two Women and Blue Snow, (Fig. 69—from Columbus Museum of Art, Ohio:Museum Purchase, Howald Fund 1958.035), and The Battery.*

Emerson Burkhart

Emerson Burkhart was born in Kalida, Ohio (Putnam County) in 1905. He demonstrated talent for drawing at an early age. He was labeled "artist" by his classmates. School instructors utilized his artistry to aid in teaching. His family moved from state to state; he grew up in Texas, California and Florida. His father wanted him

Fig. 70

Fig. 71

—both the portrait of Burkhart and the painting in upper right are from the Columbus Museum of Art, Ohio: purchased with funds donated by Loann W. Crane and A.B. and Barbara Siemer 2001.002.

to become a lawyer. He was a good student at Ohio Wesleyan University, but, before getting his degree, he transferred to the art studio and school of Charles Hawthorne in Providencetown, Massachusetts. Lacking funds, he slept in a coal shed, which he painted white. He was reduced to doing odd jobs and selling hand painted ties on the streets. The Great Depression brought him to Columbus where he found work in a federal Works Project in 1931. He painted a mural for The Ohio State University School of Social Work. He also painted the mural above the stage in the Central High School auditorium. Since then, several coats were painted over it, but it has been restored in recent years. His favorite subjects were females and self-portraits (*The Confused Process of Becoming*-portrait of Roman Johnson-Fig. 71). He had a running dispute with the Columbus Art League who would not exhibit his work and, therefore, Burkhart held annual exhibits of his work in his home on Woodland Avenue for over thirty years. Fortunately, his wife was supportive. He traveled worldwide on artistic tours, painting as he went. Recognition came from his exhibits in the Whitney Museum, Carnegie Institute, the Art Institute of Chicago and the Corcoran Gallery. Several of his paintings are in the Columbus Museum of Art. He always believed in himself and the value of his work.

David Citino

David Citino was born in Cleveland, Ohio, in 1947. In high school, he enjoyed participating in baseball and football along with creative writing. He received his B.A. degree from Ohio University and his M.A. and Ph.D. degrees from The Ohio State University. He taught English and writing at the Marion campus of The Ohio State University for eleven years. In 1995, he was appointed professor of English and Creative Writing at the main campus of The Ohio State University. He authored eleven books of poetry: *The News and Other Poems, Paperwork: Selected Prose, The Eyes of the Poet: Six Views of the Art and Craft of Poetry, The House of Memory, Broken Symmetry, The Weight of the Heart, and The Invention of Secrecy*. Among his awards were: a Poetry Fellowship from the National Endowment for the Arts, the first annual Poet Award from the Ohioana Library, a Fellowship from the Ohio Arts Council, the Dasher Award from the College English Association of Ohio, the Exemplary Faculty Award from The Ohio State University College of Humanities, the Alumni Award for Distinguished Teaching from The Ohio State University and in his last years was Poet Laureate at The Ohio State University. He was a trustee of the Greater Columbus Arts Council, poetry editor and member of the editorial board of the Ohio State University Press, a facilitator of the literature council of the Ohio Arts Council and a member and past president of the board of trustees of *Thurber House*. Citino died October 17, 2005.

Charlotte Curtis

Charlotte Curtis was born in Chicago in 1928. Her father was a prominent surgeon in Columbus. After preliminary education in Columbus, Ohio, she graduated from

Vassar College. Her first journalist position was as a reporter for the *Columbus Citizen-Journal*. Her next job was with the *New York Times*, where she ascended to the editorship of the Family/Style section. She explored the curiosities and complexities of the lives of the rich and famous, world-wide. She was fearless and did not hold them in awe. An example of her writing is, "The new, young, chic and acquisitive rich, the restless young Europeans and the beautiful people still flit from Palm Beach's polo fields to Newport's yachts with refueling stops at Gucci, Yves Saint Laurent and Tiffany." She then became the Op-Ed editor of the newspaper. She was allowed the freedom to write about anything that drew her interest. This section of the paper changed from its tradition of shopping and clothing to feminist subjects such as abortion. She was the first female senior editor of the *New York Times*. Her responsibilities included the *New York Times Sunday Magazine*. Her published books included *First Lady* (Jacqueline Kennedy) and *The Rich and Other Atrocities*. She died of cancer in Columbus in 1987.

Eric Gnezda

Fig. 72

Eric Gnezda (Fig. 72) was born in Columbus, Ohio in 1957. His grandparents were immigrants, and his parents were college graduates. His mother attained a Ph.D. degree in Education from The Ohio State University and was an Assistant Dean of their College of Dentistry. As a teenager, Eric performed with a band as its drummer. In high school, in addition to being a scholar, he participated in track and had the lead in two musicals. He received his B.A. degree in journalism from Ohio Wesleyan University. Music continued to be his main focus and for over two decades he has performed as a musical composer, pianist, singer, entertainer and keynote speaker for national corporate and other audiences. His themes are inspirational, humorous and dynamic. Among his compositions is his beloved anthem of triumph, *Blossoms of Hope,* a favorite among cancer survivorship celebrations and other organizations. *Everyone Wins* was written for the Special Olympics, *True Heroes* for September 11, 2002 remembrance, and *The Bells of Worthington* for their bicentennial celebration. In 2006, he received the Ohioana Library's Music Citation for his creative contributions. His other pursuits have included writing a newspaper column, *Just Enough Rope,* for the *Columbus Dispatch,* teaching speech at Ohio Wesleyan University and doing radio commentaries. His presentations are available in compact discs. His song, *True Heroes,* was chosen to be included in a CD sent to U.S. troops by *musicfortroops.com,* a national non-profit organization.

Asa Lord

Asa C. Lord was born in Madrid, New York, June 17, 1816. Upon completing local school education he began teaching school at age sixteen. In 1839, he was appointed Principal of the Western Reserve Seminary in Kirkland, Ohio. It was considered one of the first normal schools in the nation. In 1843, he organized the first teachers institute in Ohio. While in Kirkland, he completed medical studies and received an M.D. degree. In 1847, he was appointed the first Superintendent of Public Schools in Ohio; his residence was in Columbus. His salary was $600. per annum. In the second year he was paid $800 and $1000 for the third year, attesting to the satisfaction with his efforts. His wife taught school also. He inaugurated the first graded schools in the state as well as the first public high schools. In 1863, he completed a course in theology and was ordained and licensed to preach in the Presbyterian Church. From 1854 to 1863, he was Superintendent of the State Institute for the Blind. He was styled "one of the pioneers and master builders in the educational enterprises of Ohio." In 1863, he became Superintendent of a similar institute in Batavia, New York, holding that position until he died in 1874. He was one of the foremost educators in the history of Columbus.

Starling Loving

Dr. Starling Loving was born in Kentucky in 1828. His father was affluent, allowing Starling the time to enjoy an active outdoor life, and he especially enjoyed hunting. His basic education was achieved in a private academy. He was Lyne Starling's great nephew which drew him to migrate to Columbus in 1846. He studied medicine under local physicians and was one of the first students in the new Starling Medical College; he was given a degree to practice medicine in 1849. He served internships at Bellevue, Charity, Immigrant's and Children's Hospitals in New York City. His health failed at this time, but a short time later he began practicing medicine on the island of Nassau (Bahamas). This was followed by a stint on the Isthmus of Panama as a railroad doctor, where he acquired knowledge of tropical diseases. Upon his return to Columbus in 1854, he began to practice medicine with Dr. Francis Carter, one of his former mentors, and became an Instructor in Anatomy in the Starling Medical College (named for his great-uncle). In 1856, he married Margaret Noble, and they eventually had six children. In 1857, he was promoted to Teacher of Therapeutics. During the Civil War, he was a surgeon for the Sixth Ohio Volunteer Infantry, but for health reasons he returned to civilian life in 1862. He was recalled briefly into the army as a Captain in 1863 during General John Morgan's raid into Ohio. For the remainder of the war, he was a civilian examiner of recruits. In 1875, he was promoted to Teacher of Practical Medicine in the medical school and became its Dean in 1883. In 1894, Dr. Loving was elected president of the Ohio State Medical

Society and first vice-president of the American Medical Association. He served also as president of the Columbus Academy of Medicine and as a member of the Judicial Council of the Association of American Medical Colleges. He was very active in civic affairs and belonged to many business and social clubs. He was on the Columbus Board of Education for eighteen years, serving as its president for two years. An elementary school was named after him, as was a building in the Ohio State College of Medicine. He was known for his strong likes and dislikes, often sought for his views, and was always looking to improve the welfare of the community. He died in 1911 and is buried in Green Lawn Cemetery.

Bob Marvin as Flippo, the Clown

Fig. 73

Bob Marvin, best known to Central Ohioans as Flippo, King of the Clowns, was born in Cleveland in 1927. After stints in the army and attendance at The Ohio State University, he settled into a witty clown character, and was known for his quick retorts ("snappers") in the entertainment world. He sang and played the saxophone on radio shows early in his career. His repertoire included skits, outrageous jokes and wide-ranging comedy carried out in a red, white and blue jumpsuit studded with pom-poms. His facial makeup was that of a clown with typical headgear. He became a fixture on a Saturday morning kids' TV show and as host of afternoon TV movies in Columbus. Other television appearances included the Ohio State Fair. He was popular in parades and personal appearances. After retirement in 1983, he donated his costume to the Ohio Historical Society. In fond return, the society honored him with a ceremony on his 79th birthday and made a documentary of his career. He died in 2006.

Elijah Pierce

Fig. 74

Elijah Pierce was born in Mississippi in 1892, the son of former slaves. He attended a segregated school through eighth grade. As an adult, his first work was as an apprentice barber.

Fig. 75

During childhood, his uncle instructed him in wood carving with a pocketknife. Most of his lifetime carvings were given away. After the death of his first wife, he became a hobo and itinerate laborer. In 1920, he was "licensed" to preach in black churches. He migrated north and, with a new wife, settled in Columbus in 1923. He opened a barbershop with an attached studio where an apprentice allowed him time for his avocation. His animal carvings had Biblical themes. Pierce considered the *Book of Wood* his best effort. He held "sacred demonstrations" to explain the meaning of his works. The public gradually became aware of his work through showings at fairs and exhibits. His secular art depicted sports, comics and movie themes. Many of his carvings are owned by the Columbus Museum of Art. He was "discovered" at a YMCA exhibit by sculptor, Boris Gruenwald, in the early 1970's, who made sure that the world knew of Pierce, who died in 1984.—Figures 74 and 75 from the Columbus Museum of Art.

Aminah Robinson

Fig. 76

Aminah Brenda Lynn Robinson was born in Columbus, Ohio in 1940. She was reared in Poindexter Village, one of the first federally funded metropolitan housing developments. Her father encouraged her early emerging artistic ability and taught her book-making. From her mother she learned

Fig. 77

spinning, weaving, button and needlework. At age eight, she exhibited her paintings on a clothesline. She received formal art training at the Columbus Art School, later called the Columbus College of Art and Design. Her education was augmented by classes at Ohio State University. Her marriage to army sergeant Charles Robinson ended in divorce. During her marriage she saw much of the United States and Puerto Rico. Her only child, Sydney, graduated from Ohio State University with a degree in ceramic engineering. He took his own life at age twenty-seven. Many of her works utilize "hogmawg", a mixture of hog grease, paint, Elmer's glue, wood putty and sticks. Her inspirations came from Poindexter Village, Columbus and travels abroad. A grant from the Ohio Arts Council allowed her to visit Israel, Africa and South America. It was during her exploration of her African-American heritage after a trip to Africa that she adopted her first name in 1979. Her Doll House, containing various household objects arranged in her artistic design, has been recreated at the Columbus Museum of Art. Never-quite-finished pieces she calls "RagGonNons." A carved door, entitled "A Tree Grows in Brooklyn" has been divided into twelve woodcuts. A festive painting on cloth is labeled "Life in Sellsville" after a local circus (circa 1871-1900). One extensive painting is entitled, "The Canwoman Who Carries Her Home Through the Streets of New York." Other vibrant and expressive paintings are called "Nightmare of Horrors", "The Old City of Akko", "Lady at Sapelo Island" and "One Day in 1307 AD: King Abubakari II." Some of her renditions are in sculpture. She has been a recipient of a MacArthur Foundation Fellowship. She has exhibited at the Akron Art Museum, Oakland Art Museum, Baltimore Museum of Art, Studio Museum in Harlem, National Museum in Santiago, Chile and the Columbus Museum of Art. The latter has created a special room for a permanent exhibition of her art. She continues to work out of her home in Columbus.—photo of Robinson in Fig. 76 working on one of her "RagGonNons" called "Journeys" and "The Brownyskin Man" in Fig. 77 are from the Columbus Museum of Art, Ohio, purchased with funds donated by Wolfe Associates, 1997.010. g.

Alice Schille

Fig. 78

Alice Schille (Fig. 78) was born in Columbus, Ohio in 1869. Her parents ran a prosperous business, and were of German and French descent. They lived in an upscale neighborhood on Bryden Road. Her early interest in art was encouraged by her parents. Her father died

Fig. 79

when Alice was seventeen. In 1891 she entered the Columbus Art school which resided in the YMCA. There she won the Emerson McMillin prize for her paintings. After three years of art school, she began teaching art at the Ohio Institute for the Deaf and Dumb. In 1897, she went to New York to join the Art Students League where she studied under major American painters. Her training included visits to many prestigious art museums in Europe, Asia, North Africa and Central America. For a brief period her studio was in Paris. The people and countryside of France were the main inspiration for her paintings. Street scenes and portraits were also subjects for her art. Hundreds of exhibits took place over the next forty years, and she received many awards in the United States and abroad. In 1904, Schille returned to Columbus where she remained for the rest of her life. She taught students in the Columbus Art School (later called Columbus College of Art and Design). Return trips to France were frequent. Each summer she studied and painted abroad. She was recognized as one of the foremost American woman watercolorist. She did some work also with oils and pastels

(Fig. 79). Her paintings are owned privately and in museums in thirty states. She was featured in the Washington D.C. exhibit, *"American Women Artists, 1830-1930."* She continually mastered new modes of painting, but her style and technique is best described as impressionistic, postimpressionistic and decorative. She helped broaden the aesthetic tastes of her community who in turn gave her many accolades. She died in 1955 and is buried in Green Lawn Cemetery.

James Thurber

Fig. 81

Fig. 80

Cartoonist and humorist James Thurber (Fig. 81) was born in 1894 and educated in the public schools of Columbus, Ohio. He attended The Ohio State University from 1913 to 1918 where he worked on the college newspaper, *The Lantern,* and the humor magazine, *The Sun-Dial.* He had poor eyesight and wore thick lens glasses. Following college, he obtained a job in Washington D.C. as a code clerk in the State Department. Returning to Columbus in 1920, he became a reporter for the *Columbus Dispatch* and a correspondent for the *Christian Science Monitor.* In 1925, he moved to Paris and worked on the French edition of the *Chicago Tribune.* One year later, he returned to New York City and joined the staff of the *New York Evening Post.* Shortly thereafter, he published stories in the *New Yorker* magazine and became its managing editor. Disliking management, he transferred to the humor section of the magazine and wrote under the byline, *"Talk of the Town."* In this effort, he collaborated with E.B. White. Most of his articles centered on his hometown and Central Ohio. With White, he published his first book, *Is Sex Necessary?* (1929), followed in 1931 by *The Owl in the Attic.* His best known story was *The Secret Life of Walter Mitty,* later made into a movie in the 1940's. *My Life and Hard Times* was his autobiography. His play, *The Male Animal* (1940), was written with Eliot Nugent of Ohio. *The Thurber Carnival* (1945) was about his university experiences. In 1953, he published *Thurber Country,* and in the same year he was awarded the Ohioana Sesquicentennial medal. Most of his work was illustrated with his humorous and ironic cartoon characters. Readers enjoyed his wistful but deep psychological themes. Some of his sketches featured *Anne Honeycutts* and *How to Raise a Dog* (see Fig. 80). He is Columbus's best known humorist. The Thurber House, where he lived, is preserved today as a museum and residence for visiting writers and workshop for students. He died in 1961.

Nancy Wilson

Nancy Wilson was born in Chillicothe, Ohio in 1937. Her family moved to Columbus where she finished high school. Her earliest exposure to music was with her church choir. At age fifteen, she won a talent contest and became a regular singer on a local television show. She entered college but soon dropped out to pursue a music career. She sang with club bands, and Cannonball Adderley introduced her to her future manager, John Levy. Her first contract was with Capitol Records. Her first two singles were hits. Barry Manilow chose her to sing some Johnny Mercer songs that drew the attention of NPR Radio, and she continues to perform in their Jazz Profiles. For a period, her thirty-seven Capitol albums were second in sales only to the Beatles. She was guest artist on numerous TV shows and sang at many supper clubs. She finished her recording career with Columbia Records and enjoys semi-retirement. She won a Grammy Award for *How Glad Am I*. Other best sellers were, *If I Had My Way*, *Walk a Mile in My Shoes* and *When Did You Leave Heaven*. In 2004, her fifty years in show business was acknowledged with a Jazz Master award from the National Endowment for Arts.

Notable Clergymen in Columbus

Jerome Folkman

Jerome Folkman was born in Cincinnati, Ohio in 1909. He earned his B.A. degree from the University of Cincinnati in 1928. He received a M.A. degree from the University of Michigan in 1936 and a Ph.D. degree from The Ohio State University in 1953. His first temple served as a rabbi was in Jackson, Michigan (1931-1936). For ten years (1937-1947) he served as rabbi in Grand Rapids, Michigan. During World War II he was a civilian chaplain in the United States Air Force Weather School. He became rabbi of Temple Israel in Columbus in 1947. He held an adjunct professorship in sociology at The Ohio State University. He taught also at Capital University, Grant Hospital School of Nursing and the Pontifical Seminary of Josephinum. His tireless work was focused on marriage counseling, interfaith activities, ecumenical and political affairs. He was scholarly and authored several books that included: *Cup of Life* (1955), *Design for Jewish Living* (1955), *Interfaith Guide for all Young Couples* (1969), and *Marriage Has Many Faces* (1970). He was a recipient of the Governor's Award in 1968, the Humanitarian Award of the Orthodox Jewish Community, an honorary degree and many other awards and recognitions. He died in 1993. His son, Judah M. Folkman, M.D., was a prominent pediatric surgical researcher at Boston Children's Hospital and a Professor at Harvard Medical School.

Washington Gladden

Fig. 82

Washington Gladden was born in Pottsgrove, Pennsylvania in 1836. From early adulthood he demonstrated an aggressive advocacy of social reform. His first pastorates were in North Adam and Springfield, Massachusetts. While serving an inner-city church in Brooklyn, New York, he wrote newspaper articles attacking Boss Tweed. He was minister to the First Congregational Church in Columbus, Ohio from 1882 until his death in 1918. He challenged the conservatism of his church members. He was progressive in his ideology and preached the "Social Gospel" i.e. applying Christian principles to solving social problems. He supported temperance and worked for women's rights, the working class, and minorities. He set up a settlement house in Columbus. He advocated profit-sharing and arbitration in labor disputes where he acted as a mediator. In international relations, he was a pacifist and anti-imperialist. He believed in public ownership of local and national utilities, better education of minorities, a progressive income tax, repression of monopolies, and he was an enemy of gambling. He served on the Columbus City Council for one term. He intervened in a street-car strike in Columbus and traveled to Cleveland to openly support the rights of the workingmen in their street-car strike. He established friendly relations with Jews and Catholics. In his time, he was called "the First Citizen of Columbus." As president of the National Council of Congregational Churches, he turned down a gift of $100,000 from John D. Rockefeller, whose Standard Oil Company he thought oppressed its workers. While serving in national church affairs, he organized committees and conferences for the study of social issues. His militancy against the nativist American Protective Association prevented him from becoming president of The Ohio State University in 1892. He was the first Protestant to receive an honorary degree from Notre Dame University in 1895. Among his forty books are: *Working People and Their Employers* (1876), *Who Wrote the Bible?* (1891), *Social Salvation* (1902), and *Recollections* (1909). In 1886, he wrote an essay on *The Strength and Weakness of Socialism*. One of his best known hymns was *O Master, Let Me Walk With Thee*. His sermons were printed in a weekly newspaper.

Sylvester Rosecrans

Sylvester Rosecrans was born in Homer (Licking County), Ohio in 1827. After attending local schools, he enrolled in Kenyon College, an Episcopal school in Ohio. When he received a letter from his brother, General William Rosecrans, informing him that he had converted to Catholicism, Sylvester dropped out of college. He became a Catholic and entered St. John's College in New York where he graduated with honors. He decided to enter the priesthood and studied at the College of Propaganda in Rome. He was ordained in 1853. He returned to Cincinnati and was given a pastorate at St. Thomas's Church and appointed professor at St. Mary's College. When St. Mary's became a seminary, he taught dogmatic theology, and later was made its president. He also edited the *Catholic Telegraph*. He founded and became editor of the *Catholic Columbian*. He became an auxiliary bishop in the Cincinnati diocese in 1863. In 1868, he was appointed the first Bishop of the new Columbus diocese. His duties included building a new cathedral, starting a new seminary, beginning an orphanage, relocating St. Mary's of the Springs from Somerset to Columbus, and establishing an academy in New Lexington, Ohio. He continued to edit the *Catholic Columbian* and to teach in the new seminary, St. Aloysius. He consecrated the new cathedral, St. Joseph, on October 20, 1878, and died unexpectedly that evening. His legacy was that of being an excellent teacher and administrator. Rosecrans High School in Zanesville, Ohio is named for him. His brother, William Rosecrans, was a prominent general in the Union army during the Civil War.

Notable Political Figures from Columbus

John Bricker

John Bricker was born on a farm near Mt. Sterling, Ohio in 1893. He attended country schools and later taught for a short period. He attended The Ohio State University where he received his A.B., LL.B. and LL.D. degrees. During undergraduate days, he played on the baseball team and was a member of the debate team. He began law practice in Columbus. Results of his medical exam precluded him from active fighting in World War I; however, he was able to obtain a chaplaincy and a first lieutenant's commission. He served as solicitor in Grandview Heights, Ohio from 1920 to 1928. From 1923 to 1927, he acted as an assistant attorney general for the state. He was elected state attorney general in 1933 for two terms, after failing to be nominated for the position in 1928. In 1932, he served as legal counsel for the Ohio Public Utilities Commission. In 1938, he was elected Governor of Ohio, having lost that election two years previously. He served three terms and saw the state's financial deficit turned into a surplus. In order to achieve the surplus, two thousand state employees were fired. Old-age pensions, workmen's compensation benefits and school subsidies were increased. The state Department of Conservation and Natural Resources and the Ohio Water Supply Board were established during his tenure. He ran unsuccessfully for Vice-President of the United States as a Republican on the Dewey ticket in 1944. In 1946, he began two terms as United States Senator. He was a staunch conservative and sought to limit federal executive power in general. The Bricker Amendment that would have reduced presidential treaty-making power was defeated. He returned to the private practice of law after his defeat for a third term as senator. His defeat was blamed on his support of right-to-work legislation. He served on the The Ohio State University Board of Trustees. His law firm, Bricker & Eckler, remains active today, and occupies the renovated "old" Columbus post office, a registered historic building. He died in Columbus in 1986.

Jo Ann Davidson

Jo Ann Davidson was born in Ft. Wayne, Indiana in 1927. Her father was an appliance sales manager. She started her political career as a township clerk. In 1967, she began a ten year stint on the Reynoldsburg, Ohio City Council. She was active in Republican activities serving on committees and attending conventions. In 1981, she was elected to the Ohio House of Representatives and advanced to become the first woman to be Speaker of the Ohio House in 1995. After ten terms in the statehouse, term limitations forced her to retire from the House of Representatives. Thereupon, she founded a private consulting business. She also founded an institute to train Republican women for public service. In 2001, Governor Taft appointed her interim Director of the Department of Jobs and Family Services and to the Ohio State University Board of Trustees. During her career of public service, she was Chairperson of the Franklin County Republican Party Central Committee, Vice President of the Ohio Chamber of Commerce, member of the Ohio Turnpike Commission, member of the Ohio Constitutional Revision Commission, and on the Boards of Trustees of the University of Findlay and Franklin University. Columbus State Community College named a hall after her. She received numerous honors and awards for her achievements, including Honorary Doctorate degrees from The Ohio State University, Ohio University and Capital University. She was inducted into the Ohio Women's Hall of Fame in 1991, the same year she was named Legislator of the Year by the National Republican Legislators Association. She was given the *Good Housekeeping* Award for Women in Government in 1999. In contrast to her predecessor, iron-fisted Speaker Vern Riffe, she reached across the isle and relaxed the rules to allow free debate and amendments. As a result, she saw adoption of many of the laws she introduced: income tax cuts, welfare, health care and campaign finance reforms, revised unemployment and workman's compensation rules, deregulation of utilities, and enforcement of crime control measures. She managed several Ohio campaigns for Republicans running for the offices of governor and president. Her last job was in Washington D.C. as second in charge of the Republican National Committee.

John Janney

John J. Janney was born in Goose Creek Meetinghouse, Pennsylvania in 1812 of Quaker parents. His father died when he was one month old. He attended a Friends and Day School in Alexandria. There, he developed a belief in the abolition of slaves. He came to Warren County, Ohio in 1833 and taught school, did surveying and worked in a village store. For three years, he served as a clerk in the General Assembly. For four years he was chief clerk for the Secretary of State. In 1851, he became Secretary of the Board of Control of the State Bank of Ohio. Other positions held were Assistant Postmaster of Columbus and Secretary and Treasurer of the Columbus & Hocking Valley Railroad. He advocated free schools and the inclusion of black students. He helped establish a public library in Springboro, the Atheneum Library and Reading Room in Columbus and the first Public Library in Columbus in 1872. He served as a member or director of the following: Columbus Board of Education, the State Penitentiary, Columbus Board of Health, City Council, Police Commissioners, State Horticultural Society, Prisoners' Aid Society, and the Board of State Charities. He also taught in the Sabbath School of the Ohio Penitentiary. He served as Chairman and Treasurer of the Whig and Republican Parties. He participated in the activities of the Friends Society in Ohio and Indiana. He gave generously of his time and expertise to Columbus.

John Kasich

John Kasich was born in Pennsylvania in 1952 and graduated from public high school in McKees Rocks, Pennsylvania in 1970. The family moved to Ohio where his father became a postal carrier in Westerville. He graduated from Ohio State University in 1974 with a major in political science. In 1975, he became an administrative assistant to Ohio State Senator Donald Lukens. In 1979, he was elected to the State Legislature as a Republican. His special interests were health, welfare, energy, refugees, taxation and finance. He was elected to the United States House of Representatives in 1982 where he served for eighteen years. He acquired financial expertise as Chairman of the House Budget Committee. In 1999, he carried out an exploratory move to run for president of the United States. He emphasized presiding over a balanced national budget. Tax reduction was the center piece of his candidacy. After retirement from Congress, he headed a conservative project called New Century and had his own Fox TV News program called "Heartland with John Kasich." He continues to have an active interest in Republican political matters.

James Poindexter

James Poindexter was born in Richmond, Virginia in 1819 of mixed heritage. His mother was part African-American and part Cherokee and his father was Caucasian. His father was a reporter for the *Richmond Examiner.* His mother died when he was young, and his education was limited. He was apprenticed to a barber and barbering became his lifelong vocation. After he married at age eighteen, he left the south and settled in Dublin, Ohio. He became a leader in the black community that centered in the Mount Vernon Avenue/Long Street district in Columbus. He preached at the Second Baptist Church, was active in the "underground railroad" and became a member of the new Republican political party. He succeeded in replacing an old segregated school with a non-segregated one. Only a few whites attended the new Loving School. In 1880, he was the first African-American to be elected to serve on the Columbus City Council. Another milestone was reached in 1884 when he became a member of the Columbus Board of Education. He served on other boards and commissions. His barbershop was a focal point for anyone interested in politics. He died in 1907. In 1937, the first public housing project in Columbus was dedicated to him. He was remembered also as a man of principle with Christian convictions.

James Rhodes

Fig. 83

James Rhodes (Fig. 83) was born in Coalton, Jackson County, Ohio in 1909. At the age of seven, his father died in a coal mining accident. The family moved to Springfield, Ohio, where James finished his education in local schools. He attended The Ohio State University but found it necessary to drop out due to financial considerations. He had become interested in politics and was elected to the Columbus Public School Board in 1937. He was appointed city auditor and was elected to a four-year term. In 1944, he resigned to become Mayor of Columbus; he was re-elected twice. He demonstrated political skill in managing a huge debt Columbus had accumulated. He gathered the leading businessmen into a Metropolitan Committee who persuaded the voters to pass a large bond issue. He became nationally known when he served as a U.S. representative to the Olympic Games held in London, England. His first political defeat came in his 1952 bid for the governorship. He began a ten-year tenure as State Auditor in 1953, performing his tasks well. During that time, he published three novels. In 1962, he was elected Republican governor and served two terms. He streamlined the state government and reduced its budget. Because of the state law limiting successive terms to two, he entered the business sector as a consultant. He reentered politics to serve two more terms as governor, 1974-1982. During this time he oversaw several foreign trade missions and worked hard to improve the business climate in the state. His motto was "Profit is not a dirty word." He strongly encouraged the establishment of technical schools. He supported Central State College, whose primary mission was to meet the educational needs of

African-American students. While cutting taxes and reducing the state payroll, he used bonds to pay for his state projects. His legacy was marred by the Kent State University anti-war riots in 1970 that resulted in the tragic deaths of four students after he called out the National Guard. After another stint in business, he was unsuccessful in his campaign for a fifth term. His sixteen years as governor is a record in Ohio. He died in 2001. He lay in state in the Statehouse Rotunda, only the fourth person to do so since Abraham Lincoln. An Ohio State University medical school building and a state office building are named for him. A life sized statute of him striding with briefcase in hand stands in front of the state office tower on Broad Street.

William Saxbe

William Saxbe was born in Mechanicsburg, Ohio in 1916. After attending local schools, he enlisted in the National Guard and served in World War II from 1940 to 1945. He was recalled to active duty during the Korean War (1951-1952). After returning to civilian life, he entered The Ohio State University where he subsequently received his undergraduate and law degrees. He served two terms in the Ohio House of Representatives beginning in 1947. Two terms as Attorney General of Ohio followed in 1957. In 1968, he was elected as a Republican United States Senator from Ohio. In 1973, he was appointed Attorney General of the United States, serving under Presidents Nixon and Ford. In 1975, he was appointed Ambassador to India. In 1977, he resumed his law and consulting practices in Columbus and Washington D.C. During his career, he belonged to many military, occupational and social clubs, and received many honors.

M. E. Sensenbrenner

M. E. (Jack) Sensenbrenner was born in Circleville where his father worked as a jeweler. Jack was in charge of a religious book store on the west side of Columbus when he decided to run for mayor in 1954. Prior to that, he had been a ditch digger, Fuller Brush salesman, police-beat reporter and Hollywood stuntman. He won the mayoralty election and became a well-recognized figure, always wearing a straw boater. He was the first Democratic Mayor in twenty-two years. During his fourteen years as chief magistrate of the city, he encouraged and witnessed the expansion of the city from forty to over two hundred square miles of land. His annexation policy was made possible by offering water and sewer services to unincorporated areas. This increase in size resulted in Columbus becoming the most populated city in the state. Sensenbrenner was flamboyant, indefatigable, and the city's greatest cheerleader. Columbus was named an *All American City* in 1954. Sensenbrenner died in 1991.

Notable Business Persons in Columbus

Gordon Battelle

Gordon Battelle was a tough, hard working, assertive, unrelenting competitor, who made few friends and a lot of enemies. He was a top rated metallurgist and made a sizeable fortune. He died in 1923 and willed most of his estate to establish the Battelle Memorial Institute for the encouragement of creative research, discoveries and inventions. His son, Gordon, was mild mannered and well liked. He bought ten acres on King Avenue, immediately adjacent to The Ohio State University. There, in 1929, he established the Battelle Metallurgical Institute. It became a pre-eminent independent research organization focusing on technology and solutions for government and private industry. It occasionally carries out its multibillion dollar contracts in conjunction with The Ohio State University, conveniently situated nearby. Battelle's twenty thousand scientists and workers are located in one hundred and thirty laboratories in seven countries (eleven in Columbus). During World War II, it was involved in the Manhattan Project. Battelle developed zerography which led to the product Xerox, the forerunner of copying machines. Battelle manages seven national laboratories ($3 billion in contracts) such as those at Livermore in California and Oak Ridge in Tennessee. The institute's gross receipts are $4 billion. Since 2003, the company has placed $220 million in an independent research fund to invest in technology areas such as health and life sciences, security, energy and environment. The company generously supports local community projects, a condition of Gordon Battelle's will.

Donald Borror

Donald A. Borror was born in Columbus in 1929. He grew up in Franklinton, attended public schools and graduated from West High School. He received his undergraduate degree from The Ohio State University in 1950 and a law degree from OSU in 1954. He married Joanne in 1952. He served in the United States Air Force as a Captain. His main interest turned out to be building homes which began in the 1950's. Two decades later, he founded the Borror Corporation, a mass producer of homes in Central Ohio. During an initial public stock offering in 1997, the corporate name was changed to Dominion Homes, and the business expanded into additional states. Borror turned CEO duties over to his son, Douglas G. Borror, in 1999, when he became Chairman Emeritus. He served on the boards of the Columbus Clippers, Riverside Methodist Hospital, Capitol South Urban Redevelopment Corporation, Columbus Parks and Recreation, Pontifical College Josephinum and the Columbus Chamber of Commerce. Among his awards and honors were "Builder of the Year" from the Building Industry of Central Ohio, the Junior Achievement Award from Central Ohio Business Hall of Fame and Columbus Public School's Hall of Fame Award. He gave generously of his time and fortune to business enterprises and charitable groups in Central Ohio, and through the Borror Family Foundation and the Columbus Foundation. He died in 2006 at age 77.

Samuel Prescott Bush

Samuel Prescott Bush, grandfather of President George Herbert Bush and great-grandfather of President George Walker Bush, was born in 1863 in New Jersey. He moved to Columbus in 1901 and became president of Buckeye Malleable Iron and Coupler Company. Before that, the company's name had been Murray-Hayden (1881), Buckeye Malleable (1886) and became Buckeye Steel Castings in 1903. The company became the world's largest manufacturer of steel couplers for railroad freight cars, castings for mass transportation and specialized equipment for industrial and mining concerns. The company became bankrupt in 2002 and was purchased by a group of veteran steel industrialists in 2004. It remains viable and produces an average of 60,000 couplings for freight cars per year. Samuel Prescott Bush was well educated, a graduate of Stevens Institute of Technology, a strong and active athlete, a founding member of the Scioto Country Club and very active in civic affairs and society in Columbus. He received an honorary degree from Stevens. He died in Columbus in 1948. His son, Prescott Sheldon Bush was born in Columbus and became a New York banker and a United States Senator from Connecticut (1952 to 1963). During his tenure, he was the tallest man in the Senate. He died in New York City in 1972.

David Deshler

David Deshler (Fig. 84) arrived in Columbus in 1817 at the age of twenty-five. He first worked as a carpenter out of his two-room house, built on a site near the northwest corner of Broad and High Streets which he purchased for one thousand dollars. Little did he realize the future value of the prestigiously located piece of real estate. David continued to buy downtown property and invested in local banks. His son, William, founded a bank on the corner lot (northwest Broad and High) and his grandson, John Green Deshler (Fig. 85), continued in the successful banking business.

Fig. 84

Fig. 85

William Deshler was highly skilled in finance and was an advisor to Secretary of Treasury, Salmon Chase, during the Civil War. He was also civic minded and a philanthropist. He helped secure the Columbus Barracks (later renamed Ft. Hayes) during the Civil War and was a founding partner of the Hocking Valley Railroad. He inspired converting East Broad Street into a boulevard. John Green Deshler built the Wyandotte Office Building, was president of the Deshler Bank and established an endowment that created the Columbus Metropolitan Library. In 1915, John G. Deshler tore down the bank and built the fine Deshler Hotel on the prime northwest corner location at Broad and High Streets. The hotel supported four hundred rooms and was beautifully equipped. When six hundred rooms were added to the hotel in the attached AIU skyscraper, connected with an enclosed walkway and Hall of Mirrors with pipe organ (small-scale replica of its name-sake in the Palace of Versailles, France), it became a convention center. It was renamed the Deshler-Wallick, when the hotel's general manager, L.C. Wallick, gained ownership. Unable to compete with suburban motels and hotels and unable to afford renovation, the hotel went into receivership and was secured by the Hilton Hotels, and in 1964 by Cole and renamed the Deshler-Cole. Its final owner, Fred Beasley, renamed it, yet, again as the Beasley-Deshler. It was razed in 1969 to make way for the twenty-six story One Columbus Building, a large office building.

John Galbreath

John Galbreath was born in Derby, Ohio, in 1897. As a youth, he worked on a farm. After attending local public schools, he graduated from Ohio University in Athens, Ohio in 1922. He worked his way through college by doing cafeteria duties. He was elected class president and business manager of the yearbook. After college, he formed his own real estate company in Columbus, Ohio. During the Great Depression, he bought up foreclosed companies and properties. He used the profits to build town sites, office buildings and residences. His company became international with offices in New York, London, and Hong Kong. Management-leasing became an important part of the business. In Columbus, he is credited with developing Nationwide Plaza, America Electric Power headquarters, Banc One Corporate Center, the Borden Building, the Rhodes State Office Tower, the Ohio Center, Hyatt Regency, the Columbia Gas building and the Capitol Square office-hotel complex. His company carried out major projects in the United States and abroad. Examples of these were: USX headquarters in Pittsburgh, Mobil Corp headquarters in Virginia, the Mead Corp headquarters in Dayton and the Goldman Sachs headquarters in New York. He was a director on the boards of several large companies and received many honors and several honorary degrees. His love of sports resulted in ownership of the Pittsburgh Pirates baseball team, Darby Dan farms near Columbus, Ohio and Lexington, Kentucky, and an animal reserve near Columbus that contains buffalo, zebra, deer, elk and antelope. He raised and bred thoroughbred race horses and hunted large wild game. His private Darby Dan race track is surrounded by a thirty-two stall training barn, twenty-one large barns with stalls, a large cattle barn, a breeding barn and a stallion barn. Thirty-nine houses are on the property including his formidable home. Two of his horses won the Kentucky Derby; Chateaugay in 1963 and Proud Clarion in 1967. His horse, Roberto, won the 1972 English Derby. Galbreath was a supporter of preserving and propagating wild life and conserving the environment. The Big Darby Creek runs through his property and is protected by being designated a national and state "Scenic Waterway." His farm is named after the creek and his son, Dan. John Galbreath died in 1988. Dan took over the reins of overseeing and expanding his business empire until his death in 1995. Since then John's granddaughter, Lizzane, has managed the businesses. In addition to being a civic leader in Columbus and Pittsburgh, John Galbreath gave generously to local charities and civic institutions.

Herbert Glimcher

Herbert Glimcher was born in 1930. At age 29. he founded a lumber and buildings supply company. His current company, devoted to building and managing shopping malls, commenced in 1994 with Herbert as Chairman and CEO. Their property interests range throughout the country but principally in the eastern half. Their prime development in Central Ohio is Polaris Fashion Mall. In 2005, his son, Michael assumed the role of CEO. Herbert Glimcher, has served on the boards of other companies, as well as of the Mount Carmel Health System, the Ohio State University Foundation, the Columbus Jewish Foundation and is a member of the International Council of Shopping Centers. He is on the Executive Committee of the National Association of Real Estate Investment Trusts.

Lincoln Goodale

Dr. Lincoln Goodale, one of the earliest physicians in Central Ohio, arrived in Franklinton in 1803. His father had been a Captain in the Revolutionary War and brought his son to Marietta from his birthplace in Massachusetts (1782). The father was captured by Indians and died in 1794 while a captive. Young Goodale earned his medical degree by serving an apprenticeship under a physician in Belpre, Ohio. After one year of practice in Franklinton, he gave up his profession and became a wealthy drug and general store owner. He lived on the second floor of his store as a bachelor. He acquired considerable land in Central Ohio. Later, as a wealthy merchant, he gifted forty acres of land to Columbus that became Goodale Park and Lake. His deed specified that admission to the fenced public park was to be free. During the Civil War, it was the site of the first army camp in Columbus (Camp Jackson). Later, White Cross Methodist Hospital (later to become Riverside Methodist Hospital located elsewhere today) was erected near the grounds. Development of the park did not begin until the 1870's. The park's artificial lake allowed swimming, boating and ice skating. It is still a city park today, containing a bronze bust of the founder. Dr. Goodale died in 1848 after a distinguished business career. His legacy includes many philanthropic projects and public service. He is buried in Green Lawn Cemetery.

Henry S. Hallwood

Henry Hallwood was born in England in 1848. He received his education in private schools. His first job was with his father who owned a commercial enterprise. This was followed by apprenticeships in several businesses. In 1874, he eloped and sailed to America. On a return trip, the couple reconciled with their parents, then he returned to West Virginia. He failed in the mining business. He came to Columbus and built sewers and other public work projects. He began an illustrious career making bricks. In the 1890's, his Ohio Paving Company produced thousands of bricks per day with the imprint of Hallwood on each brick. They were used throughout the eastern half of the country. Many of Hallwood's bricks are to be found in Columbus today. He acquired patents to make a cash register which competed with the National Cash Register Company. Eventually, he was forced to sell out to his competitor (NCR). The federal government brought an anti-trust suit against NCR who settled out of court by paying a stiff fine in 1913. Hallwood died in 1918 at age of eighty.

Petetiah Webster Huntington

Petetiah Webster Huntington was born in Norwich, Connecticut in 1837. His father was a banker. After spending two years at sea, he came to Columbus and became a messenger for the Ohio State Bank. He was befriended by banker, David Deshler. Petetiah set up his own bank in a building that had a castle-like appearance at the southwest corner of Broad and High Streets. He was well liked and enjoyed meeting and greeting customers which enhanced his business. As a frugal man, he made a habit of walking to city market for shopping and to and from his bank. He served on numerous civic boards and was treasurer of Greenlawn Cemetery for thirty-seven years. He was president of the Columbus Club. He retired in 1914, and his children from three wives took over his bank and businesses. Eventually, the Huntington Bank Center moved a few buildings south of the corner; it replaced the Neil House Hotel. The modern Huntington Bank with many branches in Ohio and surrounding states is the second largest financial institution (after Bank One) originating in Columbus. After its merger with Bowling Green-based Sky Bank in 2007, it became the third largest bank in Ohio and the twenty-fourth largest in the nation. The bank and its officers are leaders in the city and contribute substantially to civic cultural groups.

Edgar Waldo Ingram

Edgar Waldo "Billy" Ingram was born in Kansas in 1880. After finishing public schooling, he became a real estate and insurance agent. In 1921, he formed a partnership with Walter Anderson, a professional cook in Wichita, Kansas, who had developed a method of making hamburgers by cooking the meat with onions on a hot griddle. The product was so popular, that three additional hamburger stands were opened. The company was incorporated as the White Castle System of Eating Houses. During the next few years, the expansion of restaurants spread to twelve major cities in the eastern part of the country. Ingram bought out his partner in 1933 and moved the headquarters to Columbus, Ohio, a more central location. The use of paper hats for employees resulted in the formation of a corporate subsidiary, the Paperlynen Company. Another notable feature of the hamburger chain was the building used for their five-stool outlets. An employee designed a small, movable, steel-framed structure enclosed in porcelain enamel panels. The buildings were modeled after the Old Water Tower in Chicago, and the distinctive design has been maintained to this day. Another subsidiary was incorporated to construct the buildings, the Porcelain Steel Building Company. The company pioneered the newspaper coupon, good for a carry-out order of five hamburgers for ten cents. Their marketing ploy also made use of coupons designed as score pads for bridge, golf and bowling on which all of their locations were listed. A company employee also introduced their hamburger to housewives by giving tours and samples. A menu book was provided with suggestions of foods to serve with the burgers. As the company expanded, so did the size of their restaurants, and curb-side service (since replaced by drive-thru), and an expanded menu were introduced. Expansion has occurred abroad, and a new subsidiary, White Castle Distributing, was created to market its frozen, microwave burgers. Highly publicized were the orders for thousands of burgers for the Marines in Lebanon, as well as in Arizona and California in 1982. The founder's son with the same name, continued leading and expanding the company until he died in 1966. His grandson, Edgar W. Ingram, III currently is CEO of the family-owned four hundred restaurants and subsidiaries. All Ingrams have been civic leaders, and the family has contributed generously to charities and educational institutions through the Ingram-White Castle Foundation; its initial funding of $11 million has increased three-fold.

Joseph Jeffrey

Joseph Jeffrey was born in Clarksville, Ohio, in Clinton County in 1836. He grew up and received a basic education in St. Mary's, Ohio. Jeffrey arrived in Columbus in 1858, age twenty-two. He worked as a bank clerk and for a carpet company before joining the Lechner Mining Company. Lechner eventually became the Jeffrey Mining Company with thousands of employees under the management of Jeffrey as the principal owner. Francis Lechner was the genius of the group and developed a machine that could dig coal efficiently and with much saving in labor. There would be a demand for coal as a fuel for many years. Francis Sessions was a banker who handled the financing for the new enterprise. The company succeeded and became one of the world's largest manufacturers of heavy coal mining machinery. In the early 1980's, the number of employees reached 4,500. Ownership was passed to Joseph's son and remained in the family long after the elder Jeffrey's death in 1928. The family was prominent in local politics and society. In 1961, a portion of the company moved into a new plant in Woodruff, South Carolina where its size reduction and feeder businesses were settled. The Carolina business was acquired by Jeffrey Specialty Equipment Corporation in 1999. Meanwhile, the original sprawling North Fourth Street enterprise was sold to Dresser Industries in 1974, and its headquarters moved to Houston, Texas. After the mining company was sold to Penn Crusher in the 1990's, the Columbus operation closed.

Today, a new large building on the former site of Jeffrey's on East First Avenue is the home of the Ohio State Library. Immediately south of the library, within the old rundown Italian Village district, a reclamation project called Jeffrey Place is being built to provide eleven hundred mixed priced residences and small businesses, supported by local and federal government money. Its forty-one acres is next to major fiber optic lines that course along rundown railroad tracks, offering high-speed internet access. The new community will contain four acres of parks and greenspace and a sixteen square feet Fitness Center with a rooftop pool and sky deck. Local residents will hold automatic membership in the Center.

Alfred Kelley

Fig. 86

Alfred Kelley, state legislator from Cleveland, was the chief promoter of the Ohio canals in the 1820's and 1830's. Governors Thomas Worthington and Ethan Allan Brown also gave considerable support to canal development. Kelley built a magnificent mansion and became the foremost politician in Columbus, his adopted home. He gave generously of his time and money for state projects, especially canals and railroads. He was a thin, austere, energetic, brilliant and honest public servant. He closely supervised public expenditures and did on-site inspections of projects. He drove hard bargains that made it easy for him to be disliked. In the Panic of 1837, he pledged his own home as collateral for state loans, saving the canal system. When the railroads came to Ohio, Kelley was one of the first to invest in their companies. He is considered "Father of the Banking System in Ohio." His mansion, four blocks east of the statehouse, built in the Greek Revival style, was the scene of numerous gay parties. It was dismantled in 1963 and the stone pieces saved in such a manner that the mansion could be reassembled in the future.

John H. McConnell

John H. McConnell was born in Pughtown, West Virginia in 1923. His father was a steel worker, and John's first job was working for Weirton Steel Company. He served in the navy during World War II. He graduated from Michigan State University with a degree in Business Administration, making good use of his GI Bill benefits and a football scholarship. Following college, he became a salesman for Weirton Steel. He took out a loan on his car, bought his first load of steel and started Worthington Steel Company in 1955. The company has been exceedingly successful under the leadership of the founder and son, John P. McConnell, the current CEO. The founder has enjoyed many awards, such as Outstanding Executive (*Financial World*), the Horatio Alger Award, the Ohio Governor's Award, Junior Achievement Business Hall of Fame and the Marco Polo Award from the government of China for fostering better international relations. The company has been honored also with "Most Admired Company" in the metal industry in 2000 and 2004, and One of Thirty Best Performing Steel Companies. Employee satisfaction is high with many benefits. McConnell was a sports enthusiast and was chief investor in a national hockey team, the Columbus Blue Jackets, and in a national soccer team, the Columbus Crew. Each team has a new arena in which McConnell was the chief benefactor. Formerly, he was part owner of the Pittsburgh Pirates baseball team. Mr. McConnell gave generously to Columbus civic projects. His prime gift of seven and one-half million dollars allowed the McConnell Heart/Health Center to be established in conjunction with Riverside Hospital. He donated one million dollars to the Worthington Arts Council for renovation of a building on the Thomas Worthington High School campus. It will be named the Peggy R. McConnell Arts Center in memory of his wife. McConnell retired from the positions of CEO and Chairman of the Board in favor of his son, John P. McConnell. John H. McConnell died in 2008.

John G., Jane and John B. McCoy

John G. McCoy, a second generation banker, was the driving force who started the acquisitions that turned the third largest bank in Columbus, City National, into a national giant, Bank One (1970). He introduced such innovations as using celebrities such as Phyllis Diller to advertise banking products, keeping decision-making local at acquired banks, acquiring the first franchise outside of California for what is today's Visa credit card, establishing the first drive-through branch in the Midwest and installing the first domestically manufactured ATM machine. He pioneered work with debit cards and home banking. Bank One was the first Ohio bank to expand beyond the state's borders. In 2006, John G. McCoy, age ninety-three, received the inaugural Pioneer in Banking award from the Ohio Bankers League. His son, John B. McCoy, was born in Columbus in 1944. He was well educated, attending the Columbus Academy where he was active in athletics and was class president. He graduated from Williams College in 1965 with a major in history. He received his M.B.A. in finance from Stanford University Graduate School of Business where his father had received a similar degree. He served in the U.S. Air Force in the 1960's before joining the family banking business in 1970. He rotated through various departments, and became president of Bank One in 1977. Upon his father's retirement in 1984, he assumed the position of CEO of the bank. In 1987, he became chairman and CEO of Banc One Corporation. In 1998, the corporation merged with First Chicago Bank and John B. moved to Chicago as the CEO. He resigned a year later. In 2004, Bank One merged with J.P. Morgan Chase bank of New York, a $1.2 trillion company, and the Bank One name was replaced by Chase. The McCoys have been very active in Columbus civic affairs and have been on many local and national company boards. Some corporate boards on which they have served are: Cardinal Health, Battelle Institute, SBC, Onex, ChoicePoint, Corrillion, General Bankwidth, Freddie Mac and InsLogic. John B. served on the advisory council of the Federal Reserve System. The McCoy family endowed Kenyon College with $1.5 million for a Distinguished Professorship. John B. had been a member of that college board for twenty-five years. He holds several honorary degrees including one from The Ohio State University. Among the local philanthropies of the McCoy family are the donation of $3 million to Children's Hospital in 2006 to subsidize care for needy children and the Jane T. McCoy and John B. McCoy Chair in Cancer Research Fund with preference for lymphoma research. Jane McCoy is an emeritus member of the James Cancer Hospital and Solove Research Institute Foundation Board, and was instrumental in the growth of LeaderSpark from a local youth leadership development organization into a national entity.

William and Hannah Neil

William and Hannah Neil (Figs. 87-88) had a strong influence on Columbus during its early years. In 1818, William Neil, born in Kentucky, came to Urbana, where he worked as a farmer, stonemason and banker. His bank in Urbana failed. William Neil, decided to try his fortune in Columbus, the new center of state government. He bought a lot and built a cabin at the northeast corner Gay and Front

Fig. 87

Fig. 88

Streets. His cabin served as a tavern and hostelry. He built a keelboat to carry products to New Orleans. This business venture failed, leaving him heavily in debt. He returned to Columbus and commenced work as a bank teller. The first financial institution in Columbus was called the Franklin Bank (1816) and its future was quite uncertain. Neil left the banking business to return to being a hotel proprietor. He also developed stage lines in Ohio and neighboring states. His first stagecoaches, owned with Peter Zinn, ran between Columbus and Circleville and Granville. In the process of expanding his business he bought another stagecoach company that included a line between Wheeling, West Virginia and Pittsburgh, Pennsylvania. Soon, he controlled most of the stagecoach business in Ohio. At the height of his business activities, seventy coaches passed through Columbus weekly. He was known to be a tough and ruthless businessman. Locally, he was called "Billy Neil, the Stagecoach King." He eventually sold his stagecoach lines to Kansas entrepreneurs. He owned considerable land in and around Columbus including three hundred acres purchased from Joseph Vance, a few miles north of downtown Columbus where Neil built a substantial home. This property eventually became the site of The Ohio State University. The country lane to his home became Neil Avenue that still traverses the campus. Neil's second inn and tavern, a two-story log structure on South High Street was rebuilt in 1839 as an upscale hotel, with two grand staircases, a ballroom, a long bar and shops facing High Street and the statehouse. Its prime location soon made it the center of political activity and social life, shared later with the Deshler Hotel. William McKinley lived in the Neil House Hotel a portion of the time he was governor. Not a sedentary creature, Neil turned the hotel management over to his children and wife. On national election night in 1860, many politicians were gathered in the Neil House to celebrate and watch the results as relayed by telegraph. A fire started in the servant's quarters and spread rapidly and consumed the entire hotel. Fortunately, no life was lost, but the futility of fighting the fire with a bucket brigade stimulated the securing of better fire fighting equipment and the building of fire houses. The Neils rebuilt a more elaborate hotel in the mid-1860s on the old High Street site. This in turn was replaced by a third new hotel in 1924. The last of the Neil Houses was demolished in the 1980's to make way for the Huntington Center. William Neil died in 1870. He was the foremost business person in early Columbus.

Neil's wife, Hannah Schwig Neil, was socially active and community service oriented. She was a founder of the Female Benevolent Society, and her Hannah

Neil Mission was a haven for destitute women and children in Columbus. She helped distribute food and clothing to the poor. She died in 1868, and her funeral attracted crowds of the poor who had benefited from her charitable acts. The Hannah Neil Mission and the Columbus Female Benevolent Society are still active today, a testament to her well deserved legacy.

Eddie Rickenbacker

Fig. 89

Eddie Rickenbacker (Fig. 89) was born in Columbus, Ohio in 1890. His father died when he was sixteen, after which Eddie helped support the family. He worked in a variety of industrial jobs including the Columbus Buggy Company and automobile manufacturing. He enhanced his meager education with correspondence courses in engineering. He practiced driving at the Columbus Driving Park and became a top rated race-car driver. In World War I, he was General John Pershing's chauffer. He entered the 94th Aero Pursuit Squadron (the name of a Columbus restaurant today), where he learned to fly. Soon he became an ace; he shot down twenty-six German planes and seven, single handedly. For this he was awarded the Medal of Honor, Distinguished Service Cross, Croix de Guerre and Legion of Honor. After the war, he organized and ran his own auto company which failed. For twenty years, he owned the Indianapolis Speedway. Employment with General Motors and American Airways followed. In 1938, he became president of Eastern Airlines, a very successful company. In 1940, like Charles Lindbergh, he opposed our entry into World War II, but supported his government when it entered the conflict. During World War II, he traveled for the U.S. Government, and in 1942, on a secret mission for General Douglas MacArthur, he crashed in the Pacific Ocean. He and six others survived for twenty-three days on small rafts. He credits his wife with saving his life by relentlessly insisting that the air force continue the search for him. He received many awards, medals and honorary degrees. He was an arch-conservative, speaking and writing his views. He died in 1973 and was buried in Green Lawn Cemetery. His boyhood home on Livingston Avenue is a National Historic Landmark.

Joseph Ridgway

In 1822, Joseph Ridgway, a Quaker and a bachelor, constructed an iron foundry and small factory on the bank of the Scioto River near downtown Columbus. Its principal product was Jethro Wood's Patent Plow. Horses, pulling a wheel, were used to provide power. The Ridgway plows were distributed in a fifty-mile radius.

Ridgway became wealthy, and in 1830, his nephew succeeded him as manager and converted the plant to steam power. Employment at the plant peaked with fifty-five laborers. The business was turned over to Peter Hayden in 1880 upon the death of Ridgway. Hayden and his sons expanded the business to include other enterprises including leather goods. He used penitentiary inmates as employees, a common practice at that time. Before Ridgway died, he hunted up creditors or their heirs who had loaned him money for an earlier business that failed and paid them his debts plus interest.

A competitor of Ridgway in the iron foundry and steel manufacturing business, John Gill, was very successful in selling improved plows, stoves and machines. Other early businessmen made cast iron products for the booming agriculture industry in the state. Some made furniture, woolen cloth, tubs, pails, saws, glass products, shoes and buggies. Eventually, Columbus had four steel mills, all on the small size. The Schoedinger Funeral Company of today started out as a furniture maker during this era.

Irving Schottenstein

Irving Schottenstein was born in Columbus, Ohio in 1929, of Jewish Lithuanian heritage. He, with cousin, Melvin Schottenstein, founded M/I Homes in 1976. They built upscale homes in Columbus and other sites in Eastern United States. In 2005, the company ranked 20th in the number of homes built in the nation. Irving was a leader in the Jewish community and participated in and gave generously to educational and charitable causes. He was a friend and supporter of the Fisher College of Business on The Ohio State University campus. The M/I Homes Foundation donates large sums of money to recruit graduate students for the college. Irving Schottenstein received numerous awards and honors in recognition of his civic involvement and philanthropy. He died at age seventy-five in 2004. The Dean of the OSU Business School, Joseph Alutto, when notified of his death stated, "Irving was a tremendous example of community leadership-his commitment to integrity and honesty touched many lives."

Jerome Schottenstein

Jerome Schottenstein was born in Columbus, Ohio in 1932. His father was a son of a Lithuanian Jewish immigrant (Ephraim L. Schottenstein) and owner of a retail discount store. Young Schottenstein attended South High School in Columbus. A boyhood friend said, "As a teenager, he was earthy and never changed." He traveled to New York to buy merchandise for the family store. His brothers and a sister worked in the store. He worked up to executive responsibilities and when his father died, became chief executive of what had become a large liquidation, retail department store business. Jerome was admired for his "computer-like" mind. He was known to close a large deal on the spur of the moment with a handshake. Jerome Schottenstein was thought to be one of the three or four wealthiest persons in central Ohio. He was quick to step in and help out civic entities threatened with extinction. He was instrumental in saving the Ohio Theater. He made significant contributions to Ohio State University Hospitals, Children's Hospital, Columbus Torah Academy, the Wexner Heritage House, the Leo Yassenoff Jewish Center, the United Negro College Fund, Catholic Charities, and the United States Holocaust Memorial Museum. He was active in his Temple and Yeshiva University. Many other charities and educational institutions received his substantial gifts. He died in 1992, leaving a legacy of hard work, keen business acumen and civic generosity. He may be remembered best for the creation, in his memory, of the Jerome Schottenstein Athletic Center with its Value City Arena on the Ohio State University campus. It was initiated with a gift of $12 million from the Schottenstein Foundation in 1996. He received many awards and was given an honorary degree by Yeshiva University. His son, Jay, succeeded Jerome as Chairman and CEO of the Jerome Schottenstein family business enterprises.

Francis Sessions

Francis Charles Sessions was born in Wilbraham, Massachusetts in 1820. His ancestor, Alexander Sessions was a deputy governor of the Massachusetts Bay Company, arriving in America in 1630. His father was an officer in the Revolutionary War. Francis's father died when the son was two years old, and Francis was raised by his uncle. He worked on the family farm and attended local schools, graduating at age sixteen. He came to Columbus to seek his fortune in 1840. After an apprenticeship in a dry goods store, he opened his own store with a partner, Ellis, Sessions & Co. His wife, Mary, was the daughter of Orange Johnson, a prominent entrepreneur in Worthington in 1847. He closed his store after nine years and began dealing in wool. During the Civil War, he was secretary of the Columbus branch of the U.S. Sanitary Commission and attended the sick and wounded in the western sector of the war. Through his efforts after the war, a soldier's home was opened in Columbus. Upon reentering business, he became president of the Commercial National Bank of Columbus and worked in that capacity until his death. He was active in religious (Congregational) and educational activities. He served as a trustee of Marietta, Oberlin and Columbus medical colleges and the state institutions for the blind, deaf and dumb. His name endures in the history of banking in Columbus. In 1929, his Commercial National Bank merged with City National Bank that eventually became Bank One and now JP Morgan Chase.

Robert Sheldon

Robert Emmet Sheldon was born in Tiffin, Ohio in 1845. His parents moved to Columbus where he spent most of his formative years. He attended public schools until age 12. After a stint as clerk in a grocery store, he entered the dry goods business. In order to improve his business prospects, he took educational lessons from a friend. During the American Civil War, he enlisted for 100 days and served in the siege of Petersburg, Virginia. He survived his enlistment period, and returned to his dry goods business in Columbus. His marriage to Mary Butler in 1869 resulted in seven children. He soon became a partner in the Miller, Green and Joyce dry goods store. In 1884, he joined two partners to form the store, Miles, Bancroft and Sheldon, which subsequently became Sheldon Dry Goods in 1901. It developed into a large Midwest company with seventy-five employees serving Ohio, Indiana and West Virginia. His interests widened, and he became President of the Columbus Railway Company, the principal city street car line. He was a founder of the Columbus Board of Trade, and later became its president in 1888. When he was not busy serving on boards of other companies, he pursued his favorite leisure sport of fishing in rivers, lakes and two oceans. His integrity, business acumen and civic participation made him one of the most admired men in the capital city. In 1894, his daughter, Flora, married recently arrived Samuel Prescott Bush, an engineer, who advanced to become president of Buckeye Steel Castings. A man of all sports, he was one of the founders of Scioto Golf and Country Club. The Bushes became the grandparents and great-grandparents of the forty-first and forty-third presidents of the nation.

Dave Thomas

Fig. 90

Dave Thomas (Fig. 90) was born in Atlantic City in 1932. He was adopted when he was six weeks old by Rex and Auleva Thomas. Auleva died when Dave was five and his adoptive father moved from state to state seeking work. His grandmother, Minnie Sinclair in Michigan taught him the right things to do as well as lessons about quality and service. At age twelve, he worked as a counterman in a Knoxville, Tennessee restaurant, and, at age fifteen, he worked at the Hobby Restaurant in Ft. Wayne, Indiana. At that time, he dropped out of school. He said later, it was his greatest mistake. Forty five years later he went back to school in Ft. Lauderdale, Florida, and received a GED certificate from Coconut Creek High School. His graduating class in 1993 named him "Most Likely To Succeed." In 1991, he published his autobiography, *Dave's Way,* and later, *Well Done* and *Franchising for Dummies.* In 1990, President George H. Bush asked him to head an initiative on adoption. He appealed to all CEO's of large companies and governors of states to make adoption benefits available to their employees. In 1997, President Clinton signed the Adoption and Safe Families Act, speeding up the adoption process and offering incentives and accountability. In 1996, he established the Dave Thomas Foundation for Adoption. The U.S. Postal Service issued a 33-cent Adoption Postage Stamp in recognition of his efforts. He gave large sums of money to support Children's Hospital in Columbus, creating a Research Professorship, a Primary Care Center and a Clinical Laboratory. He gave two million dollars to establish an outpatient chemotherapy center at Ohio State University Hospitals. He supported a Children's Home in Ft. Lauderdale, Florida, where he had retired. He gave extensively to other charities, medical centers and educational institutions. He supported the Wellington School, a private school in Columbus. After a lengthy bout with cancer, he died in 2002 in Florida at age sixty-nine. His business had expanded to over six thousand fast food restaurants in the United States and Canada.

Robert Walter

Robert Walter was born in Columbus in 1945. His father was a food broker. Young Walter was an excellent student and graduated from Ohio State University in 1967 with a B.S. degree-*summa cum laude* (majored in mechanical engineering). He immediately obtained a job with North American Rockwell Corporation in Columbus but left after six months, disillusioned by the management style and the huge size and complexity of the organization. Fortified with an M.B.A. from Harvard Business School in 1970, he started his own company, Cardinal Foods in 1971. The company acquired drug and health care businesses, sharply turning the company's focus to them. The newly named Cardinal Health became hugely successful. Walter has received many honors, including an honorary degree from Ohio University in 1997 and a Christopher Award. He stepped down from the CEO position in 2006 to devote more time to his foundation that has gifted sizeable funds to Columbus institutions and charities. He is a member of the board of several large companies.

Leslie Wexner

Leslie Wexner was born in Dayton, Ohio in 1937. After several moves, his parents opened a ladies clothing store in Columbus, Ohio. The store was named Leslie's after their son who worked in the store. The business failed. After attending local schools, Wexner graduated from Ohio State University with honors, majoring in business administration. He started law school but left to enter business. Borrowing $5,000 from an aunt and an equal loan from a bank in 1963, he started his own women's sportswear store which he named "The Limited." He added stores, and by 1969 he had five. Hard work and long hours gave him a stomach ulcer. Through stock sales, his chain rose to one hundred stores by 1976. In 1978, he opened a huge distribution center in Columbus. He began acquiring other outlets in 1982, including Victoria's Secret, Lane Bryant, Bath & Body, Intimate Brands, Express, Lerner New York, Mast Industries, Henri Bendel and White Barn Candle Company. Eventually, Wexner owned over four thousand outlets with 100,000 employees. He sold faltering stores and spun off others. In 2002, *Fortune* magazine rated him the Most Admired Specialty Retailer. He understood leverage; for example, instead of making $10,000 from one store, why not make $100,000 from ten stores. The companies' revenues reached $8.5 billion in 2002, making him one of the wealthiest men in the world. After gathering venture capitalists as partners, he opened a mammoth shopping center in Columbus called Easton Town Center. He gave money to the state to construct service roads as well as a special freeway exit to the Center. In 2007, Limited Brands sold most of the non-profitable outlets but retained the profitable Victoria's Secret, Bath & Body Works, C. O Bigelow, White Barn Candle, Henri Bendel and La Senza. Wexner's wealth allowed him to donate sizeable gifts to many educational institutions, hospitals and civic projects in Columbus. They include the Wexner Center for the Arts at Ohio State University, the Wexner Heritage House for senior citizens, the Players Theater, the Cancer Society, Buckeye Boys Ranch, BalletMet, the Central Ohio Diabetes Association, B'nai B'rith Hillel Foundation, Wexner Institute for Pediatric Research, COSI, the Columbus Foundation and educational and civic facilities in New Albany, where he maintains a home and estate. Many charitable groups such as United Way have benefited from his generosity. Many of his gifts have been distributed by the Wexner Foundation, created and funded by him for that purpose. He is on the board of several large companies and universities. He works closely with other civic leaders of Columbus. He has received many honors including honorary degrees. He is a Zionist and contributes heavily to the cause of an Israel State. His wife, Abigail, an attorney, works closely with him in distributing his wealth. She is considered one of the most effective service-givers, active in several civic organizations. She has completed two terms as a member and chairperson of the board of the Columbus Foundation.

John W. Wolfe II and Ancestry

In 1888, Robert F. Wolfe and brother, Harry Wolfe, started the Wolfe Brothers Shoe Company. They entered newspaper publishing by buying the *Ohio State Journal* in 1903. Two years later, they acquired the *Columbus Dispatch* with Robert F. Wolfe as the publisher of both papers until his death in 1927. Harry Wolfe continued the publishing and acquired banking business until he died in 1946. Robert's son, Edgar T. Wolfe, Sr., began work for the *Ohio State Journal* in 1919 and subsequently became co-publisher of both newspapers. Edgar promoted civic projects such as the airport, hospitals and charities. He and his relatives continued the family banking business also. He died in 1957. Edgar's son, John W. Wolfe, began his career with the Ohio National Bank in 1948. He became vice-president of BancOhio Corp in 1957 and chairman of the Dispatch Printing Company, parent of the *Columbus Dispatch* in 1975. Radio, television and media networks became part of the family enterprises (WBNS-TV, ONN-TV, WBNS-AM/FM, in Columbus; and, WTHR-TV and SkyTrak Weather in Indianapolis). John W. Wolfe was a community leader, actively involved in the direction and funding of The Ohio State University Health Center, Children's Hospital, Shepard Hills Hospital in Newark, the Columbus Airport, the Columbus Zoo, a Chinese Art Exhibit, Ameriflora and the family's foundations. He died in 1994, and John F. Wolfe II, son of Preston Wolfe and nephew of John W. Wolfe, became chairman of the printing company and, currently, is publisher of the *Columbus Dispatch*. John F. Wolfe II lives in Columbus, Ohio where he was born and educated. He is a graduate of Washington and Lee University (1965 with degree in Commerce), and is descendant of a family of successful newspaper publishers, active civic leaders and generous philanthropists in the Columbus community. Mr. John F. Wolfe II serves on numerous committees and boards and has received many honors and awards for his civic involvement. Nationally, he was Chairman in 1980 of the National Alliance of Businessmen, received the 1981 Distinguished Service Award from the Society of Professional Journalists, was inducted into the American Academy of Achievement in 1987, and received the 1993 Chamber of Commerce Columbus Award.

The Wolfe family has established four permanently endowed destinations: Children's Hospital, COSI, the McConnell Heart Health Center, and the Columbus Foundation. Ohio State University Hospitals has been the recipient of large grants. Annually, the Dispatch Charities collects money from a one-day newspaper sale and auction to provide clothing for needy children. Many other worthy causes are the beneficiaries of the Wolfe family philanthropies.

Chapter 21

Current Large Columbus Companies

Abercrombie & Fitch

Abercrombie & Fitch, with over nine hundred stores featuring clothing for youth, is headquartered in New Albany. It is one the country's largest clothing retailers, catering to the thirty and younger age group. The company is organized into four demographic divisions named Hollister, Ruehl, A and B stores. A fifth division was scheduled to open in 2007. The company penetrated the Canadian market successfully and is now opening a large store in London, England. Chairman Michael Jeffries is considered the creative leader of the company.

American Telephone and Telegraphy Company (AT & T)

The principal telephone company in Columbus has had a checkered and somewhat confusing past. It all started with Alexander Graham Bell's invention of the telephone in 1876 and his organizing of the Bell Telephone Company in 1877. In 1885, AT&T became a subsidiary of Bell. The table was turned in 1899, when AT&T became the parent company and held multiple Bell subsidiaries. Ohio Bell was the prime supplier of telephone service in Columbus from 1922 to 1984, when the federal courts forced AT&T to divest its self of the Bell companies. In 1993, Ohio Bell became a part of Ameritech and, in 1999, Ameritech was taken over by Southwestern Bell Company, making it the largest phone company in the nation. In 2002, AT&T reentered the competition and acquired SBC, where we stand today. AT&T is the largest supplier of long distance and local phone service. However, unlike 1984, AT&T has a host of competitors in providing telephone service, including wireless cellular type phones. The local company has several hundred employees.

American Electric Power (AEP)

Columbus has received virtually all of its electric power from AEP since 1980 when it acquired Columbus and Southern Ohio Electric Company. As one of the nation's largest electric companies, AEP started in 1906 as American Gas and Electric Company in New York state, where it was formed from a utility holding company originating in 1899. In its early days it also provided water, steam and ice. Over the years, it has acquired many smaller electric companies. Today, it services portions of Pennsylvania, West Virginia, Kentucky, Tennessee, Oklahoma, Arkansas, Louisiana, Texas, Michigan, Indiana, Illinois and Ohio. Its headquarters was moved from New York to Columbus in 1983 where AEP built a thirty-one story office structure at 1 Riverside Plaza, one of the tallest buildings in Columbus. In 1999, the company merged with Central and South West Corporation of Dallas, Texas. By 2000, it had $122.5 billion in revenues, sales of 200 million megawatts—hours, $35 billion in assets and nearly nine million customers.

Anderson Concrete

W.E. Anderson and sons began a family business of hauling gravel and stones in 1921. In the 1930's they added the concrete business aided by the development of the chain-driven agitator made by Blaw-Knox and drum mixers made by Jaeger, both Columbus companies. Ready mix concrete became available to customers in the 1940's. Today, the familiar orange colored cement trucks of the Anderson Concrete Corporation supply the largest builders in Central Ohio. The company has a fleet of over eighty mixer trucks which operate from a dozen stations and a work force of two hundred employees. The company also makes asphalt for highways.

Advanced Drainage Systems (ADS)

ADS was founded in 1966, as a privately owned manufacturer of corrugated high density polyethylene pipes. It employs thirty-eight hundred workers in forty-one factories. Ohio locations, employing seven hundred workers, are in Findlay, London, Napoleon, New Miami and Wooster. It has one hundred employees working in its headquarters at 4640 Trueman Boulevard in Hilliard, Ohio. Annual sales are over $1.2 billion. Its products are used for residential and commercial buildings, athletic fields and highway projects. A 2005 merger with its main competitor, Hancor in Findlay, Ohio made ADS number one in its industry. This position may be greatly enhanced by a 2006 federal ruling that required that corrugated polyethylene pipes must be considered as well as concrete for highway use when federal money is used.

Big Bear Supermarket (now defunct)

Wayne E. Brown opened the first self-service supermarket in Columbus on West Lane Avenue in 1933, one of the first of its kind in the country. Before that, the market site had been a dance hall, roller-skating rink, a ring for horse shows and a polo field. A second Big Bear store was started on East Main Street with free transportation for customers provided initially. In 1937, shopping carts and a motorized cashier counter were introduced. By 1947, there were eleven stores in the chain, and a large warehouse on West Goodale Boulevard in Grandview Heights. In 1948, the company formed Topco Associates to produce private labels such as Food Club and Top Frost. Hart Stores, which had operated in the basements of some of the stores, was purchased in 1954. In the following year, their largest supermarket was opened in Graceland. The founder died in 1976. Penn Traffic Company purchased all sixty-six Big Bear stores in 1989. The Hart stores were closed in 1995, and the central headquarters was moved from Grandview Heights to Syracuse, New York. Penn Traffic declared bankruptcy in 1999, and, by 2003, all Big Bear stores were sold to competitors or were closed. Thus ended a unique supermarket saga in Columbus.

Big Lots

Big Lots is a Fortune 500 retail department company with over $4 billion in annual revenue. Its primary focus is selling closeout and overstock merchandise. Its headquarters is at 300 Phillipi Road in Columbus where it was founded by Sol Shenk as Consolidated Stores in 1967. Its first closeout store was called Odd Lots. In 1983, Consolidated was purchased by Revco Drug Stores. In 1985, Consolidated became independent and started trading on the American Stock Exchange. In 1985, the first Big Lots (name of some of its holdings) store opened, and in the following year the company commenced trading on the New York Stock Exchange. The company acquired Toy Liquidators in 1994, and eighty-two stores were added. The company purchased KB Toys in 1996 but sold both toy liquidators to private equity shops in 2000. In 2001, the company began a conversion of all store names to Big Lots. Hundreds of stores were added to a peak of 1,400 in forty-seven states, including over a dozen in Central Ohio. Currently, the expansion has reversed. For a number of years, foodstuffs have been offered, replenished on a continual basis. Obviously, the items of merchandise vary greatly from day to day.

George Byers Automotive Company

The George Byers family began its involvement in Columbus transportation business in 1898 when the family moved from Chillicothe and opened a livery stable. The shift to selling automobiles occurred in 1918 when Geo. Byers Sons was incorporated as a dealership. They became the DeSoto-Plymouth-Dodge representative, selling cars and auto parts in Columbus as well as in twenty-three Central Ohio counties and, by 1940, in parts of Indiana and Kentucky. The General

Motors line was added in 1934, and, by 1955, Byers became GM's second largest truck sales and service franchise in the country. At that time, the Hertz rental agency was added. The company diversified into real estate, financial institutions, parking garages and motels. In the 1970's, the sales, parts and service for the Subaru automobile in four states was acquired. The dealership for Volvo and Triumph followed. The company has remained a family business with hundreds of employees and multi-millions in revenue. The Byers family has been a strong supporter of civic projects.

Cardinal Health

Robert Walter started his own company, Cardinal Foods, in 1971. Later, his emphasis changed to the health sector, and the company became Cardinal Health in 1994. The company was highly successful, and became a leader in pharmaceutical and surgical supplies distribution and health care. The sales in 2005 were nearly seventy-five billion dollars. Fifty-five thousand employees work in thirty facilities in nineteen countries. The company, which is headquartered at 7000 Cardinal Place in Dublin, Ohio is the largest employer in central Ohio. Walter has been described as highly competitive and a superb deal maker, many of which were acquisitions of other companies. Cardinal Health ranked seventeenth among Fortune 500 companies in 2004, and was rated number one in the Most Admired Company category. An accounting problem brought the company's stock price down briefly in 2005. In 2007, the company divested its drug-technology segment for $3.3 billion.

Columbia Gas

The Columbia Gas and Electric Company was founded in Cincinnati in 1912 as a result of finding many natural gas wells in Ohio. The company was merged with the Ohio Fuel Corporation in 1926. They built one of the largest systems of pipelines in the nation, and, in 1964, Columbia Gas of Ohio was formed. It is investor-owned. In the 1970's, the headquarters moved to Front and Long Streets in Columbus. Seven distribution companies operate out of the headquarters. Half of its three million customers are in Ohio. The primary Ohio metropolitan areas served besides Columbus are Toledo, Parma, Mansfield and Springfield. Over fourteen million feet of pipe are buried under Columbus. Currently, customers are allowed by the state mandated Customer Choice program to choose their gas supplier and are billed by Columbia, the transmitter and service provider. In 2000, Columbia Gas of Ohio (CGO) became one of ten energy distribution companies held by NiSource, a holding company headquartered in Merrillville, Indiana. NiSource serves nine states from Indiana to Maine with natural gas and electric services.

Columbus Dispatch Publishing Company

Robert F. Wolfe and brother, Harry Wolfe, arrived in Columbus in 1888 and started the Wolfe Brothers Shoe Company. In 1903, they bought the *Ohio State Journal*. They acquired the *Columbus Dispatch* in 1905 with Robert F. Wolfe as the publisher of both papers until his death in 1927. Harry Wolfe continued publishing the newspapers and acquired banking business until he died in 1946. Robert's son, Edgar T. Wolfe, Sr., began work for the *Ohio State Journal* in 1919 and became co-publisher of both newspapers later. He died in 1957. Edgar's son, John W. Wolfe, became chairman of the Dispatch Printing Company, parent of the *Columbus Dispatch,* in 1975. He died in 1994, and was succeeded by John F. Wolfe II. The *Columbus Dispatch*, long politically conservative in its editorial policy, changed with the last publisher. It is now more balanced politically and editorially often taking a reform and progressive posture. This stance is more fitting and acceptable to the political spectrum as the only daily newspaper in Columbus. John F. Wolfe II, current publisher of the *Columbus Dispatch,* lives in Columbus, Ohio where he was born and educated. He is the son of Preston Wolfe and nephew of his predecessor, John W. Wolfe.

Columbus Life Insurance Company

The originating company was Columbus Mutual Life, founded by Channing Webster Brandon in 1906 and operated as a mutual stock company. It is now a member of the Western & Southern Financial Group (home office in Cincinnati) whose assets total $40 billion. Twenty-three hundred employees conduct its financial services in forty-eight states. Its two Columbus offices are in the north and west sectors. It enjoys AA+ ratings from four insurance-rating companies.

Columbus Steel Castings

Columbus Steel Castings Company is the world's largest single site steel foundry. It manufactures steel castings for freight and passenger railroad cars, locomotives, mining equipment, industrial magnets, earth moving equipment, steel rolling mills, bridges, oil platforms and other industries. The business started in 1881 as the Murray-Hayden Foundry, serving a growing agricultural based economy, located at the corner of Scioto and Broad Streets in Franklinton. As the railroad industry expanded, the enterprise began manufacturing iron couplers for the railroad cars and engines, and, in 1891, the business name changed to Buckeye Automatic Car Coupler Company. The establishment was associated closely with railroad baron E.H. Harriman, and for a period of time was controlled by Frank Rockefeller, brother of oil magnate John D. Rockefeller. In 1894, the plant's location moved to

Russell Street, near the present Goodale Park. Within a short time, the company's name changed again to Buckeye Malleable Iron and Coupler Company, and the industrial site moved in 1902 to ninety-acres on Parsons Avenue where it remains today. As the iron industry progressed to steel production, the corporation became known as Buckeye Steel Castings. From 1908 to 1928, Samuel Prescott Bush served as president of the business (See Samuel P. Bush in biographies). In 1967, Buckeye Steel Castings became the flagship company of Buckeye International, acquired by Worthington Industries in 1980. The ownership of the company became Key Equity Capital in a leveraged buyout in 1999. A weak freight rail market and economic recession caused the company to enter bankruptcy in 2002. In 2004, a group of veteran railroad foundrymen purchased the company with the leadership of Donald Malenick, retired president of Worthington Industries (twenty-six years). Considerable damaged and wornout infrastructure had to be replaced. With 100% equity and no debt, the company has survived and appears to have a brighter future as a non-union, profit-sharing entity motivating the 950 employees to work hard and efficiently.

Commercial Vehicle Group

With annual revenues of nearly one billion dollars, Commercial Vehicle Group is a leading global supplier of cab parts for heavy-duty trucks, construction, agriculture, specialty and military vehicles. Their products include suspension seat systems, interior trim systems, instrument and door panels, headliners, molded products, cabinetry and floor systems, cab structures and components, mirrors, wiper systems, electronic wiring harness assemblies and controls and specially designed switches. CVG's headquarters is at 6530 West Campus Oval, New Albany, Ohio. Plans are being finalized to build a 89,000 square feet research and development facility along side an enlarged headquarters. This will allow combining four Central Ohio facilities. Warehouses and plants are located in twelve states, Mexico, Belgium, Sweden, England, China and Australia. The company has been actively acquiring companies that fit their manufacturing goals.

CompuServe (AOL)

CompuServe is a pioneer internet on-line information service based at 5000 Arlington Centre Boulevard in Upper Arlington, Ohio. It was founded in 1969 as Compu-Serv Network, Inc. by University of Arizona electrical engineering graduate students, Jeffrey Wilkins and John R. Goltz. Its original mission was to support the Golden United Life Insurance Company as its subsidiary and to develop an independent computer time-sharing business. It was spun off as a separate entity in 1975 and traded on NASDAQ under the symbol CMPU. In 1980,

H&R Block purchased the company and infused it with cash allowing expansion. In addition to serving consumers with electronic mail and technical service, it developed a financial service group. It entered the world-wide market in 1986 and became a wholly-owned subsidiary of AOL in 1998. CompuServe Information Services is a completely revamped version of its internet service offering broader, more convenient, easier to use and better organized enhancements. It is affordably priced for value-driven adults.

Continental Realty

Continental Realty was established in 1975, and built the twenty-six story Continental Centre at 150 East Gay Street as its headquarters. Other offices are in Cleveland, Pittsburgh and Dallas. It is a large developer and manager of real estate ventures in the Midwest. In Columbus, Continental secured property from Western Electric holdings east and north of the telephone company along East Broad Street. The Realty Company is developing retail ventures on the eastern portion of the property.

Core Molding Technologies

Core Molding was founded in Columbus in 1997. It produces fiberglass reinforced plastics and sheet molding compound material for a varied market that includes medium to heavy trucks, automobiles and watercraft. Its main plant and headquarters are at 800 Manor Park Road, about ten miles west of downtown Columbus. It has grown steadily by acquisition of several similar companies. Three of its other plants are in Cincinnati, Gaffney, South Carolina and Mexico. There are about one thousand employees at all locations.

The Crane Group

The Crane Group is a private, family-owned, holding company—a network of local, regional and global entities in the manufacturing and building trades. It was founded in 1947. Its core company is Crane Plastics located at 2141 Fairwood Avenue in Columbus with 810 employees. Operations in six states, China and Chile employ 1,300 people. The company has a history of over sixty years as a leader and innovator in custom profile thermoplastic and wood composite extrusions. It introduced the world to vinyl siding in 1957 and has continuously improved that product. The company has divisions applied to custom manufacturing, standard vinyl sidings, wood decking, water-protection (Atlanta, Georgia plant) and vinyl fence, railing, and post accessories. Annual revenues of over one-half billion dollars are expected to double that amount by 2010. The seventy-one year old founder, Jameson Crane, is chairman of the company's board.

Delphi Automotive Systems

The Delphi plant in Columbus was built in 1946 at 200 Georgesville Road, near West Broad Street, as a Turnstedt (or Fisher Guide) Division of General Motors Corporation to manufacture automobile components. In the 1950's, the plant was one of the largest manufacturers in Columbus with 5,500 employees. During its history, the company underwent seven name changes. Eventually, it became called the Delphi Corporation. Delphi was spun off of the General Motors Corporation in 1999, and soon began operating under Chapter 11 due to low demand for its products. The Columbus plant, reduced to seven hundred employees, made powered sliding doors, gates and latches for automobiles. Despite winning awards for efficiency and quality of workmanship, its future came to an end in 2007, when the plant was closed.

Diamond Innovations

The Superabrasives division of General Electric was started at Busch Boulevard and Schrock Road in 1953. The company was acquired by Littlejohn & Company and renamed Diamond Innovations in 2003. The company is a world-leading pioneer in the production of synthetic diamonds and cubic nitride crystals used in sawing, grinding, machining, drilling and polishing in a wide variety of industries. Their Bellataire diamond brand is a successful ground-breaking technical innovation. The company enjoys a reputation of introducing high-quality products, applications and service. Manufacturing is shared with a Dublin, Ireland plant. Twenty-five service and sales offices are located worldwide. Littlejohn is a private equity company that specializes in buying special opportunities, improving their profitability and then selling its acquisitions within a few years. In January, 2007, Sandvik Tooling of Sweden announced its purchase of the business. The successful management team is intended to remain unchanged, and an additional 350 employees are expected to be hired. Diamond Innovations is Worthington's largest manufacturer.

Dominion Homes

Dominion Homes, formerly known as the Borror Company, has built moderately priced homes (average price is $188,000) in Central Ohio for nearly fifty years. They make up almost twenty-five percent of the new home market in the Columbus area, in which they rank second. Their other building locations are in and around Louisville, Kentucky, Jeffersonville, Indiana and Lexington, Kentucky. Douglas G. Borror is Chairman and CEO and his son, David S. Borror, is Vice-Chairman of the company. The company headquarters is at 5000 Tuttle

Crossing Boulevard, Dublin, Ohio. For the first time since 1994, a buyout group that included Borror's BRC Properties, Angelo, Gordon & Co. and Silver Point Capital acquired Dominion Homes, returning it to private ownership in 2008.

Donatos Pizza

Donatos Pizza opened its first store in 1963 in south Columbus. Its founder, Jim Grote, is CEO and chairman of the board of the one hundred and seventy-five pizzeria chain located in six states; one hundred and thirty-five of which are company owned. McDonald's Corporation acquired and held the company briefly between 1999 and 2003, after which the chain's ownership returned to the Grote family. The company has retrenched from the McDonald experiment with larger stores and has focused on smaller parlors and the introduction of new food items. In 2007, Grote's daughter, Jane Grote Abell, assumed the role of president of the company. She was well prepared, having worked in delivery, counter sales, store management, human resources, real estate, franchising and as chief operations officer. She is a graduate of The Ohio State University.

Don Casto Organization

The Don Casto Organization has been in the business of building homes and shopping centers for sixty-five years. The founder, Don Casto Sr., was an orphan. He was a student in The Ohio State University when World War I broke out. He left school to join the French Army as an ambulance driver. After the war, he began building homes in Upper Arlington for King Thompson. In 1926, he ventured as a solitary builder of homes south of Lane Avenue. In 1928, he opened the Grandview Avenue Shopping Center which held grocery stores, banks and restaurants. Casto lost the Shopping Center during the Great Depression in 1930. After World War II, he was joined by his son, Don Casto Jr., and they re-built the company into its current size. In 1949, the father and son constructed a sizeable shopping mall in Whitehall called Town & Country. The mall had thirty-one stores including JCPenny, Kresge's, Kroger, Gray Drugs and Richman Brothers. It was acclaimed one of the first regional shopping centers in the nation. Success led to building other suburban malls in Ohio, Pennsylvania and in Independence, Missouri. Brother-in-law of Casto Jr., Frank Benson, Jr., joined the firm and became its president. In 1971, Don Casto III and Frank Benson III joined the company. A second development company was formed to raise capital. It included Frank Kass and Jack Lucks of Continental Real Estate. The joint venture built Dublin Village Center and, in 1994, the Lennox Town Center. As the company flourished, outside executives were brought aboard. Between three and four dozen projects were going on at any one time. Expansion spread to Florida. In 2001, they bought thirteen shopping centers from Duke Realty Corporation including one west of Tuttle Crossing, near Dublin. Other acquisitions were in Cincinnati, Indiana and Illinois. Some of the Casto assets were packaged and sold to Investcorp of New York. The new policy became to sell older properties and buy newer ones. In 1999, Casto merged with R. J. Solove to own or manage properties like Carriage Place on Bethel Road. One of the most exciting ventures is currently ongoing in downtown Columbus at the northeast corner of Broad and High Streets. A four story building is being renovated and will have offices and stores and a garage on lower levels and condominiums on the upper floors. TV station WCMH-4 will lease some of the space for a studio, and a huge $2.5 million video screen above the corner will mimic Times Square in New York City. Adjacent to the corner building, at 8 East Broad Street, the seventeen-story, 101-year old office building will be renovated into twenty-two upscale condominiums. Columbus is fortunate to have a civic booster and urban renewer like the Casto and Solove organization. In 2005, Casto entered the North Carolina market. They now own and/manage eighty-one retail centers nationwide.

DSW Shoes

DSW was a division of Retail Ventures with its first store located in Dublin. It is a shoe retailer that spun out of Retail Ventures as a separate entity in 2005. It offers over two thousand styles of shoes for women and men. Its headquarters is at 810 DSW Drive on the east side near the Columbus Airport. Additional buildings make up its warehouse and distribution center. The company operates 245 stores in 36 states. Plans have been made to enter the Internet retail business. Success has been aided by tax-abatements and loans from Columbus and the state.

Germain Motor Company

Germain Motor Company is owned by President Steve Germain and his brother, Rick. It is a continuation of a $1 billion car empire created by their grandfather sixty years earlier. Twenty dealerships are located in Central Ohio, Florida, Arizona and Arkansas. The headquarters is located in a new twin Cadillac/Mercedes-Benz dealership in Easton Mall in Columbus. A wide variety of automobile brands in addition to luxury models are sold. The company has fifteen hundred employees. Germain owns Teco Arena in Southwest Florida and the naming right for the Germain Amphitheatre near the Polaris Mall. The company sponsors NASCAR racecars and have a stake in the Columbus Destroyers Arena football team. The Germains support many civic projects and serve on boards of local foundations including the Nationwide Children's Hospital and the Columbus Zoo.

Glimcher Realty Trust

The Glimcher Company began in 1959 in Columbus as a lumber and building supplier. In the mid-1960's, the company expanded into building strip shopping centers and fast food franchise stores. In the 1970's, the business extended into building retail malls. Its first enclosed regional mall, Indian Mound Mall, was established in Newark/Heath, Ohio in 1986. Over the next eight years, six new and one acquired enclosed mall were developed. By 1993, the company portfolio included twenty-nine properties including super-regional malls, community centers and single tenant entities. The company's name was changed to Glimcher Realty Trust in 1994. As a result, an initial public offering was made as well as a listing on the New York Stock Exchange (GRT). During the company's forty-five year history, over one hundred shopping centers were managed, acquired or developed. The most recent acquisition is the enclosed Eastland Mall from the Jacobs Group, opened in 1968. Complete ownership of Polaris Fashion Place and Polaris Town Center made Glimcher one hundred-percent owner of all his shopping centers (10% of holdings) and malls (90%). The company's headquarters is in the Continental Center at 150 East Gay Street. In 2005, Herbert retired into the position of Chairman of the Board and Senior Advisor to the company. His son, Michael Glimcher, then became Chief Executive Officer and President of GRT. In a reversal of focus, community centers were divested and full attention was given to regional retail malls. In late 2006, Glimcher owned thirty properties in seventeen states.

Grange Mutual Insurance

The Grange Mutual Insurance Companies are headquartered in a twelve-story building at 650 South Front Street in the Brewery District of Columbus. The National Grange was formed in 1867 in response to the need of Midwestern and Southern farmers for collective bargaining with state governments and owners of grain elevators restraining farm trade. By 1874, more than 20,000 local granges existed in thirty-two states, and the organization developed considerable clout in farm states. Its membership soon reached 860,000 but started to decline in the last years of the 1800s. The initial Grange was a secret fraternal society with membership limited to farm families, and established cooperative stores, purchasing agencies and farm machine manufacturing companies. It expanded into providing club-like social and educational support for its members. Vehicular and other types of insurance was a natural extension of Grange services that began in 1935. Since then, the products of the company, open to all, increased to include life, casualty, home, farm, banking and business insurance. Like many other insurance companies, Grange established its banking division when Congress, in 1999, removed regulatory barriers that separated insurance from financial services. In a 2007 reversal, Grange sold its home-equity loans, commercial-business and real-estate loans and customer deposits to American Bank Holdings. Grange retained its $276 million assets portfolio, but plans to sell its auto-loan and residential-mortgage business. Today, the company, operating in twelve states, is a $1 billion insurance entity. The connection between client and company is performed by independent agents. Currently, the Columbus company is expanding its physical presence by adding a ten-story building on its north side, a parking garage with 1,000 spaces on its south side and a plaza. The new structure will have several "green technology" features in its windows and air conditioning. Grange is a generous supporter of civic projects in Columbus. The company purchased the naming right for the Audubon Nature Center to be built on the Whittier Pensinsula near the company headquarters on South Front Street.

Hexion Specialty Chemicals

Hexion Specialty Chemicals is a Fortune 500 company based in Columbus. It is the world's largest producer of binder, adhesive, coating and ink resins for industrial applications. The company is the world leader in thermoset resins. Hexion Specialty Chemicals is owned by an affiliate of the private investment firm Apollo Management LP. Hexion was formed in 2005 through the merger of Borden Chemical, Inc., Resolution Perfomance Products LLC, and Resolution Specialty Materials LLC, and the acquisition of Bakelite AG. In 2007, the company purchased Huntsman Corporation for $10.6 billion. This acquisition tripled the size of the corporation, and makes Hexion one of the five largest chemical companies in North America, with seven thousand employees worldwide. Houston, Texas is currently competing with Columbus for the company headquarters. If Columbus remains the headquarters, over four hundred employees will be located in Ohio's capital city. Hexion retains control over the Elsie the Cow trademark and the Borden name.

The company was founded in 1856 by Gail Borden, an eccentric Texan, inventor of condensed milk and dried meat. In 1836, he helped lay out Houston, Texas, and was a prime leader in securing independence for Texas from Mexico. Moving his operations to New York in 1857, Borden modernized the regional dairy industry by introducing many animal and production health measures. His dairy and pasta products and chemical company became the largest in the nation. The company's best known products were Gold Meadow milk, Borden Condensed Milk brands, Elmer's glue, Krazy glue and formaldehyde. The headquarters moved to Columbus in 1969 (the 180 East Broad Street location is still known as the Borden Building). The company became owned by KKR investment firm in 1995 after several years of financial reverses. Dissolution of the company began in 1997 when the dairy products division was sold to Dairy Farms of America. Krafts bought the pasta products division in 2000. In 2004, the remaining Borden Chemical Company was acquired by Apollo Management which in turn bought Bakelite. A merger with Resolution Performance Products and Resolution Specialty Materials in 2005 resulted in its present name of Hexion Specialty Chemicals.

Highlights for Children

Highlights for Children is a national children's magazine that was the brain-child of educators, Dr. Garry Myers and his wife, Caroline, in 1946. The mission of the journal was to help children grow in basic skills and knowledge, in creativeness, in ability to think and reason, in sensitivity to others, in high ideals and in worthy ways of living. They moved their venture from Pennsylvania to Columbus in the same year to be near their publisher, the Heer Printing Company. In 1946, they purchased another children's magazine, *Children's Activities*. The first office was in an old music recital hall at 37 East Long Street. They were joined by their son, Garry Jr., in 1951, and through his innovations, the company prospered. In 1960, a new sales team raised the magazine's circulation and expanded to a new home office on West Fifth Avenue. Tragically, Garry Myers Jr. and his wife, Mary, died in an airplane crash in 1960. A new management staff was installed to oversee more than eight hundred sales representatives. The founder, Dr. Garry Myers, Sr. died at age eighty-seven in 1971. His wife and co-founder, Caroline Myers, died in 1980. As the circulation passed the one million mark in 1972, *Highlights* purchased its own publishing company on North Park Street, the Zaner-Bloser Company. Zaner-Bloser had published textbooks on the art of handwriting developed by C. P. Zaner and E. W. Bloser. Garry C. Myers III continues to preside over this very successful Columbus based magazine.

Huntington Bank

The Huntington Bank is one of the oldest banking institutions in Columbus. It was founded by Petetiah Webster Huntington in 1866. Its first location at the southwest corner of High and Broad Streets has been maintained but its headquarters is now in the Huntington Center on South High Street at the site of the former Neil House Hotel that was razed in 1984. The modern Huntington Bank with many branches in Ohio and surrounding states and Florida, and all the ancillary services of large banks, is the second largest financial institution (Bank One, now Chase being first) originating in Columbus. After its merger with Bowling Green-based

Sky Bank in 2007, it had 730 branches. It became the third largest bank in Ohio and the twenty-fourth largest in the nation. Its many acquisitions include some historical banking institutions in Columbus; State Savings, Hayden-Clinton, Market Exchange and Columbus Savings.

J.P. Morgan-Chase (formerly Bank One)

J.P. Morgan-Chase Bank entered the Columbus scene in 2004 when it acquired Bank One, sixth largest national bank and the largest bank in Columbus at the time. Bank One took its name in 1970, having been known previously as City National Bank and Trust Company. The John G. McCoy family founded City National in 1866, and for a long period of time it was the third largest bank in Columbus. When interstate banking laws changed, the bank became the first one in Ohio to make acquisitions in other states, and it soon its holding company became the second largest regional bank after National City of Cleveland. It opened the first bank drive-through in 1950. It pioneered in the use of credit cards (1966) and became the largest issuer of Visa. It was an early installer of ATMs (1970). In 1998, Bank One merged with First Chicago-NBD and moved its headquarters to Chicago until its acquisition by J.P. Morgan Chase in 2004. The McCoys no longer participate in the management of their formidable bank holdings. J.P. Morgan-Chase has worldwide assets of over $1.2 trillion and Central Ohio assets of 5.6 billion, making it the second largest bank in the United States and the largest bank in Columbus. The Columbus headquarters is at 100 East Broad Street in a twenty-five story glass enclosed skyscraper. Chase's mortgage-servicing business remains in Easton, as does an operational center in Polaris. The name Chase comes from Civil War era Salmon P. Chase. Chase attended grammar school in Worthington, was U.S. Senator from Ohio (1849-1855), Governor of Ohio (1856-1860), Secretary of Treasury (1861-1864) and Chief Justice of the U.S. Supreme Court (1864-1873).

Lancaster Colony Corporation

The Lancaster Colony company received its name in 1961 when several companies merged under the principal ownership of the J. Gerlach family. The Lancaster Glass Company in Lancaster, Ohio had been in existence since 1910 and produced specialty glass products such as reflectors, cathode ray tubes and auto lamps. It acquired other companies including Indiana Glass and Bluebird Plastics. The Lancaster company merged with four other companies in the 1960's that included Colony Glass, thus its current name. Today, Lancaster Colony makes specialty foods (e.g. Marzetti salad dressings, acquired in 1969), candles and potpourri, and automotive parts and accessories. Each of its divisions operates autonomously. The company, whose headquarters is located at 37 West Broad Street, Columbus, has over one billion dollars in annual sales and has over fifty-five hundred employees. Consecutive quarterly dividends have been paid since 1963. In 2007, the company announced plans to close out its glass operations in Lancaster, Ohio, a momentous decision.

Limited Brands

In 1963, Leslie Wexner opened a women's clothing store in Columbus called *The Limited*. The corporation grew to over five thousand stores found in all states and has sales around ten billion dollars. It is the parent of several specialty clothing stores, the best known and most profitable is *Victoria's Secret*. The headquarters and distribution center is on I-270 near Morse Road. In late 2006, the Limited announced the purchase of La Senza, to be completed in early 2007, one of the world's largest intimate-apparel businesses, headquartered in Montreal. La Senza, which traces its roots to Suzy Shier company forty years ago, has 318 stores in Canada and licenses 327 in thirty-four countries. La Senza is a strategic fit with the Limited's 3,534 stores in the United States, the only country in which it has operated to date. The Limited hopes the acquisition will lead to overseas presence of Victoria's Secret, its most successful boutique. Both companies will have independent management. In 2007, Wexner surprised the retail world by selling its unprofitable specialty outlets, but Limited Brands retained the profitable Victoria's Secret, Bath & Body Works, C. O. Bigelow, White Barn Candle, Henri Bendel and La Senza. Mr. Wexner and his wife have contributed generously to Children's Hospital, The Ohio State University and other Columbus institutions and organizations. The Ohio State University has an outstanding fine arts center, The Wexner Center, named for him.

Liebert Corporation

Liebert Corporation employs twelve hundred people at its Dearborn Drive location. Ralph Liebert founded the Capital Refrigeration Company in Columbus in 1946. He focused on cooling systems for computer rooms. The key to success was precision control of temperature. In 1968, the company moved into larger quarters in Worthington. The company expanded into Canada and Ireland and became a Fortune 500 company. Liebert became a world leader in manufacturing controls for uninterrupted power supply for computers. In 1987, Liebert Corporation ceased to be family operated when it was acquired by Emerson Electric.

Lucent Technologies (formerly Western Electric, now part of Alcatel)

Lucent Technologies, a $20 billion company, has a regional plant at 6200 East Broad Street, in Columbus, that employs twelve hundred assemblers, testers and distributors of cellular phone transmission equipment. New communication lines and utility services have been upgraded in recent years. Its previous name was Western Electric, which in its zenith, was the world's largest electrical manufacturing company (1881-1995), and employed fifteen thousand in three shifts at its Columbus plant that was the size of seventeen football fields. Outdoor recreation facilities for employees occupied land north of the factory.

The first prime client of Western Electric, when founded in the last half of the 1800's, was Western Union. Much later, the Columbus plant was built shortly after World War II, adjacent to the south edge of Port Columbus Airport and adjacent to main rail lines to facilitate shipping. With fifteen thousand employees in the 1950's, it was one of the largest companies in Columbus. The main plant manufactured three "Crossbar Systems" for electro-mechanical telephone switching and support communication equipment. In addition, two personnel training facilities were located on Woodrow Avenue and Mound Street. The Western Electric Company shared its quarters with a portion of Bell Laboratories, the design and development research division of AT&T, the parent holding company of both divisions. Historically, Bell Labs had Nobel Prize winning scientists that were responsible for inventing the vacuum tube, cinema sound systems and the transistor. These innovations led to the mobile communications systems of today including answering machines, alarm devices and the cellular phone. Today, only a few of Bell Lab employees remain in Columbus. AT&T, the holding company of both divisions, was broken up in the government's anti-monopoly move in the 1980's. Eventually, in 1996, Western Electric's name was changed to Lucent Technologies. Lucent's chief clients today are AT&T and Verizon.

The uncertainty of Lucent's future is emphasized by recent developments surrounding the plant, which is strategically located near Outerbelt freeway I-270 and a large metropolitan hospital. The city of Columbus created a tax-increment financing district to pay for widening Broad Street and building roads and utility lines in the area. An acreage and a building immediately west of the factory (6150 East Broad Street) is now owned and occupied by the administrative and corporate headquarter of Mount Carmel East Hospital which is on the opposite side of East Broad Street. Six or seven medical office buildings are planned on the newly acquired East Broad Street site. Ironically, the Sisters of the Holy Cross owned all the land under discussion from the early 1900's until it sold property to Western Electric during World War II (some of the property became Forest Lawn Memorial Gardens and a portion became the site for Temple Israel).

A merger of Lucent with the French company, Alcatel, was accomplished in late 2006. The $11.8 billion purchase by Alcatel made it the world's largest supplier of equipment for mobile phone networks followed by Ericsson. The lease on the 1.4 million-square-feet Alcatel-Lucent Columbus facility terminates in 2008, making the future of the huge Lucent plant in doubt.

One hundred acres on the north side of Lucent was purchased by M/I Homes from Continental Realty in 2004. M/I Homes built Waterford Park, a residential community of 370 single-family homes and 110 town houses. The village green contains picnic shelters, a playground and a sledding hill.

M/I Homes

Irving Schottenstein was co-founder, with his cousin, Melvin, of M/I Homes, Inc. in 1976. He served as chairman of the board and chief executive officer of the company with headquarters in Easton Mall. His son, Robert, was president, and his nephew, Steven, was chief operating officer of the corporation. They built high quality homes in upscale neighborhoods and became a national leader in the industry ranking 20th in number of homes built in 2005. Since the start of the company, 56,000 homes had been built by 2005. They concentrated their operations to Central Ohio, Indiana, North Carolina and Florida. The Little Turtle complex (Columbus, 1970) with its golf course and club house is a prime example. The company has divisions in six states and the District of Columbia. The company has diversified to include ownership of real estate and buildings, management, brokerage and sales. Upon Irving's death at age 75 in 2004, Robert Schottenstein became head of the company. Melvin Schottenstein, an attorney and one of the original co-founders died in 1993.

Midland Life Insurance Company

Midland Insurance Company was established in 1905 as a stock company. In 1971, the company built a twenty-one floor skyscraper at 250 East Broad Street. The architect was Thomas E. Stanley. The mid-sized insurer demutualized in 1994 and became owned by fifty Columbus investors known as National Capital Financial Corporation. In 2000, they agreed to be acquired by Reassure American Life Insurance Company, a subsidiary of Swiss Re, the world's top life reinsurer. In 1999, Midland had assets of $1.2 billion, $199.1 million in premiums and 255 employees. In 1999, Swiss Re had $68.5 billion in assets and 8,770 employees.

Motorists Mutual Insurance Group

The company began as Motorist Mutual Insurance in 1928. It added life insurance to its products in 1965, but is known best for casualty and personal and commercial property coverage. By acquisitions, it now has clients in thirty states with assets of over one billion dollars. The company has 2,800 representatives working out of 600 independent agencies. The attractive twenty-one floor headquarters building (Motorists Mutual Building) was built in 1973 and is located at 471 East Broad Street. Architects were Maddox NBD and Brubaker/Brandt.

National City Corp. (its branch in Columbus was formerly BancOhio)

The largest bank originating in Ohio and a super-regional financial institution is National City Corporation with headquarters in Cleveland. The bank has holdings in Ohio, Illinois, Indiana, Kentucky, Michigan, Missouri and Pennsylvania. In 1984, BancOhio National Bank of Columbus, with forty branches, merged with National City to make it one of the ten largest banks in the country. BancOhio originated in Columbus in 1907 when Harry P. and Robert F. Wolfe purchased shares in Ohio Trust and merged with Citizens Savings Bank in 1920. A second merger in 1928 with First National Bank made it First Citizens Trust Company. In 1929, Ohio National Bank was brought into the fold, making BancOhio Corporation the state's first bank holding company. The holding company turned public in ownership in 1932. It opened branches in twenty counties and by 1970 had forty-one sites. In Columbus, in 1976, BancOhio National Plaza opened as a twenty-story/six tower building with a glass enclosed main lobby and a shopping Galleria complete with a restaurant. Today, National City has over $2 billion in net income and $35 billion in assets. It is ranked 213 in Fortune 500 and 260 in FT Global 500. In 2004, the corporation sold its credit card holdings to Bank of America. In 2006, the bank announced plans to expand beyond its mid-west holdings by purchasing Harbor Florida Banc-shares that operates forty offices in eight counties along central Florida's east coast for $1.1 billion. Provident Financial Group of Cincinnati was its most recent acquisition. The bank has 2,000 employees and sixty-one offices in Central Ohio. The regional headquarters is at 155 East Broad Street. Its assets in Central Ohio of $2.4 billion make it the fourth largest bank in Columbus.

Nationwide Insurance Company

Columbus is the headquarters to many insurance companies, second only to Hartford, Connecticut. The largest in Columbus, and a Fortune 100 company, is Nationwide Insurance Company. As might be expected in a leading agricultural state at the time, the company had its origin in 1925 as the Farm Bureau Mutual Automobile Insurance Company, founded by Murray Lincoln. Its goal was to provide low cost auto insurance to farmers. Three years later, it expanded into five eastern states. In 1934, through acquisition of a fire insurance company, it started writing property and urban motorists' insurance. By 1943, it operated in twelve states and the District of Columbia. In 1948, the Farm Bureau constructed an eight-story building for its headquarters on the site of the previous Pure Oil, Arcade and Schultz buildings at 246 North High Street. The building was like an art gallery with its many murals depicting various time periods. In recognition of its expansion into thirty-two states, its name was changed in 1955 to Nationwide Insurance Company. In 1978, it moved into a new headquarters at One Nationwide Boulevard. the largest single office building in Ohio (forty stories). The former headquarters building at 246 North High Street was sold to the state, and used successively for the Bureau of Workman's Compensation and the Department of Health. The company went public in 1996 as Nationwide Financial. In 1988, the company erected a second high-rise office building, Three Nationwide Plaza, adjacent to its headquarters; both in the Nationwide Plaza. The company has been a prime and generous supporter in civic affairs. In 2000, it provided a home for the National Hockey League's franchise, the Columbus Blue Jackets and the Columbus Destroyers on the Arena Football League in Nationwide Arena owned by Nationwide Insurance Company. Today, Nationwide Financial has over $157 billion in assets.

NetJets

NetJets is the name chosen in 2002 to replace *Executive Jet Aviation* founded in Columbus in 1964 by General O.F. Lassiter. The company provides individuals and businesses fractional ownership of its fleet of six hundred aircraft of fourteen different models that carry from six to eighteen passengers. Richard Santulli purchased the company in 1984 and moved its headquarters to Woodbridge, New Jersey, but retained its chief operational and training centers at Port Columbus Airport. Additional operational centers are maintained in Cincinnati, Ohio, Hilton Head, S.C., Lisbon, Portugal, and Jeddah, Saudi Arabia, Berkshire Hathaway acquired the company in 1998. In 2005, the company made 370,000 flights covering a total of 220,000,000 miles to 150 countries. It is the leader in its industry in size, safety, security and reliability. Currently, the company has 1,000 employees.

Outsourcing Solutions

Outsourcing Solutions is a collection agency that employs 655 in two locations in Franklin County; 435 in Columbus and 220 in Westerville. The local operation is focused on collecting student loans, health-care billing and customer services. A third office in Cleveland, Ohio employs 100. The home office for the fifty-five locations in North American is in St. Louis, Missouri. The company has entered into an agreement to be purchased by NCO Group for $325 million in cash. No significant changes are anticipated in the successful Franklin County offices.

Pinnacle Data Systems

Pinnacle Data Systems began in 1989 as a depot repair business for Sun Microsystems workstations and currently repairs more than half of Sun's requirements. The company has expanded through new engineering and design technology into a leading provider of application-specific hardware and global support solutions for the world's largest original equipment manufacturers (OEMs). These companies are involved in telecommunications, computers, medical devices, industrial controllers, digital imaging and the defense industry. Solutions are provided to the products' entire life-cycle: development, deployment, support, service, logistics and end-of-life management. In 1996, PDS became a publicly traded company. The company's corporate headquarters and sales office are at 6600 Port Road, Groveport, Ohio.

Pizzuti Companies

The Pizzuti enterprises began as a husband and wife real estate building operation in 1976. Since then, it has developed more than 35 million square feet of Class A office, retail, residential, mixed-use and institutional-quality industrial facilities throughout the Middlewest and Southeast regions. They also manage real estate. In 2006, they were selected to be the owner's representative for the new Franklin County Courthouse. They received awards from the National Association of Industrial and Office Properties for the CreekSide Industrial Center and SouthPark Business Center, in Franklin County in 2006. Other notable local projects include Miranova condominium and office buildings, MetroPlace in Dublin and Prescott Place condominiums in Marble Cliff. The founder, Ronald A. Pizzuti remains Chairman and CEO. The President and COO is Joel S. Pizzuti. The headquarters is at Two Miranova Place, Columbus. Regional offices are in Chicago and Orlando, Florida. Ronald Pizzuti is part owner of the Columbus Blue Jackets hockey team.

Plaskolite

Plaskolite is the largest, privately owned, manufacturer of continuously processed acrylic sheeting. The Dunn family began manufacturing its product, Optix, in 1950; it was available in various shapes of laminated, and/or flat sheets and rolls. The headquarters is 1770 Joyce Avenue in Columbus with additional manufacturing sites in Zanesville, Ohio and Compton, California. During its history, several related companies have been acquired. Additional distribution centers are in California, Holland and Canada. It employs more than 475 workers, mostly in Columbus. Annual revenues are over $180 million. The founder, James R. Dunn, continues as president.

Real Living

Real Living is a real estate brokerage company that originated in Columbus and is headquartered at 77 East Nationwide Boulevard. It was created in 2002 by merging HER of Columbus with Realty One of Cleveland and Huff Realty of Cincinnati. HER was started by Harley E. Rouda, Sr. in Columbus in 1956. It grew into the leading regional realtor in Central Ohio. Harley E. Rouda, Jr., CEO of Real Living, acquired HER from his father. Harley Rouda, Jr.'s wife, Kaira Sturdivant Rouda, is president of RL. Expansion has placed the realty company in seventeen states with one hundred and sixty-five franchises, one-half of which are company owned. Penetration of the Northwest U.S. is yet to occur. Company executives project entering all of the nation's states by 2010. Real Living's 3,360 agents and 532 non-agent employees conducted 28,008 transactions in 2006. The company also offers ancillary businesses such as mortgage and title services, relocation assistance and on-line connections between sellers and buyers with web sites for their agents. A consumer portal is called MyRealLiving.

R.G. Barry

R.G. Barry corporation was founded in 1947 by Florence Zacks Melton with co-owners, Aaron Zacks and Harry Streim. The company's name was derived from the first names of Mrs. Melton's children, Richard Streim, Gordon Zacks and Barry Zacks. Mrs. Melton introduced foam latex into women's slippers and *Angel Treads*™ became an instant success. Subsequent successful products have been *Dearfoam, EZfeet* and *Terrasoles*. Footwear accessories are now included in the business. The company estimates over one billion pair of feet have been covered by its products over the past sixty years. The company headquarters is located at 13405 Yarmouth N.W., Pickerington, Ohio.

Ricart Automotive Group

The Ricart Automotive Group was started in 1953 by Paul Ricart, Sr. In 1982, his sons, Fred and Rhett, took over ownership. Since then, the group has acquired nine Columbus dealerships that sell domestic and foreign automobiles. Their largest location is a mega-mall on South Hamilton Road. In 1998, they recorded revenue of $600 million with sales of 33,000 autos. For the past decade, they have been the country's number one Ford Dealer and rated number one dealer overall by *Ward's Dealer Business*. They have won the Consumers Choice Award four years in a row. Fred and his wife, Lynne, are well known for their "home-grown" television advertisements.

Ross Laboratories

Ross Products Division of Abbott Laboratories has long been a producer of pediatric and adult nutritional foods and the equipment for delivering the products. It is located in four areas with its main campus on Stelzer Road. It has 2,200 employees. The company had its origin as Moores & Ross Milk Company in Columbus in 1903. The company's first major product was Similac, a liquid milk substitute for infants. Ross Laboratories was created in 1956 in an effort to concentrate on making infant formulas. In 1959, iron was added to Similac and soon pre-bottled and pre-sterilized systems were introduced. The company merged with Abbott Laboratories of Illinois in 1964, making it the world's largest health care corporation. Vitamins, soy protein, lactose-free milk products, extra caloric food supplements, antibiotics and other specialized products have been produced in its own and acquired plants. Today, Ensure and Similac are its most successful sales items. Richard M. Ross, president of the family owned company until acquired by Abbott, with his wife Elizabeth, gave generously to Columbus institutions. The Ross Heart Institute at OSU is named for him, and the Chair in Management in the OSU Business College was funded by Elizabeth.

Roxane Laboratories

Roxane Laboratories began in 1885 as Columbus Pharmacal Company. It introduced the first unit doses of medicine, the first oral solutions of major drugs, and it was the first to use form, fill and seal technology for respiratory therapy. Roxane Laboratories continues to make unique contributions to infant therapy and palliative medications for pain and AIDS. Headquartered in Columbus, its eight hundred employees occupy a modern 250,000 square feet laboratory and an office complex on fifty-five acres on North Wilson Road. The company became a division of Boehringer-Ingelheim, a German pharmaceutical corporation, in 1978.

Ruscilli Construction Company

The company was started in 1945 by Louis G. Ruscilli as a specialty construction contractor. He was joined by his father, Louis Sr., and son, L. Jack Ruscilli in 1967. The latter is the current CEO and owner. A fourth generation, R. Anthony Ruscilli and Louis V. Ruscilli, are with management. The company is now one of the largest full service construction firms in the Middlewest. It is also one of the nation's largest pre-engineered building systems dealer. Some of its Columbus projects were: Franklin County Courthouse, Franklin County Correction Center, Franklin County Juvenile Detention Center, Ameriflora Horticultural Exhibit, and the George V. Voinovich Agricultural Trade Center. The company's headquarters is at 2041 Arlingate Lane, Columbus.

Safelite Group (Belron U.S.)

Safelite started in Wichita, Kansas in 1947 with a single store. Its corporate headquarters moved to 2400 Farmers Drive, Columbus in 1990. The company is composed of four divisions. Safelite AutoGlass is the nation's largest provider of auto-glass repair and replacement services in all fifty states. Over 400,000 windshields are serviced each year. Safe Solutions provides claims management for more than one hundred insurance and auto-fleet companies. It manages a network of nearly 11,000 affiliate providers and two call centers, both in Worthington. Service AutoGlass provides wholesale auto-glass products, repair materials and tools through a network of seventy-nine warehouses. Safelite Glass Corporation produces original equipment equivalent windshields for aftermarket with a manufacturing and distribution facility in Enfield, North Carolina. Sixteen hundred employees are located in Central Ohio. In 2007, the private-equity owners of the Safelite Group were acquired by Belron S.A., a Belgium company. This resulted in the world's largest auto-glass repair company. Belron U.S. (Safelite) continues to be based in Columbus.

Schottenstein Stores

Ephraim Schottenstein, a Lithuanian immigrant, started a dry goods store in Columbus in 1917. His grandson, Jerome, succeeded his father as head of the store after gaining experience in all levels of the family business. The company developed into a huge discount outlet by acquiring failing or liquidating businesses. Jerome occasionally dealt with large and expensive items for resale such as two thousand DeLorean and forty-three hundred Fiat automobiles and $35 million worth of bulldozers. The company also acquired some of the failing or bankrupt chain-stores. Eventually, the commercial enterprise was organized into a holding company known as Schottenstein's Stores. Some groups of stores were spun off as public owned corporations, but the majority ownership remained under the control of the Schottenstein family. In 2003, reorganization led to the formation of Retail Ventures that included DSL Shoes (acquired in 1998) and Filene's Basement Stores (acquired in 2000). American Eagle Outfitters, Schottenstein Department Stores and Value City Furniture Stores were controlled separately. In 2008, eighty-one percent ownership of 113 Value City Department Stores was sold. These stores were an outgrowth of a purchase of five dry goods stores in Philadelphia in 1989. In addition to department stores and real estate, the family owned a finance company, jewelry stores, beauty-aid boutiques, shopping centers, and an air freight forwarding operation. Upon Jerome's death in 1994, his son, Jay, became CEO of the business empire.

R.W. Setterlin Building Company

Robert W. Setterlin, Sr. founded the company in 1935. Continued under the guidance of his sons and their offsprings, the full service construction organization has grown to be one of the largest of its kind in central and southeastern Ohio. Its projects include health care, educational, industrial, religious and headquarters facilities, high-rise office space, retail centers, historic renovations, building additions and many others. Their quality work and excellent reputation has garnered them many citations and awards. Their headquarters is located at 4678 Larwell Drive in Columbus

State Auto Insurance

State Automobile Insurance Company was founded in 1921 by Robert Pein. The company prospered rapidly, suffering a slowdown only during World War II when autos and gasoline were rationed. It moved to its present headquarters at 518 East Broad Street in 1930 where the physical facilities have undergone several renovations/expansions. It acquired Columbus Mutual Life Insurance Company in 1962, and its expansion was aided by acquisitions of several other insurance companies allowing it to service forty-eight states. It has several regional offices. Company assets total over two billion dollars. An initial stock offering of State Auto Financial was made in 1991. *Forbes* magazine rated it "Best Managed Insurance Company" in 2006. Two thousand employees work out of the main office. Business is written by over three thousand independent agencies. The annual elaborate life-size Christmas decorations on the outside of its main office, makes it an impressive Columbus tradition.

Sterling Commerce

A pioneer in electronic data interchange and secure file transfer technology, the company has provided automation solutions to world-wide businesses, including Fortune 500 companies and some of the world's largest banks. Headquartered at 4600 Lakehurst Court, Dublin, the company is a subsidiary of AT&T with sales and support offices in many of the world's largest cities, including London, Paris, Tokyo and Sao Paulo. Prior to 2006, the company was originally part of Sterling

Software; it became independent in 1996, was acquired by SBC in 2000 and merged with AT&T in 2005. Recent acquisitions have broadened its services. It now has 30,000 customers. Eight hundred and twenty-five of its 2,300 worldwide employees are in Dublin, Ohio.

W.W. Williams Company

The W.W. Williams Company was founded in Columbus in 1912 by William Wallace Williams, Sr. It is one of the nation's oldest and largest privately owned industrial distribution firms, managed by the fourth generation of the Williams family. Initially, the company sold construction equipment but evolved into a multi-million dollar wholesaler and renter of new and reconditioned diesel engines, automotive-locomotive-marine parts, power generators and transport refrigeration systems. The company headquarters remains at 835 Goodale Boulevard in Columbus, Ohio; it maintains forty-two distribution locations in thirteen states, mostly in the middle-west.

TS Tech North America

TS Tech North America, a subsidiary of the Japanese Seat Company, is the headquarters, distribution center and manufacturing plant for stamping auto seats and interior trim, a $1.3 billion enterprise. It is a primary supplier to, and dependent upon, the Honda Automobile Company, with whom it works in tandem. It was established in Reynoldsburg in 1995 at 8400 East Broad Street. A similar subsidiary, TS Trim, is located in Canal Winchester. Of the 5,300 company employees, 1,900 are stationed in Central Ohio's four locations.

Wendy's

Dave Thomas met Colonel Sanders, founder of Kentucky Fried Chicken, whom he considered the greatest influence on his life. He entered a working partnership in some of the KFC franchises in 1962. In 1966, he sold four KFC restaurants in Columbus, Ohio that he had made profitable. In 1969, he opened the first Wendy's Old Fashioned Hamburger restaurant (named after his daughter) in Columbus. Every sandwich was served hot off the grill, none pre-made, nor pre-frozen. He innovated an old-fashioned atmosphere and the modern Pick-Up Window. He introduced the salad bar and baked potato to the menu. He became a role model for his employees by demonstrating hard work and dedication to success. He became the smiling congenial figure in over 800 commercials. Today, Wendy's is the third largest fast-food restaurant chain in the world. Thomas died in 2002.

Westinghouse Electric

Westinghouse opened a subsidiary at 300 Phillipi Road (four miles west of downtown Columbus) in 1954 to make dishwashing machines. It employed twenty-two hundred people. In 1975, the plant was sold to White Consolidated Industries, who in turn sold the plant to AB Electrolux in 1986. In 1988, the plant was closed.

White Castle

Edgar Waldo "Billy" Ingram was born in Kansas in 1880. After finishing public schooling, he became a real estate and insurance agent. In 1921, he formed a partnership with Walter Anderson, a professional cook in Wichita, Kansas, who had developed a method of making hamburgers by cooking the meat with onions on a hot griddle. The product was so popular, that three additional hamburger stands were opened. The company was incorporated as the White Castle System of Eating Houses. During the next few years, the expansion of restaurants spread to twelve major cities in the eastern part of the country. Ingram bought out his partner in 1933 and moved the headquarters to Columbus, Ohio, a more central location. The use of paper hats for employees resulted in the formation of a corporate subsidiary, the Paperlynen Company. Another notable feature of the hamburger chain was the building used for their five-stool outlets. An employee designed a small, movable, steel-framed structure enclosed in porcelain enamel panels. The buildings were modeled after the Old Water Tower in Chicago, and the distinctive design has been maintained to this day. Another subsidiary was incorporated to construct the buildings, the Porcelain Steel Building Company. The company pioneered the newspaper coupon, good for a carry-out order of five hamburgers for ten cents. Their marketing ploy also made use of coupons designed as score pads for bridge, golf and bowling on which all of their locations were listed. A company employee also introduced their hamburger to housewives by giving tours and samples. A menu book was provided with suggestions of foods to serve with the burgers. As the company expanded, so did the size of their restaurants, and curb-side service (since replaced by drive-thru), and an expanded menu were introduced. Expansion has occurred abroad, and a new subsidiary, White Castle Distributing, was created to market its frozen, microwave burgers. Highly publicized were the orders for thousands of burgers for the Marines in Lebanon, as well as in Arizona and California in 1982. New stores are financed from company cash rather than debt. Currently, the fast-food chain is undergoing restaurant design change and introduction of new menu items, a reflection of fourth generation management.

Worthington Industries

John McConnell grew up working in a West Virginia steel company. After graduating from college, he borrowed a small sum of money, mortgaged his car and formed his own company in 1955 in Columbus, Ohio called Worthington Steel Company. The enterprise had $342,000 in sales the first year. Eventually, under the new name of Worthington Industries, annual sales reached three billion dollars. The company specializes in customized processed steel products, sold mostly to the automotive industry. It also makes pressure cylinders and ceiling frames in addition to its flat steel products. Expansion increased the total number of plants to sixty-three in twenty-two states and ten foreign countries, with eight thousand employees. The "Golden Rule" is used in treatment of employees, managers, customers and shareholders. The excellence in management and high satisfaction of employees has earned many awards. The company went public in 1968 and joined the New York Stock Exchange in 2000. Rumors are rife that its success may lead to its merger or acquisition by such companies as Arcelor Mittal, the world's largest steel company. Twenty percent of ownership remains in the McConnell family; currently his son, John P. McConnell, is CEO, while the father remained Chairman of the Board. John H. McConnell died in 2008.

Anheuser-Busch, discussed elsewhere, employs 1,050 on Schrock Road.

A small, but, significant company headquartered in Columbus is Franklin International (glues, adhesives, caulks, sealants and hot melts).

Chapter 22

Columbus Chamber of Commerce, Visitor's Bureau, Convention Centers and Arenas

Columbus Chamber of Commerce

The Columbus Board of Trade was started in 1884, consisting of local businessmen interested in promoting business in Columbus and networking among themselves. Since then, it has undergone four name changes, the latest in 2004 to Columbus Chamber of Commerce. Its offices are located at 37 North High Street but soon to be moved to the Arena District. Its mission is to promote anything that will enhance positively the image of the capital city and Central Ohio. During its existence, it has given support to the Red Cross, the Columbus Airport, World War II efforts (war bonds, victory gardens, U.S.O. and war production) and urban renewal. Its 36-member board and 2,500 members have led economic growth and focused on the development and prosperity of the Greater Columbus Community. Since 1964, it has awarded annually the prestigious Columbus Award to individuals and one society who have done the most to provide leadership in their field of endeavor. The following were the winners:

1964 Jerrie Mock, Robert Lazarus, Sr. and John W. Galbreath
1965 Bertram D. Thomas, Jack Nicklaus and William E. Knepper
1966 Mayor M. E. Sensenbrenner   1967 Governor James A Rhodes
1968 Everett D. Reese   1969 W. W. "Woody" Hayes
1970 Harrison M. Sayre and Paul R. Gingher   1971 Novice G. Fawcett
1972 Charles Y. Lazarus and William S. Guthrie
1973 Edward F. Wagner, James Ralph Riley and Robert K. Levy, Sr.
1974 Chief Justice C. William O'Neill and John C. Elam
1975 Sherwood L. Fawcett and Dean W. Jeffers
1976 Walter C. Mercer, Clair E. Fultz and John G. McCoy
1977 Walter English and Robert S. Crane
1978 Roland C. W. Brown and Mayor Tom Moody
1979 C. Kenneth Smith   1980 Dr. Joseph L. Davis   1981 John H. McConnell

1982 German Village Society 1983 Rep. Chalmers P. Wylie 1984 Frank Wobst
1985 Robert Lazarus, Jr. 1986 John E. Fisher 1987 John W. Kessler
1988 Daniel M. Galbreath 1989 Melvin L. Schottenstein 1990 Robert M. Duncan
1991 Richard Moore Ross and Elizabeth McKeever Ross 1992 Vern Riffe
1993 John F. Wolfe 1994 Leslie H. Wexner 1995 John B. McCoy
1996 John B. Gerlach 1997 Bob and Dorothy Teater 1998 Jo Ann Davidson
1999 Paula Spence 2000 Ronald A. Pizzuti 2001 Robert D. Walter
2002 E. Linn Draper, Jr., Ph.D. 2003 Dimon McFerson 2004 William J. Lhota
2005 Don M. Casto III 2006 Jerry Jurgensen

Visitor's Bureau (Experience Columbus), Convention Centers and Arenas

Experience Columbus is the name of Central Ohio's Convention and Visitors bureau. Its mission is to promote Columbus as an ideal location for conventions and other large meetings. It is located at 90 North High Street. Currently, it has outgrown it facilities and plans were finalized in 2007 to move to 277 West Nationwide Boulevard in the Arena District.

Ohio Convention Center and other Meeting Sites

In 1980, The Ohio Center, a 1.7 million square feet convention-hotel complex, was opened on North High Street, the site of the former Union Station. It was designed by Peter Eisenman and Richard Trott. The convention center has exhibition halls, meeting rooms, ballrooms and a large area named Battelle Hall that seats 7,500 for various forms of entertainment. Five thousand can be served a sit-down dinner. Immediately adjacent to the convention center, at 350 North High Street, is the six hundred and thirty-one room Hyatt Regency Hotel, top rated in Columbus. The twenty-year old hotel was recently renovated. (As an interesting sidelight, in 1872, the Park Hotel, across the street from today's Hyatt, advertised itself as the only first class, $2 a day, hotel in the city.)

The Convention Center competes with a dozen or more other venues for shows, exhibits and conventions. The *Franklin County Veterans Memorial* building on West Broad Street was opened in 1955 and for four decades was a popular destination. It was renovated and enlarged at a cost of $11.3 million in 1982. Currently, its North Hall is 65,000 square feet, the East/West Hall is 45,000 square feet, Brehm Ballroom has 5,000 square feet, an auditorium seats 3,916, and the parking lot has 950 spaces which are rented on week days to downtown workers. The *Ohio Expo Center* at the fairgrounds has ten buildings, the largest of which has 155,000 square feet. Its coliseum has 6,378 seats. *Value City Arena* on the OSU campus has flexible seating from 4,500 to 20,000. *Nationwide Arena* in the downtown area can seat 18,000 in its bowl. The *Lifestyle Communities Pavilion* at 405 Neil Avenue in the Arena district has a 2,200 indoor and a 5,000 outdoor seating capacity for modern musical shows. The *Aladdin Shrine Center* on Steltzer Road in northeast Columbus has a 2,600-seat auditorium, an 11,514 square feet multipurpose room and ample parking space. The *Ohio Theater* has 2,779 seats; the *Palace Theater* seats 2,827; OSU's *Mershon Auditorium* has 2,477 seats; the OSU's *Wexner Center* holds 2,400; the *Columbus Hotel* seats 1,700; the *Hyatt Regency* has a 1,600 seat capacity; the *Southern Hotel Theater* has 933 seats; and the *Capitol Theater* in the *Riffe Center* seats 903. The *Buckeye Hall of Fame Café* at 1421 Olentangy River Road has a theater capacity for 900 and 600 for banquets. *Valley Dale Ballroom* at 1590 Sunbury Road has room for 1,000 people, as does *Villa Milano* at 1630 Schrock Road. The *Makoy Center* at 5462 Center Street in Hilliard will accommodate 1,200 and the *Columbus Athenaeum* (a restored former Masonic temple) at 32 North Fourth Street holds 1,400. The latter has a small wedding chapel and thirteen rooms that include a ballroom and two theaters. Lunch is served weekdays. *Germain Amphitheater* is in Delaware County but adjacent to the northeast Franklin County line. It seats 20,000 (7,000 under roof). Competition for these venues is keen and this has produced a hardship on the publicly owned Franklin County Veterans Memorial site. It is running a budget deficit due to an average use-rate of about fifty percent. This requires tax money infusion. The Army Corps of Engineers paid the county $1.8 millions for a small portion of the Veterans Memorial land needed for building the Columbus floodwall. This seems insignificant when considering the annual operating budget of two million dollars.

Chapter 23

Columbus Tall Buildings

Downtown buildings in Columbus, for eighty-five years, were limited in height to no more than five stories and had no elevators. People had to climb the stairs and carry or have transported the necessities for business or living. These impediments limited the number of people who could use multi-storied buildings.

Although the principles used in mechanically elevating passengers was known as early as 237 B.C., modern usage of elevators in multi-storied buildings was not introduced until the late 1800's. Before that, the few elevators in existence used ropes, pulleys, counterweights and were powered by steam hydraulic pistons. The production of more economical and reliable elevators for buildings had to await the introduction of electrical power, refinements in controls and better safety measures.

Two developments were necessary for the construction of tall buildings: improved structural steel and efficiently powered lifting mechanisms. Elisha Otis is credited with inventing the "safety elevator" in 1853 and installed it in New York City four years later. Electric power for elevators was initiated in 1880. Elevator accidents and deaths, although rare today, still occur and safety measures are continually being adopted.

The debut of tall buildings in Columbus took place in 1897 with the erection of the eleven-story Wyandotte Building at 21 West Broad Street. It was designed by widely acclaimed Chicago architect, Daniel Burnham. The brownstone structure still stands today as the oldest high-rise building in Columbus, attesting to the quality of its building materials. It is listed on the National Historic Registry. The first real "skyscraper" came to Columbus thirty years later, in 1927, when the forty-seven story AIU Citadel was completed. Currently, it is known as the LeVeque Tower. Today, Columbus has dozens of high-rise buildings for business offices, hotels, college dormitories and residences. Most of these buildings line the streets surrounding the state capitol or are within a few blocks distance.

Buildings Around Capitol Square

West

[Diagram showing layout of buildings around Capitol Square with streets: Front Street, High Street, State Street, Town Street, Broad Street, Gay Street, Long Street, Spring Street, 3rd Street, 4th Street. Numbered buildings 1-30 positioned around the State Capitol.]

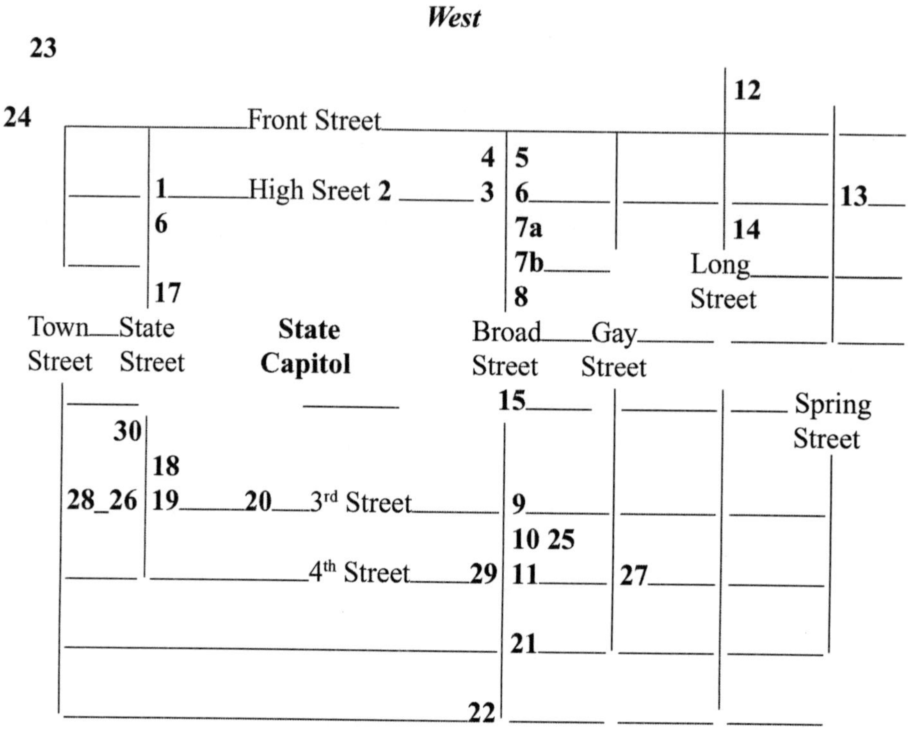

1. Riffe State Office Tower
2. Huntington Center
3. Old Huntington Bank
4. Wyandotte Building
5. LeVeque Tower/Palace Theater
6. One Columbus Center
7a. 8 East Broad Building
7b. 16 East Broad Street Building
8. Rhodes State Office Tower
9. Key Bank
10. Chase (former Bank One) Building
11. Borden Building
12. AEP Building
25. Renaissance Hotel
27. Continental Center
29. National City Bank
13. William Green Building
14. Atlas Building
15. Buckeye Building
16. Fifth/Third Bank
17. Ohio Theater
18. Capital Square Office Building
19. Hyatt Capitol Hotel
20. Columbus *Dispatch* Offices
21. Midland Insurance Building
22. Motorists Insurance Building
23. Minerva Condominiums
24. Grange Mutual
26. Old Courthouse (Bricker & Eckler)
28. U.S. Bank
30. City Center Mall

Fig. 91

Fig. 92 Aerial view of downtown Columbus buildings facing northeast.

1. AEP building
2. Top of One Nationwide Plaza
3. Three Nationwide Plaza
4. Central Police Station
5. YMCA
6. City Hall
7. LeVeque Tower

8. One Columbus Center
9. Wyandotte Building
10. Judiciary Center

11. Top of Rhodes Tower
12. Huntington Center
13. State Capitol
14. Riffe Office Tower
15. Lazarus Stores (now City and OSU)

16. Borden Building (Continental & Realty)
17. Fifth/Third Bank
19. National City Bank
20. Top of Midlands Building
21. Capitol Square Office Building
22. Miranova Condominiums
23. Waterford Condominiums & Offices
24. Broad Street Bridge
25. COSI
26. Scioto River (and Mile Long Park above it)
27. Town Street Bridge
28. William Greene Building
29. Railroad and Bridge
30. Main Street Bridge

Fig. 93 Wyandotte Building—from Columbus Metro Library

Wyandotte Building

In 1897, Columbus received its first "skyscraper," the eleven-story Wyandotte building at 21 West Broad Street, near High Street. It was designed by Chicago architect, Daniel Burnham, and named for an Indian tribe, indigenous to central Ohio. It is a simple, box-shaped structure with a brown stone exterior. It was made possible by improved structural steel and electrically powered elevators. It functioned as a commercial building and eventually was owned and used by the state for some of its offices. It is one of the few buildings remaining intact from the nineteenth century and is listed on the National Historic Registry.

Atlas Building

The Atlas Building is neither the oldest nor the tallest building in Columbus. It is known also as the Columbus Savings & Trust or the Ferris Building. Opened in 1905 at the northeast corner of Gay and High Streets, it was designed by architects John Griffith and Frank Packard in the Twentieth Century Revival style. As a commercial office building, this privately owned, twelve-story structure has been placed on the National Historic Registry. Recently a huge three piece mural was placed on its north outer side as an ad by a local insurance company. The state Department of Transportation has stated that the mural is illegal and should be removed. Whether a one hundred dollar-a-day fine will be imposed, as required by law, remains to be seen.

LeVeque Tower

The history of the LeVeque Tower is fascinating, convoluted and worthy of review. The Tower is forty-seven stories tall, and, at 555.5 feet in height, is one inch taller than the Washington Monument. It is the signature skyscraper in Columbus. At the time of its opening in 1927, it was the fifth tallest building in the world. Because of its height and weight, forty-four concrete shafts were placed on bedrock one hundred and four feet below the earth's surface to hold the tower structure. This was the slowest phase of construction. Pressurized shafts allowed only one worker at a time to dig for thirty minutes before being decompressed in a chamber for that purpose. An on-site hospital was used to treat injuries to the six hundred and fifty workmen who worked on the building. Many had helped construct the subways and skyscrapers in New York. Five laborers died during construction. The Tower served as a guide to aviators with it four searchlights and was designated as "the first aerial lighthouse." It was designed in the Art Deco/Moderne style by Detroit architect, Charles Howard Crane; his first skyscraper. It was constructed for the American Insurance Union ("since 1894") and was known originally as the AIU Citadel on the northeast corner of West Broad and North Front Streets. The ten-story base is topped by a twenty-seven floor tower which contains two apartments on the top floor. In its beginning, a radio station broadcast its programs from the tower. The steel frame is covered with brick and terra cotta. Inset into its exterior are molded figures of eagles, dragons, statuary groups, etc. (In 1944, these terra cotta figures started to fall off the building to the ground and had to be removed for safety purposes. In their place, giant color flood lights were installed.) An assembly hall in the mezzanine level was patterned after the Hall of Mirrors at Versailles, France. It contained a massive pipe organ. (In 1935, the pipe organ was sold to York Lodge of freemasons. When the lodge building was sold in 2004, the organ was sold by auction to an out-of-state museum.) A stone covered aerial walk-way connected two stories with the Deshler Hotel located at the northwest corner of High and Broad Streets. The first eighteen stories of the Tower had six hundred Deshler hotel rooms, bringing the hotel's total to one thousand rooms. The AIU offices occupied the nineteenth and twentieth floors with business offices above. A new connected building, fronting on West Broad Street contained the Keith-Albee-Palace Theater, moved from North High Street. The theater had been the principal venue for vaudeville. The newly built theater was renamed the Palace.

The company which originally owned the AIU Citadel was a secret fraternal society that sold low-cost insurance to its initiates who had secret handshakes and signals, a newspaper for its members, a radio station, made documentaries, had a male glee-club, a marching band, youth groups, planned social activities and a publishing company. Its stated mission was to promote social, moral and civic betterment. Its membership increased to 250,000 in 1,000 chapters around the country. It was spearheaded by John Jacob Lentz, an attorney and Democratic Congressman. In 1919, the AIU members voted unanimously to make him honorary president for life and granted him two-thirds of his salary annually after his retirement. It should be mentioned that he served the AIU without salary during its first ten years of existence. After World War I, he helped create Mooseheart, a progressive school for orphans, and he lectured on behalf of war relief in Europe. He was a strong believer in women's rights, laborers' rights and prohibition. He was widely recognized as a reformer.

Due to dwindling revenue during the Great Depression and an enormous debt, the AIU Tower had to be sold. It was purchased by Farm Bureau Mutual, forerunner of Nationwide Insurance, for a little more than $350,000 in 1931. In 1945, Leslie LeVeque and John Lincoln bought the building in an auction, and it became known as the LeVeque-Lincoln Tower. Court action forced a re-auction and the purchase price rose to $755,000. Leslie LeVeque owned the Olentangy Village complex and a number of warehouses, which provided him a handsome income. Lincoln lived in Columbus for a few years, and attended but did not graduate from Ohio State University. He spent most of his life in Arizona as a businessman, large land owner and inventor.

Leslie LeVeque died in an airplane crash in 1946, leaving his share of the Tower to son, Frederick, and two daughters. Frederick married Katherine Segars of South Carolina in 1948 and began building his own fortune in parking lots. Capitalizing on the fact that the LeVeque Tower had no space for parking, Frederick built a ten-story parking garage next to the tower at the corner of Front and Gay Streets, named Tower Parking. In 1969, the Deshler Hotel was razed and Frederick LeVeque and Traveler's Insurance Company bought the empty corner lot and erected a $26 million, twenty-six story office building, called One Columbus.

In 1975, due to the death of Frederick LeVeque, likewise in an air accident, and a lack of interest of Frederick's siblings, Frederick's portion of the Lincoln-LeVeque Tower and Palace Theater and all of the Tower Parking building passed to Katherine LeVeque, Frederick's widow; she bought out the step-children's trust ownerships. Katherine swapped her interest in One Columbus for Traveler's interest in Tower Parking. In 1977, Katherine bought out the Lincoln share of Lincoln-LeVeque Tower and Palace Theater. She renovated and revived the Palace Theater and turned its ownership over to CAPA. Katherine enjoyed heading her business and real estate empire and was active in the Chamber of Commerce, the Convention Bureau, and served on the boards of COSI and Children's Hospital. In 1985, she received the Christopher Columbus Award for contributions to her community, and in 1986 she was grand marshal of the Columbus Independence Day Parade.

But, the financial success of the LeVeque Tower was precarious. In 2003, the principal renter, the State of Ohio, departed. The state had been paying one million dollars annually for offices for the Department of Job and Family Services. Occupancy dropped, and the Tower began losing a considerable amount of money and difficulty arose in paying the mortgage premiums. In 2004, the mortgage holder, Lennar Partners of Miami, Florida, by default, took over ownership of the LeVeque Tower. In 2005, a group of out-of-state investors (Friedman Real Estate Group of Detroit) bought the Tower from Lennar for $8.5 million, approximately the original building cost. The new owners renovated the lobby and second floor retail concourse and increased it occupancy percentage. Its future remains uncertain; its offices are small and outdated. The LeVeque Tower continues to be beautifully illuminated with colored flood lights at night and remains the chief landmark of Columbus.

Buckeye Building

The Buckeye Federal Savings and Loan Company built one of the tallest buildings in Columbus in 1927 at the northeast corner of East Gay and Pearl Streets. It had fifteen floors above a grand banking hall on the main floor. It was constructed of limestone and granite in the Neo-Classic style and was designed by architects Hopkins and Dentz of New York City. Recently, it was placed on the National Registry of Historic Places. Marriot Hotel Company has purchased the building with plans to convert it into one of their Residence Inns. The $23 million renovation, to include 126 suites, businesses on the ground floor and a public bar on the mezzanine level, is scheduled to be completed in 2008.

Continental Center

The Continental building has twenty-six floors and was designed by the Lorenz and Brubaker groups and erected in 1973. It is located at the northwest corner of Gay (150) and North 4th Street. It is the headquarters for the Continental Realty Trust Company.

8 East Broad Street

The 8 East Broad Street office building, built in 1906, was the tallest in Columbus until 1910. The height is 222 feet with seventeen floors. The architect was Frank L. Packard of Columbus. It is now owned by the Don M. Casto Organization with plans to convert it into condominiums.

16 East Broad Street

The thirteen story 16 East Broad Street building is a twin of the one at 8 East Broad Street and was erected in 1901. It continues to serve as an office building, and is owned by the Don Casto Organization. A conversion into condominiums is projected.

One Nationwide Plaza

One Nationwide Plaza is the second Nationwide Insurance office building, completed in 1978. It is the second tallest building in Columbus with forty floors. It is bounded by Nationwide Plaza, North High Street and West Nationwide Boulevard. The architectural firms were Harrison/Abramovitz and Brubaker/Brandon.

Three Nationwide Plaza

Three Nationwide Plaza is the third Nationwide Insurance Company office tower. It has twenty-seven floors and was completed in 1988. It is situated between North Front Street and Nationwide Plaza. The architectural designer was NBBJ.

Fifth-Third Center

Fifth-Third Center is a twenty-three floor office building on the southeast corner of High and State Streets, facing the state capitol. It was re-designed in 1998 by architects Miller and Reeves. Originally, it was a low-rise structure, known as the Beggs Building, built in 1928 as a dry goods store for David Carson Beggs. It was designed by architects Smallwood, Reynolds, Stewart and Associates. Today, the principal tenant, occupying one third of its space, is Fifth-Third Bank whose headquarters is in Cincinnati. Other occupants are a California Fitness health club, an Ohio State University wellness center and a combined Wendy's and Tim Horton restaurant. The current owner, IPC US Reit, is Canadian.

Franklin County Municipal Courthouse

Franklin County replaced its courthouse in 1991 with a twenty-seven floor building, the tallest county courthouse in Ohio (164 feet). It is located at 375 South High Street, between Mound and Fulton Streets, and ranks seventh in height among city buildings.

Capitol Square Office Building

The twenty-seven story Capitol Square Office building was constructed in 1984 adjacent to and west of the Hyatt Capitol Square Hotel. It shares a parking garage with the hotel. It has a breezeway with shops leading to Columbus City Center Mall. The building changed ownership from Axa Equitable Life Insurance Company to Hertz Investment Group.

Rhodes State Office Tower

The Rhodes State Office Tower was named after James A. Rhodes, five-term Governor of Ohio (elected in 1962, 1966, 1974 and 1978). The forty-one story building was erected in 1973 and is located at 42 East Broad Street, directly across the street from the north side of the state capitol. It is the tallest building in Columbus and the highest mid-block building in the state (629 feet). Four thousand state employees work in the building. A statute of Rhodes stands in front of the structure.

Vern Riffe State Office Tower

The Vern Riffe State Office Tower was constructed in 1988 at the northwest corner of South High and State Streets. It was named for Vernal G. Riffe, Jr., long-time Speaker of the Ohio House of Representatives (1974-1984). The office complex includes two theaters; the larger one is the Capitol Theater which seats 854. The building faces the west side of the state capitol and has thirty-two floors and is five hundred and four feet in height.

Huntington Center

The Huntington Bank Center replaced the Neil House Hotel directly across South High Street from the west side of the state capitol. It is thirty-seven stories, five hundred and twelve feet in height and was constructed in 1984. It connects by walkways to its bank building to the north and to a hotel and parking garage to the west. It is immediately north of the Riffe Tower. It is one of the most attractive buildings in downtown Columbus.

Borden Building

John Galbreath managed the construction of the Borden Building for the Borden Chemical Corporation in 1974. This thirty-four story building is at 180 East Broad Street. Other tenants have been the Ohio Public Utilities Commission and Sky Bank. The latest owner of the building is a triad of Continental Realty, Nationwide Realty and Capitol Square, a subsidiary of the Dispatch Printing Company.

Midland Building

Thomas E. Stanley designed the Midland Building, a twenty-one floor building that has stood at 250 East Broad Street since 1971. It is owned and occupied by Midland Mutual Insurance Company.

The Columbus, a Renaissance Hotel

The Marriott Hotel chain is the owner of this hotel since 1997 when its latest renovation took place. The hotel was built in 1965 by the State Teachers Retirement System at 50 North 3rd Street with built-in parking since none was available on the streets. It was originally managed by the Sheraton chain and went by that name. It became the Adam Mark hotel in 1975 when it was renovated again. Currently, the twenty-one floor hotel holds four hundred and twelve rooms, three suites and sixteen meeting rooms. One restaurant with a bar is called Latitude 41. Historical research reveals that the hotel replaced the Virginia Hotel which was razed after World War II. The Virginia Hotel had been preceded by the Central Christian Church in the late 1880s.

Motorists Mutual Building

Motorists Mutual Insurance Company built its headquarters at 471 East Broad Street in 1973. The building is twenty-one floors in height and overlooks Topiary Garden, two blocks to its south, which it sponsored. Architects were Maddox NBD and Brubaker/Brandt.

One Columbus Center

One Columbus Center at 10 West Broad Street was built in 1987 by Traveler's Insurance Company. This twenty-six story office building was constructed on a surface parking space. Before that, the northwest corner of Broad and High Streets was occupied by a succession of banks and hotels. The historic Wallick Deshler Hotel was the last of the Deshler Hotels on the site. Currently, U.S. Bank plans to move its regional headquarters from 175 South 3rd Street to One

Columbus Center and is negotiating to change the name of the building to U.S. Bank Building. Eighty of the bank's four hundred employees in Franklin County work in the regional headquarters.

William Green Building

The William Green Building is the third tallest building in Columbus, and was built at 30 West Spring Street in 1990. This thirty-three story, five hundred and thirty foot structure replaced the Chittenden Hotel at the northwest corner of Spring and High Streets. It has been used as an office building, principally for state agencies and related groups.

Key Bank

Key Bank Building is a twenty-four story structure at 88 East Broad Street. It was completed in 1964 for the Republic Franklin Insurance Company. Subsequently, it was called the Society Bank building and in 1996 its name changed to the Key Bank building, its principal tenant.

The American Electric Power, Chase Bank (Bank One), Huntington Bank and Columbia Gas buildings are described in discussions of their companies.

Former Union Store

An interesting, historic, six-story, white nameless building is located at the northwest corner of Long and High Streets. Now an office building, it originated as the Union Store in 1904. It replaced the first Union Store that was destroyed by fire the previous year. Solomon M. Levy had opened the Union Clothing Store for men in 1895 at the urging of his good friend, Governor William McKinley. The store was named after the northern contestant in the Civil War. At the time, the Levy family had clothing stores also in Jacksonville, Florida and Chicago, Illinois. The structure was enlarged from four to six stories in 1923. The Union Company was sold to Manhattan Industries in 1968, and the Union Store relocated into the former Fashion Store on South High Street. It now included women's apparel. In 1980, the store was sold and closed. Subsequently, a Halle store opened on the site. It survived only a few years. The Levy family gave generously to civic groups. Solomon Levy spearheaded the fund-raising for the erection of the large statue of William McKinley on the State Capitol grounds, facing High Street.

Chapter 24

Columbus City Halls

For sixty years, Columbus lacked a genuine city hall. At first, city officials conducted their business in the state house, state office buildings, the Supreme Court building, local inns, above the city market and in a modest frame structure. The Columbus Theater was built in 1835 and closed in 1841. The interior was remodeled and used for a city hall from 1843 to 1869, when a site, where the Ohio Theater stands today, was chosen for the first real city hall.

Fig. 94 Christopher Columbus   Fig. 95 "Old" City Hall (1872-1921)
—from Columbus Metro Library

The $175,000, first city hall building was designed by R.T. Brooks. It was constructed of stone, brick and wood in Gothic style and was three stories high with a clock tower. The State Street front faced the state house to the north. It was completed in 1872 and functioned until 1921 when it burned completely. The interior was spacious with a grand staircase to the second floor where most offices and a council chamber provided the area to conduct business. A post office, library and offices for the Board of Trade occupied the first floor. A huge public hall, seating three thousand persons and illuminated by five massive chandeliers was situated on the third floor. The "old" city hall was a community center for business and other meetings for forty-nine years.

After an interim of five years, while city officials met in temporary quarters, the current city hall was built in 1926 on Marconi Boulevard near West Broad Street where a steel mill had stood. Set off in front by a statue of Christopher Columbus facing the Scioto River to the west, the hall's green copper, rectangular roof is easily recognized from the air. The twenty-foot tall, three and one-half ton, bronze figure of the discoverer of America and the city's namesake was officially unveiled in 1935. Approximately 100,000 spectators roared their approval on Columbus Day of that year. The statue was a gift from sister city, Genoa, Italy. Within a few years, a city hall annex was built on Marconi Boulevard immediately north of the city hall.

Later, Civic Center plans included a new Central Police Station (1930), and the widening the Scioto River by the Army Corps of Engineers as a flood control measure. The new police station was adjacent to and north of the annex building on Marconi Boulevard, abutting Long Street.

During the general time span (1920-1940) in which the civic center was undergoing radical changes, Columbus also embraced a new, west-side Central High School in 1924, and the construction of the AIU (LeVeque) Tower in 1927.

Chapter 25

Entertainment in Columbus

Columbus Theaters and Arenas

At one time, Columbus had seventeen theaters in the city center. The Southern Theater opened in 1896. It was the first public building to have electricity. Attendance gradually diminished, and it closed in 1979. In 2005, after a ten million dollar renovation, funded with private and state monies, it reopened as an annex of the Southern Hotel on South High Street. Its size was smaller than the Ohio and Palace theaters, with nine hundred and thirty-three seats divided between the main floor and two balconies with a good view from every seat. It is now home to the Columbus Jazz Orchestra, the Columbus Light Opera and the Chamber Music Columbus.

Columbus also features the Columbus Symphony Orchestra, BalletMet, the Contemporary American Theater, the Columbus Children's Theater, Promusica and other musical groups and theaters, such as the Riffe Theater in a state building with that name and Mershon Auditorium at Ohio State University. The Battelle Auditorium, the Schottenstein Arena and the Nationwide Arena host large traveling shows. The larger suburbs and the universities have their own musical and theatrical organizations. For years, a German-singing group in German Village, the Maennerchor Club, featured private concerts and European tours. Also, in German Village, the Actors' Theatre Company has performed in the outdoor Schiller Park Amphitheatre for twenty-five years.

The Palace Theater on West Broad Street is a delightfully renovated theater that also was saved from demolition. It is attached to the signature skyscraper in Columbus, the LeVeque Tower. The Tower was built in 1927 by the American Insurance Union (AIU Building) which defaulted during the Great Depression. The 2,827 seat theater was designed by Thomas Lamb in the spirit of the Palace of Versailles, France. The theater was originally connected to the Deshler Hotel by a stone covered bridge and a Hall of Mirrors complete with a pipe organ. The complex had its own private dressing rooms (named after cities), laundry, kitchen, billiards room, playroom for children and postoffice. The theater was used primarily for vaudeville and at first was called the Palace-Albee Keith Theater. Its $1.5 million cost and $1.5 million furnishings were provided by theater magnate Edward F. Albee. In 1929, RKO (Radio Keith Orpheum) assumed ownership of the theater and was named RKO Palace. Big bands provided entertainment. Later, movies were shown and its name changed to The Palace (the interior during this era is shown at the right. From 1975 to 1980, the theater was unused. In 1980, a three million dollar renovation by owner Catherine LeVeque made the theater an historic work of art.

Fig. 96 Palace Theater

In 1989, The Palace was purchased by CAPA, which consolidated its administration with the Ohio and other downtown theaters. It hosts the Columbus Symphony, the Jazz Arts Group, Broadway shows, opera and other sponsored shows.

Fig. 97 Ohio Theater

—both theaters from Columbus Metro Library

The Ohio Theater at 39 East State Street is the premier theater in Columbus. It was designed by Thomas Lamb as a movie center and built on the site of the "old" city hall in 1928. The exterior is beaux-arts style while the interior Spanish baroque. The theater gradually deteriorated and was destined to be razed, when public support saved it. It was beautifully renovated to become the home of the Columbus Association for the Performing Arts (CAPA). Most Columbus Symphony concerts and Broadway shows are held there.

Columbus Symphony

The Columbus Symphony began in 1951 as the Columbus Little Symphony with local violinist George Hardesty as its conductor. Performances were held in the Ohio State Archaeology and Historical Museum on the campus of The Ohio State University. The orchestra's Women's Association provided planning and fund-raising. The symphony moved to Central High School in the following year and as part of its educational commitment, included three young people's concerts in its program. Claude Monteux began a three-year tenure as conductor in 1953, and the name Columbus Symphony became official. In 1956, Evan Whallon began a twenty-six year span as conductor. By 1962, the orchestra had a Youth Symphony, an one-hundred voice chorus and a Pops Series. In 1970, the restored Ohio Theater became its home. The opera, *Barber of Seville* was produced in 1974. By 1978, a core of thirteen full-time musicians was attained. Christian Badea commenced a nine-year term as conductor in 1983. Several critically acclaimed recordings of the symphony were produced. In the same year, Picnic with the Pops was started on the lawn of Chemical Abstracts. Badea and the orchestra played a major role in launching the Lancaster, Ohio Festival in 1984. For two years, Peter Nero served as principal Pops conductor and recorded several best selling CDs of Broadway and Hollywood hit songs. In 1991, Alessandro Siciliani began a twelve-year tenure as maestro. Luciano Pavarotti sang with the orchestra in 1999. Two CDs of the orchestra and chorus performances at Carnegie Hall helped the celebration of the symphony's fiftieth anniversary in 2001. For two and one-half years, a series of conductors performed with the orchestra, and in 2006, Junichi Hirokami was chosen as the latest music director and conductor.

An important arm of the Symphony is its Youth Orchestras; a Cadet Orchestra, the Chamber Strings Orchestra and the Junior Strings Orchestra. Its goal is to expose young musicians to the highest level of orchestral music in a professional setting under the direction of experienced conductors. Their tours have taken them as distant as China.

Opera Columbus (formerly Columbus Opera)

Columbus Opera began in 1981 as an independent entity but closely aligned with the Symphony Orchestra. Initially, it was aided by the support of internationally recognized diva, Beverly Sills. Andrew Broekema, Dean of the College of Arts and Sciences at The Ohio State University, lent his talent in organizing the Columbus Opera. Grand Opera performances took place in the Ohio Theater, while Light Operas were presented in the Southern Theater. Well established opera stars and conductors are brought to Columbus to perform the leading roles in each production. Captions are used to provide English translations. Christopher Purdy offers a preview and interpretation of the opera to be seen, one hour before opening curtain time. Workshops and student residencies are offered to talented youths. In 2001, the Light and Grand Operas merged under the name Opera Columbus. Financial support is provided by corporations, grants and individuals. The business office is at 177 Naghten Street.

New to the Columbus opera scene is the Metropolitan Opera-live "movie theater" series presented at a local motion picture theater once or twice monthly. It is always a packed house.

BalletMet

In 1978, Wayne Soulant and twelve professional dancers commenced providing excellent programs as BalletMet. Their repertoire of several dozen works include full-length productions of *The Nutcracker, Dangerous Liaisons, Madame Butterfly, Beauty and the Beast, Carmen, Romeo and Juliet, Swan Lake, Dracula* and *A Midsummer Night's Dream*. Their international tours debuted in Cairo, Egypt in 1989. Their New York debut was in 1991. The world premieres of Gerard Charles' *Cinderella* and Stanton Welch's *Don Quixote* were presented in Columbus in 2002 and 2003, respectively. The company was one of eighteen chosen from sixty-six applicants to perform at the Joyce Theater in Manhattan, New York City in 2004. In addition to local and touring performances, the company has an extensive Dance Reach educational program for those age four and older. Each year they teach one thousand students. The studio is at 322 Mt. Vernon Avenue. BalletMet ranks among the fifteen largest dance companies in the nation.

The King Arts Complex and the Pythian Theater

The State of Ohio chartered the Community Arts Projects in 1982, of which the Martin Luther King Jr. Performing Arts Complex at 867 Mt. Vernon Avenue, Columbus, Ohio, is an integral part. Local community and government leaders desired to honor Dr. King by providing a center offering performing, cultural and educational programs to celebrate influential contributions of African-Americans throughout the world. The building which houses the complex was built in

Fig. 98. The Martin Luther Arts Complex at 876 Mt. Vernon Avenue (since 1987).

1926 as the Pythian Temple and was used as a lodge, social center and theater in the midst of the largest neighborhood of African-Americans in Columbus. The structure, of Colonial Revival Style, was designed by African-American architect, Samuel Plato of Louisville, Kentucky and is listed on the National Registry of Historical Places. It is the only known example of Plato's work in Columbus. The Pythian Theater was renovated at a cost of $2.7 million in 1987. Another $1.8 million was used in an additional renovation of the adjacent Garfield School, Phase II, in 1989. In addition to the theater, the complex has a grand ballroom, a dance studio, the Elijah Pierce Art Gallery, a board room and a multipurpose room. Entertainer greats such as Cab Calloway, Count Basie, Duke Ellington, the Cotton Club Dancers, Ben Vereen, Roberta Flack and Abbey Lincoln have performed in the theater.

The Lincoln Theater

The Lincoln Theater was erected at 775 East Long Street in 1928 in the near east side of Columbus in the Bronzeville area now known as the King-Lincoln-Bronzeville neighborhood. It seats five hundred and seventy, has four storefronts and a ballroom. In its zenith in the 1930s and 1940s, it was the entertainment center for the African-American community. Some of the nation's most prominent black entertainers appeared on its stage. Although it has had several renovations, its physical condition has deteriorated, and now the building is rarely used. The theater is available for rental from the city of Columbus which bought the theater in 2004 from Charles Adrian for $1 million. Mayor Coleman, with strong financial support of some commercial companies, the county and the state, has stepped forward to correct the deficiencies present in the theater. An ancillary reason for the $4 million upgrading is to spur economic development in the area. The Columbus Children's Theater has agreed to perform twice a year in the theater when renovation is completed.

Franklin Park Conservatory

Franklin Park Conservatory, located in Franklin Park on East Broad Street, between Bexley and downtown Columbus, opened in 1895. Prior to the Conservatory, the grounds were used in 1852 to hold the first county fair. The size of the park was increased in 1874, and it was made the official location for the Ohio State Fair. In 1884, the state fair moved to a new locale and Franklin Park was abandoned. It became a public park again two years later. A Victorian style Conservatory was constructed in 1894, modeled after the Glass Palace at the Columbian Exposition in Chicago in 1893. Between 1927 and 1929, animals were kept in lower rooms, but, subsequently, were moved to the newly created Columbus Zoo. The Conservatory's operation is enhanced by a multitude of volunteers supervised by professional horticulturists. It is continually modernized and now includes a glass enclosed replica of the world's ecosystems. In 1989, a renovation added new rooms, a gift shop, classrooms, a library and café. In 1992, *Ameriflora*, an international flora exhibition, was held in Franklin Park and utilized the adjacent Conservatory. In 1994, the Conservatory showcased the first seasonal butterfly exhibition in the nation. In 2003-2004, *Chihuly at the Conservatory,* a permanent glass artwork of Dale Chihuly, was acquired and is to be exhibited permanently by the Conservatory. The Conservatory is administered by the Franklin Park Joint Recreation District, a private not-for-profit organization.

Fig. 99 The Franklin Park Conservatory
—from Columbus Metro Library

Vaud-Villities

For four decades, Vaud-Villities has produced and performed an annual, popular extravagance with amateur musicians and actors in the Veterans Memorial Building in Franklinton. In 2008, the production and presentation of the show moved to a renovated movie theater in Northland at 1865 Morse Road.

Columbus Zoo and Aquarium

The Zoo originated on a large acreage in the Beechwold community, eight miles north of downtown Columbus, as the Columbus Zoological Gardens in 1905. In addition to numerous animals and a monkey house, which remains today as a barn at 150 Beechwold Boulevard, it featured rides, picnic grounds, a merry-go-round, a billiard hall and a dance pavilion. It closed after a life of only five months. The Zoo's brick entryway is still present where West Beechwold Boulevard intersects with North High Street. The Zoo reopened further north in 1927, and the city of Columbus took over its management in 1951. Today, the Columbus Zoo and Aquarium is located at 9990 Riverside Drive immediately south of Powell Road, and entirely within Delaware County. It contains six thousand animals. It has acquired the adjacent Wyandot Lake Water Park and the Safari Golf Course (both renovated). The Aquarium opened in 1999 with a retractable roof and contains manatees, sea turtles and native Florida fish. Colo, the world's first captive-born gorilla arrived in 1956. In 2006, she celebrated her fiftieth birthday. Other features are a group of pygmy chimpanzee, a breeding program for Mexican wolves that has produced twenty-nine pups, a restored 1914 Mangels-Illions carousel acquired from the former Olentangy Amusement Park in 1938, a Polar exhibit, an Australian wildlife exhibit, an African Savannah and Rain Forest, an "Asia Quest"(second phase scheduled to open in 2007), featuring tigers, sun bears, Pallas Cats in a new open air environment, muntjac, rare cranes, langurs, tufted deer, a water monitor, and a North America exhibit. The exhibits have adopted a plan of large wide open natural terrain which allows more roaming room for the animals. Currently, Wyandot Lake is closed for renovations. The popular artificial water tidal wave will be retained. Outside the exhibition grounds, the Zoo leases a lodge and retreat formerly owned by the Jeffrey Manufacturing Company for use as a research and educational facility dedicated to the preservation of mussels and other freshwater organisms. For a decade, the Aquarium has enjoyed the resources of the Ohio Department of Natural Resources and The Ohio State University in research and recovery of endangered species. For many years, the Zoo had the good fortune of having as its director, Jack Hanna, who is now Emeritus Director and active as a consultant. He has a syndicated TV show, *Jack Hanna's Animal Adventures,* and is a featured guest on other national television shows. He is chiefly responsible for the high quality reputation and international recognition of the zoo. The zoo enjoys strong local, regional and national support, and, in 2004, voters passed a measure that provides $180 million for expansion over a ten-year period. A resort-style hotel is visualized. The zoo has sustained for twenty years a conservation fund (*Partners in Conservation)* that has raised and granted millions of dollars to world wide efforts to promote sound and sustainable practices that integrate conservation research, capacity-building, education and community involvement. Other educational efforts include teacher kits, workshops, posters and publications. Many volunteers help make the zoo a success. They are members of *Face*, and fulfill the role of ambassadors of the zoo to the public. The zoo has 1.3 million visitors annually.

Television in Columbus

Three television stations began broadcasting in Columbus in 1949. The first was WLW Columbus from the Seneca Hotel. WTVN was second and WBNS was third. Today, most television comes to the customer via cable. A minority use a "dish" to receive their signal by satellite connection. Columbus now has six TV channels. They are: ONN (Ohio News Network); WBNS-TV 10 (CBS); WCMH-TV 4 (NBC); WOSU-TV 34 (Ohio State University); WSYX-TV 6 (ABC); and WTTE-TV 28 (Fox). Closed Caption for the benefit of the deaf carries a running script on the screen.

The largest cable television network in Columbus and Franklin County is Time-Warner. Another large provider of cable access is SBC. DirecTV and SBC offer television via satellite transmission.

Chapter 26

Commercial and Professional Sports and Recreation

The Columbus Clippers Baseball Team

Baseball developed its impetus as a national pastime with soldiers during the Civil War. A team was formed in Columbus in 1866, and the first game was an intrasquad affair played on the grounds of the Insane Asylum at Parsons and Broad Streets. Team A beat team B, ninety-five to forty-four. Six more teams were added to form a league. The Columbus Buckeyes became professional in 1875 and joined the International League in 1877. They were in the major leagues in 1883-1884 and again in 1889-1891, the only time in their history. In 1905, a concrete and steel stadium called Neil Park was constructed in the Near North of Columbus. In 1931, the team was renamed the Red Birds and became a farm team for Branch Rickey's St. Louis Cardinals. The present stadium on West Mound Street was completed in 1932 for $450,000. The first night game was played in that year. In 1954, there was no baseball in Columbus since Rickey moved the team to Omaha. Harold Cooper bought the Ottawa team and moved it to Columbus in 1955 as the Jets, and they became a farm team of the Kansas City Athletics. In 1960, John Galbreath's Pittsburgh Pirates made the Columbus club their farm team. The team was moved to Charleston in 1970 and, again, there was no team in Columbus until 1977 when Franklin County renovated its stadium and Pittsburgh again made the Clippers their farm team. The baseball complex was renamed Cooper Stadium in honor of the club's general manager. The New York Yankees under George Steinbrenner bought the Clippers in 1979, and they remained the New York farm team through 2006. Currently, they are a farm team of the Washington Nationals. Plans are underway to build a new stadium in the Arena District with Franklin County as its owner. Corporate donations will be added to funding by the taxpayers. The new arena will be called Huntington Stadium; Huntington Bank paid for naming rights.

Blue Jackets Hockey Team

From 1991 to 1999, Columbus had a minor league hockey team called the *Columbus Chill*. In 1997, a group of investors headed by local industrialist, John McConnell, purchased a franchise in the National Hockey League. The latter was composed of thirty United States and Canada teams. The team's name was suggested by Ohio's participation in the Civil War in which northern soldiers wore blue uniforms. The Blue Jackets' first game was in 2000. The new Nationwide Arena was the team's home ice rink. As of this date, the team has not had a winning season. Nevertheless, large and enthusiastic crowds cheer on the team. Many of the games are televised.

Fig, 100. Nationwide Arena-home of Blue Jackets Hockey Team and venue for other events.

Ice skating and related ice sports have grown in popularity in the Columbus area during the last two decades. This surge in interest was given a large boost by the presence of a major league professional hockey team, the Columbus Blue Jackets. Chiller Ice Rinks, a business venture in Franklin County, owns five ice rinks, four are under the Chiller prefix name: Chiller Dublin, Chiller Easton, Chiller North and Chiller Worthington. A fifth rink is called the Dispatch Ice Haus which is also the practice rink for the Columbus Blue Jackets. All offer public skating, lessons and facilities for private parties. Leagues for youth and adults, dressing rooms, seating for up to one thousand spectators, enclosed second-story viewing areas, party-meeting rooms, gift shops and snack bars are provided to varying degrees by all of the rinks. Major tenants are two high schools, Ohio Wesleyan University and several hockey leagues.

Columbus Crew Soccer Team

In 1994, Columbus was awarded a franchise in the newly organized Major League Soccer League composed of ten teams. Lamar Hunt and family of Kansas City were the principal owner and manager of the organization. Other investors in the franchise were Pizzuti Sports Limited, John McConnell and Wolfe Enterprises. A fan, Luis Orozca, suggested the team's name, Columbus Crew with a blue and gold logo. The first games were played in the Ohio Stadium beginning in 1996 with an attendance of 25,266. The Columbus Crew Stadium, which opened in 1999, was the first venue built in the United States solely for soccer. It is located north of the Ohio State fairgrounds, off Interstate-71. In its inaugural year, 1999, the club achieved participation in the league's playoffs. It won the U.S. Open Cup championship in 2002. The franchise has a training center in Obetz which is scheduled to be moved. The team's matches are televised nationally by ABC and ESPN2.

Columbus Destroyers Arena Football Team

The Buffalo Destroyers Arena Football Team, organized in 1999, moved its franchise to Columbus in 2003. The Destroyers were heavily supported by local corporations, and the Managing Partner was John H. McConnell, President of Worthington Industries. Home games are played in the Nationwide Arena. Attendance has been outstanding despite more games lost than won. The team's first coach was Earle Bruce (2003-2005). The second coach was Chris Spielman (2005). The third and current coach is Doug Kay (2005-). Both Bruce and Spielman were standout coach and player respectively on football teams of The Ohio State University. Most of the Destroyers' games can be seen on local television.

Ohio State Buckeyes (see Ohio State University)

Columbus Sports Figures

Fig. 101

Jack Nicklaus was born in Columbus, Ohio, in 1940, son of a successful pharmacist. As a youth, he spent most of his non-school time honing his golf game under the tutelage of the Scioto Country Club pro, Jack Grote. At five feet, eleven inches in height and weighing around two hundred pounds, he had the optimal physique for golf. His intense focus on every golf stroke and fervent desire to win were additional attributes for success. He played golf and basketball for his high school, excelling in each. The local press nicknamed him the "Golden Bear," in reference to the Upper Arlington High School mascot. Subsequently, he used this moniker on his golf equipment and accessories. He attended The Ohio State University and led his golf team to the NCAA championship as well as receiving individual honors. He became the national amateur champion twice. Lacking just one term of graduation from college, he elected to turn professional and soon dominated the PGA tour. His early image was marred by being overweight, and he was labeled "Ohio Fats" by the national press. Anger was aroused in some fans when he displaced popular Arnold Palmer as reigning top golfer in the world. His record of winning seventy-three PGA tournaments and twenty major titles remains unequalled. His six Masters, five PGA, four U.S. Open, and three British Open victories never have been paralleled. As a senior golfer, he won ten tour events. He was acclaimed the best golfer of the millennium, and most believe he has overshadowed all competitors to this date. He became a golf course architect and headed two successful related businesses. He resides in both Muirfield Village, Ohio where he designed a premier golf complex, home of the annual PGA Memorial Tournament, and in West Palm Beach, Florida, site of his business ventures. His alma mater, OSU, awarded him an honorary doctorate degree. His first priority was his family; he received three Family or Father of the Year awards from national organizations, attesting to his devotion. He retired from competitive play in 2005.

Geraldine (Jerrie) Mock was born in Newark, Ohio in 1925. After attending public schools, she worked at various jobs before becoming manager of the Columbus, Ohio airport. She began flying as a teenager and obtained her pilot's license at age twenty-three. She married a pilot in 1945 and had three children. Almost as a joke, her husband suggested that she fly around the world. Amelia Earhart, accompanied by a navigator, had attempted it in 1937 and disappeared over the Pacific Ocean. Her remains and plane have never been found. Mock accepted her husband's challenge. For eighteen months she prepared for her earth encircling flight. She modified the plane owned jointly by her husband and another man, and studied the route and weather conditions carefully. She left on her around-the-world flight from the Columbus airport on March 19, 1964 in a single engine, Cessna 180, named the *Spirit of Columbus*. The aircraft was equipped with enlarged fuel tanks, a custom built engine, and long range radio and navigational instruments. She was required to keep a daily log and she sent dispatches to the news media while enroute. She never crossed the equator. Some problems she encountered included a leaking fuel tank, a bulky radio antenna, difficulty in keeping the landing gear up and a faulty rear wheel. Repairs took place along the way, causing delays of two weeks in her journey. Another woman, also attempting to be the first woman to encircle the globe had set off two days earlier. She was never a serious contender, however; she had multiple plane problems, much bad weather and many delays. Nevertheless, Mock's husband constantly urged her to hurry during the flight. Other problems that developed during her flight were radio failure that required her to fly part of the time by dead reckoning, landing in a secret military airport in Egypt by mistake, having brakes repaired, and changing the route several times due to weather. Near the end of her journey she was welcomed in Hawaii by her husband, news reporters and a huge crowd. She touched down in Columbus on April 17, twenty five and one-half days after departure and became the first woman to fly solo around the earth. She covered 22,858 miles in 158 flying hours. Other records set during the flight were: first woman to fly over the North Atlantic Ocean from the U.S. to Africa, first woman to fly across the Pacific Ocean and first woman to fly across both oceans. President Johnson presented her with a gold medal, and other countries gave her medals and decorations, including the prestigious Louis Bleriot Silver Medal. The log of her trip is kept in Lusanne, Switzerland, and the plane was exhibited in a factory in Wichita until 1975 when it went to the National Air and Space Museum. She never flew the plane again, but the Cessna Company gave her a new model. She continued to set speed and distance records through 1969. In one interview, when asked why she attempted her historic solo flight, she replied, "to give confidence to the little pilot who is being left in the jetstream of the space age."

Bobby Rahal was born in Medina, Ohio in 1953. His paternal grandparents immigrated from Lebanon. Bobby's mother was English. His father was a graduate of Denison University, and his hobby was auto racing. Bobby was reared in Chicago, Illinois, where his father ran a wholesale food business. He began racing autos at age seventeen. He also attended and graduated from Denison University where he majored in history, English and American literature. Racing was in his blood, and he immediately embarked on a career of race car driving upon graduation from college. His twenty-nine year stint of driving race cars was punctuated by ups and downs. He won many races in Canada, Europe and the United States. He is best known for winning at Daytona, Sebring and the CART (Championship Auto Racing Teams-international schedule) three times. Most coveted of all, he was winner of the Indianapolis 500 in 1986. He moved to Columbus in 1981 to facilitate his business relationship with hotel owner, Jim Trueman. Among his other business partners is talk-show celebrity, David Letterman. Currently, he is principal owner of Rahal Letterman Racing, headquartered in Hilliard, Ohio. He enjoys playing a competitive game of golf and living the life of a celebrity. The latter has drawn him into involvement in community affairs.

Metropolitan Parks and Recreation

Columbus and Franklin County have joined forces to sponsor the Metropolitan Parks and Recreation Department. For many years, it was managed by Mel Dodge. The huge recreational facility in south Columbus on Greenlawn Avenue is named for him. It was renovated in 2005 for five and one-half million dollars. A new building was installed, featuring a library, lounge, kitchen, game room and boxing room. The outdoor portion contains many sports areas, a swimming pool, a roller hockey rink and a skateboard area. A similar facility, costing over five million dollars is located in the north side of the county on Lazelle Road. Over three dozen other recreation centers, parks and six golf courses are found placed in strategic sites in the county. They include lakes, nature educational centers and hiking trails. The locations of the major parks and trails in relation to cities in Franklin County are shown below.

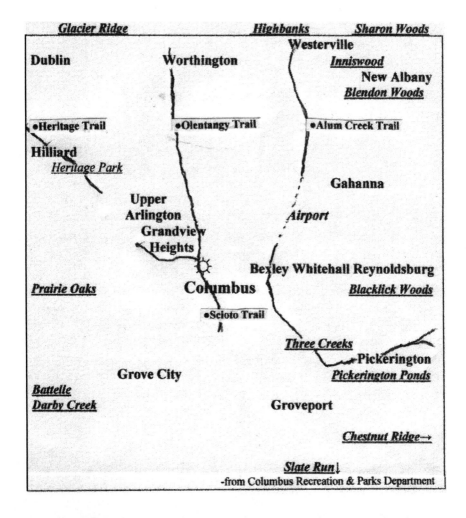

Fig. 102 Twelve metropolitan park names are in italics and underlined. The four existing trails are shown as solid lines and have a black dot in front of their names. Eight additional trails are planned.

Fort Rapids Indoor Waterpark

Fort Rapids Indoor Waterpark Resort is attached to the three hundred and thirty-eight room, Port Columbus Airport Holiday Inn. The entrance is an authentic looking mine shaft, and the scenes are surrounded by detailed wall murals and scenic waterfalls. Water activities include twelve different slides. The park is geared to birthday parties, weddings, group gatherings, corporate meetings, travelers, families and just kids. The project costing $50 million opened in 2006 and is owned by two local corporations, Platinum Ridge and FLG Hospitality Group. The Waterpark Resort competes with other waterparks in Ohio located in Newark, Mason and Sandusky.

City Based Festivities

Today, Columbus features several city-center festive attractions. In June, the Greater Columbus Arts Festival is held on the riverfront. The Fourth of July holiday is celebrated with fireworks known as Red, White and Boom in downtown Columbus. Both events draw half-a-million people. A Ribs and Jazz Festival takes place in late summer, and Oktoberfest is held in the fall. They too, attract large crowds. The suburbs have similar festivals.

Columbus Senior Centers

Columbus has six "Senior Centers" placed strategically throughout the city: Barber Roselea, Gillie, Marion Franklin, Martin Janis, McDowell and Sawyer. Barber Roselea is scheduled to be combined with the renovated Whetstone Park Center in 2008.

Columbus Golf Courses

The seven city golf courses are: Airport, Champions, Mentel, Raymond, Turnberry, Walnut Hill and Wilson Road (an executive course).

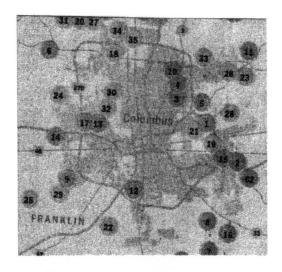

Fig. 103 Public and private golf courses in Franklin County-2007

Public golf courses		Private golf courses	
1-Airport	2-Blacklick Woods (2)	18-Brookside CC	19-Columbus CC
3-Bridgeview	4-Champions	20-CC at Muirfield Village	
5-Gahanna	6-Golf Club of Dublin	21-Eagle Eye	22-Pinnacle
7-Homestead Springs	8-Links at Groveport	23-The Golf Club	24-Heritage
9-Mentel	10-Minerva Lake	25-Hickory Hills	26-Jefferson CC
11-New Albany Links	12-Phoenix	27-Muirfield Village	28-New Albany CC
13-Raymond	14-Thorn Apple	29-Oakhurst CC	30-Ohio State U (two)
15-Walnut Hill	16-Westchester	31-Riviera	32-Scioto CC
17-Wilson Road		33-Little Turtle	
		34-Worthington Hills CC	35-York

Fig. 104 The Columbus Athletic Club, at 136 East Broad Street, opened in 1916.

—from Columbus Metro Library

Chapter 27

Notable Restaurants in Columbus

Three Columbus restaurants that were favorites, now gone, are worthy of mention.

Maramor

Mary Love opened a restaurant at 131 East Broad Street in 1920. The name was fashioned from her first name and the Latin word for her last name. It became very popular as an upscale dining place and was a special favorite with the evening theater attendees. Some of the main entrees on the menu were named for celebrities appearing on the stage. The restaurant passed on to the Sher family and, finally, to Danny Deeds, who attached his name to the marquee. The restaurant closed in 1970, and the business narrowed to making Maramor chocolate candy at a new location.

Marzetti's

Teresa came from Italy in 1896, at age thirteen. She married Joseph Marzetti, and they opened a small saloon in "Flytown," near Goodale Park in 1919. The Marzetti couple moved their business to 16 East Broad Street in 1940 where they developed a premier Italian restaurant. One of their specialties was salad dressing and patrons took home prepared bottles of their choice. When Teresa and Joseph Marzetti died, their children became the proprietors, but the success of the restaurant eluded them, and it closed in the 1970s. T. Marzetti Company at 3838 Indianola is a spin-off of the restaurant and has become an international company, famous for its salad dressings. Its business offices are on Shrock Road. It is now a subsidiary of Lancaster Colony Corporation.

Presutti's

Salvatore and Emmitt Presutti opened a saloon on West Goodale Avenue in "Flytown" in 1914. In 1928, they started a restaurant at 409 West Goodale

Street that was especially enticing to nearby Ohio State University students. The family moved the restaurant to their home at 1692 West Fifth Avenue in 1933. Later, it was called Presutti's Villa. Its original Crystalier Room was joined by the Champagne and Empire Rooms as the restaurant expanded. It became a top choice for those preferring Italian cuisine. After a fire in 1981, it failed to reopen. The building was eventually razed, and the site is now occupied by a Sherwin-Williams paint store.

Jai Lai

The Jai Lai restaurant opened at 585 North High Street in 1933. Highway construction caused it to move to 1421 Olentangy River Road in 1955. Its excellent cuisine attracted patrons from all parts of the city. Due to its proximity to The Ohio State University, it became a favorite among students and faculty, especially sports fans, players and coaches. Woody Hayes, famed football coach, was a fixture through many evenings. The walls were adorned with pictures of athletes, coaches and sports memorabilia. The Jai Lai closed in 1996 and reopened the following year as the Buckeye Hall of Fame restaurant. It remains popular attracting the same clientele.

Current Notable Restaurants Originating or Headquartered in Columbus

Bob Evans Restaurants

Bob Evans began selling sausage made on his southeastern Ohio farm at his small diner/truck stop in 1948. A little restaurant on his farm followed in 1962. The successful *Little Sausage Shop* became a tourist attraction. Today, it seats one hundred and thirty-four. Every October, fifty thousand attend the Bob Evans Farm Festival. Today, the publicly held *Bob Evans* restaurants has six hundred and eighty-three locations in the eastern half of the nation, of which forty-two are in central Ohio. There are 52,500 employees. The headquarters for the $1.5 billion revenue company is on South High Street in Columbus. The founder was a strong supporter of the Ohio State Fair and the 4-H program for farm youth. Evans died in 2007.

Clarmont

The *Clarmont Restaurant* at 684 South High Street was opened in 1947 by Frank Kondos. Its location on the eastern edge of the Brewery District was always identified with German Village, one block to its east. Known for years as a steak house, its cuisine is primarily American. This fine dining establishment has long been a favorite for business people, politicians, professionals and families. Its ownership has changed hands several times. In 1972, Barry Zacks purchased the Clarmont and in 1986 sold it to Bill Bigelow. The menu was broadened to include seafoods. In 1996, Thom Coffman became the latest owner of the restaurant. Because of the age of the building, but wishing to retain a well known and valuable landmark, plans are underway to replace the structure with an eight-story building to include an enlarged *Clarmont* on the second floor with a seating capacity of 150 and banquet rooms. Retail spaces will occupy the ground floor, and condominiums will be placed on the floors over the restaurant with underground parking. Even a crosswalk over High Street to the new corporate headquarters of Grange Insurance Company is envisioned.

Handke's Cuisine

Owner Hartman Handke, German born and former executive chef at the Greenbriar Resort in West Virginia, is the only certified master chef in Ohio. He has received over thirty-six national and international master chef gold medals. Many of his awards decorate the brick walls beneath vaulted ceilings of his below street level dining spot. His contemporary restaurant located in the former Schlee brewery rathskeller in the Brewery District of Columbus is the recipient of many "Top Ten Restaurant" awards given by the *Columbus Dispatch* since its opening in 1991. The chef is a local celebrity and conducts cooking classes.

Damon's International

The *Damon's* restaurant chain was founded in Columbus in 1979 by Irving Rossman with a single East Broad Street location. Others became part-owners in 1989. The franchises, known primarily for their baby back ribs specialty, were owned by the company or individuals and reached a maximum of one hundred and fifty, scattered over the eastern United States, Puerto and the United Kingdom. As the company expanded rapidly, it struggled financially and approximately one-third of the restaurants have closed recently. Principal owners after Rossman were Jon Self, Gene Simonetti and Shannon Foust. The headquarters is at 4645 Executive Drive, and the training center is at 4555 Knightsbridge Boulevard. In 2006, most of the chain was sold to Alliance Development Corporation of Charlotte, North Carolina followed by a sale and lease-back restructuring of its remaining holdings with Servant Investments LLC. The heavy debt load was reduced from $40 million to $5 million. The new owners have infused cash and optimism needed for success. The sports-themed restaurants are known as *Damon's Grill* today. New franchise restaurants are in the planning stages, and are expected to be smaller, brighter, airier and with new menus.

Max & Erma's

Max & Erma's is a casual bar and grill, sit-down restaurant chain with over one hundred locations. Seventy-seven of the restaurants are company owned and twenty-four are franchises. They are situated principally in the northeast sector of the Middle West. Two are in North Carolina and ten new ones are scheduled to open in Florida and Nevada. The first restaurant was opened in German Village in 1972 by founders Barry Zacks and Todd Barnum. Annual revenue is over $55 million. Long-term debt is $44 million. The company publicly trades on the stock market under the Nasdaq symbol of MAXE. The current CEO is Todd Barnum.

Cameron Mitchell Restaurants

Fig. 105

Cameron Mitchell (Fig. 105) started in the culinary business as a dishwasher in 1979. After setting goals for himself in the business he wished to succeed in, he graduated from the Culinary Institute of America in 1986 at age twenty-two. He was hired as sous chef by the 55 Restaurant Group in Columbus in 1986 and advanced to the company's operations manager in 1990. In 1993, he opened his own restaurant, *Cameron's American Bistro* in Worthington. Success resulted in creating a chain of thirty-three units in seven states and a catering service, all private-group owned. He also manages six *Rusty Bucket Corner Taverns*. Sales in the complete operation brought in over $105 million in 2006. The Columbus restaurants are: *Cap City, Martini Italian Bistro, Mitchell's Steakhouse, Mitchell's Fish Market, The Ocean Club, M and Molly Woo's Asian Bistro.* In 2007, Mitchell and his one-hundred and eighty partners sold twenty-two of his restaurants to Ruth Chris Steak House, Inc. for $94 million. The sale included all of his Fish Markets and Steakhouses. Mitchell will act as a consultant to Ruth Chris for three years and will continue to expand his eleven Italian Bistro, Rusty Bucket, Ocean Club and Marcello's concepts. Mitchell has contributed generously to civic organizations including Children's Hospital and Sera Bella, a fundraising foundation established by Cameron and his wife Bella. He has served as a member of the boards of the Ohio Restaurant Association, the National Restaurant Association and the Culinary Institute of America. He established a $250,000 scholarship fund for the last. Among his honors are Entrepreneur of the Year, Small Businessperson of the Year, a Tastemaster, Concept of Tomorrow Visionary, High Performance Restaurant Leadership and the Richard Melman Concepts of Tomorrow Award.

Refectory

The *Refectory* building was originally a Methodist Church, which was built on Bethel Road in 1853 with walnut sidings. After the church was abandoned, it became the Olde Church-House restaurant in 1972. It was purchased by the present owner, Kamal Boulus in 1980, renovated and renamed the *Refectory* (dining hall for a monastery). Since 1982, it has been acclaimed the best restaurant in Columbus. In addition to its French cuisine, it has an outstanding wine list. It has won the following awards: Grand Award *The Wine Spectator,* AAA Four-Diamond Award, DiRona Award-Distinguished Restaurants of North America, Five Stars-*Columbus Monthly,* Five Stars-*This Week Papers,* and Top Ten Dining since 1982-*Columbus Dispatch.* It is truly a distinguished Columbus business.

Bravo and Brio (Bravo! Development Inc.)

Bravo Cucina Italiana's first location was opened at 3000 Hayden Road in 1992 by Rick and Chris Doody. Since then, the BDI company's two main brands, *Brio Tuscan* and *Bravo Cucina Italiana,* have grown to sixty restaurants in twenty-one states. Rick received a master's degree in hotel and restaurant management from Cornell University in the mid-1980s, while Chris earned a similar degree from Tulane University. Their first airy, upscale *Brio* restaurant opened in the Easton Fashion Place in 1999 and remains the company's highest volume business. The company's only French café, *Brio Vie*, opened in Easton Fashion Place in 2003. The name of their Lindey's restaurant in Polaris Fashion Place was changed to *Brio* in 2007. A *Brio* is scheduled to open in Las Vegas in 2007. The company had six thousand employees in 2006 when gross sales were over $247,000. Eighty percent of BDI was sold to two private equity firms for about $180,000 in 2005. The Doody brothers removed themselves from the management team.

Lindey's

Lindey's is the latest name for a popular bistro at the corner of Beck and Mohawk Streets in German Village that opened in 1981. Sue and son, Rick Doody, were the management team among the family owners. The restaurant's décor incorporates high ceilings, big windows, walls covered with artwork, bentwood chairs, polished brass railings and hardwood floors. There are three dining rooms, several private party rooms, an outdoor terrace and a courtyard. Specialties in its upper New York City setting include steak and lamb. Carry-out is available daily. A Sunday brunch is served, and musical entertainment is furnished on Thursdays. A second venue, *Lindey's Café,* is located in Polaris Fashion Place (in 2007 the name changed to *Brio*). *Lindey's* has been voted one of Columbus' "Top Ten" restaurants for eighteen years in a row. It has been rated by national magazines as four in a scale of five. It has been featured in the *New York Times*, the *Washington Post*, *USA Today* and *Gourmet Magazine*.

Rigsby's Kitchen

Kent (at one time a chef at *Lindey's*) and Tasi Rigsby preside over one of "America's top Italian restaurants" as rated by the *Zagat Survey*. Since opening in 1986, it has made the list of Columbus' Top Ten restaurants every year as rated by the *Columbus Dispatch*. Cuisine includes Mediterranean and French meals. It was the first Columbus restaurant to be rated five stars by the *Columbus Monthly*. Located at 698 North High Street in the trendy Short North, it is open every day except Sundays.

Chapter 28

Philanthropic Organizations

There are many organizations, fraternities, social groups, service clubs, religious entities (e.g. Catholic Charities), missions (e.g. Faith Mission-Lutheran), homeless shelters, civic-minded families or individuals who have set up non-profit foundations to both receive and give money or articles to individuals or families in need. Many provide psychological or medical care. Some of the largest or better known Franklin County philanthropies are discussed below.

Salvation Army

The *Salvation Army* is one the largest relief organizations in Columbus as well as in the world. It was founded in England in 1865 by an itinerant Methodist evangelist, William Booth. His missionary zeal and mainstream Christian beliefs motivated him to create and administer a world relief group patterned after a military organization. The professional staff wear uniforms and are ranked as in an army. The uniform, badge and familiar red kettle used to gather donations at Christmas time make its members easily recognizable. The American branch of the *Salvation Army* began in the early 1880s. Officer training is carried out in special schools. As the name suggests, the group is intensely interested in a person's salvation as well as providing shelter, food, health care, freedom from abuse, psychological support, spiritual guidance and correction of social evils. The leaders conduct church services and musical groups. Their motto is "Heart to God and Hand to Man." Women share an equal role with men. The Army's mission is carried out in 109 countries despite cultural and geographical differences. Some of their major efforts are in third-world and war-torn countries. They are one of the first relief organizations to appear in emergencies or disasters such as earthquakes, tornadoes, hurricanes and tsunamis. Their programs are focused on education, shelter, food, water and sanitation, alternative energy, employment and health care including AIDS/HIV treatment in hospitals and clinics. Orphans and vulnerable children are special recipients of attention.

Their local churches are called corps and in Columbus there are five. Seven Thrift Stores situated in Central Ohio (four in Columbus) are made possible by donations of clothes, household furnishings and appliances. The main Columbus headquarters is at 966 East Main Street. The Adult Rehabilitation Center is at 570 South Front Street. The *Salvation Army* is funded by individual, group and corporate donations, foundations and fund-raisers. The word emergency instantly calls them to mind.

Volunteers of America

Volunteers of America is one of the largest national, non-profit, religious-based (ecumenical), charitable organizations in the nation. Its Central Ohio headquarters is at 1776 East Broad Street in the historic former Moody Nolan building, which at one time was a home for elderly ladies. Divisions of the Columbus agency are found in eleven sites. For seventy-three years (since 1832) the Columbus arm resided in the historic T&OC Railroad Depot on West Broad Street. The national organization was founded by Maud and Ballington Booth in New York City in 1896. It separated itself from the *Salvation Army*, founded by William Booth in England, over administrative differences, mainly related to the issue of sending money to the English headquarters. Currently, the fourth generation of Booths are involved administratively. The group is professionally staffed by over three-hundred persons of varied talents and served by thousands of volunteers. Funding is derived from donations from individuals, groups, corporations, foundations, fund-raising events and governmental agencies. Believing that every needy individual deserves another chance, structured, personalized services are provided. The Great Depression stretched resources, but the strong organization continued to provide shelter, food, work and personalized aid to the unfortunate. During wartime, scrap metal, rubber and fiber were collected by the charity for governmental use and housing. Food and canteens were provided to civilians and the armed forces. In peacetime, affordable housing has been built for the homeless, long-term nursing care for the disabled and elderly and other aids have been offered as well as spiritual (non-denominational) and psychological nurturing. Emergency services include drug rehabilitation, shelters, aid in catastrophes such as earthquakes, tornadoes, fire, and family problems caused by partner and child abuse. Community Centers provide educational skills, adult learning, mentoring, computer instruction, job preparation, job placement, after-school and summer programs, family strengthening and spiritual support. There is networking with schools and churches. There is a home-pickup service for collecting clothing, furniture, household items and autos. The charity's Thrift Stores are located throughout Central Ohio.

Goodwill Columbus

Goodwill Industries was founded in 1902 by Reverend Edgar J. Helms, a Boston Methodist clergyman. He collected used clothing and household goods from the wealthier citizens. He followed this up by training and hiring poor people and immigrants to repair the used goods for sale or for giving to the needy. His philosophy of "a hand up, not a hand out" worked. The organization was incorporated in 1910 and expanded to include the teaching of work skills and an employment placement service. Today, the international organization functions in thirty-six countries with 181 autonomous members in the United States and Canada.

Goodwill Columbus was founded in 1939, beginning as a used goods business and employment service. It functions in eleven stores and satellite divisions in Central Ohio. In 1977, it closed the stores and focused on rehabilitation and employment services. It is now the fourth largest not-for-profit organization in Central Ohio, assisting more than 1,500 people with disabilities or in need. In 2000-2002, four thrift stores were opened. They are located in Morse Centre, Hunter's Ridge, Clintonville and Central Point. Its mission of empowering the less fortunate through quality education, productivity, independence, job training and employment continues.

The Columbus Foundation

The Columbus Foundation was created after World War II to assist philanthropists who donate money for the benefit of Columbus and its citizens. During its sixty years of existence, it has grown to rank fifth in the nation in terms of assets and gifts received. In 2003, the non-profit organization received $78.9 million from individuals, estates, groups and corporations. In the same year the foundation made grants of $63.3 million from its assets of $742 million. The foundation operates under the close scrutiny of a board and professional advisors. Its office is in the former governor's mansion at 1234 East Broad Street. The mansion was designed by architect Frank Packard in 1904 as a residence for Charles H. Lindenberg. It was purchased by the state for $86,540 in 1919 to be used as the governor's residence. Ten governors lived in the mansion until 1957, after which the Ohio Historical Society used it as a repository from 1958 to 1970. In 1972, the U.S. Department of the Interior placed the building on the National Register of Historic Places. In 1977, it was purchased by two restaurateurs for $224,000, and for four years it was operated as an upscale restaurant called the Mansion. In 1982, it was leased for office use. In 1987, the Columbus Foundation purchased the mansion and began renovations. This was made possible by generous gifts from Bella C. Wexner, Leslie Wexner and Robert F. Wolfe. Hundreds of non-profit organizations in Central Ohio have been the recipients of the Columbus Foundation grants.

Heinzerling Foundation

Mildred and Otto Heinzerling mortgaged their home in Whitehall in 1959 to secure money to buy a home to care for babies. It was named *Peck O' Wee Ones*. The babies had medical problems, usually birth defects. Many required surgical attention that parents could not afford. In 1979, a new and larger facility was opened on forty-seven acres in southwest Franklin County near the junction of Clime Road and Harrisburg Pike, ten minutes from downtown Columbus. Within two years, the Foundation outreach was expanded to include disabled adults unable to finance their required care on their own. The twenty-one million dollar annual budget is largely supported by Medicaid, but voluntary contributions and support groups are important to its success. The founder's children, Dr. Robert A. and Kathryn Heinzerling, continued the family medical support facility. Today, grandchildren, Linda, a nurse, Karen, a veterinarian, and Robert Heinzerling, the chief executive, keep the passion of the foundation going strong. Dr. Heinzerling is well prepared for his job, having had a career in a business-form company, and spending six years in every department of the foundation. The foundation is licensed by the state. The complex holds two hundred patients and employs five hundred and fifty people.

United Way

The main philanthropic organization of individual and corporate donors in Central Ohio is United Way, established in 1885. It is a member, but under independent control, of the national group with the same name. A new leader of its large group of local volunteers is chosen annually. The United Way attempts to coordinate all community efforts to improve the quality of life of its citizen recipients regardless of age, race or ethnic background through an annual fund-raising drive and with the support of hundreds of caring people, groups and corporations. Its primary mission is to give support to local non-profit, charitable and cultural organizations. Examples of agencies supported by United Way are Godman Guild's first Settlement House, established in "Fly Town" in 1898, and Goodwill Columbus which builds independence, quality of life and work opportunities for individuals with disabilities and other barriers.

Charity Newsies

Charity Newsies is an one hundred-year old non-profit charity that has been sponsored by the *Columbus Dispatch* since 1986. Before the *Dispatch* took over sponsorship, that service was supplied first by *The Ohio State Journal* until 1959, and then *The Columbus Citizen Journal* until 1986. On the second Saturday of each December, over seven hundred volunteers, wearing logo white coveralls, disregarding the weather, sell a special issue of the *Columbus Dispatch* to automobile drivers at street corners and elsewhere. Additional funds are raised by a pre-drive corporate auction and voluntary contributions. For forty-two years an annual motorcycle race was used to raise funds. This was discontinued in 1980 but restarted in 2006. Donations thus derived are used to provide new clothes for needy school children (12,765 in 2004) and victims of flood and fire disasters in Franklin County. A record amount of $1,257,392 was raised in 2005. None of the contributions are used for overhead expenses.

LifeCare Alliance

One organization that distinguished itself because of its longivity, widely varied programs and volunteerism is LifeCare Alliance. It was started in 1898 in Columbus by Catherine Nelson Black, the mayor's wife, along with seventeen of her friends. They established an in-home nursing group called The Instructive District Nursing Association. Over time, the organization's name changed to LifeCare Alliance. They hire a few staff members to provide specific professional services, but the main care is tendered by over one hundred volunteers. The primary focus is the care of indigent/elderly in need, but other ages may be served in a limited fashion. For thirty years, they have provided Meals-on-Wheels to indigent, chronically-ill, elderly adults in Franklin and Madison Counties. Their unique Project OpenHand-Columbus, since 1994, has provided services to patients with the HIV virus or Aids. Additional services include visiting nurses, dieticians, home health aides, day-care for children and adults, after-school programs and community health clinics. Referrals from physicians, hospitals, patients and families are accepted.

Chapter 29

Urban Renewal by Columbus

Like many aging American cities, Columbus has been concerned with the effects of decay, neglect, crime, reduced business and loss of population in its central city. To counteract and reverse these problems, studies, commissions and generous amounts of tax money have been utilized. Results have varied with success usually temporary or lacking. Some of these efforts by Columbus are examined.

Urban Renewal

The *Marconi Building*, located at 140 Marconi Boulevard, housed a shoe factory and warehouse until it was purchased by the city. It underwent a $5.6 million renovation in 1977, and the building became offices for hundreds of city employees. When the building started to crumble prematurely due to faulty building material, the city settled its grievance with Dow Chemical for $4 million in 1988 and razed the building.

Other landmark buildings demolished during the 1970s were: *Hartman Theater*, 1971; *Chittenden Hotel*, 1971; *Franklin County Courthouse*, 1975; *Union Station*, 1976; and the *Fort Hayes Hotel*, 1977. Taking their places were: the forty-one story Rhodes State Office Building (tallest in Columbus), 1974; the forty-story Nationwide Headquarters (1978); the Hyatt Regency Hotel-connected by walkway to the Convention Center, 1980; Hyatt on Capitol Square Hotel, 1984; and the Capitol Square Office building, 1984.

The *Central Market* was demolished in 1966 as part of the Market-Mohawk Project to make room for Franklin University, a Holiday Inn, a bus terminal, apartments and offices. The project cost of $13 million was spread over a quarter-century before completion.

City Center Shopping Mall

A non-profit private group called Capitol South Urban Redevelopment Corporation was created in 1972 to oversee revitalization of fifteen acres in the two blocks immediately south of State Capitol Square. Its northern boundary was East State Street and the east and west sides were South 3rd Street and South High Street, respectively. The southern boundary was East Rich Street. The city of Columbus bought the land in the 1970s from over four-dozen business owners with $31 million collected from taxpayers and $12 million from federal government low-interest loans. Buildings were razed and the area cleared for a three-story parking garage and the occupancy of over one hundred and fifty companies in a new, three-level, *City Center Shopping Mall*. The State Street side had already been occupied by a row of buildings facing capitol square to the north. The Beggs Building (now Fifth/Third Bank Building) is situated at the southwest corner of East State and South High Streets. The Ohio Theater, renovated in 1984, the Capitol Square Office Building (1984) and the Hyatt-on-Capitol Square Hotel (1984) were side by side, as one advanced east on State Street to South Third Street. The new *City Center Mall*, in the interior of the block could be accessed from South High Street, the parking building to its south and through the Capitol Square Office Building. *City Center* was connected to an important "anchor store", Lazarus, across South High Street, by an enclosed, over-the-street walkway. Soon other "anchor stores" within the mall, Jacobson's, Marshall Fields and all of the Limited Brands specialty clothing stores, made shopping at *City Center* very attractive to central Ohioans. By 1990, the mall was 96% occupied and business was thriving. The entire mall was managed by private companies; the third was Taubman Realty Group. Columbus collected rental fees. Unfortunately, the *Center's* success was related to attracting business from suburban malls (Kingsdale, Eastland, Northern Lights, Westland, Northland and Southland), causing their demise. In the 1990's, three new, upscale suburban malls were established; Tuttle Crossing, Easton Town Center and Polaris Fashion Place. They in turn drew business away from *City Center*. Even it its zenith, downtown businesses surrounding the mall failed to prosper due to a lack of participation by *City Center's* affluent clientele. Out-of-county shoppers felt Columbus offered too few close-by attractions to supplement their shopping. As a result, all of the *City Center* anchor stores closed, followed by the departure of most of the smaller companies. Today, only a few stores remain and the *Center's* occupancy is down to twenty-percent.

One of the last anchor stores to close, Lazarus, was saved from demolition and its buildings currently are being renovated. It is the "green cornerstone" of Mayor Michael Coleman's program to make businesses more environmentally efficient by reducing operating time for heating and cooling. This will be accomplished by a 1,500-square-feet rooftop garden and recycling rain water for use in toilets and other systems. The National Association of Office and Industrial Properties has proclaimed the Lazarus renovation to be one of the two best examples of environmentally friendly developments in the country.

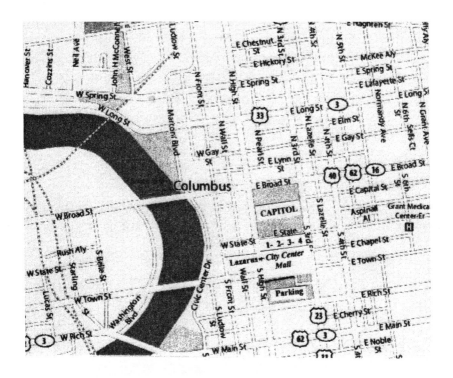

Fig. 106 *City Center Mall* and its parking garage are shown within the two city blocks south of the State Capitol. Between the mall and the Capitol are four buildings: 1)Fifth/Third Bank building; 2) Ohio Theater; 3) Capitol Square Office building; and 4) Hyatt Capitol Square Hotel. Lazarus Store is connected by a covered, elevated walk way to the west of the mall. As you look at the map, north is at the top.

The Mills Corporation took over management of *City Center* in 2004 but soon lost its financial viability and sold its assets to TL-Columbus (Simon Property Group and General Motors Pension Trust), the fifth manager of the *Center*. In mid-2007, failure of TL-Columbus to pay its leasing fees to Columbus resulted in a lawsuit filed by the city of Columbus to recover back payments and take over control of its property. The matter was settled out of court in October, 2007, and Columbus now owns and manages all of the property of *City Center*. Meanwhile, concerned businesses and other interested institutions in Columbus formed a new private overview corporation in 2002, called The Strategic Business Plan for Downtown Columbus, and in 2007 combined it with the also private Capitol South *Community* Urban Redevelopment Corporation to represent its interests. Its board is a compendium of senior business and institutional leaders. Initial funding of two million dollars from both Nationwide Insurance Company and the Columbus Foundation met half of their operational goal. To date, their public pronouncements seem to lean in the direction of utilizing the *Center's* space for small businesses and condominiums. The Columbus Downtown Commission (1997) cooperates fully with these private corporations. Its office at 20 East Broad Street serves as a home and resource center for all cooperating commissions and corporations concerned with downtown urban revitalization and redevelopment.

In 1973, the city of Columbus paid MCQ Industries $1.8 million for a quarry near Trabue Road and McKinley Avenue to be used to receive lime sludge via pipelines from the two city water treatment plants. It is still operational and considered an excellent investment.

A city project that backfired, was the purchase of the aging, three-building *Columbus Academy for Boys* at Nelson and Bryden Roads for $500,000 in 1981. Battelle provided half of the cost. The buildings were to be used for a recreational center and a training site for police and firemen. Instead, the buildings were left vacant and were vandalized. In 1983, renovations worth $175,000 made possible a police substation. Deterioration caused the buildings to be razed in 1984. In 1991, a four-court sports complex was placed on the site, operated by the city's Recreation and Parks Department.

The city bought *Wehrle High School* and thirty acres on Parsons Avenue for $1.4 million in 1992. The city renovated the building for $3.4 million, and made it a fire administration and training center.

Northern Lights Shopping Center, in eastern Clinton Township, is located on Cleveland Avenue at its juncture with Innis Road. Its many small shops and fast-food restaurants were anchored by a large Schottenstein department store nearby that has ceased business. A VFW hall is nearby. The huge Shoe Company of America, that was adjacent to the shopping center, is long gone.

Northland Mall, a thriving shopping center anchored by Sears, J.C. Penny and Lazarus, closed in 2002. Immediately, the city began buying parts of the fifty-five acre site whose northwest corner was bounded by Morse and Karl Roads. A total of $9.5 million collected in taxes was expended. Plans were made for new stores, city administrative offices ($15 million cost), condominiums, restaurants and recreational venues. The former eight-screen movie theater was purchased in 2005 and became the Northland Performing Arts Center and the home of Vaud-Villities Productions, who presents an annual amateur musical extravaganza.

The *Lennox Town Center* sprang up on the site of the former Lennox furnace factory in 1996. It is located where Kinnear Road meets Olentangy River Road, between The Ohio State University and Upper Arlington. It contains a variety of stores, eating establishments and a large movie theater.

Columbus owns twenty-nine acres of the one hundred and sixty acre *Whittier Peninsula* wedged between the Brewery District and the Scioto River in downtown Columbus. The city has negotiated for the right to develop half of the peninsula. At one-time, the former Chesapeake and Ohio Railroad transected the property and maintained a repair shop and scrap yard for its locomotives. The CSX railroad now uses the rail line. In the mid-1800s, the Ohio-Erie feeder canal passed through the land. This attracted warehouses, some industrial scrap yards, an asphalt plant, a concrete company, a quarry and a railroad. The city used part of the peninsula for a dump, and now uses it as an auto impound lot and a Parks and Recreation office. But, it attracted many bird-watchers. Currently, the city is developing a metro park on the western rim of property next to the Scioto River. Grange Mutual Insurance Company announced a gift of four million dollars to the Audubon Society to facilitate the construction of a 12,000 square-foot nature center in this park that will include a 200-seat meeting room, a library, a classroom and a gift shop. The latest developments within the park will begin in 2008. The rest of the peninsula has heavily contaminated soil from the railroad locomotive repair shop and scrap yards. The southern edge of the peninsula harbored a lime-stone quarry that the city converted into a dump for garbage and covered it with soil. This chemical waste land and other environment issues have placed a damper on residential and commercial development on the peninsula. Also, the levee constructed many years ago to protect this area from the Scioto River might be unable to prevent damage from a major flood. The peninsula holds a dream that the city hopes to fulfill.

In 1993, the *State Capitol* underwent a $110,000 restoration. The result was a beautiful interior, with gold leaf, fine hardwood edgings, restored murals and a capitol building that could make all citizens proud. Daily tours are available.

Harrison West, a commercial and residential neighborhood, is located between Victorian Village on its east side and the Olentangy River to the west. West 2nd Avenue is the northern boundary, State Route 315 is the southern border and Harrison Avenue is the eastern limit. Its need for rejuvenation was deterred by the presence of the AC Humko dairy plant on West 1st Avenue. The dairy enterprise, making margarine and cooking oils, began in 1883 as the Capital City Dairy Company and ceased to exist in 2001. The state gave $3 million to raze the plant and the city granted $3 million to clean up the site. Beginning in 2004 with $44 million, a sixteen-acre housing project commenced, centered at 525 West 1st Avenue. It included 222 two and three-story apartments on Percy and Perry Streets, 107 upscale condominiums at Perry Place, a community center and pool, and a four-acre river-front park. Construction was performed by the Wagenbrenner

Company, supported by Inland Products. Further aid was given to the project by the city through tax-abatements and tax-increment financing.

Wheatland Park, a three and four-bedroom residential project, was commenced in 2004 by Dominion Homes, with the city's promise to grant home buyers a 100% property tax abatement for fifteen years. The homes, on Wheatland Avenue, north of West Broad Street in Franklinton were priced to sell between $120,000 and $180,000. The area, located in the Hilltop neighborhood, was part of the former Central Ohio Psychiatric Hospital complex. City officials hope that neighborhood pride will reduce the drug trafficking and other crimes prevalent in the area.

Columbus Metropolitan Housing Authority

The Columbus Housing Authority works with collaborative partners to help low income people gain access to affordable housing, employment and social services. Columbus is divided into three regions, each with a coordinator for three to ten areas within each region. CMHA assists in the renovation, maintenance and revitalization of existing houses, apartments and neighborhoods. The CMHA commenced in Ohio in 1934, and Columbus opened its first federally funded low-income housing project in Poindexter Village on North Champion Avenue in 1939. The opening ceremony was presided over by President Franklin Roosevelt.

Columbus Area Commissions

In 1980, Columbus City Council, upon urging by local historical groups, established the *Historic Structures Preservation Commission* with the mission to identify, inventory and preserve historic structures in Columbus. Key players included representation from Landmarks Foundation, realtors and historical and preservation societies. A Negotiated Investment Strategy (NIS), adopted from work of the Kettering Foundation, was utilized. This commission was instrumental in the saving and restoring a number of historic buildings that might have been lost to wrecking crews.

In the 1980's, the Columbus Department of Development established area commissions to act as liaisons between neighborhood groups, property owners, residents, developers and city officials. Currently, there are fourteen area commissions (Figure 7): Clintonville, Driving Park, 5th by Northwest, Franklinton, Greater Hilltop, Milo-Grogan, Near East, North Central, North East, North Linden, South Linden, South West, University and Westland. These areas have definite boundaries established. Residents are encouraged to express their concerns to their commission toward a resolution of any problems that arise. In the past, some of the concerns have been related to zoning, development problems and the appearance of the community.

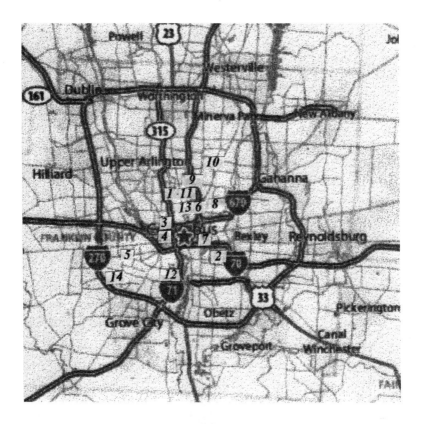

Fig. 107 Columbus Neighborhood Commission Areas

Neighborhood Areas	Boundaries			
	East	West	North	South
1 Clintonville	Railroad	Olentangy River	Worthington	Glen Echo Ravine
2 Driving Park	Railroad	Studer Avenue	I-70	E. Whittier Street
3 5th by Northwest	Olentangy R.	Wyandotte Rd	Kinnear Rd	3rd Avenue
4 Franklinton	River & Harmon	Schultz & I-70	Scioto River	Mound & Greenlawn
5 Greater Hilltop	B & O Railroad	I-270	I-70	I-270
6 Milo-Grogan	St. Clair Ave	Railroad	11th Avenue	I-670
7 Near East	Alum Creek	I-71	Railroad	I-70
8 North Central	Alum Creek	Railroad	Hudson/Mock	I-670
9 North Linden	Railroad	Railroad	Cooke/Ferris	Hudson
10 Northeast	I-270/I-62	Railroad	Morse Road	Hudson/I-62
11 South Linden	Railroad/Joyce	I-71	Hudson Street	Bonham
12 Southwest	Scioto River	Railroad	Mound Street	I-270
13 University	Railroad/Parker	Olentangy R.	Glen Echo Ravine	5th Avenue
14 Westland	I-270/Big Run S.	Hellbranch Cr.	Railroad	Grove City Rd

Chapter 30

Cities and Villages in Franklin County

Columbus has a fine array of suburbs. In 2004, a listing of the most desirable cities in the United States showed Columbus to be ranked twenty-seventh, trailing behind other Ohio cities, Cincinnati seventh and Cleveland twelfth. The village of Marble Cliff has the highest median home cost and cost of living, followed by Upper Arlington, Dublin, Bexley, New Albany, Worthington and Grandview Heights.

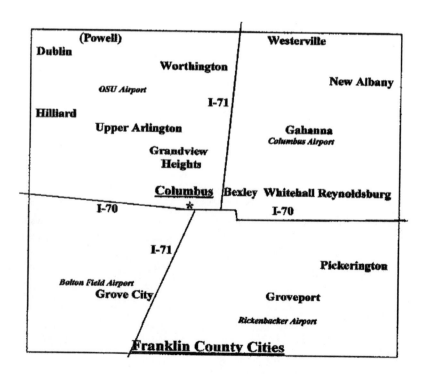

Fig. 108

Bexley

Bexley is a small upscale residential community located a short distance east of downtown Columbus. It is bounded on the west by Alum Creek (Nelson Road), on the east by Gould and Kenwick Roads, on the north by Delmar Drive and on the south by Livingston Avenue. The area along Alum Creek is believed to have been the site of an Adena burial mound, two thousand years earlier. The first settlers were farmers who saw their land divided by the Turnpike Plank Road (Broad Street) and in 1833 by the National Road (Main Street-U.S. Route 40). A one room schoolhouse was erected at the corner of Livingston and College Avenues in 1864. A second schoolhouse was constructed on Pleasant Ridge in 1875.

Fig. 109 Capital University as it appeared near Goodale Park (1850-1875).
—from Columbus Metro Library

In 1876, the most important event in Bexley's history occurred. Capital University moved to the southeast corner of College and Main Streets from Goodale Park in Columbus. This attracted academic staff and students to the community. Today, Capital University ranks among the top fifteen national colleges offering sixty major and minor programs leading to B.A., M.A., nursing and law degrees. The music department is widely acclaimed, and the university offers a strong sports program. The school was founded by the Lutheran Church in 1830 and today has an enrollment of four thousand students.

Trinity Lutheran Seminary is a theological graduate school closely associated with Capital University and is situated on its campus. It offers five graduate and postgraduate degrees to three hundred students. It, too, was founded in 1830.

Capital's Law School was founded in 1903 as an independent evening school at the YMCA on South Third Street where the *Columbus Dispatch* now stands. Women were admitted in 1918 and the first female to receive a law degree from Capital Law School was in 1926. The school's first African-American graduated in 1931. The Ohio Supreme Court empowered the school to grant an LL.B. degree in 1921. In 1923, the school moved with the YMCA to new quarters at 40 East Long Street where is continued under the name of the Columbus College of Law. The school's name changed to Franklin University Law School in 1948. The law school received full legal accreditation and admission to the American Bar Association in 1954. The law school became part of Capital University in 1966, and moved to its campus in Bexley, and assumed the new name of Franklin Law School of Capital University. The school finally became Capital University Law School in 1972, as it is currently known. In 1980, the law school relocated its campus to 665 South High Street in the former Grange Mutual Insurance building. It was recognized as a full-time day school. In 1997, the school moved to its current location at 303 East Broad Street, the former home of the Columbus Life Insurance Company. Its graduates receive the revised degree of J.D. The school has received national recognition for its Night Prosecutor Mediation Program using third-year law students to represent clients; the program was founded in 1971. Also renown, is its Center for Dispute Resolution. The school has conducted summer programs in Denmark, Greece, Poland and Germany. The school now offers additional master's degrees in taxation, business, theology, science and sports administration. Currently, the Board of Trustees is focused on: becoming more selective in admissions; providing higher quality academics; attracting and retaining world-class teachers; and developing a stronger resource base (it has a $19 million operating budget and an endowment fund of $6 million). The entering class enrollment averages 250 students. The college deliberately keeps its number steady to ensure that high standards for admission are maintained.

Capital's School of Nursing was established in 1950 as a department in the College of Arts and Science. In 1965, Nursing was upgraded to an independent College. During its history, students have participated in space research at Wright-Patterson Air Force Base in Dayton, served in the military, incorporated holistic health concepts, utilized advanced computer and audio-visual technology and have participated in off-campus learning experiences involving other cultures, community health and psychiatric care (in Jamaica, Washington D.C., England and Sweden). Nursing degrees offered are Master of Science (MSN), Registered Nurse (RN), and dual-degrees with the School of Management (MSN/MBA), School of Law (MSN/JD) and Trinity Seminary (MSN/MTS). Five hundred students are enrolled currently in these programs. Over 2,000 Capital University nurse graduates practice throughout the United States and around the world, continually earning a reputation for caring and critical thinking.

In 1898, at the onset of the Spanish-American War, Governor Asa Bushnell chose the area around Broad Street and Drexel Avenue for a camp site that sheltered eight thousand troops for three weeks. Water and sewer lines extended into the camp promoted subsequent real estate development in the area. Later, trolleys and the automobile encouraged more residents to move to Bexley. In 1905, prominent Columbus residents began the development of an exclusive community, a forerunner of Bexley as we know it today. The leaders in this effort were Robert H. Jeffrey, former mayor of Columbus, E.N. Huggins and Colonel Lincoln Kilbourne. They built stately mansions. A rigid building code was enacted that governed roads, street lights, beautification of lawns and property and excluded unsightly signs. In 1908, the Association of Land Owners incorporated the village and named it Bexley, after the parish house on the Kilbourne estate in Kent, England. It had reached a population of one thousand. Frank P. Holzman was elected the first mayor. Ordinances prohibited the grazing of cattle in the village, outlawed public intoxication, assault and the discharge of firearms. The Ohio Supreme Court settled a suit in Bexley's favor when Columbus tried to annex the village and collect taxes. The only telephone was located in a barber shop across from the university; the town marshal rode a bicycle instead of a horse, and the village owned a road scraper and wheelbarrow. By 1921, the town had grown to two thousand, and five streets had been paved. A zoning commission and a more rigid building code were enacted. Schools, a municipal building and underground electric lighting were installed. During the 1920's the population tripled. The 1930 census of five thousand citizens allowed Bexley to be recognized as a city. A new city hall was completed in 1952. Today, the 2.5 square miles within the city limits encases tree line streets, extensive parks, and an award winning school system that includes one public high school, three elementary and one middle school. Three other schools are private: Columbus School for Girls, St. Catherine School and St. Charles Preparatory School. Churches in Bexley include five synagogues, three Presbyterian congregations, two Lutheran churches, two Catholic churches and one each of Episcopal and Methodist denomination. Bexley is governed by an elected Mayor and seven council persons. The city contains no significant large business or industry, and because of its landlocked geography, its population of just over thirteen thousand is stable. The new Bexley Gateway provides an exciting Main Street entrance to the city. It has street level retail stores and restaurants, three levels of offices, three town houses and five levels of luxury condominiums. Ninety-six percent of the thirteen thousand Bexley residents are of Caucasian ethnicity, and three percent are African-Americans. The median cost of a home is $246,500, and the median cost of living is at the 109 percentile. Cultural amenities include lectures, musicals and plays given by Capital University and the high schools, superior public library programs, the Jewish Centers (Community, Foundation and Historical), churches, the Bexley Historical Society, Summerfest and the Drexel Theater (foreign and unusual films). Bexley has been the residence of many prominent civic and business leaders and outstanding educational and professional individuals and is considered a premium residential location in Franklin County. But it comes at a prime cost; it has one of the highest property tax rates in the county. It should come as no surprise that the mansions for the Governor of the State and for the President of Ohio State University are in Bexley.

Dublin

Dublin is located in the northwest corner of Franklin County in central Ohio. It lies on the banks of the Scioto River, is intersected by U.S. Route 33 (northwest/south), State Routes 161 (east/west), 745 (north) and the Columbus Outerbelt, I-270. Rich farm land originally attracted settlers, and a small trading center ensued. The Scioto River provides fishing and water sports, but Dublin was never on a canal or railroad route. The CSX rail lines are six miles to the east, and two miles to the west. These lines are shared with NS and Conrail.

Prehistoric people and later Indians roamed the countryside. By the time pioneers came to settle, the Indians were gone. Lieutenant James Holt was granted 2,000 acres for service in the Revolutionary War. In turn, he sold 400 acres (now downtown Dublin) to Pennsylvanians Peter and John Sells in 1808. The Sells brothers offered some of their land in an unsuccessful bid for the state capital in 1810. Subsequently, the land was surveyed by John Shields, who chose the name Dublin, naming it after his birthplace in Ireland. To this day, the city unabashedly embraces the Shamrock as its symbol, calls itself the "Emerald City" and celebrates an annual Irish Festival. The abundance of native limestone is evident in its use for low stone fences, an attractive border for the main streets. Many of the old buildings have been preserved, but, unfortunately, the downtown has narrow streets and traffic jams. Small industries abound, but the largest employers are the Ashland Chemical Company, Metro Center, Midwestern Volkswagen, Sterling Commerce and Cardinal Health. The thirty-nine year old, non-profit, Online Computer Library Center (OCLC) is headquartered on Franz Road. It consolidates resources for more than 50,000 international libraries. It maintains fifteen offices in seven countries and has $189 million in annual revenue. The city is fringed by many large businesses and shopping centers. The Columbus Outerbelt induced considerable growth. When Jack Nicklaus, Columbus native and world renown golf champion, built Muirfield Village Golf Club, the area north of Dublin grew rapidly. Upscale residences and other golf courses were constructed making it one of the most rapidly growing areas in the state. The annual Memorial Golf Tournament, sponsored by Nicklaus, attracts thousands. Many foreign guests come to Dublin just to play the golf course, a premier layout. A new Community Center provides a myriad of activities for youth, adults and seniors. The public library is well provided and used. The increase in population from 5,520 in 1960 to over 40,000 today portrays the remarkable growth story well.

Dublin has three relatively new high schools. Each has a Performing Arts Center. The school system also includes four middle and eleven elementary schools. The school district has reached the highest level in regional accreditation. Athletics, important to the community, has produced individuals and teams that have performed well. Ninety-three percent of the graduates go on to college.

This primarily upscale residential city is minutes away from downtown Columbus, Worthington, Upper Arlington and Hilliard. Those cities provide an additional wealth of educational and culture opportunities as well as hospitals and other needed services to Dublin. Recently opened in 2007, is the ninety-four bed Dublin Methodist Hospital. Ohio State University also plans an auxiliary health facility. The median cost of a home is $262,400, and the median cost of living is at the 112 percentile. The city is governed by a mayor and council. The population mix shows ninety percent Caucasian, seven percent Asian and two percent African-American.

Gahanna

Gahanna is located in central Ohio on the eastern edge of central Franklin County. It is traversed north/south by Big Walnut Creek. The founder was Joseph Clark who purchased the land from Governor Worthington in 1814 and named it Gahanna Plantation. The name of Gahanna is derived from an American Indian expression meaning three creeks joining into one. The current city seal refers to "Three in One." Bridgeport, located on the other bank of the Creek was merged with Gahanna, and the latter became the official name for the corporation in 1881. The surrounding land was conducive to rich farms and a trading center.

Today, the city lies adjacent to and north of the Columbus International Airport, eight miles from downtown Columbus via interstate expressway, I-670, and thirty minutes from Rickenbacker Freight Airport in south Franklin County. Conrail and CSX provide rail transportation for freight. I-70, I-71 and U.S. 62 are expressways serving the community.

Educational facilities include the Gahanna Jefferson Public Schools, the Columbus Academy and two other private schools. The library is a branch of the Columbus Metropolitan system. A large number of parks and recreational activities are supplemented by a Senior Center. There are forty-one active civic associations. Several public and private golf courses are close by. Columbus and its northern suburbs share many cultural amenities. Residents enjoy annual Herb, Bar-B-Q and Jazz Festivals and colorful holiday parades. Industry which is light is office and technology oriented. The demographic breakdown reveals eighty-six percent Caucasian, nine percent African-American, three percent Asian and two percent Hispanic. The median cost of homes is $145,000, and the median cost of living is at the 92 percentile. The present population is 32,636 and growing due to participation in the flight from Columbus to the suburbs.

Grandview Heights/Marble Cliff

The southern part of Grandview Heights was originally located at the extreme northwest corner of the Refugee Tract. The Tract was established by the Continental Congress to provide land grants to Canadians who had lost their possessions due to sympathy and support for the colonists during the Revolutionary War. The Tract was forty-two miles in length, extending from the Scioto River to the Muskingum River and with a width of five miles, from present Fifth Avenue to Refugee Road. The town site was first surveyed and platted by Hutchins, Matthew and Buckingham when Columbus was formed in 1812. In 1842, the area was divided into twelve plots. Two O'Haras, A. and J., and A. Sperry owned most of what came to be called Marble Cliff.

Marble Cliff was the small, extreme northwestern corner of Grandview Heights, just east of a large limestone deposit that became an important quarry. The Marble Cliff Quarry Company opened in the mid-1800's and was owned by the Kaufman family until most of it was sold in the 1980's for residential and commercial development. The northern section is still quarried. Marble Cliff split off from Grandview Heights as a separate village in 1901. It is governed by an elected mayor and council but utilizes police and fire protection and schools belonging to Grandview Heights. A large and nationally prominent church, First Community, started in 1910, is located in Marble Cliff. To accommodate its 4,000 membership, a satellite church was constructed in 1991 immediately south of Hilliard. A twelve million dollar expansion is planned, beginning in 2008. The village of Marble Cliff, with six hundred and forty-six residents, has the highest median cost of homes in Franklin County at $405,000 and the highest median cost of living at the 136 percentile.

Grandview Heights extends from the Scioto River on the west to the Olentangy River on the east through annexations. Today, the southern boundary is the Scioto River after it bends, and the northern edge is roughly Third Avenue. It was incorporated as a village in 1906. It became a city in 1931 when it reached five thousand in population. The area has always been primarily residential with small shops, theaters and ten churches. During World War I, Camp Willis was located in Grandview Heights. After the war, King Thompson developed a large part of northeast Grandview into an incorporated village he called Upper Arlington. A strip of Columbus between Fifth and Third Avenues, running east/west separates the two villages. The three villages have come to be known as the Tri-Village area with upscale single family residencies, condominiums and apartments. The villages remain portions of Franklin, Clinton and Perry Townships. The first separate High School was built in 1923 and included a public library. Before that, students had to go to Columbus to obtain more than an eighth grade education. With the aid of federal funds, athletic fields and a stadium were finished in 1938. Today, the school has a state-of-the-art running track. Its school system and public library are top-rated. The city has several parks, a swimming pool, celebrates several festivals and provides free band concerts. Further cultural advantages are provided by the Grandview Heights/Marble Cliff Historical Society. Until it closed in 2004, the Big Bear Grocery Company had its headquarters in Grandview Heights. Current plans for the large site, include placement of national and regional retailers and offices called Grandview Yard to be developed by Nationwide Realty Investors. The ten-year, $650 million makeover could add 5,000 jobs, a thousand new residents and $5 million in new tax income, doubling Grandview's current tax base. Grandview Heights is governed by an elected mayor and council. The city has a median cost of homes of $212,900, and a median cost of living at the 103 percentile. Today's population is sixty seven hundred with 96 percent Caucasian, 1.3 percent African-American and 1.2 percent of Hispanic ethnic background. Thirty-nine percent claim British heritage, while thirty-two purport German and ten percent Italian lineage. The villages are close to excellent hospitals (University, Riverside and Mt. Carmel), The Ohio State University and downtown Columbus. Four expressways pass nearby; U.S. 33, U.S. 315, I-670 and I-70.

Grove City

Grove City is located in southwest Franklin County, fifteen minutes southwest of downtown Columbus. The city can trace its origin to 1846 when William Breck purchased fifteen acres from the Grant family who had been given the land for service in the Revolutionary War. Breck and three other men laid out Grove City in 1852. It was a sleepy little village until steady growth allowed it to become incorporated in 1866. Joseph Bulen, a physician, was elected to be the first Mayor. In its early years it was a farming/trade center. Its position as a bedroom community for Columbus was fortified by the Greenlawn Street trolley that functioned until the 1920. The title of city became official in 1959. Today, Grove City is the destination for moderate priced residences and light industry. It is home to Beulah Park harness racing. Both Mott's Military Museum and Bolton Airfield are nearby. The airfield is used by private planes. Education for school children is provided by the large Southwestern School District that encompasses three high schools, seventeen elementary and nine middle schools. There are also three parochial and three special needs schools. In 1891, a private subscription library was formed. It became public in 1917. Rented rooms were used until a free standing library was built in 1954. Repeated failure of library levies has made the library dependent on state aid and on a working consortium headed by the Columbus Metropolitan Library System. Several branches have been operational irregularly. The residents share the amenities of Columbus for culture, recreation and work in addition to their own city parks and recreational centers. Annually, there is an art and music festival, free outdoor summer band concerts, a July Homecoming celebration, Little Theater-Off-Broadway presentations, Fourth of July fireworks and an Easter Egg Hunt. Fryer Park offers tennis, basketball, other sports and picnic shelters. In the vicinity are several golf courses. Located in the city are Nationwide's Eastern U.S. Medicare offices, Nissan Motor's regional training facility, the high-tech firm, Tosoh, a Wal-Mart regional distribution facility and Banana Republic's catalog operation. The governance is by an elected mayor and council. Historic landmarks include St. John's Evangelical Lutheran Church, Plank's on Broadway, the Railway Station and the Ganz Farmhouse. The city of 27,000 is a short distance from I-71 (north/south), the Columbus outerbelt (I-270) and I-70 (east/west). The demographics show ninety-six percent Caucasians, one and one-half percent African-Americans and one percent Hispanics. The median cost of homes is $160,200, and the median cost of living is at the 94 percentile.

Groveport

Groveport was formed and derived its name in 1847 when the two hundred and fifty inhabitants of two settlements, Wert's Grove and Rarey's Port, merged. The opening of the Ohio-Erie Canal in the 1830's made Groveport a "canal town." This brought warehouses, mills and factories, tanneries, stores, taverns and four churches (Baptist, Methodist, Presbyterian and United Brethren; a Catholic Church came later). Jacob Wert became the first postmaster in 1844. In 1868, a railroad passed through the village further enhancing transportation. Today, the CXS line passes through the north edge of the village. A Town Hall, built for $10,000 dollars, provided jointly by Madison Township, the Village, the Masons and the Odd Fellows, was finished in 1876. The first floor was occupied by businesses and used for school functions and theatrical productions. Rest rooms were added two years later. Many remodelings later, the Hall is still available for civic affairs. The hall is host to five theatrical companies, two of which are sponsored by the village. A trolley system made transportation easier for workers going to nearby Canal Winchester, east of the village. It was discontinued in the 1930's. Streets were paved, beginning in 1909. Local clay led to brick manufacturing. A number of residential annexations have brought the current population to thirty-eight hundred. The largest industry is the Spiegel/Eddie Bauer distribution complex. Route 317 enters from the north from Reynoldsburg, as does South Hamilton Road. The Mott Military Museum is located on this road. The Willows Golf Course, a championship layout, occupies a large acreage on the southeast edge of the village. U.S. 33, coursing from Columbus to Lancaster, is located three miles to the east, and Outerbelt I-270 is a similar distance to the northwest. Rickenbacker Airport is found two miles to the southwest. The Groveport Madison School District has two elementary, one middle, one junior and one high school. Heritage Park and its Log House and an Aquatic Center are part of the city park system. A number of festive events take place annually in addition to national holiday celebrations. The Hometown Classic Car Show, Apple Butter Day, and the Music In The Park series are of keen interest and local pride. The Groveport Heritage Museum preserves artifacts and memorabilia. The village is governed by an elected mayor and council. The median cost of homes is $142,500, and the median cost of living is at the 91 percentile.

Hilliard

Hilliard is located in Norwich Township on the west edge of Franklin County and close to east/west running interstate I-70 and the Columbus outerbelt (I-270) which skirts its eastern boundary. The distance to downtown Columbus is ten miles. The city was founded by John Reed Hilliard who purchased two tracts of land in 1853 along the new Columbus, Piqua & Indiana railroad and was called Hilliard's Station. The village served as a farm and commercial trading center for the rich agricultural region. Growth of the village was slow, registering only seventy-seven adults in 1860. The town's name was shortened to Hilliard in 1854, the same year the post office was established, and incorporation took place in 1869. The population increased to 5,633 during the next one hundred years, and Hilliard was declared a city in 1960. The placement of the Columbus outerbelt in its vicinity in the 1980's produced a spurt in population to 19,500 by 1996. Growth continues at a quick pace with 28,800 residents in 2007. The demographics show ninety-three percent Caucasians, three percent Asians and one and one-half percent African-Americans. It is projected that the population will be 50,000 by 2025. The key to its growth is its location near the state capital, the flight of Columbus residents to the suburbs, the highly rated school system, and the accessibility to excellent transportation. Hilliard is the site of the annual Franklin County Fair. Hilliard shares the amenities of Columbus and nearby suburbs of Upper Arlington (to the east), Dublin (to the north) and Tuttle Crossing shopping mall to the east, making it primarily a residential city. Industry is light manufacturing, with many warehouses, technology oriented businesses and office buildings. Conrail runs through the city and is connected to the large CSX Buckeye Yards, a switching and marshalling center south of the city. Columbus provides much of the infrastructure, such as water and sewers. The median cost of homes is $157,600, and the median cost of living is at the 94 percentile. The city is governed by a mayor and council. There are two high, four middle and thirteen elementary public schools. An additional middle school is private. Several weekly newspapers supplement the *Columbus Dispatch*. The public library is a branch of the Columbus Metro System. There are many parks, recreational centers and a walking trail. Several public and private golf courses are in the vicinity. The Arts Council, an Historical Society and a Senior Center provide cultural and educational opportunities. The original train station is preserved and is located in Weaver Park.

New Albany

New Albany is located in Plains Township in the extreme east central section of Franklin County. Its midsection is traversed by State Route 161 and its bypass running east/west and U.S. Route 62 (Main Street or Johnstown Road) running diagonally southwest to northeast. The northern city limit is Walnut Street, the southern edge is Morse Road, the west boundary is the New Albany Country Club and the eastern boundary extends into Jersey Township in Licking County.

The rich farmland was first developed by Noble Landon and William Yantes in 1837 as the Village of Hope. It was incorporated in 1856 as the Village of New Albany. Its population reached 213 by 1883 and 300 by 1908. The latest population is over 6,400 and growing rapidly as a prime upscale residential area (from 307 in 1960). Demographics show ninety-four percent Caucasian, one and one-half percent African-American, two and one-half percent Asian and 0.8 percent Hispanic. Growth of the village was dormant until upscale country clubs sprang up nearby in the 1980's (The Golf Club, New Albany Country Club and the Winding Hollow Country Club). The largest impetus, however, was the erection of billionaire Les Wexner's mansion in the locale. His development organization purchased thousands of acres surrounded by a white board-rail fence enclosing horse stables and very expensive homes. His money was used also to modernize the utilities' infrastructure and build a first class high school. Upkeep necessitates a high property and school tax rate. The first-class school system includes two elementary, one middle and one high school. A new library is a branch of the Columbus Metropolitan Libraries and offers extensive educational programs for children. The New Albany/Plains Township Historical Society, founded in 1975, preserves artifacts, documents and the upkeep of the restored 1881 Kern-Harrington House, certified as a museum. In 2007, the New Albany Surgical Hospital, a specialty facility emphasizing orthopedic and neurological surgery, merged with the Mount Carmel Health System. The town celebrates Founder's Day, the Harvest of Arts Festival (sponsored by the Arts

Council), senior seminars, theatrical presentations, concerts and a community chorus. Recreational opportunities are provided by parks, a swimming pool and several nearby public golf courses, including the New Albany Links. The large metropolitan park, Blendon Woods, is just west of the city. For recreational and educational activities there are hiking trails, a nature and exhibit center and lake with water fowl. Limited has its headquarters for Too in New Albany, a five hundred and fifty store company, catering to girls aged between seven and twelve. Another large retail clothier, catering to youth, Abercromie & Fitch, has its headquarters in New Albany. Discover Financial Services in New Albany is one of twelve U.S. locations of Discover, the fourth largest credit card company in the nation. When its spin-off from Morgan Stanley is complete, it will be publicly traded on the New York Stock Exchange (DFS). It is a call center employing 2,100 workers locally. Many other new businesses include banks, retail stores, service companies, a specialty hospital and restaurants. Formerly, only small businesses were present in the city, which is governed by an elected mayor and council. The median cost of homes is $243,000, and the median cost of living is at the 108 percentile.

Pickerington

Pickerington began as a tiny settlement called Jacksontown on Sycamore Creek in Fairfield County in 1808. It actually straddled the line between Franklin and Fairfield Counties (its county seat) with less than ten percent of it land in Franklin County. The city is situated half-way between Columbus and Lancaster, fifteen miles each way. The portion lying in Franklin County is in its northwest quadrant. Abraham Pickerington is credited with organizing the village in 1815, and it assumed his name thereafter. The area was originally used for grain and dairy farming. A railroad (no longer used), entered the village in 1879. The state certified it as a city in 1991, and in 1995 it was officially named the "Violet Capital of Ohio." The main thoroughfares are Refugee Road on the north edge, running east/west and State Route 256 coursing through the center, running north/south. The east/west interstate highway, I-70, is five miles to the north. The population is 14,400 (from 634 in 1960). Governance is by an elected mayor and council, and a city manager is appointed. The school system includes five elementary, two middle, two junior high and two high schools. A Carnegie Public Library was built in 1915 and replaced in 1993. Local points of interest are preserved by the Pickerington Violet Township Historical Society. Pickerington has a Senior Center and five parks. A Violet Festival is held annually. In close proximity to the west and northwest are two Columbus Metropolitan golf courses, Turnbury and Blacklick Woods. The latter includes a large park with shelter house, a lake and trails. Recently, the upscale Jefferson Golf and Country Club, surrounded by expensive homes, became a valuable addition. Today, Pickerington is considered a bedroom community for Columbus and Lancaster. The median cost of homes is $223,600, and the median cost of living is at the 105 percentile.

Reynoldsburg

Reynoldsburg is located on the extreme east edge of Columbus on U.S. Route 40 (Main Street) and I-70 (east/west) and State Route 256, going south to Pickerington. Parts of it lie within three counties: Licking to the east, Fairfield to the south and most of it in Franklin to the north and west. It is close to the east rim of the Columbus Outerbelt (I-270). Although James C. Reynolds founded the city, it is best known as the "Birthplace of the Tomato" due to the life work of Alexander Livingston. Livingston was a self-taught horticulturalist and performed many tomato breeding experiments. This resulted in two early superior tomato plants, the Paragon and Acme. The A.W. Livingston Buckeye Seed Gardens catalogued and sold his seeds and plants. His research is commemorated by the annual Tomato Festival. His home, which was constructed in 1864, in the high fashion of the time, is a landmark. It is maintained and shown by the Reynoldsburg/Truro Historical Society. Mr. Livingston was deeply religious. He was committed to the freeing of slaves and participated in the "underground railroad." He was an active member of the Truro Seceders Congregation, where he taught Sunday School. He also taught Sunday School at the Ohio Penitentiary. In addition to the Tomato Festival, the city sponsors Founders Day and Tartan Days, the latter in honor of those with Scottish heritage. The school system includes a high, one junior, one middle and five elementary schools. The Columbus airport is twenty minutes away. The city is governed by a mayor and council. Reynoldsburg has an active Senior Center. Among its parks and recreational facilities is Blacklick Woods Metropolitan Park. It includes a shelter house and two fine golf courses. All are located on the east boundary of the city where Blacklick Creek flows. Most businesses are small or service oriented. The largest is the J.C. Penney Outlet Center. Mount Carmel East Hospital is a sizeable general health facility. The current population is 32,000 with eighty percent Caucasian, ten percent African-American, five percent Latinos and two percent Asian. The median cost of homes is $163,400, and the median cost of living is at the 85 percentile.

Upper Arlington

Upper Arlington's ten square mile city, a few miles northwest of downtown Columbus, is nestled between the Scioto River on the west and The Ohio State University on the east. Grandview Heights and Marble Cliff lie to the south and Columbus surrounds it on the north. It became a premier planned city when King Thompson converted the farm land into streets and homes in 1914. The town resembled an armed encampment for a few months in 1916; Camp Willis was located there. Upper Arlington became incorporated in 1918 and has served as a choice residential suburb with easy access to Columbus and the The Ohio State University. The terrain is flat and the streets are tree lined. One of the nation's premier country clubs, Scioto Country Club, as well as two University golf courses are located within the city limits. Likewise, private Riverside Methodist and public University Hospitals are on its edge. The city is proud of its public school system and libraries rated among the best in the Middlewest. Proficiency tests are perennially high, and the high school matriculates many national merit finalists and commended scholars. Many teachers have been selected for national recognition. A high proportion of high school graduates attend college. The school athletic teams usually perform in the upper rung. The Upper Arlington School District is the only one in Ohio to be fully accredited by the North Central Association of Schools and Colleges. There are two middle, five elementary, one high and one private school. The city has three charter schools; one elementary and two high schools, and each receives state and federal aid. Each has its own board of directors that report to the city school board. The elementary charter school works with the Harvard Graduate School of Education. Five thousand of the city's residents participate in its Life Long Learning Programs. The Historical Society collects archival materials and conducts educational programs. All major service clubs are represented. The city has seventeen parks, thirty-five tennis courts, three swimming pools, four shelter houses, 120 recreational programs for all ages, a very active senior center and a fitness trail. Seventeen churches of all denominations are represented. While heavy industry is prohibited, there are a number of small businesses and service companies. The two major shopping centers are Shops on Lane Avenue and Kingsdale. The latter is under severe economic stress. The main highways are U.S. Routes 33 and 315, each running north and south. No trains pass through Upper Arlington, but the University Airport is within two miles and the Columbus Airport is within twenty miles via I-670. The most spectacular community event is the Fourth of July Parade followed later by the Labor Day Arts Festival. The University athletic facilities are a few minutes away. All the cultural benefits of Columbus and the University are within easy access. The City Council is elected and a City Manager is appointed. Homes range in price between $100,000 to $1,500,000. The median cost of homes is $285,000, and the median cost of living is at the 116 percentile. Property taxes are the highest in Franklin County, and the city has a two percent income tax. The median male income is $66,850. The population of 34,100 is composed of ninety-five percent Caucasian, three percent Asian, 0.6% African American and the rest "other."

In 1963, First Community Church sponsored one of the first upscale retirement living quarters in Central Ohio called First Community Village. It is located at the northeast corner of Riverside Drive (U.S. Route 33) and 5th Avenue. Its address is 1800 Riverside Drive, but its entrance is on 5th Avenue. In 2001, it became an independently operated nonprofit organization, paying its property taxes to the Upper Arlington School District. Its thirty-acre campus includes independent living in an apartment building, an assisted-living building, Alzheimer's care cottages, a nursing-home, an indoor swimming pool, a fitness center with personal trainers, formal and casual dining facilities, an exercise area with aerobics room, a library, game rooms, a theatre, medical clinic/offices, beauty/barber shop, bank, and landscaped walking paths and courtyards. Entry fees range from $188,000 to $555,000 (ninety percent refunded when residents leave), with monthly usage fees ranging from $2,725 to $4,352.

Westerville

Westerville is located on the extreme northeastern edge of Franklin County and ten miles northeast of Columbus; it serves as a residential suburb. It is partly situated in Delaware County. Settlers moved into the area along Alum Creek in 1806, three years after Ohio statehood and its neighboring town of Worthington were created. Today, its southwest corner blends into Worthington. Garrit Sharp and family are credited with being the first inhabitants. In 1817, the Westervelt families built their cabins in what is now downtown Westerville and after whom the town is named. The 1820 home of Gideon Hart is still standing. The first postmaster was appointed in 1840 when the population reached 900, and the town's name became official. In 1837, a Methodist Church was started; the land was a gift from the Westervelts. They also donated land for the Blendon Young Men's Seminary. In 1847, the United Brethren opened Otterbein College which had the distinction of being one of the earliest colleges to admit women students and appoint females to the faculty. Otterbein was also one of first to take students of color. The local school district was created in 1855. By this time, an inn and health spa had been added to the town. Local participation in the "underground railroad" was active. In 1853, a toll plank road was constructed between Westerville and Columbus. The settlement was incorporated as a Village in 1858, and the first mayor was elected. A volunteer fire department became part of the establishment in 1860 and remained volunteer for one hundred years. The first railroad passed through Westerville in 1873 and reduced the travel time to Columbus from four and one-half hours to forty-five minutes. This spurred economic activity that included some mills and the Everal Tile Company. Everal bricks were used to pave several streets. The Everal family barn and homestead are focal points of interest in Heritage Park today. The Westerville Electric Division opened in 1898 and the first water treatment plant three years later. In 1895, an electric interurban line connected Westerville with Columbus. The first automobile in Westerville (a Cadillac) appeared in 1904. The dirt roads made travel uncomfortable and soon the streets were paved with brick.

Westerville had a "Whiskey War" in 1875. The focus of irate citizens favoring prohibition was Henry Corbin's saloon and his unwillingness to cease operations. An unexplained explosion blew the roof and windows out of the saloon and subdued the controversy for a time. Four years later, fifty-two pounds of gunpowder produced a similar result at Corbin's new location. No liquor has been sold in the city until very recently. Many women and some men were active in the prohibition movement of the early 1900's. In recognition of this, the Anti-Saloon League moved its national headquarters to Westerville in 1909. Thus, Westerville was the center of one of the main socio-political issues of the day. The crusade against the consumption of alcohol attracted heated debate until the Volstead Act was enacted in 1920. Even after probation was lifted in 1933, Westerville remained dry for over seventy years. The Anti-Saloon League headquarters building was turned into the first public library in 1930. In 1998, the library underwent a considerable renovation and expansion for the second time.

In the "roaring twenties" the Winter Garden Motion Picture Theater thrived, a Masonic Temple and new high school were built, and the Kilgore Manufacturing Company which made children's toy guns and caps employed 175 people. The Great Depression hit the town in 1931 when a bank failed, and unemployment rose to unheard of levels. The WPA was a town saver; it built a park, post office, a city office building, an armory, storm drains and other projects besides providing much needed employment. World War II brought prosperity. Hand grenades, flares and land mines were produced at the Kilgore Company. There was a rapid increase in new homes, the roads were enlarged and improved and new businesses arrived. The public schools and Otterbein College added more students. In 1961, Westerville became incorporated as a city. A quarter of a century later the Brooksedge, Eastwind and Commerce Centers added new business opportunities. Nearby Polaris Center offers stiff competition. The population is steadily growing. Today, Westerville and Dublin vie for the honor of becoming the largest suburb of Columbus.

The North American headquarters for the paper products and automation divisions for the Swiss company, ABB, is at 579 Executive Campus Drive in Westerville. The company gives customers an "ABB University" crash course in how to use the products they have purchased. ABB, a $19 billion company, is the number one automation technology supplier in the world. Formerly it was located on Ackerman Road in Columbus; since 1952. ABB employs two hundred and fifty people.

President Coolidge dedicated Westerville's first high school, Hanby, in 1920, and the building is still in use. He also toured Otterbein College, where he placed a wreath on *Soldier's Monument*, dedicated to Civil War participants. The monument remains today in front of Towers Hall.

Benjamin Hanby lived in Westerville and was one of the first graduates of Otterbein College. He was a minister and composer of popular music. He wrote *Darling Nellie Gray* and *Up On The Housetop*. He married Kate Winter, the first female to graduate from Otterbein (incidentally, she was a distant cousin of the author of this book). Hanby died at a young age. The Westerville Historical Society operates the Hanby House and Gift Shop. The Winter House is preserved a few blocks away. Many of the old historic homes and civic buildings are maintained and are entered in the National Registry.

Otterbein College was co-founded in 1847 by Bishop William Hanby and Lewis Davis. It is named after Phillip William Otterbein, a German immigrant who became a prominent American clergyman and evangelist and founded the United Brethren in Christ denomination. After a merger in 1968, the college was supported by the United Methodist Church. This fine four-year liberal arts college is private and coeducational. It has an enrollment of over 3,000 students and offers twenty-five majors and grants bachelor and master of business administration degrees. The school has outstanding theater and athletic programs. The theater group continues its presentations throughout the entire year. The new Frank Art Museum, limited to African and Asian art, opened in a renovated church building in 2004. Gordon Jump, screen and television actor, is an alumnus of Otterbein College.

Alum Creek Park was initiated in 1934 as a WPA project. Schools, churches, parks, utilities and new buildings proliferated in the mid-1900's. The city always has been administered by a manager and council. In the 1980's, when the population reached 24,000 and 90% of the land was residential, attention was focused on business development to ease the tax burden. St. Ann's Hospital opened in 1984, and the old water treatment plant nearby was converted into a Senior Center. By 1990, the population of Westerville had burgeoned to 32,270, and several shopping/business malls and commerce center were thriving. Today, the population is 36,000 and growing. Ninety-four percent of the populace is Caucasian, three percent African-American and one and one-half percent Asian. A part of the growth may be attributed to annexation of land, but the attraction to residents who work in Columbus with its easy access and the excellent education system are chiefly responsible. Recently, *Columbus Parent* recognized Westerville as the best place to raise a family in Central Ohio. Three high schools are in operation. Other schools include four middle and eighteen elementary. The Westerville Parks and Recreation Department received a national gold medal for its excellent service. It includes a Community Center. In 1972, Grace and Mary Innis donated their Westerville home and many acres of gardens and woods to the Columbus Metro Parks. The Inniswoods Gardens contained 2,000 species of flowers and herbs, including over 250 varieties of roses. Their three park trails have waterfalls and trellis arches. A large metropolitan park, Sharon Woods, complete with nature trails and an educational center abuts the western edge of the city. The federal government awarded the city's postal system a top rating for its delivery program. Almost a thousand individuals are employed in some form of government service. State Route 3 passes through the heart of Westerville and for years was the main artery from Cleveland to Cincinnati, passing through Columbus. It was known as the 3-C highway and was beneficial to downtown business. Today I-71 parallels that route. The Columbus outerbelt (I-270) and State Route 161 skirt the southern border of the city. The rail lines are long gone. Port Columbus International Airport is only fifteen miles to the southeast. The median cost of homes is $188,000, and the median cost of living is at the 99 percentile.

Whitehall

Whitehall is a small residential area with a population of nineteen thousand situated between Bexley to the west and Reynoldsburg to the east. The residents are of average income and mostly blue collar workers. Demographics reveal that seventy-five percent of the populace is Caucasian, eighteen percent African-American and two percent Hispanic. The Town and Country Shopping Center, developed by Don M. Casto in 1949, was the first such center in Central Ohio. Now, only a few shops and small businesses remain. One former sizeable store, Wal-Mart, moved elsewhere. The largest industry and the employer of six thousand people is the Defense Supply Depot of Columbus. Most of this huge defense facility, present since 1918, is within the city limits of Whitehall, the remainder is in Columbus. It is found in the northwest quadrant of the city where a railroad mainline skirts the city. The Columbus Airport is two miles directly north. Three major roadways transect the flat terrain; Hamilton Road runs north-south and Main Street (Old National Road-U.S. 40) and East Broad Street courses east-west. Reynoldsburg is directly east, Bexley is directly west and Gahanna is three miles to the northeast. At one time, a trolley line connected Whitehall with Columbus. Interstate I-70 is two miles to the south and the I-270 outerbelt is one mile to the east. Big Walnut Creek, two city parks and the Columbus Country Club form the eastern boundary. The southern limit is formed by Mound and Main Streets. Maplewood Avenue is the last street on the west side. Since Whitehall is landlocked, growth is restricted. There is one high school, one junior high and three elementary schools. A Public Library and Historical Society are educational attributes. An elected mayor and city council govern the residents. The median cost of homes is $167,400, and the cost of living is at the 85 percentile.

Worthington

The same year Ohio became a state in 1803, the city of Worthington was founded by a group of Connecticut and Massachusetts citizens, some of whom were Revolutionary War veterans anxious to try their luck on the western frontier. They formed the Scioto Company with forty-two subscribers and purchased sixteen thousand acres along the "Scioto Trail" in United States Military Land, ten miles north of Columbus. Half of the footage rested against the Whetstone River (later renamed Olentangy). The cost was $1.25 per acre: thirteen thousand dollars paid by a four-year mortgage requiring six percent interest per annum and the remaining seven thousand dollars given as real estate owned by the subscribers. The early settlers were a close knit group; many were related. Their common religion was Episcopalian.

The land in the Northwest Territory that became Worthington had been a collection of parcels purchased by eastern speculators, Jonas Stanbury and Jonathon Dayton, directly from veterans of the Revolutionary War who had been issued land warrants by Congress in payment for their services in the war. The two middlemen realtors made a hefty fifty percent profit. The land had been surveyed in 1797, using 1/8 mile long chains and blazing trees at 2½ mile intervals. Two representatives of the Scioto Company had made a scouting trip to Ohio and talked to land agent Thomas Worthington in Chillicothe. They backed out of their tentative agreement with Worthington to buy land at two dollars an acre. In a change of plans, a different portion of land was purchased from Stanbury and Dayton without being viewed by the buyers. But, upon seeing their purchase for the first time in 1803, they were completely satisfied with its location and the appearance of the soil. Each subscriber was allotted a town lot of three-quarters of an acre and an out lot measuring .9875 acre. They named the town Worthington in honor of Thomas Worthington whom they had come to admire. The land proved fertile and the harvests satisfactory. A small dam was constructed on the Whetstone River and mills were erected. The principal leader of the group was businessman, soldier, farmer, surveyor, mechanic and Episcopalian Deacon, James Kilbourne. Other important members of the company were Joseph Topping, a physician; Ezra Griswold, a merchant; and Nathaniel Little, a store keeper. They sent an advance party of young men to erect temporary shelters, clear some land and plant crops (corn and potatoes). The remaining migrants, including women and children, came in small groups during the next year. They traveled the six to eight-week journey by boat, horseback or mostly walking. Horses or oxen pulled wagons and often were assisted over rough terrain by man power. The journey was a severe ordeal as many of the routes followed were Indian trails or unimproved roads full of wheel-ruts, potholes and rocks.

Upon arrival at the new land purchase, two squatters were found. Their primitive shelters and fruit orchards were bought and found useful at once. Other settlers resided five miles to the north. Several prehistoric burial mounds were located on the land near the river (Jeffers Mound on Pleasanton Drive, has been preserved to this day by the local historical society). No significant Indian presence was encountered. The first cabins erected in Worthington were composed of eighty logs assembled in sixteen by twenty feet rectangles with a fireplace. One of the early acts was to build a school house which also served as a town hall and church (presided over by Deacon Kilbourne). A small dam was constructed on the Whetstone River and sawmill and gristmill were constructed. Work was commenced to build more substantial dwellings. Only minimal belongings were brought from their homes in the east. They included eating and cooking utensils made of wood, iron, tin and pewter and building implements, such as an axe, saw, nails, hammer, rasp, chisel and knives. Farming equipment and animals included plows, harnesses, hoes, spades, sickles, horses, oxen, pigs and cows. Some equipment was purchased along the way and some animals upon arrival. Chillicothe was the nearest center of commerce. Supplements to their diet included berries, fruit and roots. Some of the wooden furniture and china did not stand the roughness of the trip; however, spinning wheels and looms for making yarn and clothes did survive and were useful at once. Clothes made of wool, coarse cloth, calico and buckskin could be purchased at local trading posts. Pillows containing feathers, corn husks or leaves, plus sheets and blankets on rope springs and mattresses (feathers, leaves, corn husks) completed their needs. Stills for making whiskey, bee hives for collecting honey, maple syrup from tapped trees and means for making beer were added as soon as possible. Trapped and shot animals supplemented the need for meat. Fishing furnished occasional supplements. Chickens provided meat and eggs. Cows provided milk, and cream was churned for butter. Much of the day was spent by all in farming, making shelters and preparing food. There was little time for recreation, reading or idle talk. Prior to coming, subscribers had been signed up at two dollars per person for a library, and books were purchased or donated from the east. School teachers were hired, and subscribers placed their children in school for a maximum eighth grade education in reading, writing and ciphering. A Masonic Lodge was established in the first year (in 1820 a Masonic Temple was built in Worthington and still stands). Both the forthcoming Episcopal Church and the Worthington Academy were given an eighty-acre farm lot and a twenty-acre wood lot to provide financial support. Quickly a blacksmith, merchants and tavern keepers set up businesses. Within a short time a double wedding took place, and new arrivals swelled the populace. The state approved a road from Newark to Columbus with Worthington as a cross center. Eventually, a toll road to Delaware was built. Only the low land next to the river was susceptible to flooding. Most of the town was situated on high ground. Worthington's subsequent history included a college and medical school, both long gone. The first newspaper in Central Ohio, *The Western Intelligencer,* was started in Worthington in 1811.

The War of 1812 attracted few participants from Worthington. The only local casualty in the conflict was Zophar Topping, who was serving with Indian scouts.

President James Monroe visited Worthington in 1817 while on a tour of the nation.

The leader of the Scioto Company, James Kilbourne, was born in New Britain, Connecticut in 1770. He worked on his father's farm until age fifteen. When the farm could no longer provide him a livelihood, he left home and became an apprentice clothier for seven months of the year and worked on a farm the other five months. He also achieved ability in surveying. He was befriended by an Episcopalian Bishop who instructed him in the classics and mathematics. He was then placed in charge of the bishop's business and farm. He soon gained competence in merchandising and manufacturing and continued his education. He joined the Episcopal Church, became a lay-reader and in 1790 was ordained as a deacon. In 1789, he married Lucy Fitch, daughter of the inventor and builder of the first steamboat. Mrs. Kilbourne was the mother of two sons and five daughters; giving birth to one enroute to Ohio. She died four years later. Mr. Kilbourne remarried to Cynthia Goodale Barnes who was the sister of Lincoln Goodale, a prominent pioneer in Franklinton and Columbus.

Fig. 110 James Kilbourne (1770-1850), principal founder of Worthington.
—from Columbus Metro Library

In addition to farming and surveying for income, Kilbourne obtained funds from eastern entrepreneurs and established the Worthington Company that made clothing, household utensils, bricks and building supplies. A dormitory was provided for the workers who ran his mill and made his products. He commenced the first newspaper in Franklin County, the *Western Intelligencer*. He also acted as Rector of St. John's Episcopal Church. He was appointed a civic magistrate and an officer in the state militia. After rising in rank to Colonel, he resigned his commission. He was appointed a United States surveyor and explored the southern shore of Lake Erie and selected the site for the town of Sandusky. He was made a trustee of Ohio University in Athens. He was one of three commissioners appointed to select a site for Miami University of Ohio. In 1812, he organized Worthington College and served as its President. President Monroe appointed him a commissioner to resolve boundary disputes between the State of Virginia and the United States. He served two terms as a United States Representative to Congress. During the War of 1812, his company made a large profit by manufacturing woolen uniforms. The post-war recession forced his company into bankruptcy, and he was destitute at age fifty. He returned to surveying and accumulated land and acquired another fortune. He was elected to the State Legislature in 1823 and helped select lands upon which the Ohio-Erie Canal was constructed. He presided over the laying of the cornerstone for the new state capitol in 1839, and the State Convention of Whigs in 1840. He declined all other public offices except that of Franklin County Assessor of Property. He retired in 1848 and died in Worthington in 1850. He led an energetic life of service to his community and state.

In 1830, a medical school, *Ohio Reformed Medical College*, was established in Worthington. Six qualified physicians formed the faculty. In 1839, members of the school were suspected of stealing bodies from local cemeteries to use as cadavers for anatomical dissections. A riot occurred and the faculty fled. This ended the medical school.

In 1861, at the beginning of the Civil War, fifteen residents became members of Company E of James Worthington, Jr.'s 46th Ohio Volunteer Infantry regiment, which trained at Camp Lyon on the site of the former Worthington Manufacturing Company. The unit lost almost half of its members in the Battle of Shiloh in 1862.

Worthington, located on high, dry, rich farmland nine miles north of Columbus, on the Whetstone River (later renamed Olentangy) might have made a much better location for the state capital. It had an important north-south route through its center (State Route 23, today), subsequently, paralleled by Interstate I-71. Columbus had the more important east-west thoroughfare (National Route 40, later superceded by Interstate I-70).

Thus was the early history of one of the first towns in the new state of Ohio. It thrives today as a suburb of Columbus with a static population of about 14,000 and is known for its superb school system and libraries. A special section of

Worthington is called Rush Creek Village. Martha and Richard Wakefield built the first home there. It was designed by Theodore van Fossen in the Frank Lloyd Wright style. Subsequently, van Fossen designed thirty additional homes in the area, each with a distinctive Wright inspiration. The Rush Creek Company, a non-profit organization, oversees the neighborhood. Ninety-four percent of Worthington's population is Caucasian; three percent is Asian and two percent is African-American. The city is administered by an elected council which appoints a city manager and mayor. The mayor presides over a court, issues proclamations, and honors appropriate gatherings with his presence. Civic buildings include a police and a fire station much admired and supported by the city and townships. A new community center sports a swimming pool, weight room and large meeting and class rooms. The Griswold Senior Center has an extensive program housed in its own building shared with an Arts Council. Landlocked by Columbus, the population has reached its zenith in numbers, and the student rolls are decreasing. Due to maintenance of the high quality of education and other amenities, Worthington is considered a choice suburban community. The Worthington library system has two large sites and a third temporary location in the northeast sector with active educational programs. The Old Worthington library is on High Street and the Northwest Library is on Hard Road. The libraries have a close working relationship with the Columbus Metropolitan Library which co-operates the Northwest branch. In 2007, the library received a prestigious honor, the Gale/Library Journal's Library of the Year award. It was based on service to the community, creative programming, increase in library use and leadership. In addition to being designated the best community library in the nation, a gift of $10,000 accompanied the award. There are three high (one private parochial), four middle and twelve elementary schools. The two highly rated public high schools were the only ones in Franklin County to meet all state standards for three consecutive years. The school district sponsors an alternative high school in Linworth. A private Christian school encompasses all grades. The Vatican administers the Pontifical College Josephinum, a local Catholic seminary.

In 2007, the Worthington Public Schools announced the introduction of four new exciting alternative middle school programs. The *Kinesthetic Learning School* would appeal to students who learn primarily through movement, touch and active involvement. It would replace the traditional primary focus on visual and auditory instruction. The *Global Experimental Middle School* would focus on problem solving, environmental awareness, cultural awareness and service in a background of the world as a global community. The *Worthington Experimental Middle School* would emphasize experimental problem-based learning, focusing on "real-life problems that require real-life solutions." The background of this school would be a cooperative venture with Worthington and the surrounding communities aimed at producing well-rounded lifelong learners with both the education and experience necessary to succeed. The key would be to create "synergy" by combining core classes into a cohesive whole. Finally, the *Phoenix Project,* which is nearing its first year in operation, creates in students a deeper understanding of themselves and the world in which they live, while using creative scheduling to offer varied opportunities. The program focuses on connections among language, social studies, art and mathematics. Several of these school innovations include plans for town-hall style student governments. Also, students may be sent to "home" middle schools for core classes. These four alternative schools are housed in an existing middle school building.

The Phoenix project opened at Perry Middle School with eighty seventh-graders, selected by lottery, in August 2007. Its 8 a.m.-5 p.m. class day commences with Creative Start each morning. It includes art, music appreciation, instrumental music, voice, graphic design, industrial arts, fiber arts, drama and other fine arts courses. The next Foundation course includes silent sustained reading, followed by a class in reading, writing, technology, research, speech and media literacy. Other blocks of learning deal with math, social studies, physical activities, academic options with guest speakers, language studies, cultural and behavioral issues and integrated science/extension classes. The goal for each student is to attain a ninety percent achievement evaluation before proceeding to the next level of academic activities. Consideration is given to after-school activities.

In 2005, Worthington citizens voted to create an arts center. John McConnell, founder of Worthington Industries, gave one million dollars for the development of the project. It has been named the Peggy McConnell Cultural Arts Center. The original high school building on the Thomas Worthington High grounds is being renovated for this purpose and will be funded by taxpayer, corporate and private sources. An auditorium will be included.

An active Worthington Historical Society successfully preserves historic buildings (including the Episcopal Rectory-1841 and the Orange Johnson House-1811). The city's zoning and architectural commissions have retained the New England motif so that the city resembles a Colonial village with its central village green within a square anchored by St. John's Episcopal Church (from 1803), the Presbyterian Church (from 1830/1927) and an educational building. Worthington celebrated its bicentennial anniversary in 2003 with a year long program of informational and theatrical enjoyment. Entertainment programs on the village green each summer, Saturday Market Days, programs presented by the schools and two art galleries offer additional amenities for the residents. Within ten miles are first class colleges, a state university, highly rated hospitals, theaters, symphony orchestras, ballet and sports arenas. Worthington is surrounded by large shopping malls and a modest sized one within its midst (Worthington

Mall). Many small commercial plants and service businesses abound. The chief industries include one of the largest breweries in the country (Anheuser Busch), a steel processing company (Worthington Industries) and Diamond Innovations, a maker of superabrasives.

Worthington is a two to three hour drive from Cincinnati, Cleveland and Pittsburgh and is located halfway between Chicago and New York City. The state, county and city maintain excellent paved access. Several north/south, freight hauling trains toot frequently on the edges of the city; the CSX line passes through Linworth to the west, and both NS and CSX are situated on the eastern boundary. Both lines share their tracks with Conrail. There is a local museum of original railroad engines and cars. An interurban line between Columbus and Marion served Worthington for several years but was abandoned in 1933. The Columbus International Airport is thirty minutes driving time to the northeast. The median cost of homes is $217,000, and the median cost of living is at the 104 percentile.

*Powell

Powell is a rapidly growing premier residential community in southern Delaware County*, extending into the northern edge of Franklin County. It is considered a bedroom suburb of Columbus due to its geographic location, fourteen miles north of downtown Columbus. It is bisected by north/south Liberty Road and east/west State Route 750 (Olentangy Street or Powell Road). It lies midway between the Scioto River to the west and the Olentangy River to the east. The village was settled in 1801 as Middlebury since the first settlers came from the Middlebury, Connecticut area. In 1857, Judge Thomas Powell established a post office in the village, and his name was adopted for the community. It was incorporated as a city in 1947. The northern spread of suburban growth from Columbus reached Powell in the 1980's, increasing its population from 400 to over 10,000. In 2005, CNN/Money and *Money* magazine ranked Powell eighteenth on their list of the 100 Best Places to Live in the United States. In 2000, the medium household income was $115,904. Only 0.45% of the population is below the poverty line of which none are over the age of sixty-five. The growth has been so rapid that the city lags badly in development of its infrastructure. The narrow main streets cause traffic congestion and impacts on shopping development. Antique shops and restaurants are the main attractions for visitors. The racial makeup is ninety-four percent Caucasian and less than one percent African-American, Asian or native Americans; one percent are Hispanic. Its schools remain in the Olentangy Local School District (county), and there are two private schools; Powell Preparatory Academy and Village Academy. Its library is a branch of the Delaware County District Library. The governance is by a City Council of seven elected members who choose the President (Mayor) and Vice-President. A Parks and Recreation

Program was organized in 2000. Close by are the Columbus Zoo/Wyandot Lake complex, Highbanks Metropolitan Park, Olentangy Indian Caverns and Alum Creek State Park. The city has its own Police Department but utilizes the Liberty Township Fire Department.

Incorporated Villages in Franklin County

Amlin

Amlin is a tiny cluster of single family dwellings found on six streets immediately adjacent to the southwest corner of Dublin. It is approached by Rings (Main) Road. It is in Washington Township, whose trustees administer village affairs. It has a post office but no businesses and is in a rural setting. CSX/Conrail passes through the village, chiefly hauling coal.

Brice

Brice is a tiny village of seventy people living in twenty-seven housing units on four streets in Truro Township in east central Franklin County. It has no commercial or public buildings or parks. It is governed by an elected mayor. All police, fire and emergencies are handled by the township. Over ninety-seven percent of the inhabitants are Caucasian with no African-Americans. Brice Road runs north/south through the village and intersects with Refugee Road from the west and south. Reynoldsburg is two miles north and Pickerington three miles east. Farmland surrounds most of the village. A CSX/Conrail line courses through the center of the village. The median cost of homes is $125,700, and the median cost of living is at the 88 percentile.

Canal Winchester

Canal Winchester is a town of 6,500 people in Madison Township, located in the extreme southeast corner of Franklin County. Two brothers, Reuben and Jacob Dove, owned rich farm land in the area and sold part of it to plat a town on the Ohio-Erie Canal that passed through in 1828. The first boat appeared in 1831 and soon passengers, canal workers and the transport of local farm products brought growth to the village. Stores, taverns and churches were started. In 1841, the first post office was established, and the village officially became Canal Winchester. The village was annexed to Madison Township in 1851, and was incorporated in 1866. In 1869, the Columbus Hocking Valley Railroad made its appearance, and local commerce benefited from the speedier transportation. The Scioto Valley Traction Company connected the community to Columbus and neighboring towns from 1904 to 1930. A tri-weekly stagecoach service to Columbus existed in the mid-1800's. The last passenger train passed through in 1949, and now only CXS freight trains are seen. The first bankers were grain dealers. The first bank was the Canal Winchester Bank in 1887. It became the Central Trust Bank in 1973 and Bank One in 1991 (now JPMorgan/Chase). The People's Bank, organized in 1904, became a branch of Huntington Bank in 1962. TS Trim Industries, a manufacturer of auto door panels, headliners and other interior parts, has been headquartered in Canal Winchester since 1986. It is a subsidiary of the Tokyo Seat Company and chiefly supplies the Honda Automobile Company. Canal Winchester's main highway is Route 33 which connects with Lancaster, eight miles southeast, and to Columbus, fifteen miles northwest. The village has a community center with special programs for all ages including seniors. Festivities include "Christmas in the Village," Harvest Festival, Farmer's Market and concerts at Stradley Place Plaza. There are seven Protestant and one Catholic church. Education is conducted in two elementary, two middle and one high schools. The town is administered by an elected mayor and seven members of council. There are an additional eleven staff personnel. The unique private Wagnalls Memorial Library (originally funded and named after one of the editors of the Funk-Wagnalls Dictionary) is in near-by Lithopolis. Demographics reveal ninety-five percent of the residents are Caucasian and three percent are African-American.

Harrisburg

Harrisburg is a small village in Pleasant Township in southwest Franklin County. It was platted in 1836 by Joseph Chenowith and Frederick Cole. Before that the area was known as Darby Cross Roads. Within fifteen years it was incorporated, had thirty families, two taverns, four stores, two physicians, a Methodist Church and a post office. Today, the village of 335 residents rests on the Pickaway County line. It is five and ten miles southwest of Grove City and Columbus, respectively. One mile north is Interstate I-71 and U.S. Route 62 passes through the village on its way south five miles to Mount Sterling. Harrisburg has a modest library, a community center, but only a few businesses. Children attend school in Grove City. Ninety-six percent of the residents are Caucasian, and two and one-half percent are American Indian. They are governed by an elected mayor and council. The median cost of homes is $124,300, and the median cost of living is at the 83 percentile.

Lockbourne

Lockbourne received the first half of its name from the village's proximity to the Ohio-Erie Canal and the last half from Colonel James Kilbourne who laid out the town in 1831. The village is located in Hamilton Township on the mid-southern boundary of Franklin County. U.S. Route 23 running north/south, three miles to the east, is connected by Rowe Road. Lockbourne Road, coursing north/south, transects the village. Canal business caused the village to thrive initially, and within fifteen years it contained a Methodist and a United Brethren Church, a post office, two mills, two dry goods stores, three grocery stores, two taverns and three physicians. Its growth accelerated during World War II, when the Army established Lockbourne Airbase immediately east of the village. Norfolk & Western Railroad laid a line between the airfield and the village. In 1942, the airbase became a glider and B-17 training facility. The primary unit at the base was the all-black 447th Composite Group also known as the Tuskegee Airmen. In 1947, it became the 332nd Fighter Wing in the newly created United States Air Force. In 1949, the base was deactivated, and control was transferred to the Ohio Air National Guard who used it for training. During the Korean War, Lockbourne Air Force Base was reactivated by the defense department. Hangers were expanded, runways lengthened and a control tower was erected. It was now under control of the Strategic Air Command. Eighteen thousand service people were stationed at the base in the peak year of 1967. In 1974, the facility was renamed Rickenbacker Air Force Base in honor of the World War I flying ace from Columbus.

By 1980, the number of personnel at the airbase had reduced to 2,800, and the base was closed. While active, the base covered 4,400 acres and contained 265 buildings; many were living quarters. The Ohio Air National Guard resumed control of the facility. A port authority was formed to allow civilian freight flights and formation of an industrial park. Federal Express, Spiegel/Eddie Bauer and Siemens were some of the lease holders. Currently, the airport has two 12,000-foot runways, long enough to accommodate any aircraft in the world. It is recognized as the seventh fasting-growing cargo airport in the world, having moved 112,907 metric tons of cargo in 2005 and expecting this amount to double in a decade. A $64 million intermodal facility is under construction surrounding the airbase to facilitate long distant freight haulage by air, train and highway. Norfolk Southern Railroad desires to create a "Heartland Corridor" from Columbus to east coast ports. Use of double-stacked railcars, a prime ingredient for such a corridor, must await the raising of bridges and tunnels for height clearance by the railroad. Federal, state and private funding has been forthcoming. Tax-abatements for fifteen years have been granted to developers in the industrial area which contains one hundred and twenty-five companies. Currently the airport authority and Duke Realty, Capitol Square (a subsidiary of The Dispatch Printing Company) are the developers. The local Hamilton School District agreed to the abatements when they were reimbursed for the closing of an elementary school and for property-tax benefits it would lose when homes are acquired. Necessary infrastructures are underway. Eventually, Columbus will annex the industrial area. Intermittently, civilian airplanes and commercial airlines have been allowed use of the airport. The federal government provided fire protection and subsidized management costs. In 2002, a merger with Port Columbus airport resulted in the formation of the Columbus Regional Airport Authority with a U.S. Customs office.

The village of Lockbourne currently has two hundred and seventy residents which are ninety-nine percent Caucasian and twenty-eight percent of German heritage and nineteen percent of American Indian descent. There are three elementary, three middle and one high school. The town has one hundred homes, five churches and a single store. All are contained in a landlocked rectangle, two blocks wide and six blocks long. An elected mayor and council govern the village. The Landings at Rickenbacker is a public golf course hugging the airbase and close to the village. The median cost of homes is $104,300, and the median cost of living is at the 84 percentile. Lockbourne hopes to annex three farms west of the town for its own industrial development. Columbus would have to agree to provide water and sewer service, currently prohibiting the annexation plan by the village.

Minerva Park

Minerva Park commenced as a small farm settlement in Blendon Township in northeast Franklin County. From 1895 until 1902, it was the location of the largest amusement park in the county. It had a zoo, museum, roller coaster, water slide, lake for swimming and boating, baseball diamond, a large dance pavilion, pony rides, fireworks, theater and restaurants. A stone water tower/ jail was available to handle ruffians. The original dance hall burned in 1896 and was quickly rebuilt. Gambling and intoxicants were prohibited. The amusement center quickly died when the Olentangy Amusement Park opened closer to downtown Columbus. Only the lake remains. A trolley line from Columbus to Westerville passed nearby. The village is four miles southwest of Westerville and a similar distance southeast of Worthington. Its western boundary is Cleveland Avenue and Westerville Road (3C highway) marks the eastern village limits. State Route 161 abuts it on the north and Footloose Drive on the south. It is best known for the Minerva Lake Golf Course that occupies its southeastern portion. The Village of twelve hundred and fifty residents is governed by an elected mayor and council and has its own fire and police departments. Children go to schools outside the village limits. The village is entirely residential.

Obetz

Obetz is a small village of residences and small businesses in Hamilton Township, five miles southeast of Columbus, criss-crossed by Groveport Road and I-270, the Columbus outerbelt. It was settled by farmers who saw it grow into a railroad junction in 1838. It became incorporated as a village in 1928. For years, a low-level security state correctional facility was located within its town limits. Its eastern and southern boundaries are contiguous with Groveport. Williams Road delineates its northern border, as Rohr Road forms its southern edge. The U.S. Route 23 runs north and south, three miles to the west. Hamilton Road is placed a similar distance to the east. The village of four thousand residents has six parks, a senior service center, adult day trips and children's programs, a food pantry and is governed by an elected mayor and council. Special festivities were held to celebrate the seventy-fifth anniversary of its incorporation in 2003. The median cost of homes is $131,300, and the median cost of living is at the 81 percentile.

Riverlea

Riverlea can trace its land ownership to a grant of four thousand acres given by Congress to Reverend John Dunlop in 1800, for service in the Revolutionary War. This became Sharon Township. In 1802, Dunlop sold the land to Dr. Jonas Stansbury who in turn sold the land to the founders of Worthington in 1803. A part of the Worthington area, known as Maynard Farm in 1806, was sold to Jacob and Clara Artz and was secured by the Van De Boe-Hager Company of Cleveland in 1923. Twenty-five residences were built in the area during the next sixteen years. Thus, Riverlea came into existence as a tiny upscale residential area without shops or public buildings, nestled between the Olentangy River and North High Street (U.S. Route 23), completely surrounded by the south end of Worthington, and less than a twenty minute drive from downtown Columbus. It was incorporated in 1939 as a non-chartered Village. It has an elected mayor and council who appoint a clerk-treasurer, solicitor, marshal, street commissioner and a planning commission. The first mayor was Harold Barber, and Alvin Potter was the first treasurer. Riverlea pays Worthington for fire and police protection. Its children use the Worthington School system. The village of five hundred residents celebrates several holidays with festive events.

Urbancrest

Urbancrest is a tiny residential area (0.4 square miles) with a few small shops in southwest Franklin County laying within the boundaries of Grove City. Also, it is close to the Columbus Outerbelt (I-270) on the north and Interstate I-71 on the east. Grove City provides Urbancrest with all services including schools. The population is 868 with 58% African-American, 22% Caucasian, 10% Asian and 1.5% Hispanic. The Caucasian ancestry is revealed to be 9% German, 6% a mix of Irish, French and Italian. The median cost of homes is $94,800, and the median cost of living is at the 83 percentile.

Valleyview

Valleyview is small village in Franklin Township in west central Franklin County. When Franklinton, its predecessor was founded in 1797, Valleyview was farm land belonging to Lucas Sullivant. It is situated on a hilltop between Interstate I-70 on its north side, West Broad Street (U.S. Route 40) near its southern boundary, Hague Avenue to the west and the State Psychiatric Hospital on the southeast edge. Its population of six hundred is ninety-six percent Caucasian and one percent African-American. Twenty-four percent claim to be of German heritage while nineteen percent are believed to be English, fourteen percent Irish, five percent Italian and four percent Welsh. The mayor and council are elected. Fire, police and schools are provided by Columbus. A few stores are present. The median cost of homes is $112,800, and the median cost of living is at the 87 percentile.

Communities in Franklin County

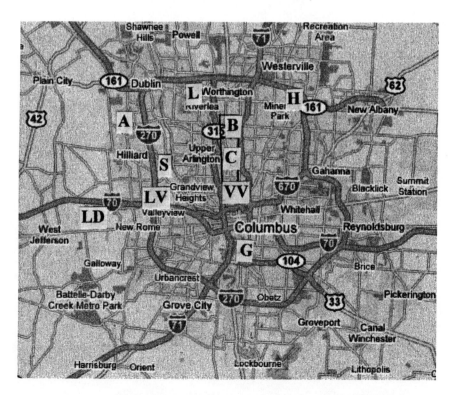

Fig. 111 The ten unincorporated communities are: *A*mlin, *B*eechwold, *C*lintonville, German Village, *H*uber Ridge, Lake *D*arby, Lincoln *V*illage, *L*inworth, *S*an Margherita, and *V*ictorian *V*illage.

Unincorporated Communities in Columbus and Franklin County

Clintonville-Beechwold

Clintonville and Beechwold are strong, longstanding communities with imprecise boundries that have been annexed to Columbus. Still, they are bound by strong community spirit. Thomas Bull, a Methodist minister and his family first settled the area on six hundred acres derived from the U.S. Military District. He made his purchase in 1813 from John Rathbone, a Revolutionary War veteran. The parcel of land lay along North High Street (U.S. Route 23) and immediately south of Worthington. Parts are in Sharon and Clinton Townships, hence Clintonville's name. The first post office in the area was designated Clintonville (named after George Clinton, a Governor of New York State and Vice-President under Presidents Jefferson and Madison), and was located at the corner of Oakland Park Avenue and High Street. This occurred in 1847, and Clintonville accepts this as its founding date. The introduction of auto travel advanced the development of new homes, schools, churches and small businesses, including service stations, banks and theaters. The Clintonville area extends roughly from Arcadia/Dodridge Avenues on its southern edge to Cooke/Henderson Roads on the north, while Beechwold extends further north to Fenway and Chase Roads. Both have the Olentangy River as their western boundary. Beechwold contains the Graceland Shopping Center near the western terminus of Morse Road. Tradition has it that the name came from Grace, who ran a brothel in Columbus and was the steady companion of gambling figure, Maurice Murnan, also of Columbus. The Joseph A. Jeffrey summer home (*Beechwolde*) on Jeffrey Place in Old Beechwold is of historic interest. Both communities extend east to Indianola Street and the Norfolk Southern Railroad. Some of the neighborhoods in the larger Clintonville are: Amazon Place, Crestview, Walhalla, Dominion Park, Northmor, Webster Park, Northridge, Overbrook, Rosemary Park and Indian Springs. The latter was the name of a public golf course in Clintonville. Wyandotte Country Club, on the northern edge, was replaced by the Ohio School for the Blind. Whetstone Park of Roses, Whetstone Library and the Clintonville Women's Club are assets to the community. The Park of Roses was established in 1944 at which time Columbus paid $75,000 for 161 acres from the Miller farm, and formed a commission to insure its proper development. More than 500 Victory Gardens were planted on the grounds during World War II. Roses were planted on 35 acres, and the park was opened to the public in 1953. Eventually, six thousand rose bushes were grown, some originals. A portion of the northern park contains the Barber-Roselea Senior Center. From World War II until the mid-1970's, the park was the showplace of the American Rose Society with its center in Columbus. After that, the headquarters moved to Portland, Oregon, because of its more temperate climate. For many years, a "Maid of Roses" pageant was held annually in the park.

The gardens have been the site of many weddings. Both communities have active civic organizations and festivities. Clintonville has an active historical society. The first log schoolhouse was built at California and High Streets in 1818. Clinton School served all grades from 1895 until 1922 when it was rebuilt, complete with a subway under High Street for the safety of school children. Current schools are Crestview and Indian Springs elementary, Dominion Middle and Whetstone High. Parochial schools are Immaculate Conception, Our Lady of Peace and Bishop Watterson High School. For four months in 1905, the Columbus Zoo was located in Beechwold. In addition to animals, the 21 acres contained rides, picnic grounds, a merry-go-round, a billiard hall and a dance pavilion. The population of the two communities is about ten thousand.

(German Village presented elsewhere)

Huber Ridge

Huber Ridge is located in Blendon Township, south and west of curving outerbelt I-270, north of State Route 161 (Dublin/Granville Road) and east of State Route 3 (Westerville Road). Its population is 4,883 with a racial makeup of ninety-two percent Caucasian and seven percent African-American. Students attend Westerville schools. The median home cost is $135,200, and the median cost of living is at the 90 percentile.

Lake Darby

Lake Darby is an unincorporated, census designated village located on the extreme west/central edge of Franklin County, partly in Prairie and Brown Townships. It name comes from the Big Darby River, passing from north to south on the west side of the village and the small lake in the northwest corner of the village. It lies between I-70 to the north and U.S. Route 40 (West Broad Street) to the south. It is between Plain City/Georgesville Road to the west and Amity Road to the east. It is ten miles west of downtown Columbus. A NS railroad line hugs the southern edge of the village. The population of 3,727 is ninety-eight percent Caucasian, two percent Hispanic and one percent African-American. The median cost of homes is $141,800, and the median cost of living is at the 91 percentile.

Lincoln Village

Lincoln Village is a planned, unincorporated, census designated village straddling West Broad Street (U.S. Route 40), seven miles due west of the center of Columbus. Outerbelt I-270 passes through the village, running north/south. New Rome is adjacent to the west and Valleyview is off from its northeast edge. The village was planned by Murray D. Lincoln, president of Nationwide Insurance Company in 1954. The second phase commenced in 1957. Nine thousand and four hundred and eighty-two people live on its eleven hundred and seventy acres. Children attend the Columbus public schools. In addition to homes and apartments, the village maintains churches, parks, a library, a fire station, a shopping center and an industrial park. Doctor's Hospital was placed in the village purposely. Streets are wide and curving for safety. The village is in Prairie Township. Ninety-three percent of the inhabitants are Caucasian, five percent are Hispanic and three percent are African-American. The median house cost is $116,000, and the median cost of living is at the 86 percentile. NBC produced a documentary about the village in 1954.

Linworth

Linworth is a small community situated half-way between the cities of Dub*lin* and *Worth*ington which explains the conception of its name. It is primarily residential and most of its land is in Worthington, with a western portion in Columbus. Its center is where north/south Linworth and West Dublin-Granville (State Route 161) Roads cross. The population is estimated to be several hundred. The original name of the village was Elmwood Station. The name was derived from a grove of Elm trees where the Columbus-Toledo Railroad placed its fueling and water stop in 1877. A post office was added to the station but mail was often delivered to the town of Elmwood in southern Ohio, hence the name change to Linworth in 1910. The ill-defined boundaries are Olentangy River Road on the east, Brookside Country Club and Don Scott Airport to the west, Perry Park on the north and Godown Road on the south. Pioneer farm owners, such as Hard, Case, Snouffer and Tuller have their names preserved on local street signs.

Today, Linworth has more than a dozen businesses located on a short strip of Dublin-Granville Road. Included are Cameron's American Bistro Restaurant (the first of nine Cameron Mitchell dining establishments), a summer-time farmer's market, two gas stations, the Village Bookstore and the Worthington Alternative High School.

The Village Bookstore occupies the historic Methodist Church on Dublin-Granville Road, built in 1889 and abandoned in 1958 when a second Methodist Church was constructed on Linworth Road. In turn, a third replacement Methodist Church was opened on Bent Tree Boulevard in 1997. Other churches and fraternal lodges are in the vicinity.

The Worthington Alternative High School (since 1975), offers several non-traditional programs for students from Worthington's two traditional high schools.

Some of their educational requirements and athletic programs are provided by the traditional high schools. Unique to the school are its town meetings, the "Walkabout" for seniors, a week-long experimental venture called "Interim," two-day camps, an Art House and a Maypole. Camp Akita, near Logan, Ohio is used to help those seniors preparing for college and for the "Walkabout." Camp Christian (non-religious) is a joint project with the community that sponsors an art show, a talent show and is for freshman, sophomores and juniors. The "Interim" week, gives students an opportunity to examine careers and academic goals, offer community service and hone practical and survival skills. The "Walkabout" is designed to develop skills, attitudes and values for responsible adulthood and an opportunity to test what he or she can do as an individual. Community service and interaction with adults is stressed in all school activities. Attendance at university classes is permitted after meeting minimal high school graduation requirements.

New Rome

New Rome is an unincorporated, census designated village of sixty individuals, centering on West Broad Street (U.S. Route 40), eight miles due west of the center of Columbus and immediately west of Lincoln Village. The median cost of housing is $105,000 and the median cost of living is at the 84 percentile. Due to harassment of citizens with speeding tickets and local governing corruption, the 1947 incorporation was legally dissolved by a Franklin Common Pleas Court in 2004.

San Margherita

San Margherita is a tiny unincorporated hamlet located on Trabue Road between the Scioto River on the east and Wilson Road on the west. Most of its space is taken up by the Columbus owned Raymond Golf Course. The village was heavily populated by Italian immigrants and their offsprings, but now most have moved away. Many had worked in the nearby limestone quarry, and the boys were caddies for the golf course. A railroad passes between the village and the quarry. Only small businesses are found in the settlement. Approximately one mile southeast of the village, between the CXS railroad tracks and the Scioto River, rests Shrum Mound, a prehistorically made small hill of earth, believed to be a cemetery. It is preserved and administered by the Ohio Historical Society. It is best approached on McKinley Avenue, one-half mile north of Fifth Avenue.

Victorian Village

Victorian Village is a relatively new residential area adjacent to Battelle Memorial Institute to its west and Ohio State University to the north. It is bounded on the east by North High Street and on the south by Goodale Boulevard. Prior to the 1870s, the land was part of William Neil's farm. After The Ohio State University was established, a large number of substantial homes of various Victorian Era styles were built on the land directly south of the university. Many of the homes were built of brick, and the more impressive ones along Neil Avenue and around Goodale Park were 2 1/2 to 3 stories in height. In 1879, a streetcar line along Neil Avenue connected downtown Columbus to the university. Many of the residents were professional and business people. The area entered into a decline after World War II. In 1973, Columbus declared the historic district to be called "Victorian Village." An Architectural Review Commission was established to protect and preserve the treasured homes. About eighty percent of one thousand buildings in the district have since been renovated in various Victorian styles. The village is within walking distance from the Short North, the Arena district and Ohio State University.

Chapter 31

Demographics of Columbus and Franklin County

According to the 2000 census, the population of Columbus was 711,470, making it the largest city in Ohio, almost double that of Cleveland's 478,403 and more than twice of Cincinnati's 331,285; it ranks 15th in the nation. Its population continues to climb in contrast to other large cities in Ohio. The greater metropolitan area is 1,670,000, making it third in the state after Cleveland and Cincinnati, and thirty-first in the country. The Columbus land area is 212 square miles. The city remains the seat of Franklin County. Some of the cities in the county extend slightly into Delaware, Union and Fairfield Counties. The racial makeup is 70% Caucasian, 25% African-American, 3% Asian and 2% other. The climate is moderate, with humid summers and cold winters; the highest temperature was 106°F in the 1930's with a low of -22°F in 1994. Annual rainfall averages 38".

The huge Ohio State University, one of its largest employers, is a dominant influence on the city. Its football stadium seats over 106,000 and is always filled to overflowing, a testament to winning ways. Other sizeable institutions of higher learning in the county are Columbus State Community College, Franklin University, Capital University, Ohio Dominican University, Otterbein University and DeVry Techology University. Battelle Memorial Research Institute is a world renown technology company. *Forbes* Magazine in 2008, ranked Columbus first nationally as an up-and-coming technology center. In the same time period, *Site Selection* listed Columbus first nationwide in landing industrial and corporate operations and expansions.

Culturally, the city boasts of a Museum of Art, Columbus College for Art and Design, the Wexner Art Center, a Center of Science and Industry, State, City and County Historical Societies, a highly rated metropolitan library system, a state library, many theaters, ballet, symphony and museums, many parks and athletic fields and a world class zoo. The *Columbus Dispatch* is the sole daily newspaper and is of high, balanced quality. The *Columbus Monthly* and *CEO* are published twelve times annually. There is a legal daily and several weekly papers. Columbus is home to the Ohio State Fair and professional sports teams (*Clippers*-baseball, *Bluejackets*-hockey, *Crew*-soccer and *Destroyers*-football and Jack Nicklaus's *Memorial* golf tournament). Each has its own sports arena. Many parades, festivals (arts and music) and fireworks are used to celebrate holidays.

The oldest skyscraper, Leveque Tower, is the city's landmark, colorfully illuminated at night. The city has been tagged the "Arch City" and the "Discovery City." A statue of Christopher Columbus fronts the city hall and a replica of his flagship, the Santa Maria, is anchored downtown on the Scioto River. Genoa, Italy is Columbus's sister city. Several large national and some international businesses began in Columbus, notably Nationwide Insurance, Bank One (now merged with J.P. Morgan Chase), The Limited clothing stores, Ross Laboratories, Worthington Industries, Borden Chemical, Chemical Abstracts, On-line Computer Library Center, Cardinal Health, Sterling Commerce, Wendy's Restaurants, White Castle Restaurants, Damons Restaurants and Cameron Restaurants. The Mall at Tuttle Crossing (1997), Easton Town Center (1999) and Polaris Fashion Place (2001) have replaced City Center (1989) as the upscale shopping centers. Anheuser-Busch has one of its largest breweries in the suburbs. The huge Honda auto and motorcycle manufacturing complex is near Dublin. McGraw-Hill has a large office branch in Columbus as does United Parcel Service. Three large hospital systems (Ohio State University, OhioHealth and the Mt. Carmels) provide first class health care and are large employers. Transportation is supported by six interstate highways: I-70 (east/west), I-71 (north/south), I-270 (outerbelt), U.S. Route 23 (north/south), U.S. Route 33 (northwest/southeast) and I-670 to the airport. Freight traffic on CSX, NS and Conrail railroads is heavy, but there are no passenger trains. Air travel is provided by Port Columbus International Airport, Rickenbacker Airport, Bolton Field and Don Scott Field. Delta Airlines has been the largest tenant at Port Columbus. However, the airline is bankrupt and is being sought by US Airways in a merger. In 2006, a new airline, Skybus, signed an agreement with the airport to use 100,000 square feet of empty office and hanger space and open a headquarters on nearby Fifth Avenue adjacent to its runway. This new tenant will receive $57 million in state and local incentives. They intend to have two hundred employees. Great plans are being addressed by Rickenbacker Airport for interstate freight haulage with a huge industrial park. Some infrastructure placement has commenced funded by federal, state and private corporate sources.

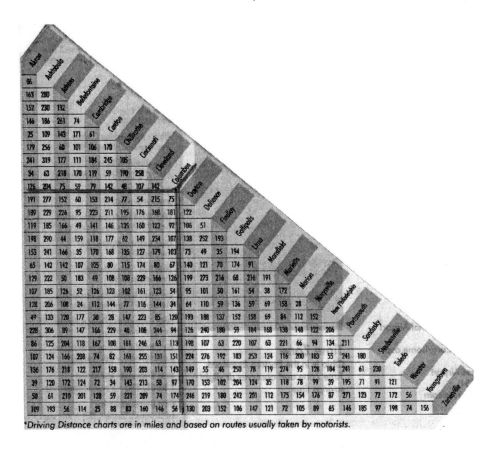

Fig. 112 Driving distances from Columbus to principal cities in Ohio

Fortune Magazine has rated Columbus as one of the top five cities in terms of innovative firms and quality of its labor force. Within its radius of one thousand miles, it has access to 78% of the country's gross domestic products and 80% of Canada's business activity. Two-thirds of the nation's population and seven of the ten largest cities reside within a radius of five hundred and fifty miles. Having no heavy industry, Columbus depends on commerce in banking, insurance, electronic services, research, education and light industry.

Columbus is frequently compared demographically with Indianapolis, Indiana because of similarities in geographic location, size and each as capital of its state. The following tabulation provides current statistics on metropolitan population, growth rate, new businesses, Fortune 1000 companies, median household income, foreclosures, percent of college graduates and violent crimes per 100,000.

Metro. Pop.	Grow. Rate/ New Bus.	Fort 1000	Med. House. Income	Foreclosures	Coll. Grads	Crime
Col 1.73 mil	7. % 3,733	15	$48,475	4,602	20.7%	441.5
Ind 1.67 mil	9.2% 4,392	7	$49,888	10,120	19.3%	574.4

Fig. 113 Statistical comparison of Columbus with Indianapolis

The current mayor of Columbus is Michael Coleman, an African-American attorney. He and all members of the city council belong to the Democratic Party. They are intensely focused on improving the inner city economically and culturally. The mayor's $25 million six-year effort to demolish or repair vacant homes has been highlighted. He is dedicated to improving the quality of inner city life.

African-Americans make up approximately one-quarter of the city's population. *Black Entertainment Television* in 2002 named Columbus as number one nationally for black families. In 2007, *Black Enterprise* magazine ranked Columbus number nine as a place for blacks to "live, work and play." Featured were a nine-percent unemployment rate, 8,771 black business owners, 5.4% of blacks earning more than $100,000 annually, health initiatives and educational opportunities. The median annual black household income is $32,347. Forty percent of blacks own their own homes. The National Conference of Black Mayors met in Columbus in 2005, and, in 2007, the National Society of Black Engineers convened in the city. Black leadership in Columbus includes the Mayor, School Superintendent, Chief of Police and Fire Chief.

Who are the shakers and movers of Columbus and Franklin County? It is not difficult to know. Their ranks change slowly since it took some time for them to get established. They are the heads of large local businesses or organizations, newspaper publishers, bank presidents, university presidents, mayors, city councilpersons, county commissioners, judges, clergypersons, some legislators, and an occasional wealthy benefactor or outspoken individual with good credentials and communication skills. If you fulfill any of these positions, you have clout and may apply.

It is obvious that the most prosperous portions of Franklin County lie north of U.S. I-70. Why has the southern half lagged behind? One explanation is that the trend was set early by laborers settling around their sites of employment that were predominantly south. The railroads added considerable coal smoke, soot and noise to the atmosphere. Small iron and steel foundries, sewage disposal and treatment plants, animal tanning and rendering facilities and, finally, the trash disposal sites and the huge trash burning plant rendered the south of Columbus more polluted visibly and to the nostrils than elsewhere. Today, efforts to correct these environmental problems are succeeding, and housing developments with higher home values are evident in the southern regions of the county. The sweet odor from the Anheuser Busch plant in north Columbus was quickly corrected, and the long standing sour odor from the distant Circleville and Chillicothe paper companies has largely disappeared. According to an FBI report in 2006, Columbus is the ninth most dangerous city (re: crime) among those with a population over a half-million in the nation, but is not listed among the twentieth overall.

Table 2
Comparison of Cost of Living and Cost of Homes in Franklin County

Municipality	Median Cost of Living	Median Cost of Homes
Bexley	109 percentile	$246,500
Dublin	112%	$262,400
Gahanna	92% estimate	$145,000
Grandview Heights	103%	$212,900
Grove City	94%	$160,200
Groveport	91%	$142,500
Hilliard	94% estimate	$157,600
Marble Cliff	136%	$405,000
New Albany	108%	$243,000
Pickerington	105%	$223,600
Reynoldsburg	95%	$163,400
Upper Arlington	116%	$285,000
Westerville	99%	$188,000
Whitehall	85%	$109,400
Worthington	104%	$217,000

Villages	Median Cost of Living	Median Cost of Homes
Amlin		
Brice	88%	$125,700
Canal Winchester		
Harrisburg	83%	$124,300
Lockbourne	84%	$104,300
Minerva Park		
Obetz	81%	$131,300
Riverlea		
Urbancrest	83%	$ 94,800
Valleyview	87%	$112,800

Unincorporated Communities

Beechwold		
Clintonville		
Huber Ridge	90%	$135,200
Lake Darby	91%	$141,800
Lincoln Village	86%	$116,000
Linworth	104%	$217,000
New Rome	84%	$105,000
San Margherita	NA	NA
Victorian Village	NA	NA

The two largest home builders in Central Ohio are Dominion Homes and M/I Homes, selling 2,450 and 2,200 units respectively in 2004.

Table 3
Populations of Columbus and Franklin County

	Columbus	Franklin County
1820	1,450	10,292
1830	2,437	14,741
1840	6,000	25,049
1860	18,500	50,361
1880	51,600	87,000
1900	125,500	164,460
1930	290,500	361,055
1960	471,300	683,000
2000	692,640	1,068,978

Table 4
Populations of Counties in Columbus Metropolitan Area

Counties and Principal Cities	Population (2000)
Franklin	1,068,978
Columbus, Upper Arlington, Bexley	
Dublin, Westerville, Hilliard, Gahanna,	
Worthington, Reynoldsburg, Whitehall,	
Grandview, Grove City, Groveport,	
Pickerington, New Albany	
Licking	145,491
Newark, Granville	
Fairfield	122,759
Lancaster	
Delaware	109,989
Delaware, Powell	
Pickaway	52,727
Circleville	
Union	40,909
Marysville	
Madison	40,213
London	
Morrow	31,628
Mount Gilead	
Total	1,612,694

Table 5
Columbus Mayors

Fig. 114 Mayor M.E. Sensenbrenner 1954-1959; 1964-1971

Fig. 115 Mayor Michael Coleman 2000-

Jarvis Pike	1816-17		Gilbert Collins	1879-80
John Kerr	1818-19		George Peters	1881-82
Eli King	1820-22		Charles Walcutt	1883-86
John Laughrey	1823		Philip Bruck	1887-90
William Martin	1824-26		George Karb	1891-94
James Robinson	1827		Cotton Allen	1895-96
William Long	1827-33		Samuel Black	1897-98
Philo Olmsted	1833		Samuel Swartz	1899-00
John Brooks	1834		John Hinkle	1901-02
John Bailhache	1835		Robert Jeffrey	1903-05
Warren Jenkins	1836-37		Dewitt Badger	1906-07
Philo Olmsted	1838-39		Charles Bone	1908-09
John Miller	1840-41		George Marshall	1910-11
Thomas Wood	1841		George Karb	1912-19
Abram McDowell	1842		James Thomas	1920-31
Smithson Wright	1843-44		Henry Worley	1932-35
Alexander Patton	1845		Myron Gessaman	1936-39
Augustus Decker	1846		Floyd Green	1940-43
Alexander Patton	1847-49		James Rhodes	1944-52 R
Lorenzo English	1850-61		Robert Oestreicher	1953 R
Wray Thomas	1861-64		M.E. Sensenbrenner	1954-59 D
James Bull	1865-68		Ralston Westlake	1960-63 R
George Meeker	1869-70		M.E. Sensenbrenner	1964-71 R
James Bull	1871-75		Tom Moody	1972-83 R
John Heitmann	1875-78		Dana Rinehart	1984-91 R
			Greg Lashutka	1992-99 R
			Michael Coleman	2000- D

Table 6
Ranking of Franklin County Banks by 2005 Deposits

Name of Bank	Amount of Deposits
J P Morgan Chase	$5.6 billion
Huntington National*	$4.5 billion
Fifth Third	$3.7 billion
National City	$2.4 billion
Key	$1.3 billion
Park National*	$1.2 billion
U.S. Bank	$1.0 billion
Ohio Savings	$620 million
Heartland	$378 million
Commerce National	$324 million
Sky	$259 million
First Merit	$180 million
Arlington	$143 million
First Community	$100 million
First City	$ 44 million
Grange	$ 39 million

* In 2006, *Bank Director Magazine* ranked Park National fifth in a list of the best managed banks. Huntington was the only other central Ohio bank ranked, at seventy-fourth.—from *Columbus CEO*

Table 7
Forbes Magazine's 2008 National Ranking of Up-and-Coming Technology Centers

1. Columbus
2. Sante Fe, N.M.
3. Palm Beach County, Fla.
4. Houston
5. Milwaukee
6. Pittsburgh
7. Boise City, Idaho
8. Iowa City, Iowa
9. Lake Charles, La.
10. Yuma, Ariz.

Table 8
Top Ten Commercial Real Estate Developers in Central Ohio—2006

Casto—Columbus
Steiner + Associates—Columbus
Duke Realty Corporation—Dublin
Equity—Worthington
Daimler Group—Columbus
Skilken—Columbus
N. P. Limited Partnership—Columbus
Pizzuti—Columbus
Plaza Properties—Columbus
Centerpoint Development—Columbus

—from *Columbus CEO*

Table 9
Central Ohio General Contractors—ranked by value

Gilbane Building Company
Turner Construction Company
Elford Company
Ruscilli Construction Company
Corna/Losing Construction Co.
Messer Construction Company
Danis Building Construction Co.
Miles/McClellan Construction Co.
R. W. Setterlin Building Co.
Quandel Group
Hanlin Rainaldi Construction Corp.
Robertson Construction Co.
Equity Company
Construction One Company
Opus North Company
Roslovic Building Company
Renier Construction Company
Gutknecht Construction Company
Ferguson Construction Company
Barton Malow Company

—from *Columbus C. E. O.*

Table 10
Largest Employers in Central Ohio-2004

Organization	Sector	Local Full-time Employees
The Ohio State University*	Public Education	17,361
United States Government	Government	13,300
JP Morgan Chase & Co.	Financial/Banking	12,130
Nationwide	Financial/Insurance	11,293
OhioHealth	Heath Care	8,398
Columbus Public Schools	Public Education	8,024
City of Columbus	Government	7,919
Limited Brands	Retail Trade/Corp. Mgt.	7,200
Honda of America-Union Cnty	Vehicle Manufacturing	6,350
Franklin County	Government	6,218
Wal-Mart Stores	Retail Trade	6,100
Mount Carmel Hospitals	Health Care	5,558
Kroger Company	Retail Food Trade	4,632
Wendy's Intnl, Inc	Retail Food Trade/Mgt.	4,500
American Electric Power	Electric Utilities	3,900
Huntington Bancshares	Financial/ Banking	3,500
SBC Ohio	Communications	3,000
Ross Products/Abbott Labs	Health Products Mfg.	2,800
Nationwide Children's Hosp.	Health Care	2,706
Medco Health Solutions, Inc	Health Care/Wholsel Trade	2,528
South-Western Public Schools	Public Education	2,516
Battelle Memorial Institute	Research Services	2,368
Retail Ventures, Inc	Corp. Mgt. /Retail Trade	2,170
Big Lots, Inc	Corp. Mgt. /Retail Trade	2,100
Discover Financial Services	Financial Activities	2,100
Cardinal Health	Health Care/Wholsel Trade	2,000
Dispatch Printing Company	News Information	1,900
State Farm Insurance	Financial/Insurance Activities	1,795
National City Corp.	Financial/Banking Activities	1,780
Alliance Data Systems	Information	1,757
Hilliard City Schools	Public Education	1,688
Owens Corning	Manufacturing	1,531
ARC Industries	Manufacturing	1,500

* Includes Health Care. In 2007, Ohio State University Medical Center employed 11,350 which would rank it fifth if separated from OSU.

—continuation of Table 10

CallTech Communications	Professional Services	1,500
Dublin City Schools	Public Education	1,482
United Parcel Service	Transportation	1,445
Westerville City Schools	Public Education	1,441
Ashland, Inc.	Wholesale Petroleum Trade	1,362

References

Barrett, Richard. *Postcards from Columbus: Senior Times.* Columbus, Ohio.
Columbus CEO. A monthly magazine published by CM Media Inc., Columbus, Ohio.
Cole Jr., Charles C. *A Fragile Capital, Identity and the Early Years of Columbus, Ohio.* Columbus, Ohio, State University Press, 2001.
Columbus Dispatch. A Columbus, Ohio, daily newspaper.
Darbee, Jeffrey T. and Recchie, Nancy A. *Images of America: German Columbus.* Chicago, Illinois, Arcadia Publishing, 2005.
Garrett, Betty and Lentz, Edward. *Columbus, America's Crossroads.* Tulsa, Oklahoma, Continental Heritage Press, 1980.
Henderson, Andrew. *Images of Forgotten Columbus.* Arcadia Publishing, Chicago, Illinois, 2002.
Harden, Mike. *Columbus Celebrates the Millenium.* Montgomery, Alabama. Community Communications, 2000.
Hooper, Osman C. *History of Columbus, Ohio,* 1920.
Hudson, N. Paul. *The Ohio State University College of Medicine, Volume II, 1934-1958.* The Ohio State University, Columbus, Ohio. 1961.
Hunker, Henry L. *Columbus, Ohio, A Personal Geography.* Columbus, Ohio, Ohio State University Press, 2000.
Lee, Alfred E. *History of Columbus, 2 vols.* New York, Munsell & Company, 1892.
Lentz, Ed. *As It Were: Story of Old Columbus, 2 vols.* Red Mountain Press, Seattle, Washington, 2001.
Lore, David. *Inside the Pen.* Columbus, Ohio, *The Columbus Dispatch,* October 28, 1984.
Martin, William T. *History of Franklin County.* Columbus, Ohio, Follett, Foster & Company, 1858. Reprinted 1969.
Moore, Opha. *History of Franklin County.* 1858.
Palmer, Angela. *Charters and Dollars, Columbus CEO.* Columbus, Ohio, CM Media, Inc., February, 2006.
Paulson, George W. *The Ohio State College of Medicine, Vol III.* Columbus, Ohio, The Ohio State University Press, 1998.
Perkins, Michael A. *Leveque.* Bloomington, Indiana, Authorhouse, 2005.
Raphael, Marc L. *Jews and Judaism in a Midwestern Community: Columbus, Ohio, 1840-1975.* Columbus, Ohio, Ohio Historical Society, 1979.

Rippley, La Vern J. *The Columbus Germans.* Baltimore, Maryland, J. H. Furst Company, 1968.

The Senior Times, an Ohio monthly news magazine, Columbus, Ohio, Senior Publishing Company.

Sterling, Lea Ann. *Historic Homes of Olde Towne, Columbus, Ohio.* Dublin, Ohio, Victory Postcards, Inc., 1999.

Studer, Jacob. *History of Columbus, Ohio.* 1872

Thompson, James. *History of Linworth,* Columbus, Ohio, Self-Published

White, Ruth Y. *We Too Built Columbus.* Columbus, Ohio, Stoneman Press, 1936.

Wills, Garry. *Head and Heart: American Christianities.* New York, The Penguin Press, 2007.

Winter, Chester C. *A Bicentennial History of the State of Ohio.* Worthington, Ohio, Caldwell Publishers, 2003.

Winter, Chester C. *Ohio Cities: Historical Descriptions.* Worthington, Ohio, Caldwell Publishers, 2004.

Winter, Chester C. *Concise Biographies of Notable Ohioans.* Worthington, Ohio, Caldwell Publishers, 2005.

Wikipedia.rg. A computer internet, on-line encyclopedia. Wikimedia Foundation, 2006.

www.OhioCities.Org

Index

Abell, Jane Grote 197
Abercrombie & Fitch 189, 277
Actors' Theater 232
Ackerman, Kenneth Company 124
ADS (Advanced Drainage Systems viii,190
Advantage Academy 122
African-Americans 89, 235
Africentric High School 126, 139
Agriculture Department, State 34
airlines
   Netjets 207
   Trans World Airline 93
airports
   Bolton Field 303
   Don Scott Field 303
   Port Columbus 93, 294, 303
   Rickenbacker Airport 293, 303
AIU Citadel 223
Aladdin Shrine Center 218
Alcatel *See* Lucent Technologies 203-205
Allegemaine Zeitung des Judentums 62
Allen, Nimrod 102
American Electric Power (AEP) 51, 100, 189
American Federation of Labor 57, 100
American Kidney Stone Management (AKSM) 114
American Telephone & Telegraphy Company (AT&T) 189, 204, 212
Amicon Produce Company 87
Anderson Concrete Company 190
Anderson, Walter E. 177, 190, 214
Anheuser-Busch 303

animals on Ohio frontier 9,10
Anti-Saloon League 281
AOL (Compuserve) 194
Arboretum, Chadwick 129
architects, notable
   Bellows, George 70, 91
   Ireland, Byron 147
   Moody-Nolan 69
   Packard, Frank 91
Army Corp of Engineers 218, 231
Arts Council 276, 288
Ashcan School 157
Ashland University, branch 141
Athenaeum Building 169, 218
automobiles racing 93
Awl, William 69

Baber, Richard P. 79
baby camp 89
Bailey, J.A. 91
Baldwin, James F. 114
Balentine, Robert 18
Ball, John 19
BalletMet 89, 187, 235
balloon rides 58, 93
BancOhio National, Columbus 188, 206
Bank, Franklin 181
basketball, OSU 137
Battelle, Gordon 126, 172
Battelle Memorial Institute 126, 172
Beck Park 64
Beechwold 237, 297
Bellows, George Jr. 75, 150, 156
Bellows, George Sr. 70, 152, 156

317

benevolent institutions 68
Benson, Frank III 197
Benson, Frank, Jr. 197
Berry Bolt Works, 87
Beulah Park racing 93
Big Bear Grocery Company 190, 273
Big Lots 191
Black, Catherine Nelson 258
Blue Jackets, hockey team 241
Bob Evans Restaurants xi, 249
Book Loft 63
Booth, William 254
Borror, Corporation 172,
Borror, Donald A. 172
Bostic, Les 72
Bott Brothers 94
Breck, William 273
breweries 18, 60-65
  Barley 61
  Biersch 61
  Blenker 18, 60
  Born 60
  Capital 60
  Columbus 60
  Elevator 61
  Hoster 18, 61
  Schlee 60
  Schlegel 60
  Wagner 60
Brice, xii, 291, 308
Bricker & Eckler Office 81, 168
Bricker, John 167
Bricknell, J. 7
bridges, 17, 23, 83
Broekema, Andrew 234
Brooks, Albert L. 90
Brough, John 79
Brown, Wayne 190
Browns, Cleveland football 136
Bruce, Earl 135
Buckeye Hall of Fame Café 218
Buckeye Building ix, 225

Buckeye Lake Dance Hall 93
Buckeye Railroad Yard (CSX) 56
Buckeye Ranch 71
Buggy Capital of World 84
Burkhart, Emerson, 157
Bush, President George H. 61, 185
Bush, Samuel Prescott 173, 185, 194
Byrd, Admiral Richard 129

Cameron Mitchell Restaurants xi, 251
camps, army in Franklin County
  Bushnell 269
  Chase 77
  Columbus Barracks 78
  Fort Hayes 78
  Jackson 77
  Lew Wallace 79
  Lorenzo Thomas 79
  Tod Barracks 79
  Willis 278
Canal Winchester 41, 291
canals 40, 45, 60, 178
Canzani, Joseph V. 140
Capital University 75, 141, 143, 302
  Law School vi, xvii, 268
  Nursing School 141, 268
  Theology Seminary 60, 75, 141, 165, 267
Capitol of Ohio 14, 24, 33, 83, 263
  first 33
  renovation 33
  second 33
Capitol South Urban Redevelopment Corporation 260
Capitol Square Office Building 227, 260
Cardinal Health 186, 192
care for disturbed children 71
Carrington, Henry 101
Carter, President Jimmy 90
Casto, Don Sr. 197
Catholic Church 71, 74, 138, 166, 274
  Pontifical College Josephinum 75
celebrations, Columbus 275

cemeteries 76
  Confederate 76
  East Graveyard 76
  Franklinton 10, 76
  Green Lawn 10, 76
  Jewish 76
  Mt. Calvary 76
  North Graveyard 76
  St. Joseph 76
  Union 76
Center of Science and Industry (COSI) 149
Central Ohio Transit Authority (COTA) 85
Central High School 120
Central Michigan University 141
Central Ohio newspapers & magazines 144
C.E.O. monthly magazine 145
Chamber Music Columbus 232
Charity Newsies xi, 257
Chase Bank (Bank One) 202
  McCoy family 179, 216
Chase, Salmon 12, 33, 46, 77, 78, 174
Chemical Abstracts Service 144
Chihuly, Dale 237
children's homes 71
  Buckeye Ranch 71
  Methodist 72
children's activities 201
Chillicothe 4, 13
Chittenden, Henry 96
  Hotel 96, 155
churches 12, 74, 269, 272, 274, 279, 282, 293, 296, 299
Circus, Sells Brothers 91
cities & villages, Franklin County 266
Citino, David 158
City Center Shopping Mall xi, 260
City National Bank, 179, 184, 202
Civil War 287
Claims Court 35
Clark Grave Vault Company 87
Clark, Joseph 271
Clarmont Restaurant xi, 249

Clayton, Richard 93
Cleveland 145
Clinton, DeWitt 39
Clintonville 297
  Park of Roses 297
Clock Restaurant 94
clubs 62, 93, 148, 150, 154, 165, 254, 276, 279
Coleman, Michael 90, 260, 310
Colleges & Universities 127
  Capital University 75, 267
  Columbus School of Art and Design 139
  Columbus State Community College 139
  DeVry University 140
  Franklin University 139
  Ivy Tech Community College 141
  Ohio Dominican University 138
  Ohio State University 127-138
  Otterbein College 280
Colonel Crawford Inn 147
colonies 1
  Connecticut Western Reserve 1
  Massachusetts 1
  New York 1
  Virginia Military District 1
Columbia Gas of Ohio 192
Columbus
  1830's 37, 41
  1840-50's 57
  aerial view 221
  arches of light 83
  banks 43, 48
  before statehood 5
  buildings 220
  celebrations 83
  cemeteries 76
  charter and "on-line schools 125
  Chill Hockey Club 241
  Christopher Columbus statue 230
  churches 12, 74
  city, county and state fairs 47
  city government vi, 22, 230, 259
  city halls 230

city markets iv, 44
Civil War 77
convention centers 216
demographics 302-5
Department of Development 264
divisions, electricity 98, water *50*
early coffee houses iv, 16
early epidemics vi, 117
early newspapers 38
early political campaigns iv, 45
early refrigeration v, 98
early road connections iii, 17, 23
early taverns iv, 39
early theatrical presentations 46
education 119
entertainment 47, 91, 93, 232
feeder canal 41
fires 49
floods 52
floodwall 52
gas lights 48, 81
German immigrants 59
German Village 63
hotels iv, 45
immigrant villages v, 87, 89
mayors 18, 310
medical 7, 42, 106
metropolitan parks 244
mid-19th century iv, 37, 41, 50, 82
Montessori Schools vi, 124
notable persons 155
  arts and science 156
  architects 155
  clergy 165
  politics 45, 167
  business 172
officials 22
penal institutions 21
population 41, 308
Post-Civil War 82-96
Progressive Era 100
public schools 120

real estate developers 14, 43, 312
relationship to Virginia 1, 2
sectarian schools vi, 124
senior centers 246
streets 15, 17, 23
urban renewal 259
water and waste v, 18, 50
Columbus Academy 123, 262, 271
Columbus Africentric High School 126
  Early College 126, 139
Columbus Agricultural Society 47
Columbus Association for the
  Performing Arts (CAPA) 148
Columbus Athenaeum 218
Columbus Awards 216
Columbus Blue Jackets Hockey 241
Columbus Buggy Company 84, 182
Columbus Call and Post 145
Columbus Chamber of Commerce 216
Columbus Children's Theater 232
Columbus Citizens Journal 258
Columbus Club 154
Columbus Crew Soccer Team 242
Columbus Destroyers Arena Football Team
  x, 242
Columbus Dispatch Publishing Co. 193
Columbus Feeder Canal iv, 40
Columbus Foundation xi, 256
Columbus gas lights 48
Columbus Gazette 38
Columbus Historical Society vii, 146, 153
Columbus Home for the Aged 68
Columbus Jewish Historical Society 147
Columbus Landmarks Foundation 152
Columbus Life Insurance Company 193
Columbus Medical Association 116
  Free Medical Clinic 116
Columbus Metropolitan Club 150
Columbus Metropolitan Library 142
Columbus Monthly 253
Columbus Museum of Art 150
Columbus Opera 234

Columbus Poor House 68
Columbus public schools 120, 299
Columbus Railway & Light Co. 85
Columbus Railway Company 92, 185
Columbus School of Art & Design 139
Columbus School for Girls 123
Columbus Sentinal 38
Columbus and Southern Ohio Electric Company 85
Columbus State Community College 139, 302
Columbus Steel Castings 193
Columbus Symphony Orchestra 233
Columbus Telephone Exchange 99
Columbus, The (Renaissance Hotel) 228
Columbus Theater 230, 232
Columbus Zoo and Aquarium 237
Commercial Vehicle Group viii, 194
Community Shelter Board 102
CompuServe (AOL) 194
Congress, Continental
  first members 35
Congressional Military District 3, 27
Congressional Ordinances
  of 1785 2
  of 1787 2
Continental Realty 195
Cooper Stadium (Harold Cooper) 240
Core Molding Technologies viii, 195
Court House, first U.S. 28
courts 22
  Claims 22, 35
  Common Pleas 22, 35
  Domestic Relations 22, 35
  Juveniles 22, 35
  Mayors 22, 35
  Municipal 22, 35
  Ohio Supreme 22, 35
  Probate 22, 35
Cox, Governor James M. 103
Crane Group 195
Crane, Jameson 195

criminal sentencing 21, 35
Cross and Journal 38
Crystal Ice Company 98
cultural activities 148
Curtis, Lucille 100
Curtis, Charlotte 159
Curtiss-Wright Aircraft Plant 105
Cyclorama (Gettysburg) 92

D'Angelo, Gene 87
  Beverly 87
Damon's Restaurant 250
dams in county,
  Griggs 9, 51
  O'Shaughnessy 9, 51
Darby Creek 27
Davidson Hotel 84
Davidson, Jo Ann 168
Deaf School 70, 153
Deardurff, Abraham 6
Defense Construction Supply Depot (DCSD) 103
Delphi Automotive Systems viii, 196
Dennison, Governor William 79
dentistry 106, 111
Der Westbote 60
Deshler, John Green 173
Deshler, David xvii, 49, 173, 176
Deshler Hotel 101, 174, 181, 224, 228, 232
Deshler, William 173
DeVry University vi, 122, 140
Diamond Innovations 196
Dickens, Charles 39
diseases 42, 82
  cholera 21, 42, 82, 117
  in early Ohio 42, 82, 117
Dispatch Ice Haus 241
Doan, Dr. Charles 109, 110
Dodge, Mel 244
Dominion Homes 196, 264
Don Scott Airfield 299, 303
Don Casto Organization 197

Donatos Pizza 197
Doody family 252
driving distances from Columbus 305
Dublin 270
Duncan, Judge Robert 122

East High School 121
economy 43, 81
education 19, 119
8 East Broad Street 226
electric power 51
entertainment 46
Episcopal Church 12, 74, 284
Esther Institute 120
Evans, Bob 249
Experience Columbus 217

fairs 47
Farm Bureau Insurance 206
Fashion Store 229
Federated Department Stores 65
Fetch, Frank 63
fires 45, 47
Firestone, Clinton 84
First Community Village 279
Flippo, King of Clowns 161
floods, 1893, 1913; 41, 52, 84, 258, 263
Flytown 45, 63, 87, 88, 248
Folkman, Jerome 165
food supply, early Ohio 10
Foos, Joseph 15, 36
football, Ohio State University, 131-136
Ford, Henry 93
Fort Steuben 2
France 1
  Indians 1
  New France 1
  Quebec 1
Frankenberg, Louisa 121
Franklin, Benjamin 5
Franklin Park & Conservatory 48, 236
Franklin County iii, 26, 56

banks 21, 25, 275, 287
colleges and universities 127-141
cost of living iii, iv, 307
courthouse iii, iv, 26
demographics 302-314
early churches v, 12, 74
early newspapers iv, 37
formation of 14, 26
Genealogical & Historical Society 146
Oberdier House iii, iv, 8
general contractors iii,iv, 15, 312
Germans 59
largest employers 313
population 308
railroads 56, 86
townships 26
Franklin University 139
Franklinton iv, 5-11, 39, 175
French & Indian War 1, 4

Galbreath, John 174, 228
Garfield, James 78
gas lights 48, 83
Gee, E. Gordon 130
Genealogical Society, County 146
George, Eddie 136
George Byers Auto Company 191
Germain Motor Company 198
Germans in County 59-63, 87, 103
Gill, John 183
Gladden, Washington 166
Glenn, John 129
Glimcher, Herbert 175
  Trust Company 199
Gnezda, Eric 159
Godman, Henry 88
Guild/Settlement House 88
golf 73, 247
Goodale, Lincoln 175
Goodale Park 45, 75, 92, 107, 175
Goodwill Columbus 256
governors 36, 45

Grand Army of the Republic (GAR) 83
Grange Mutual Insurance 199
Grant, Ulysses 36, 78
Grant Hospital vi, 107, 114
great depression 104
Greek Orthodox Church 74
Green Lawn Cemetery 76
Green, William Office Building 96
Griffin, Archie 135
Grote, Jim 197
Grove City 273
Groveport 274

Halleck, Sanford 149
Hallwood, Henry S. 176
Hanby Benjamin 282
Handke, Hartman & Cuisine xi, 250
Hanna, Jack 238
Harrisburg 292, 308
Harrison West 263
Harrison House (Oberdier) 7, 146
Harrison, William Henry 11, 12, 45
Hartman, Samuel Brubaker 94
  Hotel 94
  medicine 94
  Office building 94
  Theater 94
Havlicek, John 138
Hawkes, W.B. 115
Hayden Bank 61
Hayes, President Rutherford 36, 55
Hayes, Woodrow "Woody" 133
Heinzerling Foundation xi, 257
Heinzerling, Mildred 257
Heinzerling, Otto 257
Helms, Edgar J. 256
Henrietta Theater 96
Hexion Specialty Chemicals 200
Heyl, Christian Lewis, 16, 59, 120
Hightlights for Children 201
Hilander Research Library 129
Hilliard, John Reed 275

Hilliard 275
historic homes 152, 282
Beers, D. 7
Deardurff, A. 6
Deardurff, D. 6
Oberdier 6-8
Historic Structures Preservation 264
Historical Society, Columbus 146, 153
  county 7, 146
Hoge, Reverend James 12
Holbrook, Karen 130
Hosec, Adam 7
hospitals 107, 112, 129
  Alcorn (Dr. John Alcorn) 116
  Doctor's 115
  Dublin Methodist 114
  Grant 114
  Harding 113
  Lawrence 116
  Lincoln Memorial 116
  McKinley 116
  Mercy 116
  Mount Carmel East & West 115
  Nationwide Children's 113
  Ohio State University group (8) 112
  Protestant 113
  Riverside Methodist 113
  Select Specialty 116
  St. Ann's 115
  Starling-Loving 107
  St. Claire 116
  St. Francis 107
  White Cross 113
hotels iv
  American House iv
  Atlas iv
  Chittenden 96
  Columbus iv
  Davidson iv
  Deshler iv, 95
  Hartman iv, 94
  Hyatt (Capitol Square & Regency) iv

Irving House iv
Neil House iv, 98
Norwich iv
Park (Northern) iv, 45, 96
Seneca iv, 96
Southern iv, 60, 96
Howells, William 79
Huntington Bank Center 201
Huntington, Petetiah Webster 176

Idiot Asylum 69
immigration 80
Indianola Amusement Park 91
Indianola Informal School 122
Indians 1, 3, 6, 11, 175
Industrial Commission 34
Ingram, Edgar Waldo 177, 214
Insane Asylum 69
Ireland, Byron 147
Irish 270
Italian Festival 87
Italian Village 87
Ivy Tech Community College 141

J.P. Morgan-Chase Bank 90, 202
Jaeger, Christian 117
Jai Lai Restaurant 249
Jails 10, 22
James, Dr. Arthur 109
Jamestown, Virginia 1
Janis, Elsie 103
Janney, John 168
Jefferson, President Thomas 24
Jefferson Center 153
Jeffrey Mining Company 87, 178
Jeffrey, Joseph 177
Jessing, Joseph 75
Jews 12, 62, 74
Johnston, Alice 100
Johnston, James 15, 17
judidiary 33-35
  annex 33

conference 34
number of Supreme Court Justices 35
Junior League of Columbus 151

Kappa Kappa Gamma House 152
Karb, George 64, 310
Kasich, John 169
Kay, Doug 242
Kelley, Alford 178
Kelley, Florence 123
Kelton, Fernando & House 151
Kent State University, branch 171
Kentucky 4
Kerr, John 15, 17, 76, 117, 310
Kilbourne, James 7, 11, 23, 35, 38, 286
King Arts Complex 235
King, Martin Luther, Jr. 235
Kingwood Cemetery 67
Knight, Bobby 136
Kondos, Frank 249

labor unions 57
  AFL 57
  UMW 57
Lake Darby 298
Lake Erie 2
Lancaster Colony Corporation 202
Land Grant Districts 3
Landon, Noble 276
Lassiter, O.F. 207
Lazarus Family 66
  Lazarus Stores iv, 64, 261
League of Women Voters 151
Leatherlips, Wyandotte Indian Chief 37
legislature iii, 16, 35
Lennox Town Center 262
Lentz, John J. 224
LeVeque family 92, 223
LeVeque Tower 34, 223, 232
Levy, Solomon 229
libraries 142
Liebert Corporation 203

Liebert, Ralph 203
LifeCare Alliance 258
lighting, electric, gas 48, 269
Limited Brands 203
Lincoln, President A. 33, 40, 77, 80
Lincoln, Murray 206, 299
Lincoln Theater 236
Lincoln Village 298
Lindbergh, Charles 93, 182
Linden, North 264
Linden, South 264
Linworth 299
   Village Bookstore
   Worthington Alternative School 288
Lithotripter, Electric Shock Wave 114
Little Ireland 53
Livingston, Alexander 278
Lockbourne 41, 292
   Norfolk Southern Railroad
   Rickenbacker Air Field 293
Love, Mary 248
Loving, Starling 160
Lucas, Jerry 137
Lucent Technologies 203
Lutheran Church 12, 74
   seminary 75

Maennerchor Club 62
malls, shopping 175
Maramor xi, 248
Marble Cliff 272
Marconi Building 259
markets, city iv, 44
Marrapese, Father Casto 87
Marvin, Bob 161
Marzetti Restaurant 248
Matta, Coach Thad 137
mayors of Columbus 16, 320
McClellan, George 80
McConnell, John H. 179
   Peggy McConnell Arts Center 179
McCoy family 179, 217

McDowell, Irvin 101
McKinley, William 78
McLaughlin, Alexander 15, 17
medicine 106-117
   Columbus Medical Association 116
   education 106
   mental institutions 69, 106, 113, 117
   OSU College of Medicine 106
Meiling, Dr. Richard 109
Melton, Florence Zacks 209
Memorial Golf Tournament 243, 270
Mercy Hospital 116
Mershon Center for International
   Security Studies 129
Mershon, Ralph D. 129
Methodist Church 12, 74, 252, 299
   Children's Home 72
   Wesley Chapel 75
Metro High School 126
Metropolitan Opera Live-in local
   theaters 234
Metropolitan Parks and Recreation 244
M/I Homes 205, 308
Midland Building 228
Midland Life Insurance Company 205
military districts 2
Milo-Grogan Village 88, 264
Minerva Park 294
Mississippi River 1, 2
Mock, Geraldine 243
Monroe, President James 39
Montessori Schools 124
Monypeny William 68
Morgan, John 79, 160
Morrill Act 127
Motorist Mutual Life Insurance Co. 228
Mount Vernon Nazarene University,
   branch 141
Mount Carmel College of Nursing 115
Mount Carmel Hospitals 115, 141
Muirfield Village Golf Club 243
museums 150

Myers family 201

NAACP (National Association for the Advancement of Colored People) 102
National Road 25, 42, 267
National Trails 93
National City Bank 206, 301
Nationwide Children's Hospital 113
Nationwide Insurance Company 206, 217, 226
Neil, Hannah 180
Neil, William 180, 301
New Rome 300
New Albany 276
  golf 276
  Surgical Hospital 276
  Wexner, Abigail and Les 276
newspapers iv, 17, 144
  C.E.O., Columbus Dispatch, Columbus Call and Post, Columbus Monthly, German Westbote, OhioState Journal, Ohio Statesman, Politics, The Other Paper, Suburban News, ThisWeek, Western Intelligencer
Nicklaus, Jack 138, 242
Nixon, President Richard 85, 134
Nixon, Frank 85
North Adult Educational Center 121
North American Aviation Plant 105
North High School 121, 155
Northern Lights Shopping Center, 262
Northland Mall 262
Northwest Territory 2, 3
notable persons, vii, 39, 40, 155
  architechs, arts, science, business, clergy, politics, visitors
Nugent, Eliot 164
nursing schools
  Capital University 140, 302
  Mount Carmel 115
  Ohio State University 111
  Payne 109

O'Neill, Eugene 95
Oberdier House 7
Official Columbus 145
Ohio capitals 13
  first members of Congress 35
Ohioana Library 143
Ohio Centennial 82
Ohio Convention Center 217
Ohio counties 26
Ohio Dominican University 138, 302
  Charles School 126, 138
  Early College 126
Ohio-Erie Canal 41, 178
  feeder canal to Columbus 263
Ohio Expedition Center 82
Ohio Historical Society 146
Ohio Judiciary 33
Ohio Legislature 31
Ohio Monitor 38
Ohio Political Register 38
Ohio River 2
Ohio Stadium 131
Ohio State Bulletin 38
Ohio State Capitol 33, 83, 261
Ohio State Journal 38
Ohio State Printer 38
Ohio State University 127
  College of Dentistry 111
  College of Medicine 101
  College of Nursing 111
  hospitals 112
Ohio Territory 1-7
  land grants & agents/offices, Seven Ranges, purchasing, ordinances, pre-statehood, statehood
Ohio Theater 148
Ohio Tribune 38
old Tuberculosis Hospital 112
Ohio Village 147
Olde Town East District 152
  Myers Home 152
Oldfield, Barney 93

Olentangy
  Amusement Park 91, 238
  Village 91, 294
One Nationwide Plaza 226
Online Computer Library Center 143
Opera Columbus 234
O'Shaughnessy Dam 9
  hydroelectric generator 9
Osteopathic Hospital 115
The Other Paper 145
Otterbein College 141, 282
Outsourcing Solutions 207

Packard, Frank L. 155
Palatines to America 64, 147
  library 143
Park Hotel 217
parks
  Beck 64
  Driving 93
  Franklin 47, 236
  Goodale 45, 93
  Metropolitan 244
  Roses 297
  Schiller 64
Parson Railroad Yard 56
Pe-Ru-Na 94
Pein, Robert 212
penitentiary 14, 19, 21
  inmate labor 21
  medical care 21
Peter's Run 89
Peters Brothers 84
philanthropies 254
Physicians Free Clinic 116
Pickerington 277
  Jefferson Golf & Country Club
Pickerington, Abraham 277
Pinnacle Data Systems 208
Pizzuti Companies 208
Plaskolite 208
Poindexter, James 169

police 12, 20, 22
political parties 46
pollution 42
Pontifical College Josephinum 75
post offices 7, 81
postmaster, first
  Columbus-Matthews 7, 18
  Franklinton-Hosec 7, 18
Powell 290
Powell, Thomas 290
Presbyterian Church 12, 155, 160, 289
Progressive Era 100
Psychiatric Hospital 69, 264
public utilities 51
Pythian Theater 235

Rahal, Bobby 244
railroads and depots 53-57
  county map of railroads 56
  manufacture of railcars 57
  strikes 55
  Union Station 53
  West Broad Street Station 53
rainfall 50
Ralston Steel Car Company 57
rapid transit 86
real estate 109
Real Living (HER) 209
recreation 237
Refectory Restaurant 252
Refugee Tract 3, 13, 14, 29, 272
religion 12, 74, 272-4
Resch, Charles 61
reservoirs 9, 51
  Alum Creek 9, 51
  Hoover (Walnut Creek) 9, 51
  Scioto 9, 51
restaurants 177, 248
Resurrection Cemetery 76
Revolutionary War 1-4, 175
Reynolds, James C. 278
Reynoldsburg 278

Alexander Livingston 278
  Mount Carmel East Hospital 115
R.G. Barry 209
Rhodes, James 170
Rhodes State Office Tower 227
Ricart Automotive Group 209
Ricart family 209
Rickenbacker, Eddie 103, 182
Rickenbacker Airfield 271
Rickey, Branch 240
Ridgway, Joseph 182
Riffe, Vern 217
Rigsby, Kent and Tasi 253
  Rigsby Kitchen 253
rivers 2, 9, 23, 51
  Alum Creek 51
  Darby Creek 51
  Little Miami 2, 51
  Mississippi 2
  Ohio 2
  Olentangy (Whetstone) 2, 9, 51
  Scioto 2, 5, 8, 18, 51
  Walnut Creek 9, 51
Riverside Methodist Hospital 113
Roaring Twenties 104
Robinson, Aminah 162
Rockwell-North American Plant 105
Roosevelt, President Franklin 264
Rosecrans, Sylvester 166
Ross, Richard and family 210
  Heart Hospital 109
  Laboratories 109
Rossman, Irving 250
ROTC 105
Rouda, Harley E. Sr. 209
Roxane Laboratories 210
Ruscilli Construction Company 210
Ruscilli, Jack and Louis 210
Rush Creek 288
Russell, James 148
Russell, Robert 16

Safelite Group 211
Salvation Army 254
Sanfilippo, Dr. Fred 109
San Margherita 296, 300
Sanders, Harland 213
Saxbe, William 171
Schille, Alice 163
Schiller Park 64
Schlesinger, Arthur, Jr., 143
Schmidt, William 75
Schoedinger Company 66
  F. Oscar 66
  Funeral Homes and Cemeteries 67
  Phillip 66
Schoenbaum family 90
schools 119, 122
  Advantage Academy 122
  African-American 108, 122
  Alternative 108
  Blind 70
  Central High 120
  Charter 125
  Columbus Academy 123
  Columbus School for Girls 123
  Columbus Public 120, 122
  Deaf 70
  desegregation 122
  early 10, 19, 119
  Early College 126
  Africentric 122, 126,
  Charles 126
  Esther 120
  first in Columbus 10, 119
  foundations 122
  Hispanic 122
  Indianola Junior High 122
  kindergarten 121
  Metro High 126
  Montessori 124
  North High 120

on-line 124
sectarian 124
taxation 119
University 123
Wellington 124
Schottenstein, Ephraim L. 211
Schottenstein, Irving 133, 183, 211
  OSU Athletic Center 133, 183, 211
  Stores 133, 183, 211
Schrum Mound 300
Scott, Mary Bole 123
Select Specialty Hospital 116
Sells Brothers Circus 91
Sells, Lewis, Peter and William 91
senior centers 246
Senior Times 145
Senter, Mahala and Mary 106
Sessions, Francis C. 99, 184
Setterlin, Robert W. Sr. 212
settlers, early 15
Seven Ranges, Ohio 2
sewage 18, 99
Shephard, Dr. William 58
  sanitarium 58
Sheridan, Phillip 78
sheriff, 61
Sherman, William T. 79, 83
Sisters of St. Francis 107
Smith Brothers Hardware 87
Snowden-Gray House 152
Snowden, Philip 152
soil in Franklin County 8
Solove, Richard 109
Soulant, Wayne 235
Spain 1
sports 240
  Blue Jackets, hockey 241
  Clippers, baseball 240
  Crew, soccer 242
  Destroyers, football 242
  golf 242, 280
  OSU 131

Harley, Chic 132
Hayes, Woody 133
Matta, Thad 137
Ohio Stadium 131
Schottenstein Center 133
Taylor, Fred 136
Tressel, Jim 134
St. Ann's Hospital 115
St. Joseph Cemetery 76
St. Vincent de Paul Orpanage 71
Stanton, Edwin 35, 39, 78
Starling, Lyne 6, 10, 15, 106, 160
  Sarah 6
  Medical School 15, 17, 106, 160
Starling Middle School 121
State Auto Insurance 212
State Bank 169
state buildings 14, 15, 31, 43, 232
State House 17, 31, 43
  fire 33
  first 33
  grounds used as farm 32
  renovation 1933 33, 263
  second 33
  statues 78
State Library, Ohio 142, 178
state offices 31
Steinbrenner, George 240
Sterling, Commerce 212
Sterling, Lea Ann 152
streetcars 85
Streim, Harry 209
Strickland, Governor Ted 125
Suburban News 145
Sullivant, Lucas 5, 10, 15, 23, 26, 35
  Eliza 10
  Joseph 10
  Michael 10
  Sarah (Starling) 6
  William 10
Swayne, Noah 79

Tarhe ("The Crane") Indian Chief 11
taverns 16, 39
taxation 119
Taylor, Coach Fred 136
Tecumseh, Indian Chief 11, 12, 34
telephone, early company 99
   Central 99
   Midland 99
   Western Union 99
television providers 238
   cable 238
   local stations 238
   sattelite 238
Theological Seminary, Capital 60, 75, 141
This Week 145
Thomas, Dave 185, 213
Thompson, King 197
Three Nationwide Plaza 226
Thurber, James 143, 164
   Thurber House 164
Tiffin, Edward 36
Tiffin University, branch 141
Timken Roller Bearings 87
T & OC Railroad Depot 255
Tod Barracks 78
Tod, Governor David 79, 152
Todd, Dr. Hiram 106
Topiary Garden 153
townships, Franklin County 2, 26
trade 313
Trans World Airline 93
Tressel, Coach Jim 134
Trinity Lutheran Seminary 60, 75, 267
TS Tech North America 213
Twiss, George 99

unincorporated villages 171, 297
Union Cemetery 76
Union Store 229
United Mine Workers 57, 100

Univeralist Church 74
Upper Arlington 207, 278
Urban League 102
urban renewal 259
Urbancrest 295, 308
U.S. Court House, first 16

Vallandigham, Clement 80
Valleydale Party Hall 93, 218
Vaud-Villities 237
Vern Riffe State Office Tower 227
Villa Milano Banquet Facility 218
Village Book Store 299
Virginia 1, 2
Visitors Bureau 217
visitors, notable to Ohio 29
Volstead Act 281
Volunteers for America 255
Von Steuben 2

Walter, Henry 33
Walter, Robert 186
wars
   Civil 77
   French & Indian 1,
   Gulf
   Iraq
   Korean
   Mexican
   1812 11, 286
   Revolutionary 1-4
   Spanish-American
   Vietnam
   World War I 103
   World War II 104
Washington, President George 2
waste water 269
water supply & treatment 42
Watkins Railroad Yard 56
Weiland Park 88
Wellington School 124

Wendy's 185, 213
Westbote 39, 81
Western Electric 203
Western Intelligencer 38, 286
Westerville 280
Westinghouse Electric 214
Wexner, Abigail and Les 122, 186, 276
Wheeling, Virginia 24
Whig Battering Ram 38
White Castle Restaurants 105, 214
Whitehall 283
Whittier Peninsula 200
William Green Building 221, 229
Williams, William Wallace, Sr. 213
Willis, Bill 136
Wilson, Nancy 165
Wise, Dr. Henry A. 114
Wolf Ridge 13
Wolfe Brothers Shoe Co. 187, 193
Wolfe, John F., II 144, 188, 193
Wolfe, John W. 188, 193
Wolfe, Preston 149, 188, 193
Wolfe, Robert F. 187, 193, 206, 256
women in early Ohio 10
Worthington 285
Worthington, Governor Thomas 11, 284
Wyandotte Building 222

YMCA 101
YWCA 102
Zollinger, Dr. Robert 110
zoo 237

Chester C. Winter

B. A. University of Iowa
M. D. University of Iowa

Captain, United States Medical Corp

Surgery/Urology Residency, University of California, Los Angeles

Professor and Head of Urological Surgery,
The Ohio State University

Professor Emeritus of Surgery/Urology,
The Ohio State University

Medical publications: 8 books, 150 articles and 24 chapters

History books published

A Concise History of the United States and of the State of Ohio, 2002

A Bicentennial History of the State of Ohio, 2003

Ohio Cities: Historical Descriptions, 2004

Concise Biographies of Notable Ohioans, 2005